NORWAY

Oslo

SWEDEN

Stockholm

FIN

Helsinki

GOTLAND

BALTIC SEA

SCOTLAND

NORTH SEA

DENMARK

Copenhagen

E

LITH

EIRE

Dublin

ENGLAND

London

NETHERLANDS

Amsterdam

Hamburg

Bremen
(BR.)

Berlin
(U.S.S.R.)

Stettin

U.S.S.R.
(POL.)

POLAND

Warsaw

ATLANTIC OCEAN

Brussels

BELGIUM

GERMANY

Dresden

Breslau

Paris

FRANCE

Frankfort
(FR.)

Frankfort
(U.S.)

Rhine

Prague

CZECHOSLOVAKIA

SWITZERLAND

Vienna

AUSTRIA

Budapest

HUNGARY

Trieste

Genoa

Belgrade

YUGOSLAVIA

PORTUGAL

Lisbon

SPAIN

Madrid

CORSICA

Rome

ITALY

ALBANIA

Gibraltar

SARDINIA

MEDITERRANEAN

MOROCCO

SP. MOROCCO

MOROCCO

ALGERIA

TUNISIA

SICILY

Tripoli

TRIPOLITANIA

LIBYA

Frontier of
Western Democracies

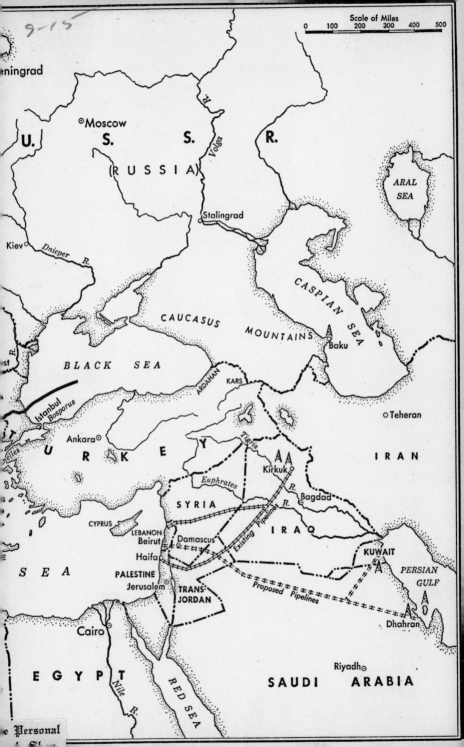

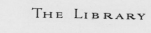

◉

Profile of Europe

◉

PROFILE
OF
EUROPE

By SAM WELLES

HARPER & BROTHERS
PUBLISHERS   NEW YORK

9-8

PROFILE OF EUROPE

COPYRIGHT, 1948, BY SAMUEL GARDNER WELLES

PRINTED IN THE UNITED STATES OF AMERICA

FIRST EDITION

G-X

To the Memory of
HENRY ALLISON PAGE III
born at
Aberdeen, North Carolina, October 19, 1913
killed in action off
Okinawa, May 4, 1945

H ENRY PAGE was the finest person of my generation I have known.

During the oral examination for his Rhodes scholarship, he was asked, "What is it that more than anything else makes you hot under the collar?" A southerner answering southerners, in Georgia, he said (one of the astounded examiners later told), "To see anyone be unfair to a Negro." When he saw a beggar, he crossed the street if necessary, not to avoid giving but to give. He was one of the best linguists and wittiest talkers I ever heard. He was never unkind, caustic, or fulsome—yet no one could deflate any sort of pretension more neatly and sweetly.

As a small boy he could identify any star, and would drag people out of bed on frosty nights to come peer through his telescope. At Asheville School his achievements included a 100 in the English college-entrance examination. His Princeton record, from track to phonetics, was topped with the highest undergraduate award, the Pyne Honor Prize. At Oxford his rare combination of great intelligence and warm, human naturalness caused a teacher to say, "He writes on philosophy as if he were writing to his mother."

From 1938 to 1940 he had a fellowship at Harvard, and was nearing his Ph.D. in government when he volunteered for the Navy in June, 1940.

At Princeton he was a pacifist. In Europe during the late 1930s he saw totalitarianism and decided there were principles for which men must fight if necessary. A commission would have been his for the asking. He characteristically chose a method that would make him a line, not a desk, officer: a six-month training course, starting as apprentice seaman. The Navy several times offered him good shore posts. While no one more valued peace, quiet, pleasure, the amenities of life, seeing friends and having solitude— all the things a warship so seldom provides—Henry felt the issues of World War II so deeply that only the most active possible part in it could satisfy him. He rejected every shore assignment and was on sea duty from early 1941 until his death.

During the worst of the submarine war in the Atlantic he did convoy work, spending two winters off Iceland in a destroyer. I had often seen him sick in even a mild sea, and marveled. With the twinkle no friend will ever forget Henry assured me, "After a week on a destroyer in dirty weather, you can never be seasick again!"

He was at the landings in North Africa, Normandy, and southern France. When action lessened in the Atlantic, he applied for transfer to the Pacific. There he took part in the naval actions off the Philippines, Iwo Jima, and Okinawa.

The Navy found good use for his precision, skill, and stubborn sense of duty. He was communications officer on the staff of the admiral commanding the bombardment group off Okinawa. He was on the command ship, at the nerve center. All the messages, in and out, that co-ordinated the air, ground, and sea bombardment passed through him. He did his complex job under the strain of the continued Japanese suicide attacks that turned Okinawa into the longest and bloodiest battle in American naval history. In April he narrowly escaped death from a Japanese hit on the

Tennessee. In May he was killed when a suicide plane struck the *Birmingham*.

His admiral took the time to write a letter longhand, stating "I have seen no finer officer in this war." Regulars do not say that lightly of reservists. The admiral added that Henry was one of the few truly saintly men he had ever known.

He did have a saint's faith, gentleness, and sheer unselfishness. He also had the flaming temper characteristic of saints when they step out of stained glass. I once told him I was glad to have been one of a large family of children who rubbed off each other's rough edges. Henry grinned and retorted: "My sister and I knocked 'em off." As he grew up he learned to control his wrath. But cruelty, meanness, or injustice always aroused it.

Being friendliness incarnate under all other circumstances, Henry made friends wherever he went. He kept them because his cordiality and beautiful manners were no veneer but his true character. I saw him under many kinds of pressure and he never once struck a false note. He came as close to the ideal as a normal, lovable human can; in any situation, he gave the best he had. He accordingly brought out the best in anyone who met him and I know scores of people in many lands and all walks of life who still use him as a touchstone for their own and others' actions, cheer themselves with his cheerfulness, and cherish him as a companion because his integrity, decency, and humanity mean as much as ever.

When his fiancée expressed a fear that because she did not have his education she would disappoint him as a wife, Henry wrote: "At seventeen you knew more than I do about life and beauty and charity; and those are what are important. I went to school many years, but I am a very simple person—indeed, I have always been afraid it would be you who was disappointed."

On his last leave, Henry managed to walk for a few days in the Great Smoky Mountains he loved so well. He wrote me: "Go as far as I may, I do not think I will ever find a more heavenly country than the Smokies in October with the full glory of autumn upon them. It is unbelievable, even while you are looking at it. Make a date for some October, please." Only a few days before his instant death, he wrote of the Germany we had known together and the Japan that had already almost killed him: "The chaos and misery in Germany must be absolutely inconceivable, though no greater than others suffered at the Germans' hand. The sentiments of *Dover Beach* thrust themselves almost forcibly upon you these days. And now we propose to do the same to Japan. I, for one, am reluctant to do so."

Some things are said whenever the good die young. Friends of Henry have claimed he was too fine for this world, that he was not meant for earthly success, that he might have been frustrated had he outlived the war. I do not believe it. He had great charm and just as great firmness of character. His gentleness was not weakness; his idealism had a strong inner core.

Henry was not ambitious. But because he did not seek honors and offices, they often sought him. True success would always have been his. If he had lived to be a hundred, all he did would have been done well and all his life would have added to the happiness of others. He could have done more in peace than he did in war.

He would have laughed at anyone calling him a hero. Service, not heroism, motivated him. He did not thirst to lead a charge or storm a barricade; he merely wanted to do his duty. That led him, who hated war, into active service long before most Americans thought we had responsibilities toward the rest of the world. He believed that nations too had their duty.

Those who have said good-by to someone in wartime will know why, in a period of uneasy peace, this book is dedicated to Henry Page.

Contents

◉

Profile of Europe

◉

◉

PART I

Chapter 1. EUROPE BETWEEN THE MAGNETS

JOSEPH STALIN is the man who has put most bluntly the tug of the two magnets. In 1927, Stalin told a group of American workers who visited him in the Kremlin:

"There will emerge two centers of world significance: a socialist center, drawing to itself the countries which tend toward socialism, and a capitalist center, drawing to itself the countries that incline toward capitalism. The battle between these two centers for command of the world economy will decide the fate of capitalism and of communism in the entire world."

Today those two centers, or magnets, do exist. They are Russia and America. As Stalin predicted, the tug between the two has drawn in the whole world. It centers in Europe, where the last two world wars began.

In 1939, when World War II started, seven nations could be called major powers. Alphabetically, they were America, France, Germany, Great Britain, Italy, Japan, and Russia. China was not then and is not now a major power in the sense that any such nation must be a strong one, unified enough at home to be able to intervene decisively in affairs abroad.

By 1948, when the dust of World War II had settled somewhat, the world had no major powers. It had two superpowers: America and Russia. Germany and Japan were under military occupation. Britain, France, and Italy were so much weaker, and so busy trying to recover at home, that they had only a fraction of their former world influence. If these three make a good recovery they may be major powers again. Their best chance for such a recovery lies in their forming, with as much of the rest of Europe as they can, a close-knit political and economic federation. They cannot do even this much without a great deal of American aid.

That means, as Stalin predicted more than twenty years ago, that many countries are being drawn toward America, the capitalist center of the world. These nations are not necessarily capitalist—Britain, for example, has a socialist government—but they all have more sympathy with capitalism than with Communism. It also means that many other areas, from Albania to those held by the Chinese Communists, are being drawn toward Russia, the world's Communist center. Stalin oversimplified. Many people in many countries want other systems than these two. But he was right in calling capitalism the chief opponent of Communism. He was wrong in using the word "battle," Stalin's euphemism for "war" when speaking to non-Communists. War between the two great magnets is not necessary and can be avoided.

While Soviet Russia can never have warm, friendly relations with America or other nations, America and the rest of the world can have a lasting, peaceful relationship with Soviet Russia if they are prepared to be patient, firm and above all *consistent*.

That is controversial and not easily proved. I shall spend the rest of this book trying to prove it. I cannot conceivably cover all its aspects. Areas like the Far East and Latin America, where there are certainly important U.S.-Soviet differences, are not discussed. I concentrate on Europe, with a short side glance at the Middle East. Europe is where the effort to develop a lasting, peaceful world relationship is most critical. There is where world wars have begun. If America and Russia cannot solve their differences peacefully in Europe, they cannot do it anywhere. I think they can.

After any war, there must be a new equilibrium before there can be peace. The British have long called it "the balance of power" and thought of it chiefly in European terms. Ever since 1918 an effort has been going on to find, for the first time in human history, a *world* balance of power. As late as 1939, one could still think of it primarily as a European balance; four of the seven major powers were concentrated in central and western Europe; Russia and America seemed more concerned with domestic than world affairs.

Now the most important forces are outside the Europe which

Britons from Cardinal Wolsey to Neville Chamberlain attempted to keep in a balance of power.

Europe is between the magnets.

2

I spent eight months of 1947, early March to late October, in Europe and the Middle East. My first ten weeks were in Russia. One episode before I started the trip was to me symbolic of the whole complicated Soviet-American relationship.

Molotov, wishing to have the Council of Foreign Ministers meet in Moscow, promised that reporters could cover the session as fully and freely as they were then covering the autumn-1946 meeting of the CFM in New York. Two months after Molotov's promise, Russia limited the American reporters' group to twenty. After a violent argument, the State Department got the group raised to thirty-six—less than half the reporters who had arranged to go. The State Department arranged even this small concession only by cutting its own official delegation and by yielding some of its allotted Moscow office space to be used as bedrooms.

This episode shows how Russia negotiates. Promise a principle (full press coverage) to get a specific (agreement to meet in Moscow). Once you have the specific clutched safe in your bosom, slash the principle to the least you could get away with (not full coverage, but only twenty U.S. reporters). If the other fellow not merely objects but fights long and hard, yield a little more of the principle you promised (thirty-six, instead of the far greater number who believing you made arrangements). Never yield all the original promise if you can avoid doing so, and yield a bit above minimum only if you get further specific concessions (a smaller U.S. delegation and less space for it).

This explains why negotiations with Russia are slow. It also indicates that Russia does negotiate, in its way, and doubtless always will. The Russians know that Americans are impatient people. That encourages them to be slow. They know they can take advantage of American impatience to get this or that matter settled, even if not on the terms we would like. Yet there is seldom if ever a good reason why America should be in any greater hurry than Russia to settle any given issue. Just as long as we are patient, the talks will go on—and we can simultaneously use the time to get the non-Russian world back on its feet.

The thirty-six reporters who did get to Moscow found that Soviet officials occasionally tried to co-operate. We were offered some guided tours in Moscow plus a guided trip to Stalingrad. Those who wished could have a few days in Leningrad, which I did on my own. Of the few regular visas Russia grants to foreigners, only twenty are held by reporters from countries beyond the Soviet security belt. These twenty must live in Moscow, and are lucky to get one trip a year to another part of Russia, usually in a Soviet-escorted group of those free to go at that moment. So the treatment the thirty-six of us had was better than the Soviet average—though well below that of any other country I ever worked in as a reporter.

In short, Russia did fulfill a perceptible part of the promise Molotov had made to get the CFM meeting held in Moscow. Ordinary Russians could not enter our hotel, and each corridor on which we roomed had secret police agents on twenty-four-hour watch. But I could go about the city (I walked over three hundred miles in Moscow), or rent a Soviet-driven car to go out into the country. Though I had to give my destination whenever I hired a car, the drivers also stopped at any other place I asked. In this way I visited collective farms and other places on my own. I never felt I was being followed. I had more freedom than foreigners normally have, but then Moscow had more than twice its normal number of foreigners during the conference and the system was not geared to check up on them all.

The breakdown of control showed in the petulant half-panic I once saw on a Soviet official's face. Thirty foreign reporters whom he was shepherding round an institution (nameless, so he can stay blameless) suddenly came to a place where they could scatter in all directions. They did. He started one way, then another, then a third. When he saw how hopeless it was he stopped, shrugged his shoulders, turned up his palms and said to me with Russian fatalism, *"Nichevo,* I cannot keep track of so many."

Such American initiative and Russian resignation are more widespread than you might think.

3

These are the conclusions with which I returned from my eight months in Europe:

(1) There is little chance of a major war in the next fifteen years—that is, before 1960 or 1965—*if America pursues firm, consistent, intelligent policies in that period.* Russia is not ready for major aggressive war. Stalin himself has stated that his country will not be prepared for "any eventuality" before 1960 at the earliest—in his speech of February 9, 1946, a very full statement of Russia's intentions for the next fifteen years.

Russia will keep pressing at soft spots like Greece, Palestine, Persia, Korea and China. It will do this to hinder reconstruction in every way possible. Russia might have some of its satellites invade Greece, let Yugoslavia try to take Trieste, or encourage Chinese Communists still further. Such maneuvers would be mainly to test America. If America reacted firmly, Russia's stooges would retreat and Russia would have lost no face because it would not have been directly involved. If America ever failed to react firmly, Russia would of course expand its interests in the area as fast and far as possible.

(2) Few Russians, including the men in the Kremlin, want war. The ordinary Russian wants only peace. Most of the men in the Kremlin, until Russia is as strong as it can be in the 1960s, want only what can be got without war.

(3) The most important single factor in what seems like Russian aggressiveness and expansionism is the Kremlin's realization of Russian weakness. It thinks the best defense is to stay on the offense—to keep every other nation in the world as far off balance and as internally disturbed as possible.

(4) Central and Western Europe—the region from the Stettin-Trieste line westward, including the American, British and French zones of Germany and Austria—can recover. It will take years, perhaps more than a decade. It will require a lot of effort, and both self-help and American help. But it can be done. It is worth it.

(5) Eastern Europe—the Soviet security belt and from the Balkans to the Adriatic—can also recover. If these countries can depend only on Russia and not on America for help, it will take them even longer to recover than western and central Europe.

The local Communists are doing their best to take these countries over. They may not succeed in Finland; Communists dropped from first to third place in the July 1948 Finnish elections. They are not having complete success in the Soviet zone of Germany. They are succeeding everywhere else.

That is, they are having physical but not 100 percent psychological success. I was struck by the way even native Communists in these countries wanted American aid—and would eagerly have entered the Marshall Plan had Moscow let them.

(6) The local Communists to whom I talked—in eastern, central and western Europe—were unanimous on one point that is not publicized. I think it should be. While the Kremlin wants Communist unanimity, I doubt if it had bargained on this unanimity. I asked every local Communist I met in every country I visited: "Do you want the Soviet system in its present form in your country?" Every one of them vehemently assured me that he did not. Nearly every one of them mentioned "Soviet excesses" or "Russian extremes" that they never wanted to see in their country. Nearly every one of them said, in varying but similar words, "We intend to avoid Russia's mistakes."

They are Communist all right. They know what they are doing. They know that Communist control of a state economy also means control of every citizen's thoughts, words, and private life. They know that experience has proved what Bismarck predicted of Marxism in 1878, almost forty years before the first durable Communist state:

If every man has to have his share allotted to him from above, we arrive at a kind of prison existence where everyone is at the mercy of the warders. And in our modern prisons the warder is at any rate a recognized official, against whom one can lodge a complaint. But who will be the warders in the general socialist prison? There will be no question of lodging complaints against them; they will be the most merciless tyrants ever seen, and the rest will be the slaves of these tyrants.

Why then are so many Europeans Communist? Because Marxism simultaneously offers excitement, ritualistic trappings, the feeling of a "cause," and a blessed relief from the necessity for individual thought, action and responsibility which is a nearly unbearable strain in much of Europe today. Democracy under tough, troubled conditions requires a good deal of initiative, courage, conviction, and the moral equivalents of physical food in the belly. It requires those qualities even under the uneasily easy conditions of America.

Marxism has an emotional appeal to broad human types: outward-looking people truly moved by humanity and pity for their fellow men; inward-looking people moved by self-pity, hatred, and a desire for revenge against real or assumed injustices; and shrewd, emotionless people who love power.

The first type of Marxist—for example, Socialists in Scandinavia and England, and even some Communists—are men America can work with. One Danish Communist I met was well grounded in Marxism but was far more eager to talk about the unfair distribution of vegetables in Copenhagen. He was sorry for the people who could not get their share. When Communists of that type run into the harsher sides of their creed, they usually leave Communism in a hurry—if they live in a country where they can.

The second type of Marxist is very hard for others to work with. The third type is hardest of all for non-Communists to get along with.

Every country in Europe is being tugged, to some degree, toward Moscow. Every one of them may become more Communist than it now is. Every country that the Communists take over will have terror of the sort Lady Astor meant when she asked Stalin, twenty years after the Communist Revolution, "How long will you go on killing people?" Stalin answered: "Until it is no longer necessary." The unanimous fear among local Communists of becoming like Soviet Russia has even moved Yugoslavia's Tito, a tough Marxist of the third type. In June 1948 he defied the Kremlin, causing great repercussions in the satellites.

(7) Soviet Russia has few material assets to show for thirty-one years of Communist dialectical materialism. This is not solely, or even primarily, the fault of World War II, tremendous as the war damage was. Most Americans realize Russia's lack of freedom. Few realize how much that lack of freedom, when combined with the other inefficiencies of the Soviet system, handicaps Russia's physical progress.

Russia might well be further advanced materially if the October 1917 Revolution had never occurred. Thoughtful Russians, including those in the Kremlin, in some ways realize that. It does not mean another revolution is in the offing. There are no signs of one. But even the Party stalwarts are not above backsliding. In 1947, Georgy Alexandrov, who for years had been head of all Soviet propaganda, was haled up before a Party jury headed by Politburo member Zhdanov and fired from his job because he had "burned incense before bourgeois philosophers." Alexandrov had been one of the thirty most important men in the Soviet Union. The official spokesman of Communist orthodoxy was found to be unorthodox. The archbishop in charge of the missionary work was shown to be a heretic!

There is not a year since the Bolshevik Revolution that this has not happened in the Party hierarchy. When not even Party bigwigs can be sure of their doctrinal ground, the lot of lesser Communists and of the great herd of non-Communist Russians is even more uncertain. Soviet Russia merges politics and economics to an extent that can scarcely be grasped by people who have not seen it firsthand. In America, with the foundation of the Bill of Rights, there is not much political interference with productive processes—Americans are fairly free to live and produce as they like. In Russia, no one has any such sure foundation. There are constant Party purifications and purges—and every political quiver shakes everything else. A poorly designed engine has a frictional loss that makes it waste fuel and produce less power than a better engine. Soviet society is so poorly designed that in all its activities it has a frictional loss almost beyond belief. Size and drive can make up some—not all—of the engine's deficiency.

As a direct result, Russia had the worst food, clothing, and housing of any war-affected country I saw on my trip—Finland, Denmark, Poland, Czechoslovakia, Germany, Austria, Greece, Italy, France, Belgium, and Britain. Russia was making a slower recovery than eight of these war-affected nations—faster only than Germany, Austria, and Greece.

4

On the rare occasions you can get a Russian Communist away from his safe doctrinal platitudes, you can have a very interesting talk. In Europe I had five talks with Russian Communists—two in their native land, three elsewhere. I cannot be more specific about time, place or person. It was fascinating, and somewhat reassuring, to find at firsthand that Russian Communists do not invariably believe what they must officially say. They played the standard tunes, but after a while came variations.

All five said America was aggressive and cited our policy in Greece and Turkey. My defense was this: "Your leaders could put you to war tomorrow if they wished. [None of them disputed that.] Our leaders cannot put America to war that way; America can go to war only when the great majority of the American people think it should. [None of them disputed that either, though it does not square with the Kremlin line.] The last world war started over Poland. Britain and France had guaranteed Poland, but the Nazis did not think that enough to stop them. They took care of the only other possible objection by agreeing to split Poland with you Russians. The Nazi leaders could start war without consulting their people, just as your leaders can. They thought they could win a quick, cheap war—and instead the whole world got six years of the most frightful destruction it had ever known. There are many Americans who believe that Russia wants Greece and Turkey, especially the Dardanelles, the way Hitler wanted Poland. Now who is to guarantee Greece and Turkey as Poland was guaranteed? The United Nations? Russia can veto any action there. Britain and France? If they could not warn the Germans off Poland in 1939, how could a much weaker Britain and France warn the Russians off Greece and Turkey now? America, or a combination of countries that includes us, is the only power on earth that can guarantee Greece and Turkey in a way that might warn the Kremlin off an invasion that could start a third world war. The Russian people cannot check their leaders. Only America can check the Kremlin."

Each of those five Russian Communists listened without argument. Then three of them quietly changed the subject. Two of them, a thousand miles apart, said: "It is as well there is such a check."

All five of them said that the West in general, and America in particular, would soon have an economic collapse that would make 1929 look like peanuts. On that I could not budge any of them an inch. There they did argue fervently, even passionately.

That is real Communist conviction—and of course they may be right.

They used this belief in various ways to justify Soviet policy. One with whom I had been arguing Soviet economic isolation said: "Why should we trade outside our sphere any more than we can help? The more ties we have with Western economy, the more adversely we will be affected when you have your inevitable capitalist collapse."

Another used it to explain Russian slowness to agree to any German peace treaty terms. "Why bind ourselves to a treaty?" he asked. "Soon you will be so concerned about your depression at home that you will stop caring anything about Germany. Then we can do whatever we want, in Germany and many other places."

Many Europeans find such Russian arguments exceedingly persuasive. America cannot change this wide European belief by counter argument. America can change it only by demonstrating —over a period of years—that the U.S. need not have a disastrous collapse. It may not be easy. But it is a fair test. If capitalism is going to have worse and worse depressions closer and closer together—as the Communists so confidently say—it is not a system that will long survive in the world, even if the Communists stay quite neutral.

The greatest single boost that world Communism has ever had was the 1929-37 American depression. The first Soviet Five Year Plan had begun in 1928. Communists all over the world are still making effective contrasts between capitalism, which "cuts production when the people's need is greatest," and the "Planned State Which Forges Ever Forward." Molotov did it in one devastating sentence in 1932, when as Soviet premier he was outlining the next twelve months of the Five Year Plan: "Russia will build as many new blast furnaces in the next year as America shuts down." Communists always concentrate on that sort of remark, and avoid actual comparative facts and figures—which would be even more devastating the other way. Russia, with a population nearly 50 percent larger than America, had an over-all production less than half America's even at the depth of the great American depression. The Soviet standard of living in 1938-40, the best period Russians have yet had or can have before the 1960s, is well below the worst Americans have had at any time in the twentieth century.

The long frank hours of discussion I spent with each of those five Russian Communists produced only this one economic point on which their views on world affairs differed fiercely from mine. The other differences, while many, were ones that countries could still live with, like a husband and wife with different hobbies. That is why America can eventually work out a lasting, peaceful relationship with Soviet Russia.

The Marxists are not like the Millerites, those strange American sectarians who proclaimed that the world would end on October 22, 1844, eagerly awaited the Last Judgment—and had their faith thoroughly disrupted. Marxism is a far more adjustable theology. Its prophecy of a last judgment for capitalism has no exact date attached. If fifteen years or so go by without a fulfillment, Communist theologians—even those on the Politburo—will be inclined to proclaim the judgment "eventual," not "immediate."

It will take America some fifteen years to prove that capitalism is not going to collapse and that isolationism is truly dead. It will take Russia some fifteen years to prove that it can finish its recovery and reach Stalin's 1960 "or later" goal, which amounts to a heavy industry less than that which America had in 1941. It will take the world's other war-damaged areas, notably those of Europe, some fifteen years to prove that they can recover their strength and stability.

These are America's years of opportunity. If America uses them to increase its own and friendly nations' production, to help restore world trade and strengthen its associates, and to do what it can in co-operation with other countries to eliminate the politico-economic conditions that breed war, the opportunity will not be lost. By then the world outside the Soviet sphere of influence should be healthy enough to withstand Communist contagion. Communism feeds best on diseased tissue.

No world balance of power of the sort that could last a century is likely until the world regains its health. Not until then could the United Nations become properly effective. Not until then would the Russians conceivably agree to the American proposals on the atom, which have already been seconded by every country outside the Soviet sphere. That would be an essential part of military stability.

You cannot have military stability, on which a durable world balance of power depends, unless economic stability and political stability have first been developed.

5

Winston Churchill has called Soviet policy "a riddle wrapped in a mystery inside an enigma." Soviet policy, though it moves in many and mysterious ways its wonders to perform, is clear enough in its bold, over-all objectives. It wants to make its magnet strong enough to pull the whole world into Communism.

Communist strategy, and the tactics to implement it, have not changed much since Marx himself. When Europe had its series of revolutions in 1848, Marx founded a Paris workers' club and instructed its operators to talk not of Communism but of democracy. The agents he sent to Germany were told to set up Communist cells but to act like worthy, energetic liberals. The masthead of Marx's paper called it an "organ of democracy." As Marx admitted: "It was in reality nothing but a plan of war against democracy."

The Soviet Union is the chief single embodiment of Communism, and the key body in Communist world-wide strategy is its fourteen-man Politburo. All over Europe, people I met wanted to discuss the riddle of Russia. But there was something that puzzled them more, on which they asked me far more questions. I could give much less exact opinions on it than on Russia—and no sure answers at all.

Their root question was "What is American policy?" As it came to me again and again, country by country, I realized what nation was the real enigma. America is the most mysterious country of all.

At least fourteen men know what Russia is up to. Outsiders can make a fairly well-informed guess. Stalin has outlined a series of specific Russian goals for 1960.

Nobody I have ever heard of knows with any assurance what America is up to. Who knows in advance what we will do in world affairs in 1949 or 1950, let alone 1960? As long as no one on earth knows what we are going to do next, nothing can be settled. Until we realize that we are more mysterious than the Sphinx and answer that root question, by getting an American policy, the world will not have peace.

6

The two magnets, America and Russia, are the world's greatest forces. Neither is as strong as it looks. Candidly, neither the Russians nor the Americans have a very high morale. It is odd but significant that I have seen more citizens of these two great powers show feelings of inferiority than people show anywhere else.

All five of those Russian Communists who spoke frankly to me managed to imply, in one way or another, that America faced not only an economic but a moral crisis. They all avoided putting it that bluntly and in none of the talks did we ever come fully to grips with the subject. First, because it is a hard one to pin down in talk at any time; second, because people who live in glass houses dare not throw stones. Each of those Russians knew that I knew his country's morale was low too.

Intelligent Communists have inner doubts about Communism. Intelligent Americans know that capitalist democracy has not fulfilled all its dreams. It has fulfilled far more than Communism, but few would claim that its present state was wholly satisfactory.

A shrewd observer once said to me: "The worst morale I know is that in American government employees. It's the weakest major segment of American life." It is not the world's worst morale; I have seen Russian government employees. But I know what he meant. A man from Mars would not have to be a Marxist to see serious weaknesses in American morale.

In discussing America and Russia as the two great magnets tugging on the world, we are in the realm of possible war. In wartime every state is, in a real sense, a total state. Low morale is even more serious in a nontotalitarian state when it faces the prospect of war—as America now does—than in a totalitarian state. If a war arises between Russia and America—and it well may, though it need not—American will be at least as total (the less unpleasant side of totalitarian) a state as it was in World War II.

Soviet Russia is more total all the time. Czarist Russia was before it. Take the Marquis de Custine's *Lettres de Russie*, published in 1842, after that French nobleman had paid a long visit to the court of Czar Nicholas I:

"The Russian state is a country where the government says what it wishes, because it alone has the right to speak. . . . The government of Russia is the discipline of a camp substituted for the order of a city; martial law has become the normal state of society. . . . Political obedience has become for the Russians a cult, a religion."

However, any American who thinks that bad conditions or low Russian morale means Russia would not fight well is as wrong as any Russian who thinks the same about America. Soviet living standards are the worst of any country that has seen much of the Machine Age. Yet there is no reason to say that under-privileged people are less able to fight than the better privileged. Russia's civilian supply during the last war was frightful. Yet the Russians held, then hit. Once Russia has repaired its scars and got stockpiles high enough to keep supply no worse than in 1941-45 (two tasks that will take years), poor conditions otherwise would not necessarily keep the Kremlin from starting war. This group controls all Russian sources of information, and could make the war sound defensive even when it was aggressive.

"The wicked capitalist encirclement gets plainer and plainer," the Moscow radio would blare, "so we are striking before it strangles us."

Precisely because the Russian people have so little, the Kremlin could make them that much angrier at "rich, bloated Americans trying to take your last crust."

Soviet propaganda has already made ordinary Russians furious about American aid to Turkey and Greece. I saw that myself. The Kremlin now uses the same line against America's Economic Co-operation Administration. I was able to tell some Russians what I thought was the truth and they at least halfway believed. But almost no Americans get that chance with Russians; for thirty years the Kremlin has controlled news sources. It uses the monopoly coldly and well. So Russians might fight effectively if the Kremlin sent them to war—though the farther they got from Russia the less patriotic they would feel.

American aid to Europe and the Middle East is similar, in nature and purpose, to our wartime lend-lease. We are helping those who want the sort of peaceful, stabilized world we do. But it *can* look very encircling and menacing indeed to a powerful, suspicious clique in another country. The Kremlin feels that way. Japan's rulers did.

America had a problem in the Orient before Pearl Harbor. In Europe, Nazi Germany clearly endangered the peaceful world we wanted. So we sent lend-lease aid to Britain, to Russia (after June 1941) and other nations fighting Germany. In the Pacific, Japan was just as dangerous as Germany. But there was no one to whom we could send effective lend-lease; Japan held China's seacoast. Tokyo decided that sooner or later we would find some way to send aid that would hurt them, so they tried to forestall us with Pearl Harbor, thinking they could paralyze America until they had safely consolidated all their Pacific and Asiatic gains.

Some day Moscow may strike for a somewhat similar reason. But the fear of such action should not cow America into stopping aid it can give with as clear a conscience as it did in 1940 and 1941. This time we have probably begun aid soon enough to stop the war. Russia's leaders are more cautious than Japan's. *If* they believe the other side is prepared, they will hesitate to start the sort of war that risks a nation's life.

There are no longer many illusions among Russian people as to the moral and spiritual quality of all that the Soviet state represents. The fires of revolutionary Communism have somewhat died down in Russia itself. There is still patriotism and nationalist sentiment. But the Revolution can no longer command that ultimate fund of human idealism upon which it, like the churches of all ages, could once draw. The Kremlin has a tractable but no longer an inspired array of followers. It has obtained that which is Caesar's. Its initial bid to obtain also that which is God's has been quietly and decisively rejected. Russia's Communists do not have the burning fervor of Communists elsewhere. They live in the reality of the Promised Land, not in a dream of it like those others. They know it is not all milk and honey.

Americans too have doubts about their system. Many Americans do not know what they want and do not prize what they have. Some actually think that free enterprise means to jail Communists or outlaw them as a party. It is not that easy. Nothing is easy in politics, except to drift into a system where a stern government will relieve you of the need to think or act or live.

Any political system is a mixture of the ideal and the material.

The two are symbolized, respectively, by freedom and goods. America's system of capitalist democracy, for all its faults, has far and away outproduced any other system. Stalin is the best witness of its superiority in goods. He is constantly telling Russians that they must "overtake and surpass America," and setting up production goals for them that America surpassed years ago.

Capitalism has also left men far more freedom than Communism. No American need be ashamed to compare his system with any other system. He can have his justified doubts about it, and he certainly ought to be sweating to improve it. But since 1935 I have seen, firsthand, German Naziism, Italian Fascism, Greek despotism (1938 Metaxas variety) and chaos (1947 variety), English conservatism and socialism, Portugal's "corporative state," Sweden's "middle way," Dutch constitutional monarchy, Arabian feudalism, Russian Communism and many other systems.

I have never seen a system that offered as much, in the present or for the future, as capitalist democracy when it is fairly applied.

PART II

A Look at Russia

⊙

Chapter 2. THE SURPRISES

A T FIVE on a sunny mid-May morning the train from Leningrad on which I was leaving the Soviet Union stopped near the Finnish frontier. A captain in the green-tabbed uniform of the Soviet security police and a buxom, middle-aged woman interpreter whose uniform had similar green piping came into my compartment. When they learned I was an American reporter leaving Russia with all my effects, they visibly grew more alert. Everything, including myself, got a more thorough going-over than I had ever encountered at any frontier, even in wartime.

"How much Russian money have you?" asked the woman. I showed her the hundred rubles I had kept for last-minute contingencies.

"You can't take any with you," she said.

"What can I do with it?" I asked.

"The porter can buy you some breakfast in the station," she said, and called in the female porter. For the hundred rubles, $18.87 at the absurd Soviet exchange rate, the girl got me two sandwiches of butterless black bread, each with a thin slice of smoked beef, and two cookies. (Hereafter I shall use the old diplomatic rate of twelve rubles to $1, which is nearer the ruble's real value.)

While the girl porter was gone, the two Soviet inspectors began examining everything in the compartment. The woman even turned over the thin Russian mattress, felt along and under the wooden berth, and climbed up to examine the baggage rack. As she sorted through my third bag, I said: "It's terrible to travel with so many clothes."

"The clothes are no trouble," she replied. "It's the papers."

Soon she pounced on one of my notebooks and started through its close-crammed writing. It was the one that included my stay in Stalingrad, so I told her how Laurenty Makoyed, director of the Stalingrad tractor works, had watched me busily take down everything he said during a two-hour interview and then do a lot more jotting during a long, thorough tour of his plant. As we were standing by the factory gate at the end, a fellow reporter asked Makoyed about the number of Stakhanovites (workers with an output above average) he had. Before answering, Makoyed pointed at me and, smiling, said: "You are a Stakhanovite among reporters."

The woman translated this to the security-police captain. They laughed heartily—and kept right on going through my notes and other papers. Only one really pleased them: my embossed lavender-colored pass to Red Square to watch the May Day parade. Both eagerly examined it. As the woman said, "Neither of us has ever seen one of these." They are something of a rarity; less than eight thousand people among Moscow's seven million get them.

"Did you see Stalin?" she asked.

"Very clearly," I said, "through good field glasses from about sixty feet. He is getting grayer, but his face has more animation than I would have guessed from his pictures. He climbed the steps to the top of Lenin's tomb without any pause to catch his breath. He stood there the whole five hours the parade lasted."

She told all this to the captain, who said with feeling, "We too would like to see Stalin."

At long last everything I had was okayed. Again the woman turned to me, this time with a new note in her voice. The tone was no longer official, but personal.

"When you write about Russia," she said, "you will have your opinion. But write with the heart. We don't want any more war. We had enough. Remember the terrible destruction we suffered and the pale faces of our children."

Again she translated to the captain. He vehemently echoed "Da, da, da (yes, yes, yes)."

As she spoke, her intense eyes looked straight into mine. I knew she was giving me, as a reporter, a final message to take away from Russia, doubtless inspired by the continual Soviet attacks on America for "warmongering." Whatever spurred her remarks, they sounded like the sincere words spoken to me all over Russia by Soviet officials and ordinary people. Everyone I talked to was genuinely anxious to avoid another war.

The security policewoman was correct. You cannot write truly of Russia without using the heart as well as the head. One must use the head; trying to understand the Soviet Union in Communist principle and practice takes quite as much intellectual effort as trying to understand Aristotle, Aquinas or astrophysics. One also—always—must use the heart.

Two qualities the West should never lose in dealing with the Soviet Union are understanding and compassion. Other qualities, such as firmness and patience, are needed too. But understanding and compassion are quite as important.

2

Soviet Russia is a very controversial subject. Anyone writing on it should submit his credentials. I have long studied Russia and, for a year before I went there, headed the *Time* group that analyzed all news and background available on it. My 1942-45 service in the U. S. State Department included much work on Russia. During my stay in the Soviet Union, I took notes that would fill eight hundred printed pages. Stalin has said, "Facts are stubborn things"—I try to be fair and factual.

This book uses about one-sixth of my Russian notes. A reporter learns to winnow, and I have earned my own living primarily as a reporter ever since entering college in 1931. During the eight months of 1947 I spent in Europe, I talked to hundreds of experts and to thousands of plain people. Through these conversations plus reading and firsthand observation, I have amassed bushels and bushels of facts. They cannot merely be dumped in the reader's lap. A reporter uses his judgment and sense of values to sift the facts and find their pattern. People who saw my *Time* pieces asked how I ran across such lively, realistic remarks. One answer is a self-invented game called "Twenty Quotations." The game was won when I had twenty different quotations from people in that country which were fresh, pungent, or penetrating. With twenty, I could write about a country with some intelligence. On the average, it took 1,500 quotations to collect my score. The other 1,480 have their function, like the roots of a rose bush.

Wherever I was, I walked at least five miles a day, moseying about the city or countryside to get the firsthand feel for which there is no substitute. For longer distances I usually went by car, tourist style, avoiding the good hotels in the capital cities and stopping to ask questions when anything looked interesting. I traveled some twenty-five thousand miles that way. One could even rent a car in Russia (for about $30 a day) and I motored 1,200 miles with only one small political hindrance. (In no country was driving as easy or pleasant as in the 30s, when I logged over 100,-000 miles in Europe.) I had to carry food, extra cans of gas, plenty of tools and spare tires, and piles of documents. It could be done. It was worth the trouble.

I have rusty French and a little Russian and German. More and more Europeans are speaking at least some English; the change between the 30s and the 40s is quite perceptible. When I needed interpreters, I was careful to use several and first test each one not only for English-language but human qualities. Information and quotations derived through interpretation are used only when I am reasonably certain they are right.

There is the job of getting people to say what they really think. I have often been asked why on earth Communists spoke so fully and frankly to me. They wanted to talk and decided they could trust me. A reporter who cannot as a rule discover in five minutes whether a person has something to say and in fifteen minutes make him feel free to say it, is not much of a reporter. It also pays to know something of the subject. At the end of a three-hour conversation, a Russian Communist who spoke fluent English tapped my knee and said: "You know, I have never been able to *talk* to an American before. They know little about Russia and less about Marxism, and won't try to understand either. I have enjoyed talking with you. When I made a point, you could follow it."

A reporter should be honest, thorough, and impartial. The better American journals and journalists are; they cover many sides of the news. Soviet reporters and newspapers are not. One tragedy of Russia's rulers, whose subordinates on every level carefully select what information it is safe to show their boss, is that the Soviet press mirrors the Kremlin so slavishly that the Politburo cannot even learn anything new in the papers. In America it is different. A government official almost invariably learns something new to him in any newspaper or magazine he picks up. He never knows when something his subordinates have tried to hide from him will pop up on the front page. That is a very healthy uncertainty for all levels of any bureaucracy to have.

3

A man who had lived two years in Russia said to me, shortly after I returned: "The question that really stumped me when I got back was, 'What did you find in Russia that you didn't expect before you went?' I couldn't think of a thing that had surprised me."

I have found surprises wherever I went; they are part of the fun of moving about—though you can also have them sitting down, as that remark to me shows. The first thing I noticed after our Berlin-to-Moscow plane crossed the Soviet border surprised me: the lack of motion. Russia has a static quality. America is a large country with static stretches. I remember once rising before dawn on the Utah-Nevada border and driving west; in the first 150 miles along the road I saw only two cars. But I am here talking about the great area of European Russia which is as thickly settled as America's Middle West, with towns or villages every few miles or oftener. You see surprisingly little motion there. When you fly in America, even over mountain or arid areas, you see railroads and paved highways; in the middle west you see a maze of them, carrying heavy traffic. We flew into Russia at 1,500 feet. It was diamond-clear; I saw men walking along the roads. But in the five hundred miles to the outskirts of Moscow, I saw just two trains. Not one single motor vehicle was visible, even in cities like Vilno and Vitebsk.

Nor will I soon forget a Soviet airplane ride from Stalingrad to Moscow, when we flew almost the whole six hundred miles at a hundred-foot altitude, on occasion dropping to forty feet or less, so that I sometimes looked up at church steeples beyond our wingtips. The pilot sent back word that he wanted the Americans on board "to see Russia," and then zoomed down to ten feet over the river Don so that our propellers sucked up drops of water and turned them into a misty rainbow spray. Flying at a hundred feet for hundreds of miles, you do see everything—with a new and startling clarity. I saw the terrible scars of war: the still-raw trenches zigzagging through the fields and up the hillsides; the gun emplacements in gulches and on bluffs; the burnt-out tanks, some of them freshly plowed round and one a rusting brown-red in a vast green expanse of winter wheat that lapped up to the very tank treads. I saw two constantly recurring signs that we were in Soviet Russia: decaying churches and great collective barns. Nearly all those churches we brushed past were falling to pieces even in towns untouched by war, their roofs caved in, the plaster peeling from their walls and steeples, and the onion bulbs on top of the steeples only skeletons. The barns on collective farms were big structures, dominating their villages like grain elevators in the Dakotas or Catholic churches in Quebec. It was a bird's-eye view all right. Chickens ran for shelter from us as though we were hawks. Cows completely lost their dignity. Flocks of sheep huddled madly together from every part of their pasture. Only the roads and rails were still and lifeless as we roared past. In these six hundred thickly settled miles before Moscow's immediate suburbs, I saw one stationary train, no trains in motion, one paved road, and not one car or truck.

There is almost no motor transport in Russia in the American sense of the word. You can drive out a bit from some of the main cities; I went about a hundred miles from Moscow, much less from Leningrad and Stalingrad. The roads are bumpy and bad, and I got stuck both in winter snows and spring mud. Now I know why, as *Pravda* reported in 1946, a high Soviet official in the Stavropol district abandoned his car and fatalistically took to moving about his district on horseback! There are a few long-distance highways in Russia. I met one sturdy Englishman who had driven the five hundred miles from Minsk to Moscow. He saw only five other cars and relatively few trucks until he got close to the capital. When the gas supply he carried ran out, he had to buy some black-market from the Soviet secret police. His car had never been the same since. For a country of 8,473,444 square miles, the cur-

rent Five Year Plan calls for 7,200 miles of new surfaced roads—
or less than the total surfaced roads in Connecticut, with its mere
5,009 square miles.

Since the war, Stalin has told several American visitors that
Russia needs four times as many railroads as its 53,163 miles,
which would still give it less trackage than America's 226,696.
But the Five Year Plan calls for only 4,500 miles of new rail lines
by 1950. The plan calls for an increase in Soviet river and canal
transport to 50 billion ton miles in 1950. If this is achieved, the
Soviet inland waterways will for the first time have caught up with
the czarist system in amount of goods moved. Russia's seagoing
merchant fleet is relatively small, and the Nazis destroyed or damaged all four Soviet shipbuilding cities.

Nothing in what I'd read or heard before I went to Russia had
really prepared me for this static quality, and it may surprise
others as much as it did me.

Russia's communications system is as poor as its transport: mails
and telegrams are slow and uncertain, few Russians have phones.
As one Soviet official in Russia remarked to me: "The only way
a telephone is of much use is to have your secretary make appointments for you to go see people, or for them to come see you. A
telephone is too hard to hear over." The Soviet phone model is
almost an antique; it is hard to hear over, even when the secret
police have not tapped it.

No nation can approach its full industrial potential until it
has first-rate communications and transport. If you think of a
businessman in Nashville writing steadily for five months to a
Seattle manufacturer, finally hearing he can have one-third of his
original order, and then bombarding Seattle with intermittent
letters, phone calls and telegrams for eight more months before
finally getting a shipment of half that third—*and having something almost that slow and discouraging happen with every trans-
action involving goods and transport*—you will have some idea of
what postwar Russia is like. Naturally the war is in part responsible. But Russia was always a long way from a modern or adequate system of transport and communications. It still is.

4

Another thing that surprised me about Russia was the waste. Other nations are wasteful. We know how America has squandered resources, and have heard the Frenchwoman's crack that she could feed her family for a week on the food an English family wasted in a week (she could not do it now). But no nation in history has wasted on so prodigal a scale as the Soviet Union.

One Soviet citizen who knew his country very well told me just before I went there that an outstanding characteristic of Soviet life was the number of people it took to get anything done. He is right.

Part of it is fear, which in Russia does sometimes seem pathological. The most unlikely places are guarded, as well as every conceivable likely one. The Soviet Army is much the biggest in the world. Long after the war, I saw as many men in military uniform on the streets of Moscow as I saw at the peak of the war in London or Washington. (The count did not include the many ex-soldiers who, possessing no other clothes, still wore their old uniform with the insignia removed.) For a country as critically short of manpower as Russia since the war, that is shocking waste —to consider it from no other angle. The last thing I saw in Russia was that sort of waste. My train from Leningrad to Finland halted four times in the border area, and over one hundred able-bodied young security police guarded this one three-car train on its stops, even though it had already been searched from stem to stern with the minuteness of which my examination was a sample. A uniformed group appeared from the nearest settlement every time we stopped, and took up its stand on all sides.

What is one to make of a country that uses so many men between 18 and 30 to guard one small train near the border of a small disarmed neighbor? It seemed sheer madness to waste manpower this way. When I said as much to a Finnish Socialist, he took a more detached view: "Why worry? If Russia wants to waste men, it will suffer more than anybody else."

Another part of the waste is inefficiency, not only the unproductiveness of men in uniform and in the world's most topheavy bureaucracy, but the human inefficiency that is unavoidable under Soviet conditions. I do not primarily mean the ten to fifteen million Russians in slave-labor camps, though slave labor is almost as wasteful of output as it is of human happiness. I mean the way the average Russian and his wife have to use up almost all their energies just to keep going. As a result, and because of the lack of machinery, almost every Soviet factory and farm has to be heavily overstaffed by Western standards in order to get much of anything produced.

I gnashed my teeth or had a lump in my throat whenever I saw what Soviet waste meant to the ordinary Russian. There are pitifully few consumer goods for these poor, hard-working people; those few are so pitifully shoddy. A Kansas housewife would not be caught cleaning her cellar in most of the dresses I saw women wearing in the orchestra and dress circle of the Bolshoi Theater —Russia's Metropolitan Opera House. The stuff doesn't even last. *Crocodile*, the only humor magazine in a land where public humor must be as official as anything else, prints jokes about shoddiness so regularly that the Kremlin must be trying to get Russians to laugh off their sorrows on the subject.

A *Crocodile* cartoon showed two climbers roped together high on a mountain. One says, "Afraid of the cliff?" The other answers, "No, I'm afraid of the rope. My factory made it." In another, a woman asks: "Do you have any children's bicycles?" The clerk says: "Buy this tricycle. When your child rides it, a wheel will fall off."

To most Russians, unfortunately, *Crocodile* laughter is as hollow as crocodile tears.

Women's shoes were selling for $100 to $150 a pair while I was in Russia, with canvas shoes a bit cheaper. The average Russian wage is $42 a month. Recently the Moscow *Bolshevik* reported:

Kratovo village received a supply of canvas shoes. . . . When they were displayed in the stores, they stopped traffic. People had only to look at them, and their hands would instinctively go into their pockets for money to buy. By evening many people were wearing the season's novelty—these light elegant shoes.

But on the following day, going along the street, you'd first see the heels all by themselves—and then the owners wearing different shoes. Two days later the street scenery changed somewhat: the streets were now spangled with soles. It would be too much to say the customers were delighted.

Two purchasers—laboratory workers—prepared a *Manual of Instructions for Owners of Canvas Shoes* (1) keep shoes in hermetically sealed place, preferably under glass (2) do not wear at temperature higher than 10° (3) best of all, don't wear them at all, as it is bad for them.

These Soviet shoes had been made at the Dawn of Freedom factory.

As that memorable factory title indicates, the Soviet Union is excellent at names and slogans: collective farms, Five Year Plans, Order of the Red Banner of Labor, Mother of Maternal Glory for a woman with five children, etc., etc. Soviet Russia often manages to fool itself—and foreigners—by a stage effect or new label. A lot of waste effort arises from this practice.

Label pasting is not peculiar to the Russians. I saw a diverting instance of it during my wartime service in the State Department. When I left for London, Cordell Hull, who had long been an able secretary, was aging and less active. Under-Secretary Edward R. Stettinius, of whom Russian bureaucracy sometimes reminded me, was dashing up and down the long, high, slat-doored halls of the old State Department building with a bunch of charts in one hand and a bucket of pastel-toned paint in the other, serenely certain that with reorganization and redecoration he could change State overnight. When I returned, the paint was fading and State had undergone a second complete Stettinius "reorganization," he having become secretary. Every office, division and employee in State had had titles changed twice in my absence. Everyone I knew was sitting in the same old place, doing the same work.

The Soviet Union has done a more thorough restaging than that since 1917, but Mother Russia still speaks many lines from the old act. The farms have been "collectivized" and "tractorized" but the change on them is not anything like as thorough as I would have thought from the newsreels. Everything in Russia is now "planned"—but Soviet plans work like any other human plans, which is not perfectly. There is definitely more propaganda in Soviet plans than in those of the Western world.

One surprise I had about Soviet planning concerned the Palace of the Soviets. For years I had been hearing stories and seeing pictures of this mighty edifice, which was to outtop any building in the world and be surmounted with a three hundred-foot stainless-steel statue of Lenin infinitely more inspiring than the Empire State Building's mooring mast for blimps or the Chrysler Building's toothpick. The Palace was to be Something Symbolic, the epitome of the planned perfection of the Soviet state. When the Nazi invasion began, the unfinished steel skeleton of the Palace did serve a highly symbolic purpose. Since metal was short, Stalin decreed that the framework be taken down and turned into arms.

When I got to Moscow, someone pointed out the high board fence around the site. One slushy March afternoon I strolled over to investigate. The only gate in the long circuit of the fence was heavily crisscrossed with rusty wire. I finally found that a near-by courtyard (where a soldier, as in so many Moscow courtyards, was guarding a couple of German cars and three American lend-lease trucks) led onto a little ridge at one side of the excavation. Its circular hole, dug down some fifty feet, looked like a prodigious bomb crater. In the center were several acres of concrete foundation, flat like a pavement, and on it a double circle of huge concrete teeth—a twentieth-century Stonehenge, the base for the 1,400-foot cylindrical tower to be topped by Lenin. Four rusty cranes slanted off at an angle. That was all. It was impressive.

The next day I mentioned to a foreigner who has long lived in Moscow that I had gone over the site of the Palace of Soviets. Chuckling, "It's never going to be built," he told me the story.

When you build a skyscraper anywhere, you test the subsoil first, taking borings to see if it will stand the weight of the structure. In this planned state, they hadn't bothered about that. They simply picked the site they wanted because it was handy, right across the Moscow River from the Kremlin; blew up the city's biggest cathedral, because it was on the site; and in the early 30s dug down that fifty feet. Then they found the whole subsoil affected by river seepage. The Kremlin was quietly frantic. It had told the whole world what it was going to build, where it was going to build it—and how high it would be.

When Russian engineers admitted that they could do nothing, American engineers were called in to rescue this Soviet symbol. They warned Stalin that the task was probably hopeless, but he asked them to try anyway. They tried for two years, taking all sorts of borings, and pumping in quantities of concrete and other reinforcements. They finally licked the seepage, but at the end advised Stalin that, while the site could take a fair-sized structure, it would never bear the one planned and proclaimed.

In 1937, all work stopped on the site. The cranes have been there rusting ever since. The Kremlin found one excuse after another for delaying work until 1941, then leaped at the chance for a patriotic dismantling of what little had been erected. Since 1945, the Kremlin has used postwar reconstruction problems as justification for not resuming. A highly placed Soviet engineer told a foreign colleague who asked when work on the Palace would be resumed: "It won't be. The original plan has been officially abandoned. But that is secret. The Kremlin is still too embarrassed to admit it."

There is the hole in the ground. Russians still point pridefully at the fence, with the four cranes jutting above it like giraffes' heads. You can still see little replicas of the Palace in Moscow second-hand shops. They are no longer sold at the other stores.

A month afterward an ardent Komsomol (Young Communist) began boasting to me about the Palace of the Soviets. When I told her the truth, she was enraged.

"You are trying to blacken our dreams," she said.

Even a materialist regime must leave its people a few dreams—especially when it has done so little for them materially.

5

My greatest surprise in Soviet Russia was the sudden, deep happiness I had at being an American. I have spent more than five years of my life abroad, in over twenty countries. I have never before had that feeling with the intensity Russia gave it to me.

I am not one of those who says, "My country, right or wrong." Our country has often been wrong. It is wrong in some ways now. We must try to correct as many of the wrongs as we can; they help explain why Communism is so strong. But when you live awhile in Russia, you are very glad to be an American.

Since leaving Russia, I have often thought of that woman border inspector who asked me to "write with the heart." I could not answer her then. She and the captain were in the Soviet security police. Even if, by some chance, they had both secretly agreed with me, each of them would nevertheless have had to report fully on the "propaganda" they had heard. If only one had reported, it would have gone badly with the other.

Yes, I should have told her, I shall remember your terrible destruction and your children's pale faces. I shall remember that you want peace and many things besides peace. You want a real people's state, for instance, and freedom of movement in your own country and abroad. You cannot move anywhere, say to Moscow, without the state's permission. If you have no permit, you are sentenced to hard labor. You cannot even visit places like the Kremlin. I shall remember the Russian girl I met only once for a few minutes, during which we happened to walk past it. She said: "We Russians envy you foreigners. You can visit the Kremlin. We cannot."

I shall remember the farm youth who was born the year your farms were collectivized. He asked: "Do you have collective farms in America?" When I said no, and added that I myself owned a farm, he said: "I would like land of my own. If I farmed it well, I would get something from it. If I did badly or the weather was against me, I would be the one who suffered. Either way it would be up to me." I shall remember the Soviet intellectual to whom I quoted that statement. His comment was: "We can very seldom say it now, but Russians are more like Americans than you might think."

Your rulers tell you many harsh things about America. They paint a very grim picture of life there. Yet any American who visits the Soviet Union comes away deeply aware that, for all his country's shortcomings, America has a most precious heritage: freedom. Not the four freedoms, or this freedom or that one. Freedom.

Or would you rather consider bread than freedom? Would you rather consider the material things on which your rulers, your dialectical materialists, take their stand? Materialism cannot promise things about the next life; it denounces "pie in the sky by and by—that's a lie." It believes that there is no next life. Its pie and promises are in this material life—the present and immediate future. Your rulers, in denouncing America, never make certain specific material comparisons. They do not say, when they speak of American depressions: "The greatest prosperity Soviet Russia has ever provided you or will provide you before 1960 is a far lower standard of living than America has had at any time in the twentieth century." That is the truth—and they keep such truths from you.

"But America is a much richer country than we are," one of your young Communists told me. Potentially, you are far richer than America. You have gold—more than America, more even than South Africa. You have plains that could produce more wheat than Argentina and America combined. You have the most timber, the most ores and the most water power—perhaps the most oil. Your land, stretching almost halfway round the earth, makes America look almost puny. As people, you match any people on your human merits. Nature has given you almost everything a nation needs, not only for greatness but for abundance. You need only to be allowed to use what you have, as we do.

Visiting you has made me realize as I never did before the things I took for granted. I have been more fortunate than most Americans, but nearly every American has more privileges than all but the merest handful of you. I can leave America any time I wish, start a business if I want, choose my own job, even change jobs if I change my mind. I can buy a long-distance train ticket readily. I can motor quickly and comfortably on a great network of roads. When I go to Washington, I visit the Capitol and no one dreams of stopping me. I can live in any city or county of America that strikes my fancy. When I enter my apartment, I wish that ninetenths of your city-dwellers did not have to share yours with several other families, so that each of you has a living space not much bigger than a grave. When I am on my farm, I wish that collective lad could earn money and buy one, as I did; in America, he would at least have the chance.

We Americans hope that some day you may find out these things. We hope against hope that some day your leaders, who take such pride in having taught you how to read, will let you decide for yourselves what to read. Only then would you be able to read such a book as this without a qualm, and without worrying about a knock on the door as you read.

Chapter 3. THE PEOPLE

THE Russians are as warmhearted as their rulers are calculating. When you meet them, you realize how much these people who suffered so heavily to defend the Motherland want peace and a chance to rebuild their devastated country. You also find how friendly they are to any Americans they chance to meet, despite the steady stream of Kremlin propaganda about American hostility to Russia, of which they believe an appalling amount. It is tied into the third of their chief concerns: food, reconstruction, and the fear of war.

I had one long talk with a group of Russian workers and their children. My companion and I were the first Americans they had ever seen. We met them when a freckle-faced, seventeen-year-old stopped us to ask for a light. We in turn asked what he did for a living. He said: "Come and see." We went with alacrity.

It was a small repair shop on a side street near a school. As we walked along the lad explained he had quit the village school at his collective farm after fifth grade and come to this near-by town to get his training as an electrician.

"Why didn't you go back?"

"My collective has no electricity."

"Would you go back if it did?"

"Yes, I would like to be the electrician there. Collectives have more food."

The shop had two other workers: The foreman, a middle-aged war veteran with stainless steel false teeth whose wife and son had both been executed by the Nazis as partisan fighters, and a handsome, young, just-demobilized soldier in bright new blue overalls. An old man in a fur cap was waiting for a minor repair job on a wagon. When they heard we were Americans they welcomed us and all came outside to bask a bit in the not-too-warm sunshine of the Russian spring. We passed around cigarettes, lit up, and

31

talked about the weather, politics, and this and that in the way people do all over the world.

Before long school let out and we were waist deep in kids as cheerful as they were curious. We also asked them: "Have you ever seen Americans before?" "*Nyet* (no)," they chorused, giggling and looking us up and down.

"Is there anything you would like to know about America?"

A sharp-chinned, black-eyed, nine-year-old in a brown dress spoke up at once. Typifying the pride of country instilled in Soviet school children everywhere as soon as they can say Joseph Vissarionovich Stalin, she said firmly: "We know that it is best to live in our country."

We had not dreamed of talking politics to these children; we merely thought they might want to ask something about America, now that they had met two Americans. But they get an early drilling in politics.

A blond, blue-eyed, twelve-year-old boy wanted to know how long it took to come from America. I said, "I flew from Washington to Moscow in two days."

"Impossible. I don't believe it," he answered. He had never heard of four-motor transport planes, though very much interested in aeronautics. He did know that four-motor bombers existed. After several intelligent and fairly technical questions about the exact route and cruising speed of the plane, etc. he said: "Now I believe you. I will mark the route in my school geography."

Then young and old began firing blunt questions that showed what was on their minds. The fur-capped old man, thoughtfully pulling his gray mustache, asked: "Why does your Truman want to fight us?"

"America does not want to fight anybody."

"Then why does America attack us now?" asked the foreman. "After we have suffered so much, we don't want to fight. Look at these youngsters whose fathers were killed in the war." He pointed out several of the children pressing in around us. "Sixteen men from this one side of the street were killed during the war." (This was a town not reached by the Nazis.)

With deep feeling the young overalled veteran chimed in to express the sentiment of war survivors everywhere: "God, it's so nice just to be alive."

I asked the apprentice who had brought us to the shop if he had been in the war. He said, "No—and I hope I never will be."

"But if you want war," exclaimed the old man, "we are not afraid. Look what fine boys we have growing."

He waved his hand to the lads standing around us. One of them, a slim sensitive-featured thirteen-year-old, smiled proudly and said: "Yes, you can see that."

I asked him what he wanted to be when he grew up. "Engineer," he answered.

"Would you like to study in America?"

"Very gladly, but only if my country will send me," he said, his eyes dancing. He already knew, at thirteen, that it would be up to his rulers—not him. This thirteen-year-old, who was a Pioneer (Communist youth organization) and advanced for his age in any country, then asked: "Why have you changed from the Roosevelt policy?"

"We all won the war together," I replied. "Why did your government change its policy afterward?"

He nodded like a young Solomon and said: "Yes, we can see that change too."

Just then the foreman's little niece, a cute five-year-old in a blue bonnet, got into a mud puddle in the dirt street that went past the shop door. He quickly shooed her out, tweaking her ear reprovingly. Recalling again what German butchery had done, he said: "I am so lonely now." His native town was in the direct path of the Nazi invasion and was almost completely destroyed. "I lost my family and my home. I spent three years as a partisan hunted by the Nazis. Afterward I didn't have the heart to go back to those ruins with all their memories. I came out of the war with nothing but the shirt on my back. Now I am starting all over again here. I came to this town like a straw driven before the wind. My niece is the only family I have left."

Later this steel-toothed foreman said with a warm smile: "It's an old Russian custom to entertain strangers. It would give me pleasure to invite you to my room. But I am short of food."

That reminded the thin little Pioneer of something he had read in the Communist youth newspaper. He asked: "Is it really true that you are tossing potatoes into the sea in America and burning bread for fuel in your locomotives? That seems terrible to us. We need so much more bread and potatoes."

I said it was true that some potatoes had been wasted in America because of a bumper crop, even though they were offered free to anybody, including foreign countries who would come and get them. But the cost of transporting a product that spoiled so easily made the potatoes too expensive, and the offer was not widely accepted. The group nodded all around, and the boy said: "Yes, transportation is always a problem here too." As for bread being burned in locomotives, I said I had never heard of such a thing and thought it was not true. I mentioned in passing that America had exported over five million tons of grain to other countries in the previous year, which proved news to them all. They were very pleased to hear it. Nor had any of them heard of UNRRA's $250 million aid to two Russian republics, the Ukraine and Byelorussia.

The old man countered the reference to UNRRA aid with: "Why are you also so kind to the Germans?"

I replied: "The Russians are being kind to the Germans in Germany too."

He answered: "That is true. We have heard it from our sons in the occupation army. But why are you against our getting even ten billions in reparations when we asked for twenty billion? We need it because our country was ruined so much." (He was confusing the twenty-billion-dollar Russian request at Yalta for total reparations for all war-damaged countries with the ten-billion-dollar sum that Russia seeks for itself and Poland.)

This question and the others made it clear how much these quite average Russians had read and heard—always from Soviet sources—about world affairs, and how genuinely they were concerned by the Kremlin's one-sided version of America's "warmongering" policy.

"Why doesn't America want to trade with Russia?" asked the young veteran. "It won't sell anything to Russia now."

I explained that America was selling to Russia, as well as to other countries, but that the delivery of many things, from turbines to tractors, was delayed by so big a postwar backlog of orders that even Americans often had to wait a year or two for what they had ordered. None of them knew until I told them that

Russia has thus far refused to join every international economic agency from the World Bank to the International Trade Organization. I added that it took two to trade.

The Pioneer was ready with another economic question: "Why have prices gone up in America? Can't you control them?"

I answered: "The cost of rationed food in Russia, where as you know most food is rationed and the economy is controlled, was tripled in one day last September. America does not have rations or controls. Yet while our food prices have risen, they have not gone up nearly as much as yours. Even in a planned economy, controls by themselves don't keep prices from going up." Once more they showed willingness to grasp an explanation and viewpoint entirely new to them.

Again and again they returned to the terrible effect the war had had on Russia and told how nobody wanted another war.

"So much ruin, so much bloodshed, so much to be done again," said the young veteran. "And our reconstruction goes so very slowly."

"We too want to live in peace and prosperity," I said. "I only wish more Americans could come and talk with you and other Russians as the two of us here are doing. I wish even more that you and other Russians could come to see America and talk to us there. It doesn't help for our governments to be sitting in Washington and Moscow shouting at each other over the radio."

This rang a sympathetic chord. They all nodded and there was a fervent chorus of "Yes!" The old man, his fur cap almost shaking off in his vehemence, expressed their feelings: "The heads of our governments would better solve the problems if they sat down at a table over a glass of wine." Then he quoted an old Russian saying: "You can't solve anything without a bottle."

As we left, several in the group said: "Come and talk to us again. You will be very welcome." The voice of the foreman rang out above the rest as he lifted his little niece into his arms. "Tell them in America," he called, "that we don't want war."

2

The Russians are a fascinating people. They had a social hierarchy before 1917 and still have, despite the Communist claim to be a classless society. An official Soviet Intourist guide was surprised and annoyed when I suggested that our driver sit down to a meal with us. "That would not be fitting," she said—and the driver was embarrassed too. Russians are startled when they find that American generals and privates smoke the same kind of cigarettes. A Red Army private would spend six weeks' pay to buy a pack of cigarettes as good as his general's. Instead, the Russian private smokes what is almost sawdust.

Emotionally, nearly all Russians feel themselves part of a large family. The chief exception is the small group of Russian leaders and intellectuals. The leaders think of the mass of "common people" as objects, rather than as human beings. Stalin put it this way when he said: "People must be grown carefully and tenderly, just as a gardener grows a favorite fruit tree."

For centuries, the overwhelming majority of Russians have lived and worked with collective units of people—in czarist times, the *mir* (self-governing communes of peasants) and other fair-sized groups. The Russians had an urge for unanimity long before the Big Four or United Nations began meeting. N. P. Semenov wrote in 1894: "The decisions of the *mir* are achieved by unanimous agreement of all the members. If at the time of the meeting there are a few who are opposed, the meeting is considered as incomplete and a failure. Peasants do not understand decisions by majority vote. They know in each case there can only be one proper decision and it should belong to the most clever and truthful of all. To find the truth, all members are supposed to join, and if the solution is found, all the members have to comply with it. In consequence, a member who is in disagreement with the general consent has only one outlet—to separate from the *mir*, to be a member of the village no longer."

The *mir* did use compromise to reach its unanimous solutions, but most Russians know little of majority rule or "loyal opposition."

Some highly interesting theories about the Russian character are contained in Geoffrey Gorer's "Psychology of the People of Great Russia," in the 1948 *Annals of the New York Academy of Sciences*. Over 90 percent of Russian babies, for the first year of their lives, are swaddled so tightly as to be unable to use their limbs. Gorer believes that "this constriction of movement, particularly during the second six months of life, is felt to be supremely painful and frustrating and is reacted to with intense destructive rage, which cannot be physically expressed." Gorer suggests that this babyhood period of intense rage directed at everything around them produces in Russian adults a largely unconscious feeling of pervasive but unfocused guilt. He further conjectures that this "can make some Russians feel responsible for the sins and miseries of the whole world, and gives a general and continuous demand for either confession, atonement, or revenge."

In czarist times, and even to a certain extent today, this feeling was satisfied by Russian religious practices. Religion is still quite widespread in Russia, and I saw many baptisms there, including children of Red Army soldiers. And since most Russian children are still reared in early years by elderly women, nearly all of whom had Russian Orthodox training, a baby often learns to cross himself and to do other rituals even before he can speak. Later, when he goes to Orthodox confession, the priest cross-examines him— instead of listening to him volunteer a confession, as a Roman Catholic priest does. An Orthodox confessor is almost a prosecuting attorney as well as a judge; he can refuse to give absolution if the penitent persists in denying sins of which the confessor accuses him.

Russians reared in Orthodox religion can get temporary relief from their pervasive feeling of guilt by confession and absolution. Their belief in admission of guilt makes it possible for them to admit that others could also be absolved of guilt. But Russians who were not brought up in this belief, or who have abandoned it, have no way in which they can individually rid themselves even temporarily of their own feeling of guilt and fear—except perhaps the orgy.

Russia has long been, in so many ways, a country of feast and famine that Russians do place a great emphasis on the *quantity* of pleasure—almost any sort of pleasure—that they can occasionally obtain all at once. One American of my acquaintance, who prides himself on his virility, took a Russian girl to his room at the Hotel Astoria in Leningrad. After they had been together, she went and wallowed happily for a while in his bathtub (running hot water is a very rare luxury for Russians). When she returned to bed, they again had intercourse. Presently she had another long hot bath. She alternated all night and had four of each. In the morning she dashed her host's pride by thanking him for the night and then adding, "I don't know which I enjoyed more, the bed or the baths."

Russians enjoy sex and are quite uninhibited about it. When the opposite sex is available, there is not much Russian homosexuality. The Soviet regime made no moves against homosexuality until the 30s, when the Nazis, who never missed a trick, realized that a few Soviet officials could be reached in that fashion. They sent some handsome young Germans to Moscow in the hope of thus picking up information (as they kept handsome young Germans in Rome to squire around ladies influential in the Mussolini regime). The Kremlin promptly pounced. It was on this occasion that a high Soviet official made the remarkable statement that there are only three truly world-wide associations—those of Communists, Roman Catholics, and homosexuals. Communists want only the first of the three.

Russians are good haters. The czars developed a technique of diverting this hate away from their oppressive regime by pointing out to ordinary Russians other groups that would, if they could, oppress them still more. The czars often used the Jews as this bogey. The Communists have greatly extended the technique of implying that their removal would lay ordinary Russians open to still greater restrictions by their next rulers—whom the Kremlin has at various times identified as Trotskyists, Fascists, capitalists, all foreigners, etc. etc.

Much of this came up in one short monologue which a slightly tipsy factory director from the Urals gave an American in a Moscow restaurant early in 1947.

"When a common worker got his pay before the Revolution," this Russian of fifty-six told his chance companion, "he would look at it and say, 'Too little for boots, too much for bread, just right for vodka.' In spite of all our leaders' fine promises, it is still the same today. Russians have never been well governed. Before the Revolution, the regime was a joke. Now it's a disaster. Life is slavery here. Recently I sat behind a young soldier and his girl at an American film. The soldier said to her, 'Oh, to live like that, if only for a couple of hours.' It is terrible to hear that sort of thing. Our people were poor before the Revolution. We are poor now, but we were happier then. We had some freedom. Now there is none. But if Russia has another revolution, she will lose her importance and we will be poorer and more miserable than ever."

Many Russians feel like this man from the Urals, and say so when reckless or drunk. But despite their misery, they do believe the Soviet propaganda that they would be still worse off if Russia had another change of regime. The czars told ordinary Russians that their next rulers would be worse—and the Communists are. Now the Communists teach the same thing, so ordinary Russians have a double reason to believe it.

The Kremlin trains Russians to hate non-Communist nations. A Soviet school text declares: "The pupils of the Soviet school must realize that the feeling of Soviet patriotism is saturated with irreconcilable hatred toward the enemies of Soviet society. . . . It is necessary to learn, not only to hate the enemy, but also to struggle with him, in time to unmask him, and finally, if he does not surrender, to destroy him. . . . To vanquish the enemy is impossible without the most burning hatred of him."

3

Despite these disturbing traits in the Russian people, the more disturbing because of the way the Kremlin plays on them, you quickly feel great affection for Russians. They can be as kind as they are cruel. Very few of them know the meaning of moderation, but still fewer know the meaning of avarice. They have so little, most of their lives are so near the knife edge of terrible want that they often fight quite frantically for a toehold on a trolley or a few sticks of wood for their stove. But once they have managed to grab their tiny share, they are again very friendly. They will help the next fellow get his or, if the supply has already run out, give him some of their little. They will share their last piece of bread with a stranger—or ignore some one dying in the street. Unable to do anything about it myself, I saw this last in Moscow, where a man was bleeding to death from a motor accident and the many passers-by on the crowded street did nothing for the twenty minutes before the police arrived.

Moscow subway scrimmages are even bitterer than those in

Manhattan. But once aboard, Russians are again very generous. The Moscow subway has many beggars, and they reap a tidy harvest. One evening an old beggar with straggly gray beard passed through my car. Nearly everyone dropped something into his outstretched cap. Two factory girls sitting across from me were chewing sunflower seeds. (Russians chew these much as Americans chew gum.) The two girls whispered. Then each took a handful of the seeds from her pocket, and one girl clutching the double handful ran after him and dumped them in his cap. He smiled gratefully; this was a real windfall. Meanwhile, a bespectacled office girl with two heavy bundles seized the opportunity and the temporarily vacant seat.

When the factory girl returned a moment later, a short sharp argument ensued. "That's my seat." "You left it." "But you saw why I did—one ought to give to a beggar." "I don't care; you left it." "You selfish office pig." "Use any names you like. I'm above that—and I'm keeping this seat." The factory girl had to stand.

You get such contrasts and contradictions in Russia almost instant by instant. My first sight after the plane landed provided a striking example. There was the modern, glassy airport building and trudging toward it through the snow a string of ragged people each of whom, along with their bundles, carried a great bunch of mimosa. They were passengers of a just-landed plane from the Crimea; loving flowers like all Russians, they had brought back these that would last awhile in Moscow's bitter winter.

There are the endless contrasts of Moscow, the most isolated of the world's great capitals. When I toured the Kremlin, I found at the heart of this Soviet holy of holies, beside the soaring 16th-Century bell tower of Ivan the Terrible, a huge wooden spool of American wire stamped on the side WESTERN ELECTRIC—POST NO BILLS. The Kremlin is on a little hill above the small, sluggish, sewage-filled Moscow River; its medieval walls and towers still dominate Moscow and, with the adjacent St. Basil's Cathedral (the most beautifully incredible structure I ever saw), make the bustling city around them seem rather tawdry.

Moscow celebrated its eight hundredth birthday in September 1947. The city as a whole and its fire department and subways, received the Order of Lenin; the trolleys were presented with the Order of the Red Banner; the waterworks got the Order of the

Patriotic War, First Class. The subway system, while short and jammed, is the only clean one I know except London's; squads of women are endlessly swabbing down its stations. No non-Russian would give the other city services a medal. They are, frankly, terrible by American standards. The contrast in Russia's capital is between a few showy things for the elite and almost nothing for the masses.

Get off the occasional show avenue like Gorki Street (even the show streets are very spotty), and you soon wonder at Soviet propaganda about "Communist construction." Nearly all of Moscow is an overcrowded slum, most of which has had no street or sidewalk repair since the Revolution. These areas are littered with refuse. Within a thousand feet of the Kremlin, there are slums as bad as anything in Naples or Harlem. Moscow's best is not as good as what Naples or Harlem can offer. When the sun begins to warm the city in May, grandmothers come out with the tight-swaddled babies to sit; those of more fortunate families at the same time anxiously watch the family's one or two thin chickens scratching in the city filth. Moscow has thousands of log houses, sometimes an acre full of them alongside a ten-story apartment house. In the winter, men are constantly pushing snow off the roofs while women shovel it in the main streets. You buck through the drifts on the side streets as best you can. In the summer, the same women hose down the main streets to keep them a little less dusty. Even here, Russians know better than to disobey their set orders. A sprinkling truck was operating near the Kremlin one dry day when a storm sprang up. Though the rain was pelting down, the truck kept right on sprinkling!

To stroll even fifty miles around Moscow (I walked over three hundred there) is to realize that city planning is a meaningless term in the Soviet capital. A few streets have been widened, more or less at random; a few new buildings constructed, even more at random. In a city of little motor traffic and millions of pedestrians, sidewalks on the main thoroughfares are so narrow that many people have to walk in the streets, where they frequently get hit.

The crowds are as drab as their Communist capital. As an American said to me: "All the clothes in Russia look like one big rummage sale." Russians are so short of everything that they think a U.S. mail-order catalogue as magical as Aladdin's lamp. An old copy of *Vogue* sells for $125 because the dresses it illustrates are so much better looking than anything Russian. An American woman showed a group of Russian women a half-dozen copies of *Vogue*. They asked which was the latest year, as they wanted to see the newest styles. She explained that they were all the same year, that *Vogue* comes out twice a month. The Russians refused to believe her. "It would be impossible," one of them declared, "for any country to publish such a remarkable magazine more than once a year."

Clothes themselves cost much more than the *Vogue*. I met one Russian important enough to have been sent to Moscow by his Siberian city on a purchasing mission. He had rags wrapped round his feet. His shoes had been stolen in a public bath the day after he arrived and he could not possibly afford to buy another pair.

An American couple lived for some time in a room and bath at a Moscow hotel. One day the hotel's assistant manager came to the wife and said: "Would madam please be more fair in how she leaves things?" It developed that one maid cleaned the bath, and another the bed-living room. Each room had a wastebasket, and one of the maids' most coveted tips was what went into them. Not realizing this, the American couple had been putting most of their empty bottles, bits of food, cigarette butts, etc. in the bathroom basket—and the other maid had complained about the discrimination. After that, they were very careful to distribute these favors fairly.

There is the contrast between the dry impersonality of the regime and the joyous abandon of the people when they feel it is safe to let themselves go. The newspapers have no personal and hardly any local news; for instance, no marriage or death notices are allowed. Moscow had its greatest flood since 1908 while I was there; in America, that would have been good for an equal flood of news and human-interest stories. The Russian papers all ignored it for a week. Then all of them the same day carried the same brief article that said, in effect, "Moscow is having a flood." That was all. They never did run a picture of it. The people have their own word-of-mouth grapevine, which carries an amazing amount of information and rumors.

In one Moscow park I watched for half an hour while a father in his late thirties and his daughter of seven romped in the snow. (Russian fathers take great interest in their children.) Together the two slid step by step down a twenty-foot icy bank into a little ravine. The father clung with supposed desperation to a lamp post part way down. Then he pretended to lose his footing and let go of her. Down in the ravine he imitated an airplane, loading her aboard his shoulders, stretching out his arms for the wings (as she twined her legs round his neck and clung to the top of his head), revving up the engine with guttural throat rumbles and then, as the engine mounted to a roar, dashing down the path that served as runway. On their way back up the bank, to her great joy, he started to slip back time and again. When she finally reached the top of the bank, with her father still several feet below it, he pantomimed that he simply could *not* get up the rest of the way himself, that she would have to help; in fact, drag him up by sheer force! Giggling, gurgling and squealing with sheer delight, she tugged till he did get up.

I spent the rest of that afternoon at a market, near Pushkin Square, where collective farmers sold food grown on their own small personal holdings. City folk lined the alley that led into the stalls, selling bits of their belongings to raise money for food. Among their offerings were postcards of the Gibson-girl era, three secondhand toothbrushes, a pair of children's rubbers, two light bulbs, a battered saucepan, several hairpins and a large tin bathtub. One frail white-haired lady who strikingly resembled my seventy-four-year-old Aunt Pauline was holding up a soiled pillow with bare blue-veined hands in the freezing March weather. A woman asked her the price—$18—as I passed, and drew out a chicken feather through the one hole in the casing to test the stuffing. The $18 could buy less than two pounds of butter in the market itself.

Inside the market enclosure policemen eyed the crowd as it milled past the long unpainted wooden stalls with their tin-topped counters. I spent two hours moving slowly up and down along the stalls. People priced, haggled, and when they made a deal produced their own bottles or cans for milk, and their own newspapers to wrap the food. Russian dailies are used for a variety of other functions, from cigarette to toilet paper. An Army lieutenant and his wife were shopping for a hundred grams (about a quarter-pound) of beef. They argued quite awhile about cut and price and at last struck a bargain at $2.08 for the quarter-pound. Then he took a military textbook and several military maps from his shabby imitation-leather brief case to put the precious package safely at the bottom, so it could not possibly get lost on the way home.

As the winter twilight closed in, people began leaving. The peasants had a long way to go, first by bus or train and then on foot. City people could linger a little later, though in Moscow's slow, overburdened, bemedaled transport system they might well take a couple of hours to get a few miles. As I edged through the ice-covered alley toward the street that would lead me back to Pushkin's statue, I passed the frail old lady with the soiled pillow. She was still holding it up, her hands bluer than ever.

4

Given half a chance, Russians are as friendly and delightful as Italians. They too like a bit of leisure. They too like to joke about themselves. Like Italians under Mussolini, they too joke about their regime when they feel they dare.

A Russian joke of the last category is the definition of a Fascist as "any person who places the interests of his own country above those of the Soviet Union." Another is the question: "Have we built socialism yet—or are things going to get worse?" A third tells of two old Russian friends who encountered each other for the first time in years. "How are they treating you?" asked one. "Just like Lenin." "What do you mean?" "Oh, they won't feed me and they won't bury me."

Russians can get up to ten years' imprisonment for "anti-State anecdotes," so they are careful to whom they tell them. But they keep on telling them. A Russian told me this story: A Soviet soldier about to be discharged was up before his commanding officer, who asked, "Where were you born?" "St. Petersburg." "Where were you educated?" "Petrograd." "Where were you working when drafted?" "Leningrad." "Where do you wish to work after your discharge?" "St. Petersburg."

Students at the Marx-Engels-Lenin Institute, one of the Communist faith's leading seminaries, say that the statue of Lenin there with his arm pointing into the distance is advising everybody to get out of the Soviet Union.

Many stories are told on marshals' and generals' wives, especially their grasping and *nouveau-riche* qualities. One such wife was moving to a new apartment befitting her husband's high rank. When the movers put her piano in the living room, she ordered it moved to a smaller room. The foreman protested: "There's not enough resonance in there." "Never mind," she said. "You just move the piano and I'll tell my husband to bring back some resonance from Germany."

Russians are sometimes shocked out of their carefully practiced caution when their rulers' latest move catches them flat footed. While I was in Moscow, in Russia's official gazette for printing new laws and decrees there suddenly appeared, buried in a small notice on a back page, a rule forbidding all marriages between Soviet citizens and foreigners. When an American reporter asked a fairly high official of the Soviet Foreign Office for comment, the official said: "That is quite impossible. You have made some mistake." The Russians I told it to were incredulous. Every one of them, when finally convinced by the printed evidence of the official Soviet gazette, was embarrassed and apologetic at this fresh instance of the Kremlin's stern, unbending isolationism. The rule had been inspired by the fact that about one hundred Americans, Britons, and men of other nations stationed in Russia during the war had married Russian girls and were now desperately trying to get them out. British Foreign Secretary Bevin had just taken up the matter in person with Stalin, asking permission for fifteen Russian wives to join their husbands in Britain. Stalin had turned Bevin down flat.

The Russians to whom I showed this decree need not have been surprised. It was yet another proof that the more things change in Russia, the more they remain the same. That very week someone had shown me the English-language edition, published in Moscow in 1947, of Soviet Academician R. Wipper's *Ivan Grozny*, an historical study of sixteenth-century Russia. This highly esteemed Soviet historian had written:

The request of the Danish Government to allow the Danish Ambassador's wife, whom he had married in Moscow, to leave for Denmark was rejected. In its reply the Department for Foreign Affairs took the liberty of expressing itself in that lofty didactic tone in which Moscow usually addressed smaller states and at the same time of flaunting her cultural superiority, as if Moscow was the bulwark of freedom and the natural rights of man. "For," we read, "that woman is of our domain, and it would be unseemly to give that woman in bondage to your man Sidor."

Moscow was repeating itself, more than four hundred years later! (When I cabled that passage to *Time*, the Soviet censor stopped the entire cable.) In Russia, one does soon realize that many aspects of Soviet life are not so much Soviet as they are Russian. They actually date back to Catherine the Great, Peter the Great, Ivan the Terrible, or on into the mists of Russian antiquity.

Meanwhile, in any century, ordinary Russians scrape along any way they can. George Backer of the St. Louis *Post-Dispatch*, breakfasting with me in the ornate dining room of the Moskva Hotel the morning after we arrived, said: "Last night the waiters were stealing the sugar. This morning they're stealing the bread. What does the Kremlin expect us to think when that happens in Russia's finest hotel?" It showed not only Soviet shortages but Russian resourcefulness. As long as the conference group was there and supplies were plentiful, the waiters slid bread and lump sugar into their pockets as they cleared the tables—whenever they thought another Russian was not watching. They never bothered about a visitor watching; they were not scared of us.

You can always tell a lot about people from the way they act in a department store. The Mostorg, the best store in Moscow (pop. 7,000,000), is smaller and has a far poorer selection of goods than Swern's, one of the best in my home town of Trenton, New Jersey (pop. 124,697). But the people act much the same in it.

Take Olga. I watched her for half an hour at the Mostorg's sweater counter. She was the Soviet equivalent of a dashing young American matron. She had brought along two friends about her age—late twentyish—for company and moral support. I learned her name because they called her Olga. She waited in line awhile. Finally she got a young salesgirl in a light blue rayon smock. As in America, she then had the girl bring down half a dozen possible sweaters. Eventually she chose three—a plaid, a navy blue with red piping, and a burnt orange—to model at the mirror by the window. She took off her coat and scarf, which one friend carefully held, and tried on all three, pirouetting, fitting them carefully around her shoulders, trying the neck lines up, down and turned in, chattering a blue streak. "The orange is not quite becoming to my complexion. . . . Does the plaid go with this scarf Dmitri got me in Budapest? . . . My dear, what do *you* think?" She settled on the navy blue, got back to the counter, suddenly changed her mind again, had a few more sweaters brought down from the shelves, almost picked a brown one with yellow daisies embroidered round the cuffs, discarded it for a dusty pink one with white scallops at the neck, tried that on, and decided she really wanted the navy blue after all, while her friends clucked sympathetic noises.

The salesgirl wrote a slip. Olga took it over and stood in line by one of the cashier booths scattered about every fifty feet through the Mostorg, handed over her money, had the sale rung up on a black and chrome cash register stamped MADE IN JAPAN (and presumably Acquired In Manchuria), got her change along with the receipt, handed the receipt to the salesgirl, who did up the sweater in butcherlike wrapping paper, tucking in the ends for of course the Mostorg had no string. It is one of the few Russian stores where you don't provide your own newspaper for wrapping things. Off the trio went, looking both exhausted and relieved. I felt the same myself; I had stood a little way off, panting through each of the processes with them. Olga's last words were: "I *hope* Dmitri likes it. But you can never tell about men." I hope he did too; his girl had done her best.

As I say, it was rather like America. One difference was that the sweater, of a quality that would cost about $6 at Swern's in Trenton, had cost $71.25. It was an occasion almost the equivalent of buying a new fur coat in America. That was why Olga had brought her friends. It was probably the one major new purchase she was making for her spring and summer wardrobe—and she spent a couple of months' salary on it.

And how poorly this dashing young Russian matron was dressed. One American summed up Soviet styles succinctly by saying: "There isn't a girdle in the entire Soviet Union. You always see the bulge in their belly and the crack in back." Olga, like most Russian girls, even those lucky enough to be able to spend $71.25 on a sweater, was also cotton stockinged, coarse shoed, straight haired and sallow complexioned. Life is not very good to girls in Russia. They have to work very hard indeed. The few available fripperies are poor and expensive.

The unquenchable Russian humor flared at the Mostorg's wall-paper counter. Husband and wife had picked the paper but were quarreling about what color the ceiling was to be painted. The husband wanted cream, the wife white. Clearly they had the usual Russian one-room-for-everything apartment, for at last the spare-time paper hanger who was going to do the job for them some evening soon, settled the argument in the wife's favor by saying to the husband: "After all, comrade, which of you will look at the ceiling?"

The Soviet authorities show less humor. Some U.S. soldiers attached to the American Embassy formed a small jazz band which they named "The Kremlin Crows." Soon the Embassy got an official protest from the Soviet Foreign Office, demanding that this undignified name be removed from the band's drum. It was duly painted over. The bandsmen now call themselves—un-officially—"The Purged Pigeons."

Clowns must walk a tightrope too. Recently *Komsomol Pravda* sharply reprimanded circus performers whose acts were "unbe-comingly light in tone." (The exact note of seriousness a circus should strike was not specified.) About the same time a star of the Moscow circus, the popular clown Karandash, was jailed for one of his acts. He had sat on a sack of potatoes and when asked by his stooge why he did it, replied: "All Moscow is sitting on (i.e., hoarding) potatoes." Presently Karandash returned. The sack did not.

In Leningrad I noticed some double-headed czarist eagles along a fine, cast-iron fence. "I see they're still there," I said to the Russian guide with me. "Yes," she said. "They're beautiful. We don't mind history."

When Russia's rulers do remove something, there is little the people can say. Girdling Moscow, on the site of its old city wall, is a boulevard nearly two hundred feet wide. Muscovites call it the "B Ring." I often drove along some part or other of the B Ring. Almost every Russian who ever accompanied me on it, from minor Soviet officials to plain citizens and chauffeurs, spontaneously remarked about the green belt of trees and grass that used to run down its middle. They all volunteered that it had been much more attractive then. Clearly none of them ventured protest when the Soviet authorities had all the greenery ripped up and replaced with bare, bumpy asphalt—making the boulevard much wider than traffic required, and far too wide for pedestrians to cross with safety or comfort. In America, there can be screams of protest if the civic fathers so much as rename an alley.

5

In their quiet, patient way the Russian people have recesses which even the Kremlin cannot control. Perhaps the chief of these is religion. Religious persecution in Soviet Russia was never so bad as it was under Rome's Nero or Diocletian. There were always some churches open above ground, not just in catacombs. Now there are more, and the Kremlin has allowed more than a dozen seminaries to reopen. It has made other small but significant concessions. Russians have always liked to bake certain cakes at Easter. In years past the special ingredients for these cakes used to pop up in Soviet stores—possibly by sheer coincidence—a week or two before Easter. In 1947 it was no coincidence. Many stores had the ingredients piled on separate counters, with the sign EASTER SPECIALS.

The whole history of Christianity shows that once active persecution has ceased, religion returns with the slow steady power of a rising tide. There are at least some signs it is doing so in Russia. There are still official Soviet pronouncements against religion. *Young Bolshevik* recently had the most open antireligious attack the Soviet press has published since the Nazi invasion in 1941. It quoted Stalin: "The Communist Party must be antireligious since its activity is founded upon science, which is antireligious." The article then stated: "If a Young Communist believes in God or goes to church, he is not fulfilling his obligations." *Komsomol Pravda* has criticized Soviet teachers for failing to give their pupils "clear and firm atheistic beliefs."

Apparently the Kremlin thinks that time is on its side and that a state-fostered, materialistic outlook will in due course eliminate religion. The Kremlin might be right. But I saw nothing in Russia that approached the deep enthusiasm and emotion in tens of thousands of Russians of both sexes and all ages in Moscow on Easter eve. I went first to the Church of the Resurrection, where some two thousand had jammed every inch inside and thousands more were milling cheerfully in the square outside, holding the little tapers they would light at midnight. People were perched thick on every window sill, peering into the church. Then I went on to the Easter service at Epiphany Cathedral, conducted by the Patriarch. Some twenty thousand people were happily shouting, singing and shoving outside its doors. Inside, over seven thousand packed it to the eaves. At midnight, when the Patriarch chanted "Christ is risen!", the choir took up the refrain, and lights from the candle which the Patriarch lighted spread quickly from taper to taper throughout the whole cathedral. Their little lights flickered on the most deeply happy faces I saw in all Russia.

After the period of fairly severe religious persecution from 1923 to 1941, the Kremlin made concessions to the people's clear desire for more than a trickle of religion. The new religious literature is printed at the old Godless Press—under that imprint! Which could indicate that the Godless Press may some day be used again for its old purpose of publishing antireligious literature. The Kremlin has had the same experience with Russia's literary classics. It long restricted the reading of many works by Dostoievsky, Gogol, Ostrovsky, Pisemsky and Ouspensky. It has gradually brought them back because the people wanted to read them.

As an American who knows Russia well has said: "The strength of the Kremlin lies largely in knowing how to wait. The strength of the Russian people is in knowing how to wait longer."

6

The people were the single most impressive thing I saw in Russia. They made the Red Square May Day parade my single most impressive experience there. The Russian border inspectors were right to be moved by that little lavender-colored pass. No one who has seen Moscow's May Day Parade could ever possibly underestimate the might and magnificence of Russia. I stood at one spot and watched a million people walk by. I have seen Bastille Day crowds in Paris and Holy Week crowds jamming St. Peter's in Rome and the great square outside. I have seen the

Easter parades of Seville, Spain. In Britain I have seen the processions and vast crowds for a king's funeral and a king's coronation. I have seen the crowds at Coney Island on a hot summer Sunday. They all shrink beside a Moscow May Day.

I do not mean the military part of the parade, which took up the first hour. The troops, the tanks, the trucks, the guns were well deployed but nothing special. The 310 airplanes (which included only five four-engined planes, three of them bombers) were not impressive compared to Western nations' air spectacles. They did include 105 jet fighter planes, the first time Russia had shown jet planes publicly—and the Soviet censor, true to form, killed all references to them in reporters' cables.

Nor do I mean the appearance of Stalin and other members of the Politburo on the reviewing level atop Lenin's tomb. That was interesting, not least interesting because of the heavy array of uniformed secret police officers—not soldiers, every one of them was an officer—flung around all four sides of the tomb and kept alert through the long parade by being replaced with files of fresh officers every half hour. These officers first appeared a few minutes before the Politburo put in its appearance. After the military part of the parade, extra files of secret policemen were marched in to line the entire circuit of Red Square, before the people were allowed in for their "spontaneous demonstration." Across the hundred-yard cobbled width of Red Square, other files of troops were placed every fifteen feet, stretching the whole length of the square from the Historical Museum on the west to St. Basil's Cathedral on the east. These troops stood literally shoulder to shoulder and alternately faced opposite directions so they could watch everybody. Every third one of these troops was also a secret policeman; the rest were picked soldiers from the Kremlin's crack Guards Divisions. These twenty files of troops split the people's procession into twenty long narrow lengths, like twenty parallel pieces of spaghetti, and of course controlled and directed the people every instant they were in Red Square.

All these elaborate precautions were not perfectly successful. Just before May Day the American photographers—who had been given permission to stay on after the Moscow Conference and been promised they could take pictures of the Red Square ceremony—were suddenly informed that they could have passes but could not take pictures. To tell that to an American photographer is just to egg him on. Tom McAvoy of *Life* slung one camera around his neck and another over his shoulder, each one bulkier than a pistol or a hand grenade. During the military part of the parade he stood on a balcony just outside the square, where he could get mass-effect shots. (He had first locked the door of the balcony, as well as the door of the room, so he would not be disturbed.) When the people's parade began, Tom turned spontaneous demonstrator and came in on the far side of the square, where he spent a busy quarter of an hour getting fine pictures of the parade, with Lenin's tomb and the Kremlin as a background. Finally, still not showing his pass and still using only the one Russian word *pajolsta* (please), Tom gradually angled the entire way across the slow-moving people's parade and through its twenty interspersed files of secret police and soldiers, to a stance directly in front of the tomb. He shot pictures of Stalin and the others to his heart's content—from a few yards' distance. All the secret policemen there and elsewhere assumed he was just another photographer who had permission to move about.

To cap the climax, Molotov, standing beside Stalin, saw him busily snapping just below. Tom had photographed Molotov on his visits to America and, of course, regularly took his picture during the Moscow Conference. Molotov knew him, and had no way of knowing that scared Soviet underlings had forbidden the American photographers to take any pictures on May Day. He nodded and beamed at Tom, and then waved at him.

Tom is one of the most American Americans I know. He has all the humor, verve, nerve, and ingenuity which this episode implies. I was dumfounded then utterly delighted when, from my front-row stand in the bleacher section nearest Lenin's tomb, I saw him come through the parade and start shooting the Politburo. Then he came over to our reporters' row, where he was supposed to have been from the beginning, and with twinkling eyes told us the whole story. I felt honored when he slipped me some of his film rolls to hold in case he got searched as he left the square. His pictures made a striking display in *Life*. They held a laugh and a hope. When Americans are American enough, they have a knack of peacefully getting through impossible difficulties.

Stalin occasionally moved from side to side of the forty-foot reviewing walk on top of the tomb, to stretch his legs. But he never sat down, and he never long stopped waving in acknowledgement of the cheers. He was within sixty feet when he came to the end of the reviewing walk nearest me, and through powerful field glasses I had several good, unhurried looks at him. He is a short man, even among his short companions. He has a sallow complexion; it sees little sunlight. His hair and mustache were grayer than I expected; his features had life and expression when he talked, and once or twice chuckled, with his associates. Otherwise his face was an impassive mask, with many wrinkles and pockmarks that do not show in his official photographs. It is the strongest face I have ever seen. Stalin was right when he chose "steel" for his Party name.

When Stalin arrived, just as the Kremlin clock struck ten, he came through the gray-painted door under the small turret in the Kremlin wall directly behind the tomb. On either side of this door are the black marble squares behind which are the ashes of Communist heroes buried in the Kremlin wall, including one American, John Reed. He swung round the tomb and walked up the steps on its front, Red Square side to the lower reviewing level, accompanied by the Politburo, a few other top Soviet figures, and some bemedaled secret police officers. Then he mounted the steps to the upper reviewing level all by himself, to a patter of applause from the small crowd of pass-holders. Once he was up there in the center, alone, the other leaders started up, with Molotov in the van. They grouped themselves on either side of him. But the Leader had first made his solitary, symbolic appearance. The tailored simplicity of his plain military topcoat and uniform, with no visible medal or decoration, contrasted sharply with the other uniformed figures up there—who all dripped medals, ribbons and jeweled orders.

The only other glimpse I had of Stalin was in his box at the Bolshoi Theater. He enters this box, at stage level just to the left of the orchestra pit, after the lights have gone down and the stage curtain up, so the audience attention will be concentrated on the stage. He similarly leaves just before the end of each act, returning only when the curtain has again risen. He sits in a corner of the box shielded from the audience, so the only time one sees him there is when he draws aside the curtain at the door of the box to enter or leave. Then some people in certain parts of the theater can see him silhouetted for a moment against the ligh of the passage outside. (His favorite Bolshoi performance is re portedly Tchaikovsky's opera *Eugene Onegin*.) Hundreds o secret policemen are everywhere in the Bolshoi whenever he i there—two at the back of each box and others sprinkled thickl through the orchestra, easily recognized by their ill-fitting blue o gray suits and the fact they never talk to anybody or watch the performance.

Such are the precautions to keep Russia's leader from assassina tion—far greater than those for a president, the only American official so protected. (Three American presidents have been assas sinated since 1865; in that period only one czar, Alexander II in 1881, and one Politburo member, Sergei Kirov in 1934, have been assassinated, both in the city that is now Leningrad.) In the Soviet system, not one man but thousands are constantly protected. There seemed no real need for it, but Communist suspicion is widespread. I heard a great deal of what certainly seemed like genuine, voluntary admiration for Stalin, some for Molotov and some for Zhdanov. I never heard any Russian volunteer a word of praise for Beria, head of the secret police, who ranks third on the Politburo, behind Stalin and Molotov and just ahead of Zhdanov. Few people anywhere love policemen; Russians have less reason to love them than most.

I have missed my main point in writing this chapter if I have not made it clear that for centuries the Russian people have been accustomed to a leader and to forms of collective living. Soviet Russia is a land where a handful of sunflower seeds is a generous gift to a beggar, where a sweater costs two months' wages, where jail is risked by a joke. It is a land whose people's spirit is a strange compound of pride and inferiority, hate and friendship, gentleness and violence, patriotism and dissatisfaction, fear and hope—all flavored with tradition. It is a land of less hope and more disillusion than in the early years of Communism, but one that still has some hope, at least enough to keep many young Russians striving. It is an old land, where youth is very important. It is a land of a great, unconquerable people who have been beaten into passive silence by dictatorship. It is a land which any nation can live with, if it shows strength and patience, firmness and consistency, political health, and willingness to fight when it must for its principles. Finland and Turkey, both small nations on Russia's very borders, have been that resolute and thus far retain their own tradition.

It is a land where I could see that May Day parade. For weeks beforehand I had seen various civilian columns around Moscow practicing for their part in this "spontaneous" people's demonstration. That, plus all the guards I saw in Red Square, made me a bit cynical about this "people's" part of the proceedings before it started.

But nothing prepares one for that parade. What a milling mass of humanity it was. This, in the living, slowly moving flesh is the great flowing tide of man, woman, and child power that is the chief single characteristic of this vast land. Part of the procession was in organized groups. Most of it was people, just sauntering along. Whole families were there: mothers walking hand in hand with little girls and boys, fathers with still smaller children on their shoulders. There were not only endless pictures of Stalin and the Politburo; endless red flags; endless factory, club, shop and organization floats and banners. There were kids tugging at toy balloons and occasionally, as at any circus, losing their grip so the gay-colored bubbles floated up over the crowd.

This slow, steadily moving mass goes on hour after hour after hour the whole great width and length of Red Square, without ever a break or gap or pause. A voice over the loudspeaker regularly bade those in the square to "Hurrah for Stalin!" ("Hurrah" is the same word in Russian as in English.) Those opposite the tomb always did, though there was never a cheer from the whole crowd in Red Square at once. But everybody as they came by turned their faces quite naturally and spontaneously up toward Stalin and the leaders on the tomb. Shifting the range of my field glasses around through the crowd, I could see that most of them were smiling. The children especially would wave and cheer.

At last this seemingly endless stream of humanity did gradually taper to an end. It was Russia that had passed in the shape of her greatest strength: her patient, pliant, almost tireless people who can make up for almost any stupidity, brutality or miscalculation of their masters. The Russian people did that against the Tartars, Napoleon and the Nazis. They would do it against any other invader. No procession I am ever likely to see will have the force, impact or sheer splendor of those million ragged people.

Chapter 4. THE POWER

THE Communists have far more power over the ordinary Russian than the czars ever had; they are far more thorough. Both systems seized men and sent them to Siberia. The Communists do it at least a hundred times oftener than the czars, who never had more than fifty thousand prisoners in Siberia at any one time. The Communists have had at least five million there ever since 1930, when they started handling the kulaks, or well-to-do peasants, as they have since handled other groups in their grip (for example, the Party's own members in the great 1934-38 purge, Crimean Tartars, Volga Germans, and many people from Poland, Bessarabia, Latvia, Lithuania, and Estonia).

That is not to defend the czars. Few Americans would care to live under either regime. In the Lenin Museum in Moscow, there is a section devoted to Lenin's exile to Siberia as a czarist political prisoner. There are photographs of his log hut, of his wife Krupskaya who joined him during the exile. And there are a couple of shelves of the actual books Lenin studied while he was there, most of them quite anticzarist in their turn of thought.

I stood before that exhibit for a while and thought about the blindness of all tyranny: that of the czars in exiling Lenin and so many others; that of the Communists in placing on public exhibition, for all ordinary Russians to see, such concrete evidence that the tyranny which Communists call the worst in history let a political prisoner like Lenin have a hut of his own, his wife with him, and books against the regime. Czarist prisoners seldom had all three amenities. Soviet prisoners never have any of them and ordinary Russians know it.

Czarism persecuted only those who challenged it; a worker or intellectual who did not hamper the authorities was left alone. Communism does not leave passive people alone. It insists on active, positive participation in its activities not just by bureaucrats and soldiers but by workers and intellectuals—even clowns!

Soviet "democracy" does not reside in constitutional forms. Russia does have a constitution, which *Pravda* has proudly called "the only thoroughly democratic one in the world." When it was promulgated in 1936, *Pravda* had pictures of the document's eight chief founding fathers. At the tenth anniversary celebrations, *Pravda* ran a huge picture of Stalin and had nothing on the other seven. Kalinin had died. Chervyakov, Aitakov, Petrovsky, Musabekov, Khodzhayev and Rakhimbayev had all been shot.

In George Orwell's *Animal Farm*, the constitution was finally reduced to one article: "All animals are equal, but some animals are more equal than others." The Soviet constitution still has its original 146 articles, but two have always been more equal than others. Article 126 makes the Communist Party "the leading nucleus of all organizations . . . both public and state." Article 141 provides that officials can only be nominated by the Party and certain organizations it completely controls.

Many of the 144 other articles sound relatively democratic in the Western sense. But the Russians have a proverb for the mixture: "A spoonful of tar spoils a barrel of honey." Of course in every country the formal constitution differs from the way the government really runs. But Russia has the greatest gap of all. Its constitution promises "freedom of speech, freedom of the press, freedom of assembly," and Soviet authorities ignore all three. In the constitution Russians are "guaranteed inviolability of the person," but the secret police arrest anyone they please.

The constitution does not control the Soviet state. The Party controls the constitution. Russia's Communist Party has six million members, or less than one in thirty of Russia's people. Even this elite has no formal power over its leaders. The Party is sharply graded, like everything else in Russia. In Army terms, at most five thousand of these six million Communists are on the General Staff. Perhaps fifty thousand are officers and at most two hundred thousand are noncommissioned officers. The rest form the Party rank and file. Party members do get most of Russia's honors. Of the seven million Soviet fighters who got medals or awards in World War II, over half went to Party members or candidates. Of the eleven thousand who won the gold star of Hero of the Soviet Union (highest military award, comparable to the Congres-

sional Medal or Victoria Cross), 78 percent were Party member
or candidates.

Party members elect the All Union Party Congress of severa
thousand members, which by Party orders must meet at leas
once every three years. It last met in March 1939—which show
about how much influence even this one-thirtieth of the Russiar
people who belong to the Party wield on the Kremlin hierarchy
That ghostly "Congress" in turn elects the seventy-one-membe
Central Committee, which "directs the Party" between Congresse
—and ignores the rule about calling regular Congresses. The
Central Committee in turn relinquishes its power to three Party
organs:

(1) the *Politburo*, a group of fourteen men headed by Stalin
which decides all Soviet domestic and foreign policy and is prob
ably the most powerful group of men in the world;

(2) the *Orgburo*, a group of fifteen men headed by Stalin
which runs the Party. Its first five members form

(3) the *Secretariat*, headed by Stalin, which runs the Orgburo

There is, of course, a Soviet government, but it is not nearly sc
important. The government has a Supreme Soviet, which by the
1936 constitution "has the exclusive legislative power of the
Soviet Union"—but has never yet written any legislation. There
are about 1,300 members, each of them elected without opposi
tion on the one, hand-picked Party slate. Soviet elections draw
about 103 million voters in a population of some 200 million
They are the biggest, and most meaningless, elections on earth
The Supreme Soviet meets in St. Andrew's Hall, inside the Krem
lin walls, for a few days each year to applaud, and unanimously
endorse, the Politburo's decisions. Its members have their passe:
checked, line by line and picture with face, three times by the
secret police each and every time they enter the Kremlin for a
meeting. Not even this chosen group is trusted. In all the years
the Supreme Soviet has met, not one of its 1,300 members has
once voted "no" to anything.

For about 360 of the 365 days a year, the Supreme Soviet is no
in session. Then its functions are carried out by a Presidium of
thirty-three members with a chairman, Nikolai Shvernik, who is
sometimes called the president of the Soviet Union. Shvernik is
on the Politburo, and his two key colleagues are on the Secre

tariat. At the top of this formal governmental—as distinct from Party—structure is the seventy-six-member Council of Ministers, "the highest executive and administrative organ of state authority." Its chairman, Premier Stalin, and nine vice-chairmen, headed by senior Deputy Premier Molotov, all just happen to be on the Party's Politburo!

This handful of men who are at the top of the Communist Party, and its stooge the Soviet government, are smart as well as tough. In the Politburo itself they permit fairly free discussion. In private Party meetings at a lower level they also permit, under very careful supervision, something that at least remotely resembles free discussion. This freedom is only up to a sharp, soon-drawn point. When the decision is handed down from above at the end of the debate, that is that. Everybody obeys it or else.

But there has been some grousing and debating first, and by a political osmosis as mystifying as the way sap rises in an oak, a little of the argument somehow, sometimes gets to the Politburo at the very top of the tree. If it does not get there otherwise, it may come straight to a member of the Politburo himself. Hundreds, perhaps thousands of key men all over the vast Soviet Union have a patron on the Politburo. They keep him posted. Sometimes one of the Politburo members attends a meeting of the smaller fry and listens in. The talks they occasionally make at the end of such meetings are very revealing. One can learn more by studying such a speech than one can from the longest and most learned analysis of the Soviet political structure.

2

The most revealing Soviet speech in many years was one made by Mikhail Kalinin on August 22, 1945, at the end of just such a meeting of lesser Soviet lights—in this case, a group of regional Party secretaries, organizers and agitators (the Party word for a propagandist, who should keep things stirred up, or agitated, and generally does). A veteran member of the Politburo, Kalinin died (of old age) in 1946. Those who have heard both men say that his informal speaking style was somewhat like Stalin's: neither one a finished orator, but both able to spot the questions troubling their hearers and give them some sort of an answer, sprinkling the whole with dogmatics, dialectics, homely examples and anecdotes.

Foreigners never hear such private Party speeches. Like ordinary Russians, they get only the Soviet harangues and propaganda diatribes. Foreigners and ordinary Russians seldom even see such private speeches. They got a chance to see what Kalinin said on this occasion because the Kremlin found it a very useful answer to problems that Party officers had raised, and had the speech reprinted for select Party members to read. If something is worth reading, it will generally get read—rather widely read. Sometimes even the Kremlin's precautions do not keep what it orders printed for the Party from reaching a larger audience.

Kalinin spoke the very week after World War II ended. At that date, the Politburo already had its answers to postwar problems.. It had a far more definite idea about what it wanted, at home and abroad, than any Western nation then had. The Party officials in this particular Kalinin audience were working primarily with peasants, who are over 60 percent of Russia's population. Kalinin spoke with peasants especially in mind, but his answers apply with equal force to Soviet industrial workers, domestic problems, and foreign policy.

The following full, fair summary of Kalinin's speech repays close reading. It is in Kalinin's own words, carefully translated, and is about three-fifths of his speech. I have cut out certain repetitions, irrelevancies and technicalities; every essential passage is here. The indented passages in italics are mine. They can be skipped by those who wish to read the speech as a whole and get a good, solid chunk of Soviet speech-making at its ablest. Kalinin's words exemplify every one of the Russian psychological traits already discussed:

"Comrades. We have to understand the phenomenon which took place in Soviet villages during the war. One would suppose that the Fascist invasion and other complications might have brought agriculture to decline or fall. What actually happened was that in many districts a growth of agriculture took place. The results were amazing if you remember that the number of farm workers fell, equipment aged, and essential consumer's goods ceased being produced or if at all were produced in very small quantities. Yet it is a fact that collective farms fulfilled the tasks assigned them.

Kalinin uses the standard Communist blend of frankness and deception. The interwoven strands show all through the speech more clearly than usual because he is talking in the family circle. He constantly shows his propagandist hearers how to make propaganda work. Yet even here, speaking privately to convinced Communist leaders, he is a propagandist himself. He juggles his sentences skillfully to imply at least some "growth" of Soviet farm production during the war, when it actually fell about 40 percent.

"What is the reason for this? It seems to me it is patriotism—an outstanding rise of patriotism.

"What conclusion can be drawn? It is that when our people face great tasks of state significance which are clearly understood, then national energy rises, bursting all barriers. Such energy arose among our people when our country faced mortal danger.

"It is most significant that, apart from industrial workers whom we never doubted, we found that collective farmers at the moment of danger are capable of much heroism and are able to achieve great results on very small resources. Before the war there might have been peasants who believed that on a base of individual economics they could accomplish the necessary tasks and produce still more. But the war showed that had it not been for the collective farms, many peasants would have been ruined and there would not have been enough food to supply the Red Army. That would have been close to failure in the war. Now all the peasants fully recognize the advantages of the collective system. This means that they will now be able to understand political events better and will show the same patriotism as city workers in strengthening the Soviet system.

To this inner group, Kalinin admits that the Politburo had never trusted the peasants, and was pleasantly surprised at how well they behaved during the wartime crisis. He goes on to claim that the peasants now fully believe in the blessings of collectivism. They do not. Kalinin did not mention the four billion dollars of American lend-lease food sent to Russia.

No dictator can endure being dependent on anyone; he never feels secure until everyone in his country depends on him.

Without the food the peasants grow, the rest of Russia would starve. The Kremlin resents that. So it controls the peasants every way it can.

"What is our Party propaganda on the farms to make of all this? Four points: we have won; we have become stronger; we have improved Russia's situation territorially and strategically; now all this must be made secure.

"Our most important Party task is to define accurately and explain clearly our new aims. They must be emphasized to all our collective farmers, who must try to achieve them with the same energy and passion they used to achieve victory.

"We have first of all to explain how tremendous is our victory. Russians have known large victories in their past, for instance over Napoleon. For that time, it was a victory of world significance. But the direct results of Napoleon's defeat were much smaller. They were even insignificant compared with our present victory. In the past our people were able to attain large, even great victories, but their governors were not able to extract from victory the people's due deserts. Other states took advantage of Russian success. Now times are not the same, our people are not the same, their government not the same.

"Now we have a very strong Army capable of guaranteeing the state interests of the Soviet Union. But even now, after the very greatest victory known to history, we cannot forget for a single moment one basic fact. Our country remains the single socialist state in the world. You can say this openly to collective farmers: Victory achieved does not yet mean all dangers to our state existence and socialist system have disappeared.

The week after the Allies, including Russia, won the war, no other nation gets one iota of credit for victory. The Soviet line that Russia won singlehanded is already established. So is the line that Russia is alone in the world, encircled by dangerous enemies—"you can say this openly." The United Nations is ignored.

Kalinin also lets the blackest of Communist cats right out of the bag when he speaks, in successive breaths, of "our people . . . their governors" in czarist times and "our people . . . their government" now. This top Communist makes it clear that the Soviet system has no more provided a true "people's state" than did the czars. Referring to either, he mentions the regime separately, and as the operating force.

"We came out of the war stronger and firmer. This was due on the one side to the victories of the Red Army and on the other to the success of the collective farms and industrial plants. They were forces acting in the same direction. You must explain all this to the collective farmers. They must fully understand this process and also that the strength of our state depends on further collective farm efforts.

"Now we must raise still higher the economic and cultural power of the Soviet Union, and by this its defensive ability. This is the axis around which our propaganda must be built in all branches, but with the constant obligation to take account of local life, local conditions, actual tasks.

"Our people are waiting for great material improvement in peacetime. Collective farms must greatly increase their production, for the people's welfare depends on two things: abundance and variety of food, and enough consumer goods.

"If our government had only these tasks, we might satisfy our people fairly soon. But we face other tasks as urgent: restoration and development of the railroads, reconstruction of the enormous damage the enemy did to vast territory, etc.

"You were grumbling here that there are not enough consumer goods. Of course there aren't. Maybe the first six months will not be so very efficient, but by the end of the year consumer goods will start appearing, goods badly needed on collective farms. True, it may not be in great quantity, but still it will appear. It is very important that every one of you understand now the role in the common process and explain all this to our people.

"For instance, an agitator speaking in a weak collective farm must say openly to the workers of this weak collective that our country has won the victory but in order to use the achievement in the proper way it is necessary to make it secure. The agitator will attain what is wanted if he is able to combine the country's aims with local conditions.

By claiming fresh dangers from abroad, the Kremlin is trying to dodge the demands of ill-fed, ill-clothed, ill-housed Russians. It exaggerates the first to avoid doing anything about the second. In the 1930s, Kalinin had denounced "capitalist im-

perialists" for exploiting patriotism and national aggressiveness to take the people's minds off their bellies. By 1945, he is doing just that himself. Three years later, the consumer goods Kalinin promised are still only a trickle.

"There was talk here about plans for further development of agriculture. Certainly it is desirable to set up firm, definite programs. But remember that life itself forces planners to make changes, or demands come from above to change this or that plan. You remember Comrade Stalin said that only bureaucrats can think work is finished when the plan is made. The composition of a plan is only the beginning of planning. Sometimes a number of needs are even forgotten. True planning leadership is developed only after the plan is composed, checked at various points during its fulfillment, corrected and made more accurate by experience.

This paragraph, spoken privately by a Politburo member, is worth remembering every time one reads a story about a Soviet plan, especially a Five Year Plan. Despite all the glowing announcements, no Five Year Plan has ever been as much as 80 percent fulfilled.

The Kremlin does often "forget a number of needs" of the people—never its own needs.

"This is no easy task. It demands high attainments of our regional leaders. The secretary of the *raikom* [district party committee] or the chairman of the *ispolkom* [district Soviet executive] cover far more than prerevolutionary district officials. Then we had a district police official, a chairman of district nobility, a chairman of the elected district council, an inspector of people's education, and the dean of the cathedral. All these former leaders together carried out only a fraction of the work now done by the *raikom* secretary or *ispolkom* chairman. Not only are all economics of a district under your leadership, but also you are rulers over the folk-souls of the people. Never anywhere did men have such power or such influence. You are not only leading economy and policy, but if you fulfill the directives and principal decrees of party and government, if you yourselves understand correctly the system of Soviet power, then you are masters of the people's souls. That is a fact. Your possibilities and your responsibilities are colossal.

This is Kalinin's most horrifying yet hopeful passage. Horrifying, because here is the calm arrogance of men who think they are gods. Hopeful, to non-Communists everywhere, because history shows that once men think that, their eventual downfall is sure.

"But let's come back to the question of socialist planning and what it means. You have been saying here it would be good for every collective to build its own brick plant, mill, etc. One may continue that line further and build for every collective its own tiny enterprises. One should not forget that socialism is co-operation, collective work and co-ordination of all forces. What kind of co-ordination will we have if we build fifty mills in fifty collectives? Mills must be built on such sites, at such road junctions and such distances from collectives to insure the maximum number of collectives the use of one mill. Any attempt to build so that every collective farm woman could run quickly with a sack of grain on her back to her village mill—that is primitive. That does not tend toward mechanization or toward conservation of labor but is more like unorganized waste of it. The same approach must cover the construction of brick plants and similar enterprises. One collective has a large mill and uses it profitably, receiving income from it, and in another is built a tile plant which is also profitably exploited—here is a division of labor and co-ordination. It is still primitive but yet a step higher. In the future all brick plants will be mechanized and brick will easily be transported where needed. But this is certainly not a matter of one year.

"There have been remarks here that some districts are not given the opportunity to specialize along certain agricultural lines because they are required to produce bread and grain as well. I am for specialization. It is more profitable to build a rational economy when you produce not ten kinds of products but, let us say, five. Such conditions make it easier to distribute workers and prepare everything needed for production. But specialization must be thoroughly thought over. Out of specialization, God knows what may come.

Ever try "running quickly" with a sack of grain on your back? In effect, that is what Communists have attempted to make Russians do ever since 1917.

Kalinin speaks of mechanization to conserve human labor and adds that it is "not a matter of one year." Nor of twenty years—the great bulk of Russian work is done by hand. No wheelbarrow or other conveyance is mentioned for the grain sack—you "tote that bale." During my first country drive in Russia I passed twenty-one collective farm villages, each strung out a half-mile or so along the highway which also served as the one village street, with the log huts facing each other across it. Near the center of each was the village well, the only one except at the collective barns. The half mile would be dotted with women—mostly old women since the younger ones were in the fields or at the barns—bent under the weight of their shoulder yokes with a pail of water at each end.

This passage also shows the skillful Soviet blend of local interests and central authority, with never any doubt about which one counts most. The Kremlin is skillful at tailoring propaganda to fit specific local conditions and mentality. But there is doubt about specialization. In 1948, three years later, the Kremlin had still not made up its mind on that moot point.

"There was talk here about people coming back from Germany who have seen 'cultures' of German villages which made a certain impression on them. Our agitators must uncrown this German 'culture.' I will draw a comparison. There are people both in towns and villages who hardly ever read and are really very little developed, who yearn to dress more fashionably, to wear hats, even smoking jackets and use toilet water. They want to seem to be educated people. But by themselves and from inside themselves they are not cultured. Such seems to me to be the culture of the German burgher or rich farmer. This is pure external culture, an empty one, not grasping the depths of the human soul.

"Only German mediocrity is able to view daily the religious and sentimental mottoes which are the standard decoration of the German farmer or burgher's house, and the task of which is to deaden the brain. All this may create an impression on inexperienced people with no esthetic taste. In general, the German standardized way of life cannot blind a reasonable person. By this I don't want to place in disrepute certain organizational habits of Germans or defame German technique. One must make use of one or another, but certainly with careful selection—and without becoming enthusiastic about German buffoonery.

Kalinin here tries to cope with the embarrassing impact that the rest of Europe's higher standards had made on men in the Red Army. The Communist campaign on this has had some success. The Kremlin subjects Russian soldiers to an intensive six-month "re-education" course before allowing them back in Russia, scatters them widely, takes away possessions that "tell a story," and pounces quickly on any who "spread rumors" on their return. Kalinin shows no hatred of Germany—in fact, a selective but sincere admiration for German abilities. Communists are always willing to benefit from other people's technical advances.

The sneering reference to hats is because old-line Communists thought them terribly bourgeois. Kalinin himself, like Lenin, always wore a cap.

"Our culture in general and in villages in particular is different. We know that the culture of the Soviet village is continuously improving. The time is not far away when some of our advanced districts, such as those around Moscow, will have in their collectives many people who have had seven years of school. We must first of all try to raise the general literacy. You spoke about building reading huts and clubs. They are important. But not one of you even mentioned a word about schools.

"Surely you must understand that the significance of schools in the matter of educating the population is incomparably higher than all these other organizations put together. A person spends years in school and receives there a whole complex of knowledge. It is clear that no club, no reading hut can influence him as much. Party workers must constantly watch the school's influence on our future citizens. All our educative enterprises and first of all the schools must feel the Party's influence. You Party secretaries, organizers and agitators must look to that.

"The Party leader must watch whatever work is being done: in people's home needs, promotion of people's culture, administration, economic affairs—everything. The leader must watch the people who do it. It is his task to organize all the people, to convince them. All his work must be saturated with Communist spirit.

"You visit collectives often. Talk man to man and take the bull by the horns. Don't make general charges but give specific facts. Such an approach will be more effective. You should learn beforehand what kind of collective it is and what the people there are like, in order to be able to hurt them to the quick and make them speak for themselves. When you speak in a polished way, you very often do not touch the people you are speaking to and do not disturb their thoughts. But when you use a scraper, then movement begins.

Kalinin tells these leaders that they must minutely supervise every conceivable thing that all other Russians do—especially in education, which I discuss later. A Communist gets a tremendous kick out of running people's lives down to the last detail. That sense of power gives him the joy that other men and women get from drinking, dancing or making love. Communists have their own little refinements to their particular act of pleasure; Kalinin reminds these less skillful devotees that they should "be able to hurt people to the quick. . . . When you use a scraper, then movement begins." Communists have been prodding Russians ever since they got power. These local Communist leaders Kalinin is addressing are somewhat equivalent to the farm agents of American counties; imagine a top Washington leader telling a group of county agents to use all these tactics on American farmers.

"Certainly such a speech is more difficult than one based on ready-made formulas. It is desirable that after you talk you should be surrounded partly by protests, partly by approval. You will get something from such a schooling also. You had not the old school we once had. Our auditoriums were filled not only with adherents but enemies too.

"Once long ago I was speaking in Kazan Province. Suddenly a woman came up and said: 'Here you are walking in good boots and where are boots for us?' I looked at her and said: 'What do you want? That the chairman of the Central Executive Committee, representative of supreme power, should come to you in straw shoes?' People around cried: 'Right, right! This is a stupid woman not to understand that.'

"At present our collective farmers are in a very patriotic mood.

If work among them sometimes goes badly, it will be more the fault of you Party organizers.

"Those are the questions you raised which I considered it necessary to answer. We must all think about strengthening our state, and place that firmly in the minds of all collective and industrial workers. If we achieve that, then everything else will come very fast."

I think Kalinin made a very effective speech. I also think that any non-Communist who takes the trouble to grasp all its implications—who reads, learns and inwardly digests it—will have an understanding of the Soviet Union that will last as long as the Soviet Union does itself. Every essential of the Soviet system is there. These are the themes that crop up again and again in Communist writing, philosophy and propaganda.

If I had to sum up Kalinin's message, or all Communist doctrine, in a single word, I would choose the word "paternalism." The good feelings stirred by fatherly wisdom and guidance are among the most noble known to mankind. They occur in all the great religions and in every happy family life. They are a human universal. The Communists have taken this noble, powerful human universal and, like Kalinin in this speech, twisted it to say that they know how to run everything for everybody. Their paternalism is more pervasive, and infinitely more thorough, than that of the worst company union that ever existed. They have made one-sixth of the world's land surface into a huge company union. They want to turn the whole world into one.

At their best, as here, they are very persuasive. The date is August 22, 1945. The Western world was thrashing about in confusion as, in many ways, it still is. Even at that uncertain time, here is a man of smoothly integrated aims, who explains everything that has happened and foresees all that will happen next, who does it as wisely and paternally as an old family doctor. It was not for nothing that millions of the Russian people thought of him fondly as "Papa Kalinin."

But all the while Kalinin has the leaders more in mind than the people. At the end, he points out the advantages of such self-concern to these members of the ruling class in the "classless society." Some of his privileged hearers had been grumbling about the lack of consumer goods. He reminds them where the first such goods will go by telling them he got a good pair of shoes as a Party official ("Right, right! This is a stupid woman not to understand that." Kalinin saw no irony in that cry from the people; what combination of Communist and bureaucrat would?).

Old "Papa Kalinin," in the last year of his life, also adds an un-Soviet dash of nostalgia. He wants the people to talk back—a little—to these Soviet district officials. "You had not the old school we once had. Our auditoriums were filled not only with adherents but enemies too."

3

The revolutionary regime that runs Russia has few if any weaklings. Many of its key men who had pre-Revolutionary hardening are in their fifties. (Most of the lesser leaders are young men and women educated since 1917.) Kalinin made his speech when he was seventy-five. He was still active on the Politburo then. Everybody on the Politburo keeps active; except for Klimenty Voroshilov none of them spends much time drinking or wenching. The far-famed Kremlin feasts do occur—not very often and almost always for some good business reason. Excessive food and drink have a symbolic importance in Russia. The Communists use a big banquet in the same way the czars did, as a minor but handy propaganda instrument, intended to impress people with Russia's strength and splendor in somewhat the way that the rose festival at Portland, Oregon, is intended to impress people with Portland.

The members of the Politburo are quick-witted, iron-nerved men, attentive to the word from Stalin, their fellow member and boss. They know tragically little about the outside world. In that, as in other ways, they personify Soviet Russia. Stalin is their leader. Each of the other thirteen has his special assignments under Stalin's careful supervision. Their efforts are collective, they act just like what they are: the tough-minded, tough-operating board of directors of the world's biggest corporation—or company union.

Lavrenty Beria has operated the MVD, the dreaded secret police, since 1938. Like Stalin, he comes from the Russian province of Georgia. Born in 1899 and too young to be prominent in the Revolution, he first attracted Stalin's attention with an adulatory history of Communist pre-Revolutionary activities in Georgia. His essay featured Stalin in almost every paragraph.

An episode involving Beria shows the unconcealed love of power in these men who run Russia. Beria sat between two Americans at a banquet during the Yalta Conference. The three exchanged toasts to Stalin, to Roosevelt, to peace, to friendship. Then one American proposed "To the people."

Beria twisted his small mouth. "Why to the people?" he asked. "The people don't decide anything. The leaders decide. Now take the German people; they aren't bad people, but they got into the hands of bad leaders. Let's drink to the leaders."

Anastas Mikoyan, a suave, shrewd little Armenian runs foreign trade, through which Russia is economically (as well as politically) dominating her satellites.

Andrei Andreyev runs agriculture, which despite Kalinin's boast has required a complete, Kremlin-supervised house cleaning since the war.

Nikolai Voznesensky is head of the State Planning Board, which covers more paper with national plans, and figures out more kinds of forms for Russians to fill, than planners in any other three countries put together.

Lazar Kaganovich runs heavy industry. He is the only Jew on the Politburo and one of the very few high-ranking Jews in the Soviet Union, where anti-Semitism is, unfortunately, growing— though it is not state-inspired as it was in czarist Russia.

Nikita Khruschev, a non-Ukrainian, runs the Ukraine, over which the Politburo keeps special watch since the Ukrainians have the most Western notions to be found in any of the sixteen Soviet "republics." It is as though Washington decided that Texas had dangerous tendencies and sent a Pennsylvania political boss to run Texas down to the last lariat.

Nikolai Bulganin watches over the armed forces. Under the Politburo the services do not attain anything resembling a separate power. Bulganin, the wartime chief of the Soviet political commissars who looked over the shoulders of the fighting men, got his marshal's star in 1947 for preserving "the ideological purity of the armed forces at the end of the war."

Two of these thirteen leaders directly under Stalin may be taken as typical: Molotov, who is Stalin's No. 2 man if anybody is, and Zhdanov, who operates the Communist Party machinery for Stalin.

Vyacheslav Molotov is the chief executor of the Politburo's will in the field of foreign affairs. One foreigner who has seen him in action for fifteen years calls him "perhaps the best executor of policy in the world." He was born in 1890, the son of a store clerk in Nolinsk, 480 miles northeast of Moscow. At nineteen the czarist secret police exiled him to the Arctic (years later he jailed the policeman who had arrested him). By 1912 he was back in Russia, helping Stalin edit a small revolutionary paper called *Pravda* (Truth) which is now the leading Soviet daily. By 1917 Lenin himself had noticed Molotov; Lenin called him "the best file clerk in Russia."

Few of the ex-revolutionaries who ran the Soviet Union in the early years of civil war and chaos were first-rate administrators. Molotov's orderly mind soon put him in the van. In 1922, when Stalin became secretary-general of the Communist Party, Molotov was his chief assistant. His position has been riveted solidly to Stalin's ever since. In 1925 he became a full member of the Politburo. In 1930, Stalin made him premier, a job he held for eleven years. (He has been chief deputy premier to Stalin since 1941.) The approach of war turned the Kremlin's attention to foreign affairs. None of the top-rank surviving Old Bolsheviks had specialized in foreign relations. So in 1939, Molotov was also made Foreign Minister.

Of the Politburo as it existed in 1925 when Molotov was raised to it, three men—Stalin, Voroshilov and Molotov—are left. Tomsky committed suicide. Kalinin and Dzerzhinsky died. Trotsky, Bukharin, Zinoviev, Rykov, Rudzutak, Petrovsky, Uglanov and Kamenev were all purged. In 1930, when Molotov became premier, he told the secret of his survival in his inaugural speech:

"During recent years I have, as secretary of the Central Committee, learned Bolshevik work under the direct guidance of Lenin's best disciple, Comrade Stalin. I am proud of this. Until today I have been mainly a Party worker. I declare to you, comrades, that I am going to work in the Government also as a Party worker. I am an agent of the Party's will."

The complete subservience in that speech is what makes Molotov a typical Communist. He heads no clique, associates himself with no policy other than Stalin's; he even avoids what seminarians call "particular friendship" with his fellow Communist leaders. The system makes that a smart policy for Communists on all levels. A long-time Communist and member of the MVD recently told a foreigner that the qualities the Party now looked for in its recruits were passivity and pliability—not "natural leadership." Perfect and immediate acceptance of the entire Party line, even if it changes completely overnight, is expected of all Communists. From Molotov to the lowliest Party private, all Communists must resemble a character in Kirshon's play *Bread* who said: "The Party is a thong. . . . It often cuts into my flesh, but I can't live without it. I cannot step out of the ranks. I dare not leave. . . . I must have someone to give me orders. I must feel another shoulder next to mine."

Molotov has a wife who looked rather dowdy when I saw her in Moscow alongside the chic and charming Madame Bidault who had come with her husband, the French foreign minister. She was annoyed when Madame Bidault mentioned her shock at having seen a woman street cleaner spend five days' wages on one head of cabbage at a Moscow farmers' market. (It was winter, and the price higher than in summer.) "Perhaps it wasn't very diplomatic of me," Madame Bidault admitted afterward. But Madame Molotov has survived worse shocks. She is a remarkable woman. In the Soviet state, which asserts that it has given women full equality with men, she is one of the very few women who have ever risen as high as the Party's seventy-one-member Central Committee. No woman has ever been on the Politburo. She used to be head of the Soviet cosmetic trust, and was later the commissar of Fisheries. She has since been fired, both from that job and the Central Committee. The Molotov's one child, Svetlana, was born in 1928; she won a prize for "distinguished success" at school, and got a good bourgeois reward—a trip to the 1946 Paris peace conference with her father.

Madame Molotov's mother took her Orthodox Jewish religion so seriously that she was reluctant to pay a visit to the home of her gentile son-in-law. When the Molotovs called for her, she was ready with a crate of live chickens and said she would need a special room to do her own cooking. Madame Molotov assured her mother that she really could get kosher food in Moscow. But Molotov humored the old lady, whom he always called *Babushka* (Granny), and brought the chickens along.

There is nothing in Molotov's life or in his looks to indicate that he would not be a kindly man about the house. There is also nothing in his record, or in that of any other convinced Communist, to indicate that he would not sacrifice *Babushka,* chickens and all, if they got in the Party's way.

Andrei Zhdanov faced just that sort of human situation with complete Communist cold-bloodedness when he was Party boss in the defense of beleaguered Leningrad. The Politburo told Zhdanov not to yield the city. When, in 1942, a relief road was opened to the isolated, starving city across frozen Lake Ladoga, Zhdanov had it used primarily to bring in munitions and saw to it that the food later brought in was stocked in a strategic reserve. As a result, some 1,300,000 people died during the siege, mostly of hunger and cold. Zhdanov never lost any sleep over the problem; he was merely carrying out instructions.

Zhdanov can be quite pleasant when the Politburo so desires. When Finland sought an armistice in 1944, he was made head of the Finnish Control Commission. Zhdanov's one great mistake had been in 1939, when he told the Politburo that Finland would yield as soon as Russia attacked. (Such a boner also shows how completely Zhdanov or the entire Politburo can be fooled by overoptimistic information from subordinates who want to please.) A stout Finnish defense ended that delusion, and the Finns actually launched an offensive. Stalin somberly told Zhdanov: "Things are going normally on the Finnish front, huh? Well, when the Finns get to Bologoe (halfway between Leningrad and Moscow), let me know."

So Finns expected the worst when Zhdanov was named to supervise them. When he landed at Helsinski airport, the honor guard of Finnish soldiers lined up to meet him looked very glum. Zhdanov smiled at them and then said—in Finnish—"Hello, boys." The soldiers stood stonily a long Finnish moment, then grinned back and said—in Finnish—"Hello, General." (Zhdanov is yet another Soviet political leader who also carries a military title.) That's the way Zhdanov ran the Russian mission to Finland: no rough stuff, no looting, not much interference in Finnish affairs. Zhdanov also gets along with the few Westerners he has met. They find him a plump, well-manicured, neatly dressed little man with just the faintest touch of perfume about him and a fondness for dewberry cordial.

Unlike Lenin (*né* Ulyanov), Stalin (*né* Djugashvili), Trotsky (*né* Bronstein) and Molotov (*né* Scriabin), Zhdanov still has the name he was born (1896) with. Sharing a common root with the Russian verb *zhdat* (to wait, or to expect) it is a good name for a man who has quietly ridden up the Party escalator until he can hope for succession to the biggest political job on earth. His father was a school inspector at Tver (now Kalinin), about one hundred miles northwest of Moscow. Zhdanov had a better education (including German and French) than any present member of the Politburo. He joined the Bolsheviks in 1915 and had a routine career as an organizer (of the sort to whom Kalinin's speech was made) until, after years of fidelity to Stalin, his great chance came in 1934. Then he succeeded Stalin's assassinated friend Kirov as Party boss of Leningrad.

Since his return to Russia from Finland, Zhdanov's chief single Party-secretary task has been to lead the Party's cultural purge. His cultural approach is that any work which does not positively advance Communist doctrine is wrong. It is not enough just to be neutral; you must be for. He sees to it that the Soviet Union tolerates no sort of creative artist who, consciously or unconsciously, either by what he says or what he omits, gives any expression to the people's discontent.

Zhdanov has the usual Politburo allotment of Kremlin apartment, suburban *dacha* and Caucasus villa. Zhdanov, his wife, widowed daughter, and son generally live in the apartment. His favorite recreation is *gorodki*, a mixture of bowling and shuffleboard, which Lenin also liked. Kremlin dwellers have their own *gorodki* club; in one tournament, Zhdanov placed second to Stalin's chauffeur, Khvostov. On the official Politburo list (more important than *gorodki* scores), Zhdanov now stands fourth—after Stalin, Molotov, and Beria. The thirteen Politburo members below Stalin watch each other almost as closely as Stalin watches them. Each would like to be Stalin's successor.

4

Meanwhile the *Vozhd* (leader), Joseph Vissarionovich Stalin, still personally grips the reins of all power: Party, secret police, armed forces and government. He resigned the defense command in

1947, but as generalissimo is still the head of the armed forces. He has a deputy for each of the four important power positions—respectively Zhdanov, Beria, Bulganin, and Molotov. Stalin was born in Georgia in 1879; Russians have an old saying, "Georgians live forever." There is no way of telling whether Stalin will live another day or another decade. It seems fairly certain that he will run things as long as he can. No one remembers better than he how the real reins of power gradually slipped from the ailing Lenin in the last two years of his life, because Stalin was the man who gradually slipped into them.

The government has so little power in Soviet life that Molotov's position is the weakest of Stalin's four key deputies. He seems to be Stalin's heir apparent, and if he can grab the job the second Stalin dies he may be able to hold it. But he controls none of the three power sources that matter—Stalin has taken good care that no one overlaps on Party, Army, and secret police except himself. (Beria, Bulganin, and Zhdanov, like Stalin, do have high military titles, which Molotov does not.) Power is all important to Communists. It is the only thing they respect.

If the others ganged up on him, Molotov's position after Stalin's death could be embarrassing, to say the least. If, after Stalin dies, any Politburo member can get control of two of the three important Soviet power sources, he can then probably consolidate the third. The Army is the least important of the three; the Party has increasingly played down the generals since the end of the war. Once one man wins out, he may kill off the leaders who actively opposed him, as has so often happened in Russian history. Stalin's succession after Lenin's death, the only power transfer yet made in the thirty-one years of Soviet history (America has seen power transferred to five new presidents in that period), rocked Russia—and the international Communist movement—to its foundations. It took twelve years and a terrific purge to complete the change of power. (The outside world knew little of it at first; Politburo men have corporate as well as individual interests.) The succession to Stalin may easily rock Russia and international Communism once more. At a minimum, it may well take six years—half as long as last time—to complete. During that period, whenever it occurs, neither Russia nor world Communism will be at its fighting peak, which might give a slight breathing spell for other countries.

In his article "The Sources of Soviet Conduct" in *Foreign Affairs* for July 1947, "X" suggested that the men seeking Russia's supreme post might go to the six million members of the Party rank and file to seek support for their claims. He added: "If this were ever to happen, strange consequences could flow for the Communist Party: for the membership at large has been exercised only in the practices of iron discipline and obedience and not in the arts of compromise and accommodation. If consequently anything were ever to occur to disrupt the unity and efficacy of the Party as a political instrument, Soviet Russia might be changed overnight from one of the strongest to one of the weakest and most pitiable of national societies." This possibility is a Communist nightmare.

The Trotskyists are still arguing that Stalin stole the succession to Lenin. Trotsky's own *Life of Stalin* shows that Trotsky never knew what hit him until it was too late. Stalin's dominant position in the Communist Party (as its secretary-general, he ran the machine) was basically established before Lenin's death. Trotsky thought of the Revolution in terms of heroics and personal influence. Stalin knew the sources of power, as did Lenin. Whoever was Lenin's rightful successor, Stalin was the logical one.

Lenin was one of the greatest statesmen who ever lived, as Marx was one of the greatest emotional-philosophical forces. There has probably never been a colder, clearer, more cynical and complete logician of power than Lenin. Stalin has learned the master's lesson well. But he is an imitator, not a pioneer in Lenin's class.

Lenin kidnaped a state. Too few Americans remember that it was not the Communists who turned out the czars. In February 1917, the Russian people, without any help from Lenin (who was then an exile in Switzerland), revolted. The people overthrew the czar, freed political prisoners, speech and the press. They organized the only free election in Russia's history. The Russian people knew what they wanted; Lenin knew better. Lenin said: "The people themselves do not know what is good or bad for them."

Lenin organized not a people's but a plotter's revolution. One night, eight months after the February revolution, his men seized the key points in Petrograd. They grabbed the telegraph office to "telegraph the revolution to the provinces." They kidnaped the members of the democratic Provisional Government and took their place. That was the October 1917 Revolution, the one the Communists made. Lenin then re-established the czarist-type secret police which the democratic revolution had abolished, and used spies as well as force to keep his power. Communists, who constantly rewrite history for their own purposes, now often talk as though there had been only one 1917 Revolution. Some "scholarly" American works, deliberately or not, make the same assumption. There were two Russian revolutions that year. What might have happened had the Communists not wrecked the first, democratic revolution is one of the greatest—and saddest—if's in history.

At the time of Lenin's coup the Bolsheviks (as the Communists were then, as now, officially called) were a minor party that numbered only 200,000 in a state of 160 million people. The free election arranged by the democratic Russian government was only a month off. Lenin could not stop it and he did not have time to fake very much of it. When the Russians made their one free trip to the polls, Lenin and his Communists were voted out. They got only 156 seats in the 601-member Constituent Assembly. A clear majority, 320 seats, went to the Social Revolutionary Party. Lenin, the apostle of power, knew the answer. When the Assembly met, he at once dispersed it with the bayonets of his Lettish Regiment. Russia entered a 1918-21 civil war that killed twice as many Russians as the Germans had in 1914-18.

Lenin's genius lay in knowing how to use what little power his little party had to keep control and gradually to tighten the Communists' stranglehold on Russia. Lenin had political genius of the highest—and most ruthless—order. He said, "Religion is the opiate of the people," and then used promises to drug people with. He used fear on a prodigious scale—and "fear" is still a key word with Russians, up to and including Stalin. He originated the Communists' use of strategic retreat. He made peace with the Germans at Brest-Litovsk early in 1918, yielding vast territories so he could concentrate on his civil war to win the rest of Russia. He initiated the New Economic Policy (NEP) in 1921, which gave Russia's businessmen a chance to do their own trading in a Communist state, because Russian industry was paralyzed and the capitalist incentive was the only thing that could get it started again. He made such concessions when the Communists were too weak not to make them, never otherwise. As soon as he could, he went back on them.

Lenin said of NEP soon after he announced it: "We have met a great defeat, and are now making a strategic retreat. All our military successes were preceded by similar retreats. Afterward we began a cautious advance, finally crowned with victory." After Germany collapsed in 1918, Lenin tore up the Brest-Litovsk treaty and recovered as much of that territory as he could. He had started turning the screws on NEP before he died; Stalin completed the process and abolished it in 1928.

What Lenin said is the best clue to him—and a striking clue to Communism. Here are some quotations from him:

"There are no morals in politics; there is only expediency. A scoundrel may be of use to us just because he is a scoundrel."

"It does not matter that Comrade Krassikov has squandered party funds in a brothel, but it is scandalous that this should have disorganized the transportation of illegal literature."

(When the head of his secret police brought in the day's list of arrests and suspects): "Shoot those two, hold these five, and let the rest go."

"We shall ask: on which side are you? For or against the Revolution? If against—we shoot you! If for—follow us and work!" (Lenin's devoted wife Krupskaya offered one of her few objections when he uttered this dictum. She said: "That way you'll kill off all the best ones, all those with the courage of their convictions.")

(Before the October Revolution): "Revolutionaries should start training for war immediately, by means of practical operations: Killing a spy, blowing up a police station, robbing a bank to provide funds for the uprising, etc. Do not shrink from these experimental attacks; they may, of course, degenerate into excesses, but this is a worry of the future. Let every detachment train for action, if only by beating up a policeman."

"We cannot live in peace; memorial services will be sung either over the Soviet republic or over world capitalism. But until this takes place, the principal rule is to dodge and maneuver. We have to use any ruse, dodge, trick, cunning, unlawful methods, veiling of the truth."

"We shall destroy everything, and on the ruins we shall erect our temple. . . . Take, for instance, the bourgeoisie—or democracy, if you prefer that term. It is doomed, and in abolishing it, we are only completing the inescapable historical process."

"I don't care what will become of Russia, to hell with it! All this is only the road to a world revolution."

By the time Lenin died, the Soviet pattern was set. The "excesses" that are the present and future worry of the whole world had developed. Stalin has merely followed Lenin's lead. With minor personal variations, Trotsky or any other Russian Communist leader would have done the same. As Sir John Maynard, one of the most careful and thorough students of Russia, has written of Stalin and Trotsky: "I cannot myself, after close study of Trotsky's recorded opinions, detect with certainty any ideological difference between the two men."

Stalin has consciously modeled himself on Lenin. One revealing evidence of this is the memorial speech he gave on January 28, 1924, just after Lenin's death. Anyone who recalls how Stalin avoided the limelight (while grasping the power) until the time of the great purge, when it was necessary for him to be publicized as the Leader, and how on many occasions he still carefully emphasizes his "simplicity" or takes a back seat, can savor this passage:

I first met Lenin in December 1905 at the Bolshevik Conference in Tammerfors, Finland. . . . It is accepted as the usual thing for a "great man" to come late to meetings, so that the assembly may await his appearance with bated breath; and then, just before the great man enters, the warning whispers goes up: "Hush! . . . Silence! . . . He's coming . . ." This rite did not seem to be superfluous, because it creates an impression, inspires respect. What, then, was my disappointment to learn that Lenin had arrived at the conference before the other delegates, had settled himself somewhere in a corner, and was unassumingly carrying on a conversation, a most ordinary conversation, with the most ordinary delegates at the conference. I will not conceal from you that at that time this seemed to me to be rather a violation of certain essential rules. Only later did I realize that this simplicity and modesty, this striving to remain unobserved or, at least, not to make himself conspicuous and not to emphasize his high position, was one of Lenin's strongest points.

Many Communists in many countries have since copied this Lenin technique effectively.

Stalin has firmly, steadily continued Lenin's pursuit of absolute power. He spent the autumn months of 1945, 1946, and 1947 in his villa at Sochi on Russia's Black Sea coast. They were his first three "vacations" in fifty years. Even then, he kept in daily touch with affairs and most of the Politburo moved down from Moscow to be near him.

Stalin's personal secretariat is headed by Alexander Poskrebyshev, who in 1946 was made a general without stirring from the Kremlin. Better than any other, Poskrebyshev's job illustrates how Russia really works. Foreigners who get in to see Stalin know Poskrebyshev as the bald, tubby little man who sits in the outer office. Russians who get that far are more respectful. They know that Stalin organized his personal secretariat during that struggle for Lenin's succession. Ever since then it has been garnering all possible data on Communists who may rival Stalin. These files are kept in a steel-lined room to which Stalin and Poskrebyshev have the only keys. Communists in the inner circle call Poskrebyshev *otkormlennya vosh* ("gorged louse") behind his back.

The *Vozhd's vosh* (leader's louse) is one reason why Russia's flow of power, which according to that 1936 Soviet constitution is supposed to run from bottom to top, really runs from top to bottom.

Chapter 5. THE CONTROLS

A WORD you soon learn in Russia is *culturni* (cultured). Russians use it constantly and in all manner of ways. *Ni culturni* (not cultured) is one of their sternest reproaches. In an unheated theater so cold you can see your breath, it is *ni culturni* to wear your overcoat to your seat. Coats must be checked in the lobby. When a Leningrad factory director was accused of embezzlement, *Izvestia* thundered "Where does this man's culture end and where do his crimes begin?" A Soviet press attack on the serious shortcomings of village schools complained that their graduates lacked "elementary habits of culture in work. It is not cultured to be cruel to livestock or to leave machinery exposed to the weather." A Russian officer praised a new five-tube radio as a "cultured set." A Russian girl who offered to sing *Kobachok* (the Soviet adaptation of "Tavern in the Town") in the presence of foreigners was reminded by another Russian in the group that it was no longer wise to sing it. She replied: "I know it is not now cultured—in fact, more or less forbidden—but I like it."

The girl's remark shows how the Kremlin defines the word "culture." That is the way Kalinin used it in his speech. To Russians, "culture" has not only our meaning but these others— it means especially what is acceptable, with no taint of official displeasure. Soviet Russia is a country where all activities, even cultural activities, are under thorough state control.

It is hard for anyone who has not lived in Russia to realize the appalling completeness of that control. One story conveyed it vividly to me during my first few days in Russia. It occurred at a meeting of the administrative officers of the four delegations to the Council of Foreign Ministers. Having settled various routine operational matters, the meeting was about to adjourn when Novikov, the Russian representative suddenly said: "My three colleagues should remind their countrymen here that Russia has certain rules about taking pictures. Our police have already had to stop several delegation members from taking pictures. Such incidents are most unfortunate. They must stop."

Silence hung heavy around the table for a moment. Then the French member said, "Please tell us these rules about taking pictures, so I can pass on the information."

Novikov looked surprised. "I do not know the exact rules," he said. "It would be wise not to take pictures at all."

It *is* "wise not to take pictures at all" in Russia. One American photographer I know was arrested for snapping a farmers' market. He was told he had "violated security." Like "culture," "security" is a word with a much wider definition in Russia than America. It is as though Americans were forbidden for "security reasons" to take pictures anywhere along the Grand Canyon—because the Colorado River down at its bottom is a source of water power. That is the way the Soviet policeman's mind works and Russia is a police state.

Every Russian's life is regulated. Novikov's remark indicates one of the most effective controls: very few Russians do know the exact rules. They can get a long jail term at any moment for breaking some regulation they never heard of. So the ordinary Russian plays safe. He does and thinks as little as possible that might by any conceivable chance get him into trouble. Fear casts a blight on all Russian thought, words, and deeds.

The Kremlin keeps its finger firmly on the pulse of every significant part of Soviet life. Often this is done not by published laws or decrees, which the ordinary Russian might possibly hear about, but by private administrative orders of which he can know nothing. A Russian lawyer, himself a Party member, recently told a foreigner in Moscow whom he trusted that under a Party ruling every prosecutor must be a Party member and that "in practice" so must all judges. None of this appears in any published Soviet judicial code. It is known only among the administrative elect. The resultant control over Russia's entire legal apparatus is obvious.

The Soviet state—which is practically synonymous with the Party—similarly exercises control over every Soviet citizen with any significant amount of education or training. A group of foreign reporters including myself asked the head of Moscow University whether his graduates can do what they like. "Theoretically, they can go into any work they want," he said. "Practically, it is not that easy." It is not. We asked Dr. Andrei Lihachev, director of the First Moscow Medical Institute, said to be the best medical school in the Soviet Union, whether the new doctors graduated from his institute could choose where they wanted to work. "Nearly all our recent graduates have been assigned to villages," he said. "The posts available in cities for doctors are filled."

There is no question that Russian rural areas do need doctors. But the very matter-of-factness in Dr. Lihachev's answer emphasizes that doctors go where the Soviet state sends them. It is as though American medical graduates were compulsorily assigned to villages in Kentucky, Nebraska, and Alaska.

A Soviet candidate for a Ph.D. in Moscow said he would delay taking his doctoral degree as long as possible, to avoid being sent to teach in some provincial town where, he explained, "Vodka and cards will be the principal pastimes. Life in Moscow even on a student's allowance is better than that."

The Kremlin's view of the matter is that since its benevolence alone makes any training possible, the lucky recipient of the training should thenceforth be only too glad to do what he is told. Even in the Soviet Union, ingratitude sometimes rears its ugly head. Though all advanced students enter school knowing that they must work where the state wishes for at least several years after graduation, some of them attempt to avoid such assignments. Many professional schools now try to limit the number of women entrants, because women are exempt from the after-graduation assignment if they are either pregnant or married to an Army officer. Too many were finding themselves with child or Army husband. Nor are these the only artful dodgers.

A front-page *Izvestia* editorial pilloried a Moscow girl named Rosenblum who, after graduating from the Foreign Language Institute and being assigned to teach in Voronezh, arranged with the aid of one Chilikin, deputy director of the Moscow Power Institute, to stay on in Moscow. *Izvestia* denounced the girl's "failure to fulfil her duty" and Chilikin's "antistate act." Another girl, one Chernyavskaya, aged twenty-three, graduate of the Kiev Polytechnical Institute, was ordered to go to work in the Stalin Factory at Novo-Kramatorsk. She was not overjoyed at what the labor daily *Trud* described as "this great opportunity." *Trud* sneered: "She would not leave Kiev at any price." She pulled wires and succeeded in staying on in Kiev for months. But all her maneuvers—even getting married—did not budge Moscow. Finally she was warned that "further flouting of her liabilities" would land her in jail.

Foreigners in Russia often hear similar stories of the ceaseless struggle waged by individual Russians to slip out of the strait jacket of control. About their only weapon is what is known in Russian slang as *blatt* or pull.

The average Russian is in no position to resort to *blatt*, or even to bribery, in dealing with the Soviet system. He is armed only with patience. One new father, for example, had to obtain no less than six documents with a total length of seventy-eight inches to get a single food card for a new citizen who measured only nineteen inches. Another new father spent six weeks filling out forms before he could get a cake of soap with which to wash his baby.

An American may at this point be rejoicing that he is not affected by Soviet controls. He is. An American is subjected to Russian controls every time he picks up his paper or listens to a news broadcast. One clear, short way to describe Russia is "the country where censorship goes on in peace as in war." I could stitch quite a revealing sampler of Russian life from stray sentences the censor snipped from my cables. Here are some of them:

"The new Zis 110 resembled a 1940 Packard."

This is true, and I think the 1940 Packard an excellent car. But the Soviet censor resents anyone noticing such similarities. The Zis is the only Soviet limousine; 110 is the number of its 1946 model. Russia also manufactures one smaller passenger car (rather like a 1941 Chevrolet), three types of trucks (rather like American lend-lease models) and a jeep (rather like a jeep).

"The Mayor of Stalingrad frankly admitted that Stalingrad ration cards could not always be met because of food shortages and transportation difficulties. Stalingrad open-market prices were $1 a pound for potatoes, $3.40 a pound for black bread and $7.10 for a small chicken."

The censor refused to give me any reason for this cut. He could not cite inaccuracy.

"Russian girls and boys are not as active as American kids because they have fewer calories to burn."

The Russian food situation is discussed in the next chapter; the diet of many Russians is near or under starvation level.

"No one in this collective village possessed any sort of time-piece."

Watches and clocks are still on the scarce side in Russia, but the authorities are sensitive about any mention of the fact.

No Russian, not even the censor, could question the factual accuracy of these italicized passages. Why, then, were they cut? Because the Kremlin has a standing rule against the sending of any information from Russia which it thinks might hurt Russian interests in any way. It is impossible to send full, fair, or rounded news from Russia. Anyone reading a news dispatch or hearing a radio item datelined "Russia" should always remember that the censor may have cut its guts out—or that the correspondent, knowing it would be cut there, eliminated some material before he sent it to the censor.

There are about 150 Americans in all Russia, compared to some 3,000 Soviet citizens in America. The Kremlin is very reluctant to give foreigners visas, or to let them move about once they get to Russia. There is, for instance, a milepost outside Vladivostok beyond which members of the American Consulate there may not go without written Soviet permission. Since the war, because restrictions on Americans in Russia have steadily tightened, Washington has put some curbs on Soviet citizens in America. No impartial observer would state that the American curbs, some of which I deprecate, are as stringent as those imposed by the Russians.

Stalin's April 1947 remarks to Harold Stassen seem to show that Soviet censorship and control over foreigners in Russia will go on forever. As long as it continues, as long as American correspondents are allowed to live nowhere in the Soviet sixth of the world's land surface except Moscow, and as long as only five are allowed to live even in Moscow, the American people will not get one-tenth of the news coverage they need on the world's other great magnet.

2

Kalinin showed how strict is the Kremlin's supervision of education. Schools are agencies of the Communist Party. Their aim is to give every Russian child the Soviet gospel and train each in the functions that will carry on the Soviet state. Education is far more widespread than in czarist times. Illiteracy has been cut from about 90 percent to under 20 percent. Russians have learned to read—but the state is the sole arbiter of what they read.

Not much formal Communist ideology is taught before seventh grade and 76 percent of Russia's children leave school forever by the end of fourth grade. The Kremlin does not worry about that. It culls out the best children to form the elite governing class, and gives them lots of ideology. It makes workers of the rejects. The latter, who are the overwhelming majority, are sent to farms, offices or a compulsory industrial training course which puts them almost irretrievably into, say, coal mining or shoemaking for the rest of their lives. Soviet bureaucrats decide what course these "rejects" shall take and where they shall go. These fourteen-year-old boys and girls are often sent away from their families forever. Only families with some influence—these are relatively rare in Russia—have any chance of overruling the bureaucracy's decision as to what these fourteen-year-olds will do until they die.

Even the educated elite are under constant control. One professor of pan-Slavic literature has been a candidate for a Ph.D. for eight years and has already prepared most of his thesis on a famous nineteenth-century Russian figure. He cannot finish it because he must consult certain archives in Belgrade, where his subject spent an important period of his life. Since the war, he has repeatedly asked permission to pay a short visit to Yugoslavia. "But," he explained, "there are certain exit difficulties. There must be a great investigation. 'Was your father a peasant or a worker?' 'Oh, he was a teacher—not so good.' 'Are you a Party member?' 'No? That's bad.' "

The professor sighed. "Perhaps," he added wistfully, "there is some hope anyway, since Yugoslavia is now so like Russia."

Russian social scientists or philosophers never know when they will face the sort of trial that Georgy Alexandrov underwent in 1947 for his "toothless vegetarianism" toward non-Marxists. They never dare to formulate an original opinion; they carefully paraphrase something already accepted and hope that it will still agree with the Party line when it gets published and for long enough afterward to be forgotten—which, unfortunately for him, Alexandrov's was not. Exact scientists fare somewhat better. But they too are all under the direct control of the state and must sometimes twist their science to fit Marxism—as Soviet biologists have had to do.

In Soviet schools, open-minded tolerance, the unfettered pursuit of truth, and the free play of ideas are of course proscribed. A recent resolution to Stalin from Soviet educators declared: "Teaching cannot be separated from the policy of the Communist Party, which forms the vital base of the Soviet regime." Thus education, like all of Russia's other opinion-forming agencies, has become an instrument for the control and suppression rather than the liberation of thought.

That is not what Soviet spokesmen say. They claim that Soviet education is the freest and most democratic in the world. They claim it again and again, so often and so firmly that many foreigners believe them. Then, in turn, sincere Americans get up and say as Princeton University's Dean emeritus Christian Gauss said in May 1947: "Much as we hate to admit it, there is much less equality of opportunity for education in America than in the Soviet Union."

I read Dean Gauss's statement, which I am sure he made sincerely though I am not sure how thorough a firsthand knowledge he has of Soviet education, soon after I had read in Russia of a thirteen-year-old boy in Odessa. Many of Russia's teen-age children work an eight-hour day and then attend school at night. This thirteen-year-old, after starting such an arrangement, decided he would rather quit work and return to regular day school. For doing so, he was sentenced to two months in jail.

I am not quite certain what Dean Gauss means by stating "there is much less equality of opportunity for education in America than in the Soviet Union." The quantity of education available in America is much greater than in Russia. As far as I could judge, the quality in America is also much higher—though American education can certainly be improved.

Ilya Gaulkin, the rector (head) of Moscow University, which

is Russia's largest with 8,200 students, told a group including myself that his university could admit only one in ten of those who applied. Some applicants who cannot get into Moscow University do get into one of Russia's thirty-four universities which, he said, have about seventy thousand students in all. He said that including these seventy thousand, about six hundred thousand young Russians are in various technical schools and other institutions above the high-school level. The number of young men and women taking post-high-school courses in America, which has about two-thirds Russia's population, was 2,338,226 in 1946—almost four times the Russian total.

For secondary education, the Soviet figure is 29,300,000 and America's 26,759,099. But about ten million Russian children of school age are not in school. Only fourth-grade education is compulsory throughout Russia, and even that is not strictly enforced. Nearly all rural schools stop with fourth grade; none go beyond seventh. There are no school busses to take village children to the nearest town with a high school. For one thing, such a town is in many cases over a hundred miles away. For another, there are exceedingly few busses in rural Russia. Even when a town is fairly near, the deeply rutted Russian roads would soon bump any bus to pieces. So country children have no chance of getting beyond seventh grade unless they live near enough to walk to town, or are lucky enough to have relatives or friends in some town who can squeeze them in while they study.

Russian children are taught some surprising things about modern inventions. At one village school northeast of Moscow where I stopped to investigate, I asked a group of sixth graders: "Who invented the radio?" They all promptly said: "Popov." That is what they learn. While I was in Moscow, on May 7, Russia solemnly celebrated "Radio Day." As *Izvestia* put it: "On this day in 1895 the prominent Russian scientist, A. S. Popov, gave the first public demonstration of his marvelous invention." Older Russians, when asked "Did Popov really invent the radio?" act rather sheepish. They were taught—for quite a time even in Soviet schools—that an Italian, Marconi, had done that. Now Soviet school children learn differently. They also learn that another Russian of the czarist era, whom few foreigners ever heard of any more than they have of Popov, invented the electric light bulb long before Edison—and yet another the airplane long before the Wright brothers. Not that czarist times get any of the credit. In fact, this present Soviet teaching does double propaganda duty. It not only gives Russia the credit for these original inventions but explains that the czars kept the men who made them from exploiting their great discoveries. In 1948 Moscow claimed a host of inventions for Russia—the steam engine, penicillin, even soda crackers!

From eight to fifteen years of age, most Russians of both sexes belong to the Pioneers, a Communist outfit rather like a political Boy and Girl Scouts. Each school has a Pioneer "detachment" composed of a "link" in each classroom of the school. Pioneers wear red ties; their meetings are opened by a leader who says, "To fight for the cause of Lenin and Stalin, be prepared." The Pioneers give a military salute and reply, "Always prepared."

Even athletics are part of the preparedness program. In 1946, the magazine *Soviet Sport* denounced "the absurd illusion of sport for sport's sake," and said it could only be tolerated if it built muscles for the state's use. The first step in the development of a tenderfoot Russian athlete is a BGTO badge (Be Ready for Work & Defense), issued for skill in running, swimming, skiing— and shooting. Next comes a tougher test for the coveted GTO badge (Ready for Work & Defense). A GTO can swim fully clad, run 1.8 miles in twelve minutes—and make parachute jumps. The Russians have a type of sporting spirit which Americans would find hard to duplicate. For instance, as a Soviet soccer eleven trots out on the field, its players sing this military dedication:

> Physkultura hurrah!
> Physkultura hurrah! Hurrah! Hurrah!
> Be ready
> When the moment strikes
> To beat the enemy!
> You will drive him back
> From all our borders!
> Outside Left, Outside Right,
> Be on guard!

Soviet pupils are taught to have "irreconcilable hatred for the enemies of the Soviet Motherland," and to have "no personal interests opposed to the collective interests." One of their textbooks states that "America's huge wealth is in the hands of a small bunch of millionaires who . . . lead luxurious lives and sweat the workers as hard as they can. At the age of 45 a worker loses his health and becomes an old man. . . . Millions of workers have been thrown out on the streets. . . . Agriculture is also in decay. Many farmers have been pauperized."

In the first grade, Soviet school children are still a little shaky in some answers. At Moscow's Public School 29 for girls, as bare, boxlike and dingy as any American 1880-vintage school building, a group of us found a primary class full of adorable little girls in pinafores and pigtails. The room, like all Soviet schoolrooms and most other rooms in Russia, had pictures of Lenin and Stalin. We pointed at one and asked "Who's he?" "Lenin," they answered in chorus. We pointed at the other picture and asked the same thing. In unison they chanted "Joseph Vissarionovich Stalin." We asked, "What's the difference between them?" Only one little girl shot up her hand. The pleased teacher called on her. She bobbed up and said: "Lenin is dead and Stalin is not."

The upper grades in that same girls' school recited much more smoothly. (The small girls had rose-petal complexions; the seventeen and eighteen-year-olds had the coarse skin of women all over Russia who have little soap and almost none of it as good as American yellow laundry soap.) Class 9-A was having a lesson in international relations as we arrived. A girl was reciting: "The defeat of France in 1870 was a typical instance of Prussian aggression." The class swung abruptly to Greece and Turkey for the time we stayed. Some typical answers the girls gave to questions from the teacher: "Truman wants to help Turkey, which helped Germany and was Germany's ally." . . . "Truman has proposed helping Fascists in Greece." . . . "Russia as a great power has always wanted an outlet to the Mediterranean through the Dardanelles but Turkey has always blocked it." Surprised by this last, we asked if the class while it was on this subject was being taught about the Montreux Convention, which permits ships of all nations through the Dardanelles in peacetime and even in wartime bars only warships. None of the class had ever heard of the Montreux Convention.

The best test of any nation's education is its university system. When a group of us interviewed Rector Gaulkin of Moscow University, we asked him, "Must all your professors accept dialectical materialism? Can they believe—or teach—any other form of philosophy?" He answered promptly: "All of our professors have deeply accepted the dialectical point of view." In universities, as elsewhere in Soviet Russia, only one point of view is possible.

We ended our four hours at Moscow University in a biology classroom. The rector, who had led the tour till then, moved to the background now that we were at last actually face to face with his students. The biology professor also moved back. A slim, purposeful young man stood by the interpreter and stage-managed the proceedings. The students, who had apparently been primed for our coming, asked many more questions than we had a chance to ask them.

Toward the end, one of them asked, "Will you report the truth about this interview?" We asked, "Why do you think we won't?" Several said simultaneously: "Look what happened to Harry Smith." They were referring to the American correspondent in Konstantin Simonov's play *The Russian Question*, who wrote honestly about Russia and was punished for doing so by his American newspaper publisher. Simonov came to America in 1946 at the invitation of the American Society of Newspaper Editors on a good-will tour to improve Soviet-American relations. His play will for a long time do much to lower Russians' opinion of America. The Kremlin has directed that it be produced in five hundred Soviet theaters, more than twice the number that have shown any other play in Russian history. It gives about as accurate an overall picture of American journalism as *Tobacco Road* gives of all American farming, if you consider the people in *Tobacco Road* average American farmers. The best brief comment on *The Russian Question* came from William McGaffin of the Chicago *Daily News* who went with me to its Moscow premiere: "Simonov sure knows how to shoot dirty pool."

I mention this little dialogue about truth because four days later *Pravda* (Truth) printed a column-long account of the affair written by Student L. Polozova. Each question and answer during the interview was spoken originally in Russian or English and then translated into the other. Some were also given in French. That is a slow process. It does allow any reporter, who so desires, time to make full, careful notes.

One of the questions we were asked was: "Did the American Communists support the war?" Our answer, "Yes, after Germany invaded Russia," will be understood by any American who remembers what vehement isolationists American Communists were until that date, when they suddenly became vehement interventionists. Here is Student L. Polozova's account: " 'Have the American Communists really been slow to fight fascism?' asked Student Efron. 'They only started to fight properly against fascism when the Germans attacked the Soviet Union,' replied the American. This reply simply astounded us. We knew well enough that the war between America and Germany started after Nazi Germany attacked the Soviet Union."

One Russian student actually asked a French correspondent, "Did not the French Communists support the war against Germany from the beginning?" He was serious, for these young Marxists are no longer taught that from 1939 to 1941 Soviet Russia was allied with Germany and that during that time French Communists followed the Russian line of at least indirect support for Germany against the "Western imperialists." Neither this question nor its answer appears in Student L. Polozova's report.

Then a student asked: "Why has America changed its policy toward Russia?" I answered: "America can change its policy through elections and through the freely expressed will of the American people. We have free speech in America and so it is possible to change policy by democratic debate and discussion. We can even change governments peacefully in America by voting them out." As the Russian interpreter began to translate my reply, the slim young stage manager, who evidently understood some English, hastily muttered in his ear. The interpreter turned to me and said: "He says your reply is too long. We will pass on to the next question." None of this appears in Student L. Polozova's report.

I was interested in this purposeful young director. Afterward I went up and spoke to him. It developed that he was an instructor in genetics at the university, and also one of its Party officers. So I asked him the statistics on Party membership in the university; the rector had dodged our question on that. By now the rector had again moved up from the background and was standing at my elbow. He made no attempt to stop his junior by many years and several ranks in the university hierarchy, who said that 4,000 of the university's 8,200 students were Young Communists and that 500 of the 1,380 on the faculty were Party members. Only 3 percent of Russia's population belongs to the Party. Apparently, as Dean Gauss or *Animal Farm* might put it, there is more equality of educational opportunity in Russia if you are linked to the Party.

When the young man had finished giving the figures, the graying, dignified head of Russia's greatest university nodded meekly in agreement and said "*Da, da* (yes, yes)."

3

In the Soviet Union art may not be long but it is extra tough. During World War II, Russian creative workers hoped they would have more freedom of expression. They have had, instead, stricter and stricter control ever since 1946, when a new magazine *Culture and Life* was founded by the Kremlin's Department of Agitation and Propaganda. *Culture and Life* laid down an ominous program in its very first issue: "to carry on an unyielding struggle with the remnants of the old ideology and with undiscipline, laziness, lack of culture, bureaucracy and carelessness. Producers and writers who suppose that the Soviet people want only entertainment and amusement are hopelessly wrong. Soviet literature and art must produce works full of passion and deep thought, shot through with ideas of Soviet patriotism."

Like creative workers anywhere, Russian artists want to express their personal feelings, to experiment with various forms, and to have contacts with their fellow artists in other countries. They want to mix with politics only at their own volition and on their own terms. All this is impossible in Soviet Russia. As Simonov has said: "A playwright must be a politician." He later added: "Russia is like a front line, one sector of which is literature." Here are the propaganda trenches where this front-line fighting must be done, as charted in the Kremlin's list of compulsory themes for Soviet movies: "(1) the advantages of the Soviet regime over capitalism (2) the role of the Communist Party (3) the people's vigilance, patriotism and duties to the state (4) commemoration of outstanding war heroes and heroines (5) the Soviet way of life (6) the family (7) mothers who have ten children (8) problems facing the Soviet Union." Soviet movies betray what difficult film fare these topics make. The most absurd Hollywood restrictions are not in a class with these.

Mikhail Zoshchenko, Russia's best short-story writer since Chekhov, once explained why he had hesitated to write the epic novel on "the great theme of Soviet achievements" which is expected of all Soviet writers. "You barely start to write and the critics surround you. 'This is not correct,' they say. 'You lack a scientific basis in handling this problem. Your ideology is not the right one.' Well, you see, respected reader, it isn't easy to be a Russian writer."

It gets less easy year by year, as Zoshchenko himself has learned. In 1946, Politburo member Andrei Zhdanov barred him from all Soviet publications for "decadence" and "rotten lack of ideology." Zoshchenko had written a wry, ironic short story, "Adventures of a Monkey," in which an ape at a Soviet zoo is freed from his cage by a Nazi bomb, runs joyfully away, but after various sad experiences in Soviet society (ration problems, queueing, shortages, etc.) hurries back to his cage as being the best place. Soviet readers loved its dead-pan implications. The Kremlin loathed them; it even abolished the magazine *Leningrad* where the offending tale had appeared. Zoshchenko is now trying to expiate his heresy by writing that epic novel. His chosen theme: "Partisan activities in the Leningrad region."

Poets, painters, musicians and movie makers have been similarly condemned. Soviet Russia's two greatest poets, Boris Pasternak and Anna Akhmatova, have both been so violently attacked that Pasternak has taken refuge in translating the classics and Akhmatova has almost ceased publishing. The three Soviet musicians best known to the West—Prokofiev, Shostakovich and Khachaturian—were all denounced by Zhdanov in February 1948 because "their works smell strongly of the modern bourgeois music of Europe and America which reflect the wasting away of bourgeois culture." All three promptly recanted their sins.

Soviet painters and sculptors have long since learned to avoid modernism and to stress patriotic subjects. Many have kept busy painting and sculpting Stalin (from photographs) ever since 1936, when pictures and statues of him suddenly began appearing all over the Soviet Union during the great purge of his opponents. The veneration of Stalin has gone so far that a popular perfume among Soviet women is Stalin's Breath. The literary panegyrics of him also go the limit; he is "our sun," "the peerless adviser," even "the savior." While I was in Russia, Stalin himself publicly protested: "The constant dithyrambs to Comrade Stalin positively grate on the ears. It makes one uncomfortable to read them." Russian writers apparently believe that Stalin likes discomfort; they have continued the dithyrambs.

Sergei Eisenstein, Russia's greatest movie maker until his death in 1948, was often damned for deviation. Each time he made an abject apology and was in due course forgiven. His 1946 confession of guilt over *Ivan the Terrible* was a classic of its kind. Like the dramatic producer he was, he flood-lit the main features of Soviet culture and life: the conception of art as the mere hand-maid of politics, the condemnation of art for art's sake, the need to quell all previously held notions the instant the Party demanded it, the prompt purging of any resistance. Like the great artist of irony that his films show he was, Eisenstein left still more to the imagination. He wrote: "We must master the Lenin-Stalin method of perception of real life and history to . . . create highly ideological artistic films worthy of the Stalin epoch. . . . The center of our attention in *Ivan the Terrible* is and must be Ivan the builder, Ivan the creator of a new, powerful, united Russian power, Ivan the inexorable destroyer of everything that resisted his progressive undertaking." After that skillful, tongue-in-cheek confession, Stalin called Eisenstein to the Kremlin and personally told him to remake the film with this stirring, constructive interpretation.

Russia's creative workers swallow such crass Party orders for self-preservation plus privileges. Once they get caught in the Soviet web, even the most noted struggle but feebly. Maxim Gorki denounced czarist tyranny and wrote a famous exposé of czarist prison methods. Later he wrote the introduction and conclusion of a book glorifying Soviet slave labor. For spiritual subservience, Soviet creative workers share with leading Party members the fruits of ordinary Russians' labor. Their privileges, from cars to country houses, increase their dependence on the Party.

Writers, for example, like to see their work published, and in Russia you need Party approval for that. The sort of writing Glavlit, the Soviet bureau in charge of literature, wants printed is shown by the only five living Americans it published in 1947: Elliott Roosevelt (*As He Saw It*), John Steinbeck (reissue of *The Grapes of Wrath*), Ralph Ingersoll (*Top Secret*), Upton Sinclair (the Lanny Budd cycle) and a volume of Erskine Caldwell's stories about southern poor whites. These titles scarcely represent the entire range of recent American writing. Yet a Glavlit official explained: "We didn't see anything else in America that would interest Soviet readers." The five Americans can—and some of them do—write on highly varied subjects. A Soviet writer's subject matter and treatment of it is limited to a narrow band of the whole literary spectrum. Even Soviet fairy tales must hew to the Party line; several recent fairy tales have been denounced for "insufficient ideology."

One afternoon we visiting correspondents were entertained by the executive committee of the Union of Soviet Writers in a big nineteenth-century Moscow mansion which is now the Union's clubhouse. We were ushered into a living room with fine linen-fold paneling. This sanctum of the Writers Club had three busts: a smaller-than-life Pushkin and twice-as-large-as-life Lenin and Stalin. After cocktails, we sat down in one corner of the room around a long table covered with green baize. Boris Gorbatov, novelist and head of the union, introduced his colleagues, who included the poets Nikolai Tikhonov, Vera Inber, Samuel Marshak and Alexei Surkov, the novelists Leonid Leonov, Valentin Katayev and Leonid Sobolev, the playwright Vsevolod Vishnevsky and the critics Sabatsky and Yermilov.

As the questions and answers went on, I was reminded time and again of that centuries-old Russian yen for unanimity and indivisible truth—now reinforced by what the Kremlin expects.

Q. "How do Soviet writers work?"

A. (Gorbatov) "Our aim is to work and help each other to write. The government makes cultural decisions. We discuss them and accept them. The government very correctly pointed out those writers who stood aside during the war, like Zoshchenko. We are all distressed that Zoshchenko stood aside and wrote things false and untrue of Soviet life." (Gorbatov brought up Zoshchenko of his own accord; none of us had even mentioned him.)

(Vishnevsky, interrupting Gorbatov) "Zoshchenko was a czarist White Russian officer who wrote falsehoods about the Russian people. We're happy to state that very few are like Zoshchenko."

Q. "What's happened to Zoshchenko?"

A. (Gorbatov) "He's living in Leningrad and writing a book about the war. We're glad he's writing a book and hope it's good. We always welcome good books."

Q. "Is Zoshchenko still a member of the union?"

A. (Gorbatov) "He has been excluded."

Q. "If his book is good, will he be reinstated?"

A. (Gorbatov) "Of course."

Q. "Were Zoshchenko's books popular?"

A. (Gorbatov) "When they were correct, they were popular."

(Surkov, interrupting) "We don't get any directives. The tenets of the Communist Party are clear and we have accepted them because we think alike."

(Sabatsky, interrupting) "It's a great honor for Soviet writers to serve their people. We think the will of the Soviet government is the will of the people, so we always listen because it's the will of the people."

Q. (from Edward Crankshaw of the London *Observer*, a very perceptive writer on Russia) "What would be the attitude of the Union of Soviet Writers toward a writer who risked his life through the war and then returned and wanted to write somewhat at variance with Soviet ideology?"

There was bitter-sounding laughter among the Russians as the translation of the question ended. Then Vera Inber answered: "A writer should write what he ought to write. Imagine my wanting to write something antigovernment! It wouldn't work."

Sobolev (interrupting) "Zoshchenko writes as if our people were fools and scoundrels. What would you think of a man who talked of your wife as though she were of ill fame? You would not shake hands with such a man. For twenty-five years Zoshchenko thought of our people as something very bad. Zoshchenko was always in opposition to the government, in opposition to the Russian people."

Q. (Irving Pflaum of the Chicago *Times*) "I'm puzzled. The

government directive reflects the will of the people. People didn't like Zoshchenko. The government has educated the people. If the government reflects the people and people are against Zoshchenko, why not let him write—because the people won't buy his books anyway. Why not let him stay in the union?"

A. (Gorbatov) "Nobody prohibits him from writing. He wants to write. He understands his mistakes. It's our duty to criticize a writer and point out his mistakes."

(Marshak, interrupting) "Our life and work must embody the nation's hopes, the nation's struggles."

Q. (Crankshaw) "Writers must have a sense of responsibility. But an individual can only express himself, for better or for worse, and when he tries to express a whole people or group, his integrity is in danger."

A. (Vishnevsky) "By our suffering we learned that literature must be active."

Q. (Gorbatov) "What are American and British authors writing about?"

A. (William McGaffin, Chicago *Daily News*) "In America, largely escapist literature, because that's what writers want and find that's what their readers want. I hear that Russian people feel much the same way, that the light German musical film *Girl of My Dreams* was terrifically popular in Russia, with huge queues wherever it showed, and that Soviet scenario writers after a long day of ideological film scripting ask for private showings of American comedies for escape."

Gorbatov replied: "We writers are tired, perhaps even tireder than the Russian people. But we know we must work seriously and we do."

(Leonov, interrupting) "We have to be serious. We Russians were the first writers to fight against Hitler. When you see American escapist films you forget not only the past but the future. You forget Dachau and Maidenek, and that they can happen again. Escapist films can lead us right to the crematorium."

Crankshaw answered: "I'm a professional novelist and writer. I wrote against Hitler in 1931 and thereafter, very loudly. In 1939, at a time when Soviet writers were not writing against Hitler, the British government mobilized me against Hitler, not as a writer but as a man with two arms and two legs. And for seven years I very happily gave my two arms and two legs and fought for my country's cause. But I would never let my mind be drafted for any country or any cause."

As Crankshaw's answer was interpreted, Gorbatov rose rather abruptly and invited us all to have some more refreshments. So we had tea, cookies and little Russian candies. The formal session was adjourned, but smaller knots of Russians and Westerners talked animatedly for some time.

As I was leaving, Leonov shook hands with me and then with McGaffin just behind me. McGaffin said, in Russian, "It has been very interesting." Leonov smiled and said: "It has been very useful."

It had been both.

4

What sort of creative work is produced under this Kremlin control?

Architecture is the worst. Russia has many memorable structures, but no really good or original ones produced in the Soviet regime. As one experienced observer wrote: "At the mention of architecture, Moscow conversation has a tendency to drop, and even the warmest enthusiasts are apt to hang their heads and sigh significantly if asked to explain how Soviet creative feeling has expressed itself in architectural form."

Painting and sculpture are the next worst. I did not see a single post-1917 painting of any style that would rank among the best produced in Western countries during that period. Soviet sculpture has quantity, not quality. The bulk of it is statuary of Communist heroes; the Egyptians did far better votive statues of their pharaohs four thousand years ago.

Under the Kremlin's cultural lash, Soviet writing seems to get more sterile by the year.

In music, on the other hand, Russia has as many masters as any nation has produced in the past thirty years, perhaps more. Though Shostakovich's cacophonous opera *Lady Macbeth of Mzensk* so offended Stalin in 1936 that the composer was in disgrace for five years, music is harder than words to control ideologically—and Soviet musicians hence have had somewhat more freedom, so long as they provided a few tunes the Kremlin could carry. Musical performance standards, though fair, are not as high as the best in the West and lag especially in vocal and instrumental soloists. Soviet choral singing is as good as I have ever heard anywhere except Wales, but the soloists both at the opera and at the Red Army chorus left something to be desired. Russians say that their soloists' weakness is owing not so much to the lack of natural voices and instrumental abilities as to the lack of top-notch teachers and to the lack of experience in rubbing up against the best in other lands. The famous old czarist teachers of voice, violin, etc. have all died off, and since Communist controls keep both teachers and pupils pretty much at home, the standards have inevitably declined—as they do in tennis when they don't have Davis Cup competition.

For its seven million citizens, Moscow has only twenty-seven legitimate theaters (including the Bolshoi) and forty-three movie houses. If every seat were filled at every performance, every Muscovite could see one movie a year. He could see a stage show once every two years. The few top theater and ballet companies are splendid, but almost no Russian sees them unless he belongs to some privileged Soviet organization. I met one relatively well-to-do Russian in Moscow who had not been able to get inside the Bolshoi for ten years. Some tickets are sold by scalpers, way above the set price, but that risks jail for both seller and buyer.

Not the least of my luck in getting to Russia at all was to be there during the Moscow Conference. We could buy superb seats to anything, as part of the red carpet treatment.

One evening my companion for a performance of *The Cherry Orchard* at the Moscow Arts *Filiale* (affiliate) Theater had to back out at the last moment. I took the spare ticket along with me, and sure enough several people in the lobby offered me double the ticket's price. I chose a lanky student with thick-lensed glasses and sold it at face value. When we got to our seats, I learned that he had been coming for four months every time *The Cherry Orchard* was given in the hope he could some day get a last-minute seat. "I never get in otherwise," he added. His sudden satisfied intake of breath—a little gasp of pure pleasure—at each good bit of acting was worth cocking my ear for. The acting was beautifully smooth knit, from a long-established company which never missed a chance or a timing. The Arts Theater believes in realism. They had real hay in the rural scene and tossed it about. The fragrance, and one or two actual wisps, came to me in the second row. Chekhov's pre-Revolutionary Russia there on the stage was very realistic in all its minor-key charm, decadence, melancholia, and introspection.

It has been truly said that "Soviet dramaturgy and the theater are pleasing roughly in proportion to the age of the plays and the age of the actors." One of the few good Soviet plays I saw was Pogodin's *The Kremlin Chimes*. Etched forever on my memory is the deathly hush of the entire theater when two Soviet secret policemen came to take a man away. His wife gave one stricken look at the visitors, went and got the suitcase of clothes she had kept packed for just such a possibility, and kissed her husband good-by. He went quietly. Until the door closed behind him and the policemen, no one else on the stage or in the audience stirred —or even seemed to breathe. The Soviet theater can indeed be realistic.

Soviet films, even those of Eisenstein, have never been as good with sound as they were in the silent days. They have been handicapped by increasing ideological as well as increasing technical difficulties. Moscow's Puppet Theater is, however, the most delightful one I know, and Soviet circuses are very good—even though the clowns do have difficulty getting clearance for their jokes.

The ballet remains the Russians' favorite art form. There is simply no comparison between Russian ballet and that elsewhere. It has not really changed in sixty years; the Kremlin has continued to subsidize its czarist technical perfection. Soviet ballet is as sumptuously produced as *Boris Godunov*. It out-Hollywoods Hollywood. It also has a lyric grace and intensity that cannot well be put into words. Some of my evenings at it rank among the top theatrical experiences of my life. None of the many evenings I have watched ballet in other countries come anywhere near them. Why does the ballet stay so perfect while solo standards in music have declined? It may be because Russians so love ballet and struggle so to get into the various ballet schools. In this field, Russians do have enough rivalry among themselves to keep close to human perfection.

The ballet has remained almost free of Communism. The most successful post-1917 one is probably Prokofiev's *Cinderella*, the moral of which is that if a poor working girl is good enough to give what looks like a two days' bread ration to a helpless old woman, the latter will turn out to be her fairy godmother and manage to marry her to a prince complete with a crown and a castle. It is hard to find any Communism in that. I saw thirteen different ballets in Moscow and Leningrad. (Nearly every Russian ballet runs an entire evening by itself.) Only one of them, based on the French Revolution, was in the least ideological. The Kremlin, which knows a Russian supremacy when it sees one, has apparently decided that in ballet at least it can let well enough alone.

5

The episode that to me best symbolized the completeness of Soviet controls was my effort to see the Lenin Library in Moscow. Russians call this "the world's greatest library" and speak proudly of its twelve million volumes. It looks massive enough to hold that many. It stands at the start of Kalinin Street near the Kremlin, with a gigantic block-long book stack rising high above a central building topped with heroic statues. Strolling past it one slushy spring day, I realized I should visit this great headquarters of Soviet culture and learning. I climbed the steps to its wide, pillared porch and went in. A portress stopped me by the cloakroom just inside the stone-paved main lobby. "Where is your pass?" she demanded.

"I have no pass," I said. "I simply want to see a little of the library."

"No one can see any part of it without a pass," she proclaimed.

"But I hear this is the world's greatest library," I protested. "Surely anyone is allowed to see at least some parts of it."

"Who are you? What is your business?" she asked. I explained that I was an American correspondent, in Moscow to cover the Foreign Ministers' Conference. She became my champion. She went to a phone and began calling people. Finally she found the answer and turned to me smiling. "Go around to the far side of the library," she said, and gave careful directions. "There you can get a visitor's pass."

I went around through the slush and found the right door, which led into a much less imposing hall. Inside I was again met with suspicion and again went through the same rigmarole. Again the guardian of the gate became my champion. He began phoning people. Finally he too beamed with success.

"You must go to an office under the book stacks," he said. "There they are qualified to issue a temporary pass." I asked further direction. "You would never find it," he said. "It is underground and far too complicated. I will summon escort." He did. It turned out to be a secret police officer. What the secret police were doing in a library was never explained—and it seemed untactful to ask. But the officer gazed at me dubiously and asked why I was there. Once more my new friend was eloquent. Soon the secret policeman was also on my side. He promised to take me to the right room. Take me he did, through a maze of book stacks, in one section of which a conveyor belt whirred mysteriously just over our heads.

But the occupant of the office was as hostile as my three successive sponsors had originally been. No one could have done more for me than my secret policeman tried to do. First he argued my newest opponent into co-operation. Then when the man agreed that I ought to see the library but said he could not take the responsibility for issuing the pass, the policeman too began phoning in all directions.

At last he got some high official. This man spoke some English, so the officer turned the phone over to me. When the usual preliminary doubt was dissolved, the man at the far end was as cordial as the first four. But he, too, claimed that he could not assume the responsibility for admitting an unauthorized stranger to the library. I asked: "Not even for a short escorted view of the catalogue and reading room?"

"Not even for that," he admitted.

"But can I not see this 'world's greatest library'?" I asked. "I have never before been refused admission to any library in any country of the world. Libraries are meant to be visited and used. What could be the possible harm in my being allowed to admire this one?"

He did not attempt to answer my questions. He made the oblique reply you often get from a Soviet official who must say no

when it is unreasonable to say it. "A very fine pamphlet has been
published about the Lenin Library," he said. "Why don't you go
home and read that?"

At this point I had been talking with five people in the Lenin
Library for more than an hour about my wish to see some of it.
Perhaps if I had gone on for another hour, or a week, or a year,
I might have succeeded. But if a friendly secret police officer could
not arrange it for me, the prospects seemed dim. In the vast, enigmatic intricacies of the Soviet system, the Lenin Library is evidently one of those things that outsiders are not supposed to see.

"Thank you," I said, "Americans are not accustomed to hearing
that the best way to see a library is to read a pamphlet about it."

As I walked away from that great library—and it may well be
the world's greatest in size though not in spirit—I realized that
the hour I had spent there was the Soviet Union in miniature.
There had been the initial suspicion and then the friendliness
toward a foreigner of five individual Russians, one of them a
secret policeman. There had been the doubts and delays so common in Soviet life. There had been the well-grounded reluctance
of Soviet officials, who know their state and its penalties, to assume
even the smallest responsibility they did not have to, especially if
that responsibility needed to be put into writing—in this case a
pass that would permit someone to see for a short space a little of
the apparatus of learning. There had been the final frustration.

As I walked on I thought of the bitter but ironic article I had
been shown not long before in a Soviet learned publication—
bitter, because it warned Soviet intellectuals against "the poisons
of the West"; ironic, because it went on to say that efforts were
being made to translate as much as possible of the best Western
technical and scientific literature into Russian so that Soviet intellectuals could reap its benefits. Even Russians cannot enter the
Lenin Library without a pass. In the Soviet Union, libraries and
knowledge are part of the power system, the strategy, the secrecy.
It is sad. But it is true.

Thank God, I thought, that secrecy is not an integral part of
knowledge in the West. In America, knowledge is the people's
powerhouse. The American government has hidden its technical
knowledge of the atom bomb. Perhaps it is right for America to
keep the atom's military secrets until there is a working inter-

national body to which they can be given. The atom bombs thus far exploded have shown the real and frightful danger from its misuse.

Ordinary Russians know very little about the atom bomb, which their government has steadily minimized as, so to speak, not much worse than a bad cold. Soviet propagandists in factories and on farms have been ordered by the Kremlin to tell Russians that atom bombs "are nothing to worry about and amount to little more than imperialistic sensationalism."

During my entire stay, not a single Russian to whom I talked brought up the subject of the atom bomb—probably because the scanty, slanted information they get on it from propagandists and in the completely controlled Soviet press could not possibly make them realize how appalling it is. After a few ineffectual attempts, I did not initiate the subject myself; it is hard to talk about the atom bomb with people who know almost nothing of what it did, and as little about its implications. The Kremlin, presumably, has a more realistic attitude on the subject than ordinary Russians —though there is some evidence that even the Kremlin thinks that America exaggerates the atom for political purposes.

Perhaps it is also right that peace treaties and other grave negotiations should have some secrets, at least during the negotiating stages. All lasting agreements between men and nations with differing views must be founded on compromise, as America's big states and little states finally compromised in the Constitutional Convention of 1787. No statesman can make those adjustments if his every step is taken openly. But America must never keep any secrets whatever without full, justified cause. It must never reach any agreements, however secret their start, which cannot afterward be explained and justified as a whole. If there is reason for some secrets to be kept, that reason must always be ready and able to undergo as violent, public, thorough and deep a debate as that over keeping the secrets of the atom bomb. Every application of American foreign policy must continue to be subjected to just as searching, scorching debate until a great majority of Americans, while possibly not agreeing with every clause, unite on its main essentials.

In the Soviet people's state, such matters are not discussed or decided by the people. They are settled by the Politburo. But the

Politburo does not have as accurate information on some important matters as does the average informed American. Soviet subordinates often omit or play down information they think might vex their superiors. The Soviet observers at the Bikini atom bomb tests appear to have done just that. The Politburo, remember, had disastrously wrong information on Finland in 1939; it actually thought that Finns would welcome the Russian invasion!

The final irony of the Kremlin's complete thought control is that it too is caught in the controls. The protections it has thrown around itself protect it from something even more important than possible assassination—knowledge. It is at least twenty-five years since Stalin did anything as simple but vital as to walk down the street by himself and stop to peer in a shop window or chat with the people who passed. (Once, a few years ago, Stalin scared his secret-police escorts almost out of their wits by deciding to walk back the third of a mile from the Bolshoi to the Kremlin.) It is years since any other present member of the Politburo could do that. Practically all the information they get is on pieces of paper, after umpteen siftings and selections.

Not even the fourteen men who, out of some two hundred million Russians, are members of the Politburo, know as much about some world issues as does any American who cares enough about them to go to a library or anywhere else, or to talk with people as frankly as he likes and make himself informed.

6

In 1905, denouncing czarist tyranny, Joseph Conrad wrote: "The worst crime against humanity of that system is the ruthless destruction of innumerable minds." Communists have carried that crime much further than their predecessors. I agree fervently with Conrad that the worst you can do to human beings is to destroy or cripple their minds and souls, so I have devoted most of my chapter on Soviet controls to what they have done in this field.

You can also do terrible things to people's bodies. The Communists have surpassed the czars in this crime too.

Soviet Russia shows no present sign of great, bloody purges like the liquidation of the kulaks when Russian farms were collectivized, or the tremendous political pogrom of 1934-38 that left Stalin firmly in the saddle. "Shortening a man by a head's length" (Trotsky's phrase when he justified it, years before his own assassination) has now been officially abolished in the Soviet Union. Russia is so short of manpower that victims are shipped off to slave labor camps to do some work before they die. Russia's so-called agricultural, industrial and bureaucratic purges of 1946 were what the Russians themselves call a *chistka* (house cleaning). They were part of the Kremlin's general postwar tightening up of severe Communist standards which had necessarily been relaxed somewhat during the stresses and strains of war. Many people lost their jobs, or were transferred to poorer ones as punishment. In the Ukraine, for example, Politburo Member Nikita Khruschev announced a "mass replacement of the Party's leading personnel." Of the Ukraine's executives, "about half" were replaced—including 64 percent of the heads of regional Soviets and 67 percent of the directors of machine-tractor stations.

The worst offenders got prison sentences and were promptly put to work in the slave battalions you see all round Russia. These are something like the one-time Georgia chain gangs, though far more numerous. No outsider knows how many prisoners are in these labor camps. The guesses I got in Russia—nobody except a few top Soviet officials can be sure—ranged up to fifteen million. Everybody agreed that practically all these Russian prisoners, plus the many prisoners of war whom Russia still holds, are under secret-police control. They are used quite openly as slave labor.

I myself saw Russian and foreign prisoners working at many places in the Soviet Union, more than a thousand miles apart. Russians spoke of them, especially of the POWs, rather freely. I never did get over my dismay at the complete indifference ordinary Russians showed at the sight of slave laborers. They took them as a matter of course and walked past them with no signs of distress. One of the contrasts between Soviet Russia and Nazi Germany is that the Nazis hid their concentration camps and always worked the inmates inside. Before 1939, the only way I could ever see even the fence of a Nazi concentration camp was to go off the beaten track to locate it; I never saw the inmates. The Nazis knew they were doing a horrible thing, and tried to hide it. Neither the Kremlin nor ordinary Russians seem to feel any shame about their slave-labor camps. Perhaps it is because, as Littlepage and Bess in *In Search of Soviet Gold* observed: "From an American viewpoint, all Soviet citizens are treated very much like prisoners on parole"—and Russians "on parole" are resigned to the fact that at any moment they may become "prisoners."

Also involved in this is what I would call "the *nichevo* attitude" in Russians. *Nichevo* means, literally, "nothing." Russians use the word constantly with a primary and psychologically very significant, implication of "What does it matter?"—like that Soviet official who said *"Nichevo"* to me as the thirty reporters he was shepherding suddenly scattered.

You say to a Russian, "I'm sorry to hear your father died." He says *"Nichevo,"* meaning, "Yes, too bad, but he was an old man and had to go sometime." You say, "I'm glad to hear you were made director of the factory." He says *"Nichevo,"* in effect meaning, "It's an honor, I guess, but God knows what will happen if I don't do better than the last director." You say, "I hear Vassily was sent to Siberia." He says, *"Nichevo,"* meaning, "It's a shame. Anyway, I wasn't the one who informed on him." A peasant who gets a horse stuck in the mire or a maid who drops a valuable vase knows that punishment will come. They say *"Nichevo,"* meaning, "What will happen will happen." If you are waiting in the slush and your bus goes right past without stopping—splashing you all over as it does so—you say *"Nichevo,"* meaning, "Well, life's like that." At the Puppet Theater's marvelously realistic rendition of *Mowgli*, based on Kipling's *Jungle Book*, it seemed quite natural for the animals to be talking; the only thing that jolted me out of the illusion that I was in India's jungles was hearing Bagheera the panther say *"Nichevo"* when the monkeys ran off with Mowgli.

Perhaps Russians say *"Nichevo"* inside themselves every time they go past a labor gang.

The only attempt to conceal slave labor of any nationality that I encountered in Russia was about four blocks from my Moscow hotel. Here, on a side street just behind the great central telegraph building on Gorki Street, the Soviet secret police were building a big new red-brick addition to one of their many large places of operation. One evening at 6:30 as I strolled down this street I noticed a large canvas-covered truck backed into the low, tunnellike courtyard entrance to the new construction. Three similar trucks were lined up along the curb, evidently awaiting their turn. Several armed soldiers and secret policemen were standing about. My curiosity aroused, I looked through the crack between the truck and the wall. I saw and heard about a hundred German POWs, still in their green German uniforms, as they were lined up to go back to camp for the night. About twenty-five were put in each truck, along with two armed Russians. Canvas was then pulled down over the back so that the truck's contents were completely concealed. One prisoner's head made a bulge in the canvas. A guard outside hit it a smart rap with his rifle and the bump disappeared.

The trucks were so backed into the entrance that the prisoners could be seen only by someone standing directly beside the trucks' tailboards. Passing Russians, seeing armed soldiers and secret police, gave them far too wide a berth for that. To confirm my own observations, I went back to the same spot two other evenings at 6:30 with non-Russian companions. Exactly the same thing occurred.

Perhaps the MVD resorted to concealment here because this place is so close to the heart of Moscow, less than a quarter mile airline from the Kremlin and near the area where most of Russia's few foreigners congregate. They certainly do not bother much about concealment elsewhere. I often saw Russian and foreign prisoners working in guarded gangs of ten to a hundred. The stockaded and watch-towered enclosures where they live are a fairly frequent feature of the Soviet landscape.

The Kremlin could not recruit voluntary labor for many of its construction and mining projects in Siberia, the Russian Arctic, and elsewhere. Through the years it has cold-bloodedly and increasingly used prisoners rounded up on all sorts of pretexts. Russians can still disappear overnight toward slave-labor camps. The first week I was in Moscow an English-speaking Russian girl sat next to me at a program of folk dances. My host had asked her to explain the intricacies of Russian folk dancing to me and another newcomer. Four days later the secret police knocked on her door at midnight. None of her friends have seen her since.

At least three other Russians I also met casually in the weeks I was in Moscow later disappeared.

Russians who have contact with foreigners are careful in their dealings with them. They would be fools if they weren't. When employed by foreigners, they get twice or more the wage they would receive for similar work for a Russian, just as steeplejacks are paid more than men who work on the ground.

Since several families usually share the same apartment, and the Soviet apartment house and block-control system is more thorough than that of the Nazis, there is a steady check on every Russian. One MVD man recently told a foreigner that the MVD makes a point of having one informer out of each sixteen people in every Soviet apartment house. The MVD usually gets informers by rounding people up on some minor offense and then blackmailing them into the work by threatening Siberia. The system is so minutely worked out that any Russian who cannot keep his objections about the regime to himself is, sooner or later, pretty sure to be removed from the Soviet body politic by secret-police surgery. Ordinary Russians hate and fear the police but seldom dare to put that hate and fear into words. They have their small outlets, however. A foreigner described one: "There were few things I enjoyed more in Moscow than going to the Dynamo football stadium where eighty thousand fans cheered like mad for the Red Army team to knock hell out of the police eleven. Maybe it didn't mean a thing. Maybe it did."

Foreigners in Russia are, of course, more closely watched than the average Russian. Russians seldom mention this, but it is obvious. Once I drove with a Soviet guide past Lubianka Prison, another secret-police stronghold in Moscow. Curious to see what she would say, I asked, "What is that large, impressive building?" "Oh," she replied, "people live there." Which was the truth, but hardly the whole truth. When we were provided official guides and interpreters, they were invariably pleasant and efficient. Like the guide, they did not necessarily tell all. If a Russian-speaking American was along, we often learned more from what he told us afterward than we had at the formal sessions. Because of the extraordinary number of foreigners in Russia at the time, I never had personal surveillance. The secret police did not have the foreign-language staff to dog everybody. But some foreigners in

Russia are watched night and day. U.S. Ambassador Bedell Smith's car is always followed by an MVD car. When Smith goes skiing, secret police ski down the hill behind him.

The U.S. Embassy in Moscow has an open-door policy. Its front door is never locked. "Aren't there thieves in Moscow?" asked one startled visitor. "Oh yes," it was explained. "There are thieves all right. But the penalty for a Russian seen entering the American Embassy is stiffer than the penalty for larceny."

Ivan the Terrible gave Russia its first secret police, the black-clad *Oprichiniki*, who purged his opponents. They have since been known by many names. Under Czar Nicholas I a century ago, they were the Third Section. Under Nicholas II until the February 1917 Revolution, they were the Ochrana. The Communists, who restored them after the October 1917 Revolution, have given them four successive titles: CHEKA (Extraordinary Commission), 1917-22; GPU (State Political Management), 1922-34; NKVD (People's Commissariat for Internal Affairs), 1934-46; and, since 1946, the MVD (Ministry of Internal Security). At every new name for this old institution, the proverb-loving Russians say, "Horse-radish is not sweeter than radish."

Any secret police system grows inexorably. One Russian who was exiled by both the czars and the Communists recently remarked: "Not one officer of the old Army would shake hands with a secret-police officer. They used to say, 'It's important to defend the country and the czar, but these snakes' . . .'" Russians still feel that way about the secret police. But it now has far more power and privileges than the Red Army. Beria ranks higher than any secret-police head in Russian history. He is third on the Politburo, just behind Stalin and Molotov. Even in Soviet Russia, that would have been inconceivable fifteen years ago. Now Beria of the secret police takes precedence over Zhdanov, chief executive of the Communist Party.

A police state gets more and more dependent on the secret police. Himmler, the Gestapo chief, gradually rose in the Nazi regime until at the end he replaced Goering as Hitler's appointed successor. It is certainly possible that Beria will make himself Stalin's successor. Things gravitate his way. Almost automatically, he was put in charge of Russia's atomic-energy research. His man in any Soviet Embassy is more important than the ambassador. The secret police controls Soviet "investments" in occupied countries (for example, Austria's oil wells). The secret police honeycomb the whole Soviet state.

On a bitter March day with a temperature below freezing, I watched a prison labor gang of sixty women unloading railroad cars at Zagorsk. The women were of all ages; some were white haired, frail, and bent. Their clothes were tattered. Their bare hands were tugging at heavy loads including metal so cold that it seared the flesh which touched it. Other Russians were walking past the women without a glance. The only two people in the entire group who had on gloves, good boots and wool overcoats instead of quilted cotton jackets, were its two strapping young secret policemen. Leaning on their rifles, they watched the women work.

Chapter 6. THE ECONOMY

HOW do things really operate in a planned economy? Soviet planning covers everything from the simple necessities of daily living to the complex economic preparations that may help fulfill the Communist dream of world dominance.

Indirect taxation looms large in the Russian economy. Americans think, with some cause, that a 1 percent or 2 percent sales tax falls with especial severity on the food and other essentials which low-income groups must buy to live. The average Soviet sales tax is 350 percent. Instead of paying two cents on a dollar purchase, and handing over $1.02, you hand over $4.50—$1 for the purchase plus $3.50 for the tax. There are tremendous taxes on the commonest necessities, including bread and potatoes, the two basic items in the ordinary Russian's diet.

While I was in Moscow a truck driver was put on trial there because seven and a half tons of potatoes had disappeared when in his charge. The state prosecutor officially valued the potatoes at $5.83 a metric ton (2,200 pounds). He explained that this was the price for compulsory deliveries of potatoes to the state by collective farms. When these $5.83-a-ton potatoes disappeared, state stores were selling potatoes on ration at 10¢ a pound. Unrationed, on the farmers' market, they cost 65¢ a pound. The state was selling each ton of potatoes it had taken over at $5.83 for $220 in ration stores. Food in Moscow was so scarce that the same ton, unrationed, was worth $1,430.

In Leningrad I bought a chocolate bar, of the size that costs six cents in America, for $2.50. It had a sales tax of nearly 1,000 percent; that is, more than nine-tenths of the selling price went to the state in taxes. Vodka has a sales tax of about 2,500 percent, which may comfort an American the next time he buys a bottle of bourbon.

Soviet sales taxes are better hidden than ours. For one thing

hey are part—usually much the largest part—of the marked
price of a product, instead of being added by the clerk when you
buy it. They are called "turn-over taxes." But every economist
who has studied them agrees that for all practical purposes they
are what we know by the name of sales tax. The state derives
two-thirds of its entire income from them. A Soviet economist
said to me, with a smile: "People prefer indirect taxes."

Not all Soviet taxes are indirect. There are income and other
direct taxes. (A man or woman without children pays an extra
5 percent tax; the state wants more children.) The average Soviet
worker earns about $500 a year. Not one in ten earns over
$1,000. Including the high, indirect sales taxes, a Russian single
person earning $500 a year turns back about $230—and one
earning $1,000 about $575—to the state. An American single
person earning $500 pays no federal income tax and an average
$45 in all other taxes; on $1,000 he pays $66 federal income tax
and an average $110 in all other taxes. Most Russian wives work,
so they are taxed too. Children lower their parents' income tax—
but not the sales taxes. Practically every Russian, whatever he
earns or however numerous his dependents, pays several times as
much in taxes as does his American counterpart. The only Russian group that escapes relatively lightly is the privileged handful
with high incomes: the top Soviet income tax is 45 percent compared to 91 percent in America.

The peasants can make large profits on the open market selling
produce which they have grown on the small patches they can
cultivate for themselves. But if they buy consumer goods with the
proceeds, they pay those terrific sales taxes, so up to 90 percent of
their profit goes right back to the state. If they try to hoard the
money in their socks, the Kremlin makes it almost worthless by
inflation or devaluation.

What do ordinary Russians get for these staggering taxes? Very
little in the way of services, except the secret police. Most of the
money goes for armaments and other measures to build up military and state power. Russians do boast of their tax-paid education
and medical care. Seen at firsthand, the medical service is as unimpressive as the educational system.

The average Russian doctor is little better trained than the
average American nurse. Medical-education requirements are

kept low to meet the needs of the extensive state-health system
In 1917, Russia had only eighteen thousand doctors. Now it ha
150,000, one for every 1,300 people (America has one for every
750). There are district clinics even in rural areas and the state
does attempt to make medical care available to all. Short as Soviet
doctors are of training and equipment, the ordinary Russian un
doubtedly has better medical care than in czarist times. The state
clinics are so crowded in the daytime that Russians who can afford
it go to see doctors evenings at their homes, when—if they pay a
heavy monthly fee to the state—they can legally take private
patients. Compared to America, standards are low, though equal
to those of such countries as Portugal and Hungary. Floors at
hospitals and clinics are dirty. Some surgeons are so little con
cerned about germs that they stop in mid-operation to shake
hands with other doctors who, in street clothes, pass through the
operating room. The young women doctors who attended the
three visiting delegations to the Council of Foreign Ministers had
a truly remarkable remedy for colds: mustard powder in your
socks!

The delivery room in what Russians call "the best maternity
hospital in the Soviet Union" has flies on its ceiling, old women
washing its floor as the babies are delivered, a steady stream of
traffic through its open door, and windows (open in summer)
looking out on apartment-house balconies twenty feet away
where teen-age boys follow the obstetrical proceedings with avid
interest. A special card allows expectant mothers to buy for
$2.50 (this is not part of the "free care" but a very special extra
blessing that Russians boast about) a package of things otherwise
almost unobtainable: one rubber pants, two nipples, a can of
talcum powder, some gauze and a few other elementary necessities. Russians are frankly incredulous that any American can
buy all these and many more baby things in almost any quantity.

Housing is controlled to keep workers tied down. Most Moscow
apartments have several families living in them, sharing the one
kitchen and primitive bathroom. A Russian had me to lunch in
his room—the entire living, sleeping, and eating place for his
family of three. His wife had cooked the lunch on a stove where
three other women had simultaneously been preparing their
households' meal. An American family would have been hideously

aware of beds by their dining table, furniture fit only for a junk shop, miscellaneous personal effects piled loosely about a dingy room with only one small closet. Russians manage to take it gracefully.

Under Communism, Russian housing has fallen so far behind that the five rooms of an average American family would have had to house fourteen people in 1928, seventeen people in 1934, twenty people in 1937 and, with wartime destruction and slow reconstruction, thirty people in 1948. One two-story house in Moscow, built before the revolution for a single family, shelters fifteen families, who share one toilet in a hall closet. The small daughter of a Russian intellectual composes little pieces which she plays on the piano. A recent song of hers translates literally:

> Some day I am going to have a little house.
> It will be painted and have a nice green lawn,
> And there will be a light in the toilet.

This overcrowding breeds terrible tensions. Families will quarrel bitterly because one husband wants to bathe when the wife in another family wants to wash diapers. A woman will use a second burner of the stove just to boil water when she sees another woman coming to cook her family's meal on that burner. People have even dumped caustic soda in a neighbor's soup; some families, to play safe, use a cooking pot with a special padlocked lid. Food is so scarce that a woman will claim another has stolen a carrot or potato. There can be no privacy under such conditions, much less a decent or relaxed existence. As one man told me in Moscow: "Household accounts are the worst. How we all quarrel over them. 'You used far more cooking gas than we did last month. Once you had the oven on for five hours.' 'You keep the lights burning much later than we do. You ought to pay more of the electric bill.' 'Why do you leave the bathroom so filthy? Your whole family are swine.'"

A single room, even with such neighbors, is far better than nothing. A room, once obtained, is clung to desperately—and so is the job that makes the room available. The great bulk of Soviet city housing is owned and controlled by state agencies. If you quit your job with the state bureau or factory that runs your apartment, you and your family lose your room. A Russian girl

I met said she had been offered a better, higher-paying job with easier hours in a cooperative than the one she had in a factory. She did not dare to take it. "Where would I live?" she asked. In one court case while I was in Moscow, a boy testified that he had had to quit school at the age of twelve and go to work for the state railways. His father, a railway employee, had died; unless someone in the family took a railway job, the mother, boy, and several younger children would have had to leave their room in a railway-run apartment house.

Russian city dwellers have only three means of getting a roof over their heads: to rent from a state agency, to rent from the municipal authorities, or to own their own home. The present 1946-50 Five-Year Plan will extend state housing control still further. Soviet cities are to get 72.4 million square meters of living space built by the state. (*Pravda* has lately complained that the housing plan is "lagging badly.") Of this amount, 65 million will be controlled directly by state agencies: ministries, factories, etc. In almost every case it will be rented only to people working in those given agencies, only for so long as they work there.

The remaining 7.4 million square meters—only a tenth of the total—will be controlled by municipal authorities. You can rent city housing no matter what your job, but the waiting list is a long one. *Izvestia* lately had a sad story about the Sergeevko family in Sverdlovsk, who had been at the top of the list for seventeen straight years and had not yet got a new apartment. (They may have failed to give someone a bonus.) Quite a few people do get a municipal room sooner or later. After you have one, you can even trade it for another—in the same town or some other city if you can: (1) get permission to move to it, and (2) locate someone with a municipal room there who wants to move to your city. This awkward barter method is the only flexible joint in the Soviet housing system, and the Kremlin is stiffening it by allotting less and less housing space to municipalities.

One city worker in a thousand owns his home. This group tends to stay put, since any Russian lucky enough to get a home of his own is not likely to move before he has to. The 1946-50 Plan calls for 12 million square meters of housing for individuals building or reconstructing their homes with loans from the state. (This plan is lagging even worse than the public housing program.) A

1947 Kremlin decree, for example, ordered fifty thousand one-room homes to be built in the Urals and Siberia and sold to key workers in heavy industry for $1,250 each. The state may also help a successful artist, scientist, or bureaucrat to get a home, making labor and materials available at relatively low state prices. To hire labor and buy materials would otherwise take innumerable rubles. One of the rare Russians even to venture it was Konstantin Simonov. When his anti-American play *The Russian Question* was showing in hundreds of Soviet theaters and his 6 percent box-office royalty from each performance had piled up impressively in the bank, Simonov figured he was rich enough to build a comfortable house outside Moscow. Soon he got a letter from Stalin, awarding him "the high Soviet privilege of having no bank account." Instead, he could simply draw on the State Bank when he needed money. This ominous "privilege" meant: Simonov's royalties had vanished, if he ever lost favor he would have no savings to fall back upon, and—above all—he must justify any especially large withdrawal. That afternoon Simonov stopped the work on his new home. For all his success, he must now wait till the Kremlin decides he deserves a house.

Individuals own less than 5 percent of Russia's property—the state owns the rest. Individuals can acquire property in Russia if they earn enough to buy it. They can sell, give away, mortgage or bequeath such personal property. But it will never accumulate in more than a trickle since it can be acquired only by one-man effort. All operations that involve hiring anyone for your own profit are a Communist monopoly. For a person to do that is "exploitation" of other persons; the Soviet state reserves the sole right to exploit on the ground that when everybody is working for the Universal Good it naturally ceases to be exploitation.

Both the public and the private housing plans show the increasing importance the Kremlin puts on tying Russians down to permanent places of residence, to permanent work in some state agency—and on checking any normal human tendency for a shift now and then.

The other forms of state economic control over the people are equally thorough. Here are some Moscow court cases that occurred while I was there:

A man fined 25 percent of his pay for three months for being thirty-five minutes late for work.

A girl of nineteen, a first offender, sentenced to a year in jail for stealing five and a half pounds of flour in a store. She said she had done it for her family's "existence" as their ration cards had been stolen and they were starving. Her story was not challenged—and not examined. She was sentenced directly after telling it.

Several people sentenced to long jail terms for "illegal residence" in Moscow (i.e., living there without a permit). Any Russian who changes his residence must get the new address stamped by the secret police in the identification card he must carry at all times.

A boy of thirteen given a year of "corrective labor" for pickpocketing. His father had been killed in the war. His mother, accused of not looking after him, explained that she had to support the boy and herself. She added: "I have to leave home at 8 A.M. and do not return from work until 8.30 P.M. The boy is alone too much." The judge interrupted her: "That is not an excuse. Other mothers have many children and bring them up decently."

Like other countries, Russia has plenty of nonpolitical crimes. Theft (because of shortages) and child delinquency (because of disrupted homes) are especially numerous. The rest range from murder to bribery. No totals are published, but the court dockets are always crowded. There are no formal juries, but in each case the professional judge is flanked by "lay judges" drawn from the population. These two, who are something like American jurors, listen, occasionally ask questions, and retire with the judge to vote on the verdict. Prosecutors conduct the state's case. Defendants can be their own lawyers, hire one, or take one assigned by the judge. Defense lawyers do not hesitate to attack the state's case violently. The accused are often acquitted. When convicted, they usually get a more severe penalty than their offense would seem to warrant. Both ordinary and political prisoners fare poorly in jail.

No political trials have been held in public for the past decade. Anyone can attend nonpolitical cases. They are very casually conducted in small, dingy rooms with no witness box, a few chairs for lawyers and defendants, and the robeless judge seated with his two lay assistants on a slightly raised platform behind a long table which is also the court stenographer's desk. Spectators stand or sit by the door. The testimony is fragmentary and seldom cross-examined. The judges use their intuition—the evidence rarely makes any other course possible.

In a case at the People's Court in Kropotkinskaya Street, a war widow suffering from malaria, who was the sole support of her ten-year-old son, was accused of not paying a six-cent streetcar fare. She claimed she had offered to pay it. The girl conductor claimed she had twice refused, and a trolley inspector said she had been abusive when arrested. They were the only three witnesses. No impartial observer, such as some other passenger on the trolley, was called. After hearing the completely contradictory evidence, the judges left the room to determine the verdict. In ten minutes they returned and sentenced her to two months' forced labor. She said nothing; her face remained a malaria-yellow mask. Her small son rushed toward her, grabbed her two hands, and held them firmly in his dirty little palms.

A Russian-speaking American asked two women spectators what was meant by "forced labor."

"She will be sent to a labor camp where she will work," one of them said.

"Will she be fed by the government?"

"You can imagine how people are fed in the camps."

The second woman interrupted: "She will not be sent to a camp but to one of the factories where nobody wants to work."

"What kind of factory do you mean?"

"One where felt boots are made, for instance."

"Will she be under arrest and will she get wages?"

"She will get very little money and she will be obliged to provide her own food. But do not worry, they all steal boots. They sell them and manage to live somehow."

The accused woman, who had been listening to the trio, turned and said: "If what they said were the truth, I would not mind spending ten years in jail. But those lies!"

Neither her illness nor her child were taken into consideration. No word was said by the judges as to what would happen to the boy, who had no other relatives, while his mother served her sentence for not paying a six-cent trolley fare.

2

The state sees to it through various control measures that practically every Russian who can work has to work. Two postwar sets of decrees, each of which repays examination, show the economic stranglehold the Kremlin has on the people.

The set of decrees of September 15, 1946, tightened the screws of the Soviet rationing system. The set of decrees of December 15, 1947, ostensibly ended rationing. They are actually the two sides of the same coin, the coin of control which the Kremlin has been flipping—now this way, now that—since 1928, when Stalin felt the Soviet regime was at last strong enough to survive the rigors of the first Five Year Plan. In 1929, he introduced rationing on the theory that cutting consumer goods and making Russians tighten their belts would hasten the capital goods expansion which the plan called for. Rationing continued until 1935, when a good harvest and a few more consumer goods let Stalin flip the coin the other way. Rationing returned from 1941 (with war) to 1947, so Russians have been rationed for twelve of the last nineteen years, eight in peacetime and four in war. They will again be rationed whenever the state wishes.

The Russian people get very little, whichever side of the coin is up. In 1950, if the present Five Year Plan is completely fulfilled (none of the rest were, and this one is behind schedule), each Russian will, for example, average one-quarter of a pound of meat and less than half a pound of sugar a week for all purposes, and one pair of shoes and less than three pairs of stockings apiece per year. He now gets considerably less.

The 1946 set of decrees showed how the state can make ordinary Russians do just what it wants them to do. On September 15, the Kremlin overnight tripled the price of all rationed food, cut the rations sharply, and in compensation merely raised wages an average 20 percent. Those making between $66.67 and $83.33 a month were raised 10 percent. Anyone earning over $83.33 got no raise at all. Since in Russia the cost of food is a very large part of the cost of living, this lowered the already low living standard of almost every Russian. The top Russian ration became 2,340 calories a day for manual workers in heavy industry. Other manual workers got 2,120 calories a day; office workers, 1,567; housewives and "other unemployed persons," 892; growing children, 1,114. The two latter rations are under starvation level. The others are not far above it for adults expected to do hard work.

A family of four with a husband who had earned $75 a month —well above the $42 Russian average—got $82 a month after these September 15, 1946, changes. The wife had been occupied with housekeeping and looking after the two small children. After direct taxes and union dues, the husband's take-home pay had been about $65. Now it was up to $71. Before, it had cost $27 a month to buy the family of four's total rations, leaving it $38 for rent, clothes and other essentials such as fresh vegetables and milk for the children. After September 15, the family had to pay $64 a month for its reduced rations. The four, for instance, were getting only eighty-eight pounds of bread monthly instead of 115.5 pounds as before—and bread provides half the average Russian's total calories. And there was only $7 a month left for all the family's other expenses, which now included trying to buy some of the missing bread and other food on the expensive open market.

This was according to plan. The Kremlin planned it so that this family—and almost every other Russian family—would have to do more work. The husband could hunt a part-time job for his evenings, thus not only producing more for the Soviet state but getting a little more money for bread. Or the wife could go to work in a factory, thereby getting a worker's ration card instead of the 892-calory card she now held. The money she would earn and the extra ration points on her book meant that her family, by having both its adults working instead of one, would be no worse off for food and other consumer essentials than it was before September 15.

In every other way, of course, the family would be worse off. If the wife went to work in a factory, who would take care of the two young children? Who would do the housework? Who would stand for hours in different queues to get the bread and other lean rations or do other essential family chores? But that was the only possible solution. The wife did go to work in a factory, leaving the kids to shift for themselves as best they could, though the oldest was just reaching school age. She does not even see very much of them when out of the factory because she then has to queue for the family rations, cook, and do any shreds of house-work for which she still has time.

Throughout Russia, millions of other wives and dependents similarly had to take jobs after September 15, 1946. The nub of the Kremlin's plan, namely, to get as much manpower as possible gainfully employed, was met. What this meant to Russian family life was not considered.

The decrees of December 15, 1947, supposedly ended all these shortages. In fact, they changed conditions very little. Too many rubles were chasing too few goods. The peasants had also col-lected a large part of Russia's cash by selling hungry city folk some of their home-grown food. So the Kremlin decreed that all rubles held in cash lost nine-tenths of their value. Rubles in bank accounts—few Russians have bank accounts—lost up to two-thirds their value. It was as though the U.S. Government suddenly called in all dollar currency and handed back a dime for each dollar. Russians were assured that this would be their "last sacri-fice"—but they have heard that promise before.

Having abolished all but one-tenth of the old rubles' value and replaced them with entirely new notes (on which Lenin looked much sourer—"He must have had all his money in cash," ordi-nary Russians whispered), the Kremlin ended rationing and lowered some of its astronomical prices. Butter came down to $2.65 and sugar to 62¢ a pound. A man's shoddy suit fell from $250 to $117.67 and women's shoes from $142 to $34.20. None of the reductions were anything like as great as the 90 percent cut in the ruble—and there were none of the small 1946 wage raises. Even with their far fewer rubles, Russians so stormed the stores—to get things while they could—that the supplies the state had carefully hoarded to put on display with the end of rationing disappeared in a few days. Many items never reappeared. Milk at the new state price of 34¢ a quart was just not in the stores; you had to go to the farmers' market and pay the same old $1.60 a quart. Items the stores did have were in their former scant supply and there was unofficial rationing: You could buy only a bit at a time; for instance, two ounces of butter per customer.

By the spring of 1948, Russia's food and consumer-goods situation was little better than it had been during the 1946-47 low point. Russians had to keep on struggling. Even by their new "low" prices, they had to work seventy minutes for the pound of bread an American worker could earn in eight minutes, three hours for the glass of beer an American got in six minutes, and thirty-two hours for the woman's cotton dress an American earned in two hours and twenty-three minutes.

Perhaps the most revealing aspect of the Kremlin's 1947 decrees was that they leaked in advance. Buying panics based on detailed rumors swept Russia more than three weeks before ruble devaluation and the other measures were announced. High Soviet officials (though not as high as the Politburo) profited by their prior knowledge. The Soviet state prides itself on "secrecy" and "Communist incorruptibility." Both were shown to be far from perfect. Italy and France devalued their currencies about then without rumors or profiteering. Almost the same week, Britain fired its chancellor of the exchequer for a minor budget leak only a few minutes before he announced the budget in Parliament. Soviet morale, on either the official or unofficial level, is not nearly so high as the propaganda paints it.

The Kremlin's 1946 decrees forced almost every able-bodied Russian over fourteen, of both sexes, into a paid job. The 1947 decrees kept them there—but gave them carefully graded incentives to work better and faster. One striking thing about Communist Russia is the number of capitalist devices it has adopted. The Communists combine incentive wages with a form of speed-up that American union members would never stand. In the spring of 1947, for instance, output norms were raised 20 to 25 percent in all key industries—that is, workers were told they must produce up to a quarter more to earn their old wages. If a Pittsburgh or Detroit plant tried that stunt, it would face an immediate strike. But Soviet workers have not once dared to strike since 1923.

If they produce enough, Soviet workers do get incentive pay. And in 1946 the Kremlin began beating the drums for something suspiciously like the profit motive. *Pravda* proclaimed that the "monopolist position" of state stores was hurting trade and lowering production. It demanded "healthy competition." Politburo member Andrei Zhdanov said that co-operatives must be encouraged. (These are not exactly like American co-operatives; they are state run. But they have more freedom of action than regular state factories and shops. As in co-ops elsewhere, members sometimes get dividends.) The Kremlin promptly did so, using five capitalist incentive devices: (1) permission for Russian co-ops to make profits as high as 20 percent—and give them to their members as bonuses (2) special tax concessions (3) promise of over $200 million in favorable long-term credits to encourage speedy expansion (4) freedom to fix their own prices (5) right to buy their materials direct from farms, mines, and factories (hitherto a state monopoly).

The Kremlin gave the co-ops these capitalist incentives hoping to break the vicious circle of farmers lagging on their food deliveries because they got no goods in exchange, and industrial workers lagging in output because they got so little food. The Communist state monopoly system was not producing nearly enough; it was realized that people might work better in a modified capitalism. They did. The expanded co-ops became a $700 million business in 1947. Their extra output was marketed through thirty thousand new co-op stores and a host of state-licensed street vendors. The 1947 co-op items included: 375 million buttons (nearly two buttons apiece for Russia's entire population), 23 million pairs of stockings, 4,000 tons of kitchen utensils, 500,000 beds, and a million tons of food.

Another use of the "profit motive" is a ruling, in effect since 1946, that establishes a "director's fund" in any plant that overfulfills its planned profits. The state used to take all profits. Now part of the profit overfulfillment, on a sliding scale that starts at 5 percent, goes not to the state but to the "director's fund." The plant leaders—director, union head, secret police chief, etc.—decide how to use the money to benefit everyone in the plant.

Most Russian workers, even on farms, get paid by piece rates, and their wages do climb sharply the higher they get above norm. The December 1947 decrees give the more efficient workers an even greater opportunity to live better than ordinary workers, who get barely enough to keep alive. Those who keep on upping their output can earn enough extra to buy a bit of meat or a spare shirt. If they produce enough, their whole family may have a little more food.

It is impossible to overestimate the significance of food in Russia. People there have gone hungry so long that, as in China, plumpness carries prestige. Any fat Russian is either important or closely related to someone important. Nearly every Politburo member is fat. The fattest person I met in Russia was Mrs. Pavel F. Yudin, wife of the outstanding Soviet philosopher of Communism. Her arms, sticking out from her sleeveless party dress, were the biggest and pinkest sausages I ever saw except on a circus fat lady. Even before the introduction, or my having a chance to note the gold medal of the Stalin Prize dangling from her husband's lapel, I knew she was an Important Wife.

Yudin has richly earned the rubles that feed and clothe her so well. He can even square the circle—reconcile Communist principle to Communist practice. In 1946, for example, he used a 1938 Stalin comment to justify the revision of one of Marx's key texts: that once Communism is attained, "a special repressive force, a state, is no longer necessary. The state is not abolished, it withers away." What needed explaining was the hothouse growth—instead of "withering"—of state power in Soviet Russia. This, it developed, was not only necessary but logical: "To bring about the abolition of the state, the state itself must be extended still further." Marx had added that for a state to have an army was very repressive and backward. Yudin showed that while this applied to bourgeois nations, the Red Army was quite forward looking: "In capitalist states the army is used for home oppression. It has an introvert function. But in the Soviet Union this introvert function is no longer necessary, as the enemies of the proletariat have been liquidated here. So in the Soviet Union the army has a purely extrovert function."

Yudin's talents—he does a great mass of such writing—were recently rewarded by his appointment as editor of the new Cominform magazine of international Communism. The Cominform is also to perform that "purely extrovert function." Not every industrious Soviet laborer can expect as much for his work as Yudin. But the incentive system is undoubtedly extending as never before to every class in this "classless society."

3

The economy of the Soviet "people's state" is not run for the people. Having provided details, I will now repeat my earlier statement: Russia had the poorest food, clothing, and housing of any war-affected country I saw on my eight-month 1947 trip— Finland, Denmark, Poland, Czechoslovakia, Germany, Austria, Greece, Italy, France, Belgium, and Britain.

Russian housing, both in areas damaged and undamaged by the war, speaks for itself. As for food, it is harder to convey the hungry look in people's eyes. But no other victor nation set starvation rations for large numbers of its population at less than nine hundred calories a day, or rationed growing children at 1,114. Even these rations, as the mayor of Stalingrad and other Russians admitted to me, were not always met. In 1947 the Kremlin exported food—for political purposes—while Russians dropped of hunger at Odessa, the Dneiper Dam, and elsewhere. Rationing of food and clothes was "abolished" in December 1947—but unofficial rationing followed and there have been only the barest increases. Russia's 1950 food and consumer-goods *goals*, which will not be achieved until after 1950, are in almost every instance less than the *actual consumption* of people in the eleven other war-affected countries during 1947.

War damage is not the primary cause of this. It is the Soviet system. Soviet industrial expansion, though considerable, is far less than the Soviet claims. A survey by six recognized economists, published in the *Harvard Review of Economic Statistics* in November 1947, showed how grossly Soviet figures had exaggerated Russia's advances. Not until the second year of the second Five Year Plan (1934) did the Russian output and national income exceed its 1913 level. By 1938, it was only 50 percent more than it had been in 1913. The Soviets claim they had a spectacular 650 percent rise of industrial output between 1928 and 1940. The rise was really only 50 percent over 1913 or 1928 (two years which were almost equal in output though there is no question which was the happier for the ordinary Russian).

This is a much lower percent of increase than czarist industry had shown in each of the three decades before World War I— and each of those decades showed a successively higher rate of increase. If the Communists had not sabotaged the democratic Russian revolution of February 1917 by seizing the government eight months later and plunging Russia into a bloody civil war, it is only logical to assume that Russia would have continued its rapidly accelerating economic expansion—and avoided an incalculable amount of human suffering.

Soviet competence in economic administration is highly debatable. The Kremlin did manage to build an industry vigorous enough to defeat the Nazis—aided by a vital $11.2 billion of American lend-lease food, armaments, and technical equipment. But either the czars or the Russian democrats, especially the latter, would almost certainly have built a stronger, healthier, happier Russia—and one less dangerous to the rest of the world—in 1920, 1930, 1940, 1950 or any other decennial date. Such a Russia could have met the Nazis or any other opponent at least as effectively as the Communists did.

The cost of Russian Communism's slow, small economic advance between 1917 and the Nazi invasion of 1941 was enormous. At least fifteen million human beings were killed or worked to death; living standards were kept appallingly low; Russian housing became the worst in Europe; the Russian cottage and handicraft industry, which produced so many consumer goods, was almost entirely wiped out; Russian livestock was decimated from 1930 to 1933 and has never recovered; and family life was so disrupted that the sense of security and emotional balance of an entire Russian generation was affected. Soviet Russia is the most wasteful form of society in human history.

Nothing since World War II ended in 1945 has indicated that the Kremlin is any more enlightened, humane, or progressive (in the literal, not the fellow traveler, sense of the word) than it was from 1917 to 1941. The postwar control and incentive systems are designed not to help Russia's people but to increase Communist world influence as fast and far as possible. The Kremlin's chief concern is power. It cannot extend its power indefinitely—either in time or space—if it does not have a strong state at home, both as an arsenal and as a stirring example (which it can be made to seem by shrewdly selected propaganda) to the underprivileged all over the world of What Communism Can Accomplish.

Stalin's Russian-wide broadcast of February 9, 1946, outlined politico-economic goals for the next fifteen years. He blamed World War II entirely on capitalism—"It was the inevitable result of the development of world economic and political forces on a basis of monopolistic capitalism." He implied that World War III was inevitable for the same reason—"The catastrophe of war might be avoided if it were possible to make periodic redistribution of raw materials and markets. . . . But this is impossible under present conditions of capitalistic development." He added that the policy of "heavy industry first" had saved Russia from defeat by the Nazis and that "heavy industry first" must "accordingly continue," i.e., there are countries still loose in the world as threatening to Russia as Nazi Germany had been. Then he said that, to be sure of winning the next war—"to guarantee our country against any eventuality"—Russia would have to produce an annual 60 million metric tons of steel, 500 million tons of coal and 60 million tons of oil. He added that these goals could well require "three Five Year Plans or longer"—i.e. until 1960 or later.

The thoughts Stalin expressed are the political and economic mainspring of Soviet Russia. This is what the Kremlin wants in the next fifteen years or so, and why it wants it. Stalin, with his usual acute sense of the sources of power, picked the three key economic necessities. Steel, coal, and oil are the industrial sinews of any country that wages war. They are what make and run trucks and tanks, railways and ships, machinery on farms and industry in cities, military and civilian equipment of all kinds.

Russia's 1940 production of the three essentials was 18.3 million metric tons of steel, 166 of coal and 31.1 of oil. In 1944, under the stress of the Nazi invasion, Russia produced an estimated 16.5 million metric tons of steel, 147 of coal and 19.8 of oil. (It was lower in 1942 and 1943.) Russia's 1950 goals of the three are 25.4 of steel, 250 of coal and 35.4 of oil. Stalin's 1960 "or later" goals are, to repeat, 60 of steel, 500 of coal, 60 of oil.

What is America's production of the three essentials? In 1944 America produced 81.2 million metric tons of steel, 619.6 of coal and 226.7 of oil. That was wartime effort, but America has carried this high level over into peace. America, two-fifths Russia's size and with only two-thirds of Russia's population, has already achieved far more in Stalin's three economic essentials than Stalin has set for Russia to achieve in 1960 "or later."

Those figures bear pondering. Not only does Russia need steel, coal, and oil for future war but these materials are needed to rebuild Russia's war-ravaged cities and countryside, to develop its always inadequate transport system and that vast region beyond the Urals which the Kremlin increasingly calls "the Siberian heartland." Until Russia is inwardly much more healthy than at present, Russia's rulers cannot send the Red Army far beyond Russia's borders—if America shows vigilance and an active interest in world affairs.

Is Russia's production in other fields also far below that of America? In general, yes. The three essentials do give the essential picture. In pig iron and electricity, two other basic necessities, Russia's 1950 goal is, respectively, 35 percent and 40 percent of America's present production.

The three essentials also illustrate slow Soviet recovery—and the propaganda nature of the five year plans. Steel is not scheduled to regain its 1940 rate of 18.3 million metric tons until the start of 1949. Then it is expected to jump over 7 million tons in two years, to a 1950 production of 25.4. That will require new plants, because Russia has never had any such steel capacity. To expand steel capacity is a slow process, as America found to its cost in World War II. For Russia to expand it by 7.1 million tons, or nearly 40 percent of its original peak capacity in a mere two years, will take a Marxist miracle. Even if this 1950 goal of 25.4 is somehow met, there is still the goal of 60 which Stalin set for 1960. That will require the same annual 3.5 million ton increase for another ten straight years—a piling of Pelion on Ossa *every year*. The highest annual steel increase Russia ever had before World War II was just over a million tons.

The Nazis ruined the Donbas, Russia's most developed coal region. Though the Siberian mines have increased output and the Donbas is back in production, there is only a poor chance of Russia's achieving the 1950 goal for coal.

Oil is worse off than steel or coal. Oil is the classic instance of how slowly Soviet production actually does expand. Only 15 percent of Russia's oil wells were overrun by the Nazis. It was less touched by the war than any other major Russian product. But

Russia's 1950 plan of 35.4 million metric tons—though it is not one-sixth of America's oil production—is far below its 1937 planned goal of 44.3 and its 1942 planned goal of 48.5. By loud talk of "expansion," the Kremlin is trying to hide the horrid fact that its oil plans have actually shrunk. The Russians are just not very good at exploiting their tremendous oil reserves; they use poor, old-fashioned methods. Not one impartial oil expert in any country believes that the Russians will meet even their sharply contracted 1950 goal in oil.

That is the picture in the three essentials Stalin himself picked. Russia will require the Stalin-set minimum in those three before it can be a fully recovered, integrated country ready to wage major aggressive war against major opposition. Only an industrially efficient country can do that. Steel consumption per capita is a good measure of a nation's industrialization. In 1947, Russia's annual use of steel per head of population was less than one-sixth of America's. If Stalin's 1960 goal is met, it would still be only about one-half of America's.

Russia is not so badly off as its lack of the three essentials makes it seem. It does not need as big a production of steel, coal, and oil as America. It uses far less of them for consumer goods. In case of war, it would use them almost 100 percent for military needs. As in World War II, the American consumer—who is also a voter, in a sense the Russian consumer is not—would insure America's never doing that. The Kremlin has taught ordinary Russians to draw in their stomachs flatter than a West Point plebe's. Also, in case of war, the Russians would live off the land they were fighting across to a far greater extent than Americans ever could or would.

4

Stalin had America in mind during his 1946 speech. He had America in mind in 1927 when he spoke of the two great centers of capitalism and Communism which would become magnets to draw the rest of the world. America is constantly on Stalin's mind. Again and again, in all sorts of contexts, he has told Russians that they "must overtake and surpass America."

When I said earlier that thoughtful Communists, including

the men in the Kremlin, were themselves realizing that Russia might well be stronger if the October 1917 Revolution had never occurred, I did not mean they would ever admit that in so many words. I meant Communist actions. Long before Stalin spoke in 1927, the Kremlin had realized that mere Marxism would never bring the world to heel—that it would not even bring Russia itself to heel. To get the power for which top Communists lusted, some stronger, more lasting patterns of government than their own had to be adopted.

The men in the Kremlin have in many ways copied the czars —who lasted for centuries, as the Communists hope to last. They have taken all the cues they could from their predecessors' autocracy, repression, and skillful use of Russian patriotism. Kalinin's entire speech shows how fully the Kremlin now admits its role as the heir of the czarist dream to make Moscow "the third Rome" —i.e., capital of the world. Communist copying of the czars' nationalist traits finally made them Russian enough for the Russian people (albeit reluctantly) to accept as rulers. Communist copying of Peter the Great's crude but potent recipes for modernizing Mother Russia has slowly, bloodily, and very wastefully made Russia stronger than it was at the start of World War I. But Russia now is not nearly so strong as it could have become with the assets it had in 1917: a rapidly burgeoning industry, a prolific people, and the world's greatest natural resources. The power so expensively acquired has made Soviet Russia the center and magnet of world Communism.

That is still not enough power to fulfill the Kremlin's lust. Russia's rulers have taken all they could from the repressive example of the czars. Having adopted aspects of a longer-lasting system, they found they also had to adopt aspects of a stronger system. They began copying from American capitalism.

Ever since the early 20s, when Henry Ford and his mass-production methods were placed almost alongside Marx in the Soviet pantheon, the Kremlin has been drawn to imitate more and more of the techniques of America—which it knows is stronger than itself. It wants what America has. It has done the only thing its relatively limited imagination could think of doing: copy. It had to copy pervertedly; the two systems are very different. But copy it has—more with each passing year.

The Kremlin's economic means are not those of Marxism but of capitalism gone totalitarian. It is a capitalism more ruthless than that of any American robber baron like the first John D. Rockefeller (who if he had grown up in Soviet Russia might well have made the grade to the Politburo). Marx said that capitalists would exploit the fruits of the proletariat's labor in every way they could. Soviet economic policy takes a far bigger bite from the wormy fruit, which is all it allows the proletariat, than any American robber baron ever dared. The Kremlin has equally adopted—and perverted—many other capitalist devices that Marx denounced: for example, capitalism's incentive and penalty systems, made much sharper and harsher. Russia's rulers also proclaim, like the great capitalists, that a huge heavy industry or capital goods system is the keystone of an industrial nation's economy. The Kremlin rams that idea down the Russian people's throat far more completely—and cruelly—than private enterprise possibly could.

Of course the two systems have basic economic differences. One of them is money. The Kremlin believes that money, prices, and wages can be changed quite arbitrarily—that they are just bookkeeping devices. It cut the ruble to one-tenth its old value without turning a hair. In Stalingrad, the director of the tractor plant said that his tractors cost $600—the price tag I had seen on a man's woolen overcoat in Moscow that week. The director of the Stalingrad steel plant said that his steel cost $28.33 a ton— the price of three pounds of unrationed butter. The Kremlin can put absurdly low prices on state-made tractors and steel because only the state is allowed to buy them; it can put absurdly high prices on overcoats and butter because it has an almost complete monopoly on selling them. Rockefeller used to cut and raise the price of oil that arbitrarily when he could. But a robber baron like Rockefeller can never monopolize more than a small fragment of a private-enterprise economy and, through corruption, a small fragment of the political power. A Rockefeller can juggle oil prices but not those of overcoats and butter. Even in any one product, like oil, America usually has some competition, and always a channel through which popular pressure can flow, if it will, to correct abuses. Russia has neither competition nor a means of popular redress—also basic differences between the two economic systems.

The figure I use in this book for changing rubles to dollar values is the old diplomatic rate of twelve rubles to $1, or 8.3¢ a ruble. The official Soviet-fixed rate is 5.3 rubles to $1, which makes it worth a ridiculous 18.9¢. In terms of what money will buy in America, the ruble's value has fluctuated between 2¢ and 5¢ in recent years. The most revealing single figure is from the $110 million worth of consumer goods, mostly food, which UNRRA sent to the Soviet Ukraine. What had cost UNRRA $110 million was sold to the people by the state for 2.8 billion rubles—$528.3 million at the official rate. On that basis, the ruble is worth 3.9¢, about one fifth of the official 18.9¢.

The contrast in those figures explains why the Kremlin, which normally wants everything international put in Russian terms or in a way that glorifies Russia, always insists on having anything economic (such as the reparations specified in the Finnish peace treaty) put—and paid—not in terms of rubles but of dollars. The Kremlin, which respects only power, knows that anywhere in the world including Russia the dollar wields more power than the ruble.

Russia's top economist, as important in that field as Pavel Yudin is in Communist philosophy, was long Eugen Varga. We have seen what happened to the top Soviet propagandist, Georgy Alexandrov, who was ousted in 1947 for "burning incense" to non-Communists. Varga met the same fate early in 1948. Inner doubt about the most sacred Communist tenets pervades even the highest levels of Soviet authority. Varga had publicly backed the Kremlin's contention that the capitalist world would soon have a disastrous depression. Privately, Varga told the Politburo that: such a depression was impossible before 1955; there were no economic reasons for a struggle between Russia and the West; Russia's eastern European security zone was so weak economically as to matter relatively little in total European recovery; Western workers' living standards had actually risen during the war. All four statements were against the official Soviet line. The Kremlin told Varga to recant. He refused. The Politburo purged him and twenty other leading Soviet economists. The Institute of World Economics and World Politics, which Varga had headed, was abolished.

Alexandrov and Varga can be excommunicated for unorthodox views. Stalin, as high priest of Communism can be as non-Communist as he likes—and get away with it. He is least Communist of all when it comes to economics. There he not only pervertedly preaches certain key doctrines of capitalism but has led the Soviet Union in pervertedly practicing them. Stalin was once a seminary student. He knows the significance of a Black Mass.

5

Russia is the only other country in the world which at present has the people, the materials, and the fiery urge to become what America is now unique in being: a great nation with a great economy of industrial mass production.

Germany and Japan's militaristic efforts to achieve this aim have been defeated forever if America will help to initiate and pursue a permanent, constructive world policy: see to it that the Germans and Japanese can produce enough for their peaceful needs and only enough over that to pay for any necessary imports and reparations. Once Britain has recovered (with American aid), it will continue to be a strong industrial nation of the second rank. A few other countries—for example, India, Brazil, and China—may some day become great industrial powers, but not in the twentieth century. Russia is the one real candidate for first-rate industrial rank in the next generation.

The Kremlin certainly plans such a position of power for itself. The strong likelihood of its success is one reason why the Russian magnet exerts such drawing power. Some of the Soviet system's advantages and handicaps in this tremendous struggle have already been discussed. It is time to consider them all and make an estimate.

There is Soviet planning. Stalin has already set its goals for "1960 or later." For at least that long, the basic Soviet drive will be to rebuild and expand the military industrialization that has occupied it since the first Five Year Plan, meanwhile keeping up the world's biggest military establishment. This capital goods expansion is pursued with only the smallest regard for consumer comfort—which is so lopsided an emphasis as actually to slow down the entire program. This important Soviet defect will be shown firsthand at Stalingrad in the next chapter. It helps explain why no Soviet Five Year Plan, despite all the glowing propaganda to the contrary, has ever had an over-all fulfillment as high as 80 percent. But the heavy industry sections of the plan have always had the most emphasis and have usually been better fulfilled than, say, the housing section.

Soviet propaganda makes the claim that planning is a Communist invention, that it is a virtue in itself, and that Russia's planned economy makes it different from—and, somehow, better than—all other nations. State planning goes back at least as far as ancient Egypt's ever-normal granary. And in Soviet Russia, planning is not a virtue. It is a stark necessity. The Kremlin has removed all the economic checks and balances by which other countries operate. Without a plan that reaches down to control even the smallest unit, Russia would soon be hopelessly snarled up. As Kalinin admitted—and the hole in the ground in place of a 1,400-foot-high Palace of the Soviets shows—Russian planning is far from perfect. It is a centralized and totalitarian planned economy which had to destroy the power both of labor unions and land-holding peasants before it could operate at all.

Psychologically, one of the most fascinating figures in Soviet life is The Planner. He may live in a Kremlin turret yet he dwells in an ivory tower. He can be more irresponsible than other Russians. Though responsible for drawing up a plan, he is not responsible for fulfilling it. If he sets a plan too high and it is not met, someone may be punished—but not him. If he sets it too low, he can be charged with many grave Soviet crimes, from pessimism at Soviet possibilities to taking bribes from industry heads who did not want the plan to be too tough. He knows his plan will be examined by Higher Authority, which has almost always revised original plans upward. So he tries to please his bosses. Stalin's speech is only one of many signs that Soviet planning is not so much planning as it is wishful thinking imposed from above.

A factory director in the Donbas summed up the result in talking to Craig Thompson of *Time*: "A plan is something people in Moscow write on a piece of paper. They figure the rated capacity of my mill, add about 10 percent to it and tell me what is the plan. I look at it, and then just do the best I can." In this mill, the plan had been set so much higher than either the workers or the equipment could achieve that the bonuses for "plan-fulfillment" began to be paid when 80 percent of the plan was met.

This director in the Donbas typifies the second great problem of Russia's slowly expanding economy: the plight of The Manager. He is much more subject to purge than The Planner. The Soviet economy needs men with managerial savvy just as badly as America does. It has far fewer of them than America—and it places them under far greater handicaps than a manager faces in America or in any other industrial system. Every Soviet factory or institution of any size at all has one or more secret policemen on its staff. They check up on everything, most of all on the manager. Since their middle name is suspicion and they seldom have much technical knowledge, they smell sabotage in the most trivial mistake or in the slightest deviation from established order. Any manager anywhere must sometimes make a snap judgment or take a calculated risk if he is ever to maintain high production, let alone increase it. A Russian manager, knowing that even an honest error may speedily send him to a slave-labor gang, is half crippled before he starts. Only the better ones make some decisions regardless of the fear that always hangs heavy over them. This is one of the many uncertainties that produce so much frictional loss in that awkwardly designed engine, the Soviet state.

The Kremlin constantly thunders against "graft" in managerial ranks and has purged a great many people in that group since the war. There is undoubtedly a fair amount of corruption among managers as in other key Soviet groups. Both morale and ethics are quite low in postwar Russia. Some managers graft because Soviet shortages mean that barter and bribery are the only way they can get enough raw materials and equipment to keep their plants going. Many other managers have been caught in the "anti-State practice of falsifying reports" to collect bonuses for nonexistent production. Is is not only a yen for bonuses that leads to this. A manager who does not consistently fulfill his factory's plan is sure of trouble. If he reports "plan fulfillment," he can avoid trouble at least for a while, maybe forever. So he says *"Nichevo"*—and cooks the books.

Kremlin insistence on "plan fulfillment" produces another problem: much more attention is paid to quantity than quality. If the plan calls for fifty thousand bricks, a manager may well ship out fifty thousand—some half baked, some overbaked, and all as useless as those beautiful canvas shoes Kratovo village got from the Dawn of Freedom factory. You let the guy at the receiving end worry about the defects. At the height of the 1946 industrial purge, the Soviet humor magazine *Crocodile* ran a cover cartoon of a man filling milk cans at a water pump. Each can had the legend "100% fulfilled." The caption read: "Chief milkmaid, or how Comrade Figure-Chaser fulfills the plan." Many things are "fulfilled" in the Soviet Union by watering the milk.

Poor quality applies to capital as well as consumer goods. If production of three bulk essentials like steel, coal, and oil in satisfactory quantity and quality seems slow, the production of more complex goods is even slower on both counts. The output of such vital industrial instruments as turbines, generators, and centrifugal condensers is both poor and small. Foreign technicians who have worked in Russia agree with Vasili Kotov, a refugee Russian engineer and airplane pilot who recently wrote: "Russian engineers have not yet built a good Diesel engine or, for that matter, as good a gasoline engine as the British and Americans turn out. The M-82, our best airplane motor, fell far short of imported motors of comparable type."

The Kremlin is not going to find atom bombs easy to make. Russian scientists have the theoretical knowledge, but it takes more than theory to solve the formidable technical problems of production. Soviet Russia to date is incapable of producing the great volume and the very high standards required by such precision work. Unbelievable as it may seem, Russia is not even accurately tooled enough to provide the easy interchangeability of parts which has standardized and speeded American machine work ever since Eli Whitney invented the system over a century ago. No Russian can count on getting an engine to start up again by simply replacing a broken or worn-out part. All too often the new part won't fit.

The Kremlin has drafted German scientists and technicians for work on the atom, rockets, etc. but their work has not proved too satisfactory under Soviet masters.

Significantly, Russia still uses a great many foreign industrial experts of all sorts—and grants them special privileges. The Kremlin thus admits the imperfection of Soviet technical standards in all lines. Even foreign businessmen, like engineers and technicians, receive far more respect and freedom of movement than other foreigners. They can get things done in Russia when no one else can.

One foreign businessman in Leningrad told me that the Soviet authorities hoped to have a hundred American fur buyers come to Russia for a fur auction soon to take place. I was incredulous. The total number of Americans in Russia, including the staff of the U.S. Embassy, is only 150, and there are only twenty reporters from countries west of the Stettin-Trieste line.

The man smiled. "The Russians," he remarked, "would like to reduce embassies and reporters—and increase fur buyers."

A most significant aspect of Soviet economy is the slow tempo of work. As stated earlier, Russia is making a slower recovery than eight of the war-affected nations I visited in 1947—Finland, Denmark, Poland, Czechoslovakia, Italy, France, Belgium, and Britain. Only Germany, Austria, and Greece—two of them occupied in vital segments by Russia and the third in a state of civil war incited by Russia—were recovering more slowly than the Soviet Union.

Russia's static quality must be seen to be believed. Part of it is the bureaucracy and red tape that has plagued Soviet production from the very start. Russia has the world's hugest bureaucracy—over ten million people, including two million book-keepers! The Soviet magazine *Problems of Economy* compared two coal mines, one near Pittsburgh and the other in the Urals. The American mine produces three times as much coal—and has eight office workers to the Russian mine's sixty-seven. It then compared two power stations, one at Kemerovo in Russia and the other at South Amboy, New Jersey. They produce the same amount of electricity. The Russian plant employs 480 people, ninety-one of them office workers, while the American plant did the work with fifty-one people, only seventeen of them in the office.

Another reason for Russia's slow industrial tempo is that any Soviet product that might be needed in war must be designed accordingly, despite its civilian uses. A Soviet tractor, for instance, must be able to pull a gun as well as a plow. It is heavier, and harder to handle as a farm implement than it would be otherwise.

A third reason is that Russians, for all their efforts, still do not really understand mass-production methods. You don't get volume just by building a big plant and putting an assembly line in it. Without efficiency, bigness is slower than smallness—more is held up when you stop. Soviet factories have fallen into that industrial trap time and again. Their production costs are far higher than America's, for they have no clear concept of assembly-line technique. They have constant costly delays because of low inventories. Whenever they run out of a single item, the line must shut down indefinitely to wait for another shipment. They keep a machine running until it breaks down, halting the whole assembly line until it is repaired. They seldom think of servicing a machine before it breaks down, and the Soviet shortage of everything means that they never have a spare motor or machine to rush into the breach.

Soviet workers do not have the labor efficiency of workers in nations with longer and larger industrial experience. The Soviet lack of skilled labor is especially serious. There is nothing in Russia to compare to America's widespread technical know-how. It may well take a generation or more for Russia to reach America's 1948 volume of savvy and standards. Techniques on this scale and of this precision cannot be taught overnight.

Despite the toll of war, Russia's present industrial capacity is almost what it was when Hitler struck. But in skilled technicians Russia is back about where it was in 1927. In that key field it has lost almost a generation's hard effort.

As an American engineer will admit, really good technicians are quite as necessary as he is for any large-scale construction or production. For every trained engineer of any type, America has twenty skilled technicians who can read blueprints, understand the details of a job and see that they are all done properly, once the engineers have done the planning and explaining. Technicians are one of the chief cogs in America's otherwise almost incredible volume of production.

A Soviet engineer is much more class conscious than his American counterpart. It is beneath his caste to don overalls and show workers how to do things, or personally to smooth out wrinkles in an assembly line—both of which an American engineer does as naturally as he breathes. Russia has an even worse handicap.

Its ratio of trained engineers to trained technicians is about one to one, instead of America's one to twenty. By 1941, Russia had painfully struggled up to a ratio of four fairly good technicians for every engineer. During the war, Russia did manage to save most of its engineers. But it used up technicians prodigally, as it has so often used up even its best manpower for want of machines. These technicians were highly expendable in front-line jobs like sapping, bridging rivers, and clearing minefields. A pool of skilled manpower can be sluiced off rapidly. The pool cannot be filled with the freshets of any one spring, or even a decade of springs.

Soviet Russia does not yet even approach America's combination of quality and quantity. Probably the best single embodiment of that American combination is the motor vehicle. A lot of good motor vehicles are needed in any strong country. One fair symbol of that production, in some ways the peak of its pyramid, is the limousine. Russia's Zis 110, put into production in early 1946, resembles the 1940 Packard. That is a rather high standard. Many American motor manufacturers have reached it. In Russia there is only the one.

In Russia, as elsewhere, a good limousine does stand for something. In Moscow one Russian told me: "Do you know how Stalin rewards a man who has done especially outstanding work? He calls him in and says, 'There's a Zis waiting for you at the factory.'" The cream of the Kremlin hierarchy also rides in the Zis 110—except when in bulletproof American limousines (which Stalin—and others—believe are more reliable than the Zis). But the respect the Zis draws in Russia shows that it is fairly near the mechanical, technical, know-how top of the Soviet Union.

A group of us went through the Zis plant in Moscow. We interviewed Ivan Likhachev, who has directed the plant since Russia first started making cars of its own in the 20s. Likhachev has twice studied in America, mostly at auto plants in Detroit. When we asked about the resemblance of the Zis 110 to the prewar Packard, he conceded: "When we started to produce a new car, we took a bit here and a bit there."

That is, of course, the technique Soviet Russia has used for many if not most of its "new" products. (Every machine tool I saw in the Zis plant—I inspected over two hundred—came from outside Russia. Most of them were from America.)

Asked "How many Zis 110s are now on the road in Russia?"
Likhachev answered: "About six hundred," and said the present
production was "about one car a day." His plant also produced
"about forty thousand" trucks in 1946. We asked: "What is the
total auto and truck production in Russia?" He replied: "I don't
know; I know only about my own plant." That is a very common
answer in Russia. The segments of Soviet life are strictly segre-
gated. (Russia's peak prewar production of motor vehicles was
about 220,000 a year, compared to America's 4,800,000 in 1941.
Russia's 1950 goal is 500,000 motor vehicles.)

Afterward we went along this one limousine assembly line in
all Russia. It is 170 feet long. That afternoon nine men and two
women were working along it on different stages of hand-assemb-
ling chassis, body and motor. The pace was that of a large American garage which specializes in repairing good cars and charges
its patrons more by the hour than the accomplishment. The Zis
at the last stage of the assembly line was almost ready to roll off.
I looked at its serial number. It was not 601. It was 463. After
that I made a point of looking under the hood for the serial
number of every Zis 110 in which I rode. The highest number
I ever drew was 322.

This Russian tempo is not confined to heavy industry. It applies even to movies. In Moscow I remarked to a Russian who
knows the Soviet arts quite well that I could not understand why
movies, preferably color movies, were not made of the various
great ballets which in their superb, uncut Russian versions run a
full evening—like *Swan Lake, Giselle* and *The Fountain of Bak-
chisirai.*

"There could be few better advertisements of Russia than your
Russian ballet," I said.

The Russian agreed. Then he added: "Our Soviet slowness
means it would take most of a year to film one ballet properly.
We would probably have to keep the entire ballet corps out of
the Bolshoi that whole time, or—if we filmed it in the Bolshoi—
close the theater that long."

He went on in still more significant detail: "Our trouble is
that we make relatively so few pictures and make them relatively
so slowly. So our actors do not get enough actual movie experience. Experience is as important in movies as in any other branch

of activity. And our directors have a tendency to star their wife or mistress in picture after picture. That would not be so bad if they made several pictures a year, like many of your good Hollywood directors, because they could not possibly star the same people in all of them. Then we would get more experience and some fresh blood. But each does only one film a year and can keep on using his favorites."

Neither limousines nor movies are the whole story of Soviet production or of the continual Soviet tendency to use the same people over and over again in any line of activity. Both do typify the slow motion of Russia's economy.

6

How soon will Russia become a first-rate industrial power?

My own belief is: "Some time in the 1960s." It will not "overtake and surpass" American industry that soon. It may never do so. Russia is much bigger than America, and has far more people and raw materials. But the Kremlin's peculiar perversion of capitalism makes industrial expansion so slow, so wasteful of every human and material value, that America's smallness might not ever be too heavy a handicap.

This chapter on the Soviet economy may possibly be misinterpreted both by those who think Russia is no threat to the world and those who think it is. It should not be misinterpreted either way. I have tried to make it frank and factual. To write on the Soviet economy is not easy. Russia has issued no annual statistics since 1940 and a Soviet official told me: "Statistics are a military secret." The figures for 1940 and earlier, scattered figures since, the 1950 goals of the present Five Year Plan, and Stalin's aims for "1960 or later" do provide a framework.

One explanation of why the Kremlin publishes so few figures, allows so few foreigners into Russia, lets them see so little while they are there, and permits only selected Russians to do its work outside, is because it wishes to prevent careful, revealing economic comparisons. Mine have been made by utilizing hundreds of sources.

Secrecy can be an advantage in many ways, and the Kremlin has certainly profited all over the world by its use of secrecy. Not

simply by spying and undercover troublemaking, but by successfully hiding the real nature of the Communist state. In no field
has Soviet secrecy been more effective than in concealing the
rounded story of the Russian economy, from food and housing
to oil and technology.

Secrecy is a two-edged weapon. The Kremlin has hurt itself
with it as much as it has hurt others. We have already seen the
disastrous effect which fear and concealment of knowledge have
on Soviet political life up to and including the Politburo. It
handicaps the Soviet economy, especially Soviet industry, still
more.

Any American is free to learn and decide things for himself.
Even leaders in Russia have no freedom to learn in the full
American meaning of the word. There is no quick, easy, Amer-
ican-style transmission of serious and technical information to
anybody who wants it. With some reason, America's atom scientists complained about "the army mind," and how its sometimes
unnecessary stress on secrecy "compartmentalized" their knowledge and kept them from the cross-fertilizing intellectual contacts
which produce some of the mind's richest fruit.

Bees are the only living thing fully free to do useful cross-
fertilizing in the Soviet Union; they are still allowed to spread
pollen as they choose. What American scientists meant by "the
army mind" and "compartmentalization" is infinitely more pervasive in Russia. It goes on in peace as well as war. It is not
limited to things like atom research.

America's atmosphere of free knowledge is far too precious to
abrogate in any way except for a reason as grave—and justified
by a year of violent public debate—as the atomic bomb. America
must not even try to retaliate against Soviet secrecy. We should
follow our own tradition with knowledge and not copy the Kremlin. Let them continue to do the copying. Let them copy the 1940
Packard, or later models when eventually they get round to them.
America will have still newer cars by then. Let them continue to
buy, as they now do, more copies than anybody else of every
publication we make of patents and processes we found in Nazi
Germany—even if they continue to claim, as they now do, that
they found not one blessed thing in the Soviet zone of Germany
and accordingly have nothing to transmit to us. Let them keep

on translating whatever we discover and print in America, even if they attack us in the same breath and even if they continue to hide the few striking new processes they have apparently discovered, like the use of pure oxygen in steel making, about which they boast cryptically while withholding details.

What has America to lose? We have our freedom to go right on discovering and disseminating knowledge as far and as fast as we possibly can. If America and the West keep themselves free to do that, the hobbles and perversions that Russia's rulers put on knowledge and industry mean that Russia cannot possibly "overtake and surpass America." It would be like a man with a ball and chain trying to win a footrace.

Few Americans will believe that the Soviet economic system can outproduce an America that keeps itself healthy, or that the Communist regime can provide Russia's people with a standard of life and knowledge comparable to America's. Two key American governmental agencies took that sensible view early in 1948.

The Office of Technical Services decided to publish microfilms covering the whole vast range of German research and sell them to all comers—even though Russia had been so big a buyer of its earlier publications. The OTS figures that if it cut off the Russians, they could buy through dummies. More importantly, it stated that wide distribution of German technical knowledge would do more to increase America's industrial lead over the rest of the world than any attempt at secrecy.

The Atomic Energy Commission began to publish over sixty volumes, averaging five hundred pages each, on America's atomic discoveries, keeping only military secrets. The general public can buy these books; Russia will undoubtedly get hold of them. In developing the varied and appallingly complex processes of making atomic-bomb materials, America had to solve innumerable problems that produced new instruments, machines, and techniques. The AEC has decided that wide knowledge of these will increase America's entire technological efficiency—and that the sole way to keep America safely ahead in the atomic field is to have American industry well versed in the methods of nuclear science. If, as, and when Russia or other nations discover the atom's "military secrets" for themselves, America will still have more commanding industrial lead in the field than it would have without those sixty volumes.

The Office of Technical Services and the Atomic Energy Commission each took an adult, realistic, American attitude. They were not panicked either into undue fear of Russia or into undue caution toward it. They knew America would have to go on living in the same world with Russia—and that Russia was as much interested as America in the types of technology that are the two agencies' concern. They considered all the factors and took a calculated risk, just as America is doing with the Economic Cooperation Administration and must do in all other matters that involve world affairs, however remotely.

Americans must show that same adult realism, that same knowledgeable attitude of calculated risk, in considering the future possibilities of Soviet industry. Some Americans may say that my economic evidence merely confirms what they knew all along: that Soviet Russia is a backward place which will never equal America industrially and can therefore be safely ignored for the next generation or two. Such a stand is criminal folly—just as criminal as the folly of those who advocate dropping atom bombs on Russia.

Though Soviet production is a poor second to America's, it is already higher than that of any other country. With what the Kremlin has to draw on—its own ruthlessness and iron will, plus slave labor, satellites, more raw materials than possessed by any other two countries put together—its production will continue to grow. If the Soviet state survives at all in its present form, it is fairly certain to become a first-rate industrial power within the next fifteen or twenty years. It will not have America's production or living standards. It will have enough for the Kremlin's purposes.

World War II left Russia no economic or political rival in Europe or Asia. Russia is recovering on its own—plus what it can grab in other areas from Korea to Austria (both of which it guaranteed freedom and integrity by signing solemn agreements with America). Russia has got and is getting more from such grabbings and continuing reparations than any other country will get under the Economic Cooperation Administration and all other postwar American aid. Stalin's 1960 goals, while well below

America's present production, must not be underestimated. When they are achieved, the Soviet military potential will be equal to that of America—and Russia will be far better organized than America for war. The Russian people and the armed forces have long experience in doing well on much less food, equipment and foofaraw than their American counterparts. The Kremlin will have much more at its disposal than Germany or Japan had in World War II. The world will not soon forget what Germany and Japan accomplished with what they had.

There is more than one way to skin a cat. There is more than one way for Russia to "overtake and surpass America." The Kremlin has demonstrated that time after time since World War II ended. It used the Red Army in the Balkans to pick off those countries one by one, installing a Communist regime in each. It used "governments of national unity" in Poland and Czechoslovakia to get Communists in key posts like the Ministry of the Interior; when the Communists were consolidated, they struck. It is using Chinese and Greek Communists to disrupt those countries by warlike means. It is using French and Italian Communists to disrupt France and Italy by more peaceful methods. It is using various other sorts of pressure on countries like Finland, Turkey, and Persia.

Russia has accomplished all that with a postwar industrial production less than the unimpressive one—by American standards—it had in 1940. It will accomplish even more if America lags. Unless America is really effective abroad, Russia will take over most of the world.

America must be as constructive as Russia is destructive. It does have years of opportunity, because Russia will be relatively weak until 1960. Economic, political, and military stability develop in that order. If America uses the years before 1960 to get the world's non-Russian areas back firmly on their economic feet, those areas will then have a political strength that Communism—which like a fungus grows best on a dying tree—will find hard to attack. Then, and only then, can there be real military stability, a world balance of power that can usher in a long period of peace.

◉

Chapter 7. THE CITY

IT IS no accident that there are now two famous Russian cities called Leningrad and Stalingrad. Identification of cities, and the workers in them, with Communism was one of the earliest and most necessary items on the Kremlin's agenda. Lenin needed city workers. He knew how to exploit them once he had them. He made them dependent on the Soviet state for jobs, food, housing, *everything*. That utter dependency makes people, especially city workers, putty in a planned state's fist. Stalin has carried on Lenin's program.

To get "dictatorship of the proletariat," which Marx had termed the first step toward the Communist state (and which to Lenin meant at least tacit backing of the urban workers for his own tiny Communist Party), Lenin had to increase Russia's relatively small proletariat as fast as he could. He needed their aid to get rid of the non-Communist intelligentsia, businessmen, middle class and ex-ruling class as quickly as possible. He began with that bloody 1918-21 civil war which to repeat (it needs to be remembered) cost Russia twice as many lives as did the 1914-18 world war. He and his successors completed it in the tense years that followed. Lenin kept the peasants quiet, until the Kremlin could deal with them, by promising that they could keep their land.

Russia's urban population has increased from about 12 percent in 1913 to nearly 40 percent at present. (Nearly half of Russia's population is under twenty and two-thirds of it is under thirty; less than one Russian in five has any more than a child's recollection of pre-Revolutionary Russia.) This was all part of the Communist plan. No group is more defenseless against predatory attacks from other groups than are city and industrial workers. They have almost no base of defense. Few of them in any country —including America—possess more than a meager wardrobe, little furniture, and their weekly wage. The place where they live is generally rented or so heavily mortgaged that they lose it almost immediately if they lose their jobs.

The way other groups exploit the proletariat's defenselessness causes many of the abuses on which Marxism feeds and flourishes. Americans should never forget that. They do not have to look far to find exploitation in America. But one great tragedy of the exploited proletariat has been that in country after country they have listened to the shiny promises of Marxists in general and Communists in particular, and because of their own feelings of injustice have either joined or acquiesced in a Marxist taking of national power. Under the moderate Marxism of Socialism they have sometimes benefited, as in Sweden (though even Sweden is not all milk and honey). Under Communism they have invariably found themselves—when it was too late to turn back because they were by then in the toils of a police regime—more mercilessly exploited than ever.

Words will never remove the causes of discontent in any human being. It will do no good for the relatively privileged people in any country merely to *say* to the relatively underprivileged, "After all, old chaps, you'd be still worse off somewhere else." In countries where they can say that truthfully, as in America, they had better say it—with specific supporting detail—because it needs to be said. But if they are wise, they will devote much more energy to seeing to it that the fewest possible unfair advantages are taken of anybody. That feeling of injustice or being discriminated against, of not getting a square deal or some chance to advance, is the root emotion on which Marxism grows.

The American magnet cannot long exert a counterpull against the Soviet magnet unless it encourages that spirit of fairness among the privileged people of nations associated with America, China, Italy, Brazil, and the rest. Otherwise, a great deal more of the world will go Communist, leaving America as isolated as the most rabid isolationist could want.

2

The city discussed at length in this chapter is Stalingrad, that symbol of so many things Russian. It is a symbol of heroism; the battle for it was one of the great turning points of World War II. It is a symbol of Communist emphasis on planning and cities; it was the first place picked to be greatly expanded by the first Five Year Plan. (Stalin took part in its 1918 defense when it was called Tsaritsyn; he has gradually been making it more of a personal symbol ever since. He has had to rewrite history; far from being the hero of the defense, he was actually sent back to Moscow for insubordination after the Soviet military commander in the area complained to Lenin, "Stalin's activities undermine all my plans.") It is a symbol of Russia's painfully slow reconstruction.

Leningrad, Russia's largest city in czarist times and still the second largest, remains the most beautiful and stately city in the Soviet Union. Like America, Russia has its civic rivalries. Leningraders look down their noses at Muscovites with the same air of slightly seedy disdain that the inhabitants of St. Paul use toward bigger, more bustling Minneapolis. For all its long Nazi siege and shelling, and the frightful toll of human life Leningrad suffered from hunger and cold, the actual buildings were much less damaged than London's. The basic impression Leningrad gives as a city is one of intact but tarnished grandeur. Its shops are even more sparsely supplied than those of Moscow. Its people talk much more of their city's glorious history than about its future.

Many other Russian cities have their significance—Kiev, Minsk, Kharkov, Odessa, Samarkand, Tashkent, Archangel, Vladivostok, and the new cities like Magnitogorsk that dot the Urals and Siberia.

Siberian cities and industry saved Russia from complete economic disaster in World War II. Soviet statements now often refer to "the Siberian heartland." The Kremlin is getting that vast area as thickly settled, self-sufficient, and industrially strong as possible. The Kremlin always thinks of war. It wants Siberia as a stronghold to which it could retreat if it lost European Russia or the provinces on the Pacific. Siberian steel production has risen from 20 percent to over 50 percent, and coal production from 10 percent to almost 50 percent, of Russia's total since 1913. Great Siberian railway and electrification schemes are also in the gradual making.

Russia has countless smaller cities and towns. I visited a number of them. One I recall vividly is Istra, a town of about twenty thousand people, forty miles northwest of Moscow. I visited it unescorted, with two companions of my choice.

Istra was held briefly by the Nazis, who destroyed most of it before they retreated and, in a typically Nazi act of vandalism, blew up the beautiful medieval monastery on a knoll just outside town. The Nazis left Istra early in 1942; when I visited it nearly five and a half years later, only two fair-sized structures in the whole town had yet been restored. They were the Communist building for the area (the county courthouse, so to speak) and the secret-police headquarters. The twenty thousand people were living in cellars, in the corners of buildings that were nearly skeletons, and in a relatively few new one-room log huts. But a small park by the Communist building had been resodded and had new trees and flower beds. A gigantic picture of Stalin painted on canvas and attached to the one remaining wall of an adjacent building was flapping dismally in the drizzle. Istra's only form of public entertainment was a loudspeaker in this little park. It was screeching canned music, badly off key. Few Russian settlements of Istra's size or smaller have even that much entertainment. Life is real, life is earnest, life is very drab in the Soviet "worker's paradise."

After seeing the center of town, we drove down to the railroad station, a new ten-by-thirty-foot unpainted wooden structure with a tiny separate one-window ticket booth where people were jostling to buy tickets for the train to Moscow which was due shortly. The two hundred people in the waiting crowd were on both sides of the single-track line. Except for five trim secret policemen and a few Red Army officers, all of them were very shabby. Into strips of newspapers, men in the crowd rolled cigarettes, using *mahorka*, the cheapest Russian tobacco which rather resembles sawdust. Russians call these homemade cigarettes "goat's leg" (as Americans say "crooked as a dog's hind leg"), because the paper is rolled to hold tobacco at one end while the other end is crooked up and put in the mouth to serve as a sort of holder. Matches are so scarce in Russia that people usually light up from someone already smoking. But one man produced a cigarette lighter that flared up the second try—par for any country. Soon the antique steam engine puffed slowly in, dragging seventeen small wooden cars. People piled on with bundles and bags. One old woman even took her goat aboard. The goat may have been headed for the very middle of Moscow; you sometimes see livestock, from cows to chickens, almost within stone's throw of the Kremlin walls. When all had somehow squeezed on, the train steamed off even more slowly with many standing on car steps or couplings. The train undoubtedly got to Moscow with still others perched precariously on the car roofs.

Last we visited the market. Istra is near enough the capital for Muscovites to come shopping and its prices for farm produce are enough cheaper to make the trip worth while. City as well as town folk thronged the muddy, rectangular enclosure inspecting the dreary array of food the peasants offered, such as cabbages at $2.75 each. Three peddlers were selling thread, combs, and other notions. A girl was offering ice cream from a small tub open to the dirt and flies; Istra has no drug store or soda fountain. Ranged along one side of the enclosure were three small one-room stores. The first was for meat. The second, for hardware, had a quart-size aluminum pan with lid, priced at $13.40. The third, for dry goods, had an ordinary-sized block of coarse laundry soap at $3.33; an old woman was trying on a pair of knit gloves for $17.60. The woman running this last shop was surprised at our surprise when we learned that she even had to work on holidays like May Day. "The market is open every day," she said, "and the people need this store. Where else could they buy?" She was right; this eleven-by-sixteen-foot shop is the only department store for some fifty thousand people in Istra and collective villages for miles around.

The Russians do get along, though one can see why a favorite curse of theirs is: "May you have to live only on your salary!" By barter, ingenuity, and free-lance work at night, they somehow manage a few little extras. All over the Soviet Union, from Moscow to the merest hamlet, they share certain characteristics. A foreigner who speaks Russian fluently and has traveled widely there, summed up their way of life as follows after a trip on the Trans-Siberian Railroad:

"Food, clothing, and shelter all may exist in some form for every Russian citizen. But the food is often only a small chunk of black bread, the clothing tattered, the shelter little more than dilapidated roof and walls. Yet the people bustle about, intent on the little projects by which they eke out life. As in Moscow, so in the Urals, Siberia, the Caucasus, and the Far East, the enterprising Russians manage to supplement their official earnings through extracurricular operations. Train passengers and local residents carried on a lively commerce among themselves across the country. Improvisation is the keynote everywhere.

"But with all the will in the world, makeshift methods used indefinitely lead to breakdowns. A passenger car wrecked through a wheel defect is replaced by another with a defective wheel, which in turn must be abandoned in mid-journey without substitute. Even wrapping paper which is torn in small bits and used for telegraph blanks at various stations is exhausted after a time and telegrams are simply omitted. Countless stations are closed down entirely, whether for lack of personnel, interest in passenger convenience, or equipment. Many waiting rooms are tightly locked or barred to incoming passengers.

"Yet the train completes its run, if reduced in length and a day behind schedule. The towns and villages remain alive and working on meager fare. Their women continue to turn out to meet the train with the few small wares they can trade for bread and soap. And when there is no mop for swabbing, the train porter will tie a rag round his bare foot and swab with that."

Stalingrad symbolizes all this.

3

One of my great surprises in Russia was to find Stalingrad so cheerful. After the cautious reserve of Moscow, Stalingrad had a warmhearted gaiety and friendliness. All sixteen of the Moscow Conference group of reporters and photographers who took the Soviet-guided trip to Stalingrad in April 1947 were stirred by it.

A woman saw several of us foreigners poking among the ruins, and stopped to say: "This was a beautiful city. But war ruins everything." A friendly little Russian, quietly steeping himself in vodka at the hotel bar, came over to condemn Truman and then explain that tonight he was going to get only "culturally" drunk, not stinkingly so. Another man saw us walking along the street by the theater and, because we were dressed differently from Stalingraders, took us for the orchestra of the variety show that was playing the theater that week. He smiled, doffed his cap, and called, "Hail to the musicians! Thanks that you have come to this city." There was the mild, mournful-looking master of ceremonies at the variety show, whose fishing for sturgeon in the Volga was the funniest pantomime and body-motion skit I have seen since William Gaxton's justly famous imitation of a woman getting into a girdle. He rolled the already hilarious audience almost literally into the aisles.

All this was in the worst-blitzed city of World War II. You can raze to the ground a village like Lidice. You can almost raze a small city like Kassel in Germany (Stalingrad is worse than Kassel). A large city is something else. I have seen Warsaw, Hamburg, Coventry, Dresden, and many others. Like Rotterdam and Hiroshima (two which I have not seen but heard about), in these cities some areas and suburbs were left fairly intact. Not even Warsaw compares to Stalingrad in destruction. When the Germans at Stalingrad surrendered in 1943 after five months of grim house-to-house fighting, what had been a thriving industrial city of five hundred thousand had only a few scattered, shattered buildings. Its plants were down to zero, its housing down to 5 percent, its civilian inhabitants only twenty-two thousand instead of five hundred thousand.

When I came to Stalingrad, over four years later, I found a city of great heroism and charm. I also found a 70-60-20 ratio that sums up the cold-blooded way the Kremlin treats the Russian people. By patching and building, by slapping together thousands of one-room log huts on the outskirts and clearing little dugouts in rubble-heaped cellars, Stalingrad had risen from 5 percent to 20 percent of its 1941 housing. It had three hundred thousand people—60 percent of its 1941 population. This meant that each person in Stalingrad—by the official Soviet statistics I was given there—had an average living space of three feet by seven, or little more than a grave. By 1960 the plan calls for them to have eight feet by ten. Stalingrad's two biggest factories, the steel mill and tractor works, were up from zero to 70 percent of prewar capacity. The rest of Stalingrad's industry was on about the same level. That is the Stalingrad ratio: plants at 70 percent, population at 60 percent, housing at 20 percent of what it was before the war. The Kremlin expects three-fifths of the people, living in one-fifth of the space, to turn out seven-tenths of the work.

It is a brutal 70-60-20 ratio, especially when Stalingrad's local leaders frankly said that Stalingrad's industrial output would surpass the prewar production by 1950, while the city's housing would not even get up to prewar—let alone surpass it—before 1960 at the earliest. In Stalingrad, as elsewhere in Russia, men have been put at least ten years behind machines.

On human grounds alone, that explains the relative slowness of Russia's recovery. Human beings do not—and cannot—work most effectively that way. The Kremlin has some logic in giving industrial recovery and expansion a priority over consumer comfort. You need at least some heavy industry to have the light industry that turns out the products which individual consumers need. But the Kremlin's emphasis is too lopsided to be sane. It has provided so barely marginal—often submarginal or starvation—a living standard for its people that they have to spend most of their scanty energies in the mere mechanics of living. A man or woman in that fix—90 percent of Russia's wives have to work at paying jobs, in the city or on the farm, to help provide that bare marginal living for their families—produces more slowly and poorly at any job than a better-fed, better-housed, better-clothed, better-transported worker. (One reason why many Stalingraders live in cellar holes near the center is that the city has almost no transport; people who build a little log house on the outskirts often spent two or three hours walking to work in the morning and another two or three hours walking home at night.)

If the Kremlin would, for a few years, give consumer comforts an equal—not a higher, just an equal—priority with industrial expansion, Russia's people at the end of the time could produce way above their present norms. But the Soviet leaders have had a phobia ever since 1917 that the outside world may attack at any moment. So they keep Russia on a wartime basis. The waste and human misery that fear has caused in Russia's last generation—and will clearly cause in Russia's next generation—is incalculable. The outside world has one scant comfort from it, which is more than the unfortunate Russian people have. So long as the Kremlin, in its phobia, keeps its cart-before-the-horse policy, Soviet production is not going to be anything like as big as it could be and the Soviet striking power, if the Kremlin does go to war, will be that much less.

4

The Kremlin enforces its policy through thousands of lesser leaders all over the vast Soviet Union. In Stalingrad I met three interesting and important members of this new Soviet aristocracy. They are worth a look.

One was square, swarthy Pavel Matevesyan, director of the Red October steel plant, who fully answered all questions except when asked his own salary. Then he smiled, shrugged his broad shoulders and said, "Enough."

The second was shrewd, slant-browed Dmitri Pigalev, who said with quiet pride that he had been mayor of Stalingrad "before the battle, during the battle and since the battle." When he told us of Stalingrad's difficulties in meeting all ration cards—the passage the Moscow censor later cut from my story—we asked him his own ration. He said, "That of a third-class worker." When asked how much that was he threw up his hands and exclaimed, "I'm not the housekeeper. You'll have to ask my wife." If the mayor was right about his ration class, he officially got only 1,567 calories a day—he looked plumper than that. He said that he and his own family had never failed to get their rations.

The third was soft-voiced, pockmarked Laurenty Makoyed, manager of the tractor plant, who said with a twinkle that grew to a grin at our surprise: "We have no closed shop. In this plant 5 percent of the workers don't belong to the union. They get treated like anybody else." Actually, belonging to a union brings very few privileges in Russia, where for the mass of people very few privileges of any sort are to be had. In essence, what can a union do for its members when it cannot even consider the possibility of a strike or other effective protest?

This trio impressed me as much as any three Russians I met. They are all between forty and forty-two—in other words, were just entering their teens in 1917 and have had their whole training and adult lives shaped by the Soviet system. They are about Andrei Gromyko's age. Like him, they are prototypes of the new race of Communist leaders. They have grown up under Communism. They have never possessed or thought anything that did not have a Communist tinge. That there are such men, that they hold posts of power, and that a generation like them will grow up in every country that Communists control for any length of time, is a pregnant fact that faces America in 1948 and the future.

No one could fail to be struck by these three men's sureness, firmness, and efficiency in doing what the Kremlin considers first things first. They are tough, capable, and stern, but with the glints of humor and flashes of frankness that successful revolutionaries can allow themselves even in public. Unlike mealy-mouthed bureaucrats, who are much the same from Omaha to Omsk, they know they are doing their job and do not hesitate to say it must be done that way. They have personal rewards for doing it and they enjoy that sense of power over other people which the Communist system gives them. They admitted that they had good apartments and other comforts (Matevesyan drove up to the interview with us in his Opel sedan which had been captured with its German general at Stalingrad), while ordinary Russians would keep on tightening their belts until the Kremlin-decreed capital goods recovery and expansion has been completed.

Even such men are not fully trusted. The two directors are Party members, but each had his plant's secret-police chief sitting by him as he answered our questions.

Both directors saw their plants completely destroyed. Now Makoyed is making thirty-five tractors daily compared to his prewar fifty, and Matevesyan is producing 500,000 tons of steel yearly compared to his prewar 750,000 tons. Both say they will be well above prewar capacity before 1950. They have both been given so much higher a priority than normal for reconstruction and expansion that I am sure they will.

A steel plant is a perplexing melange of noise, smoke, overalled workers doing impressively mysterious functions, and huge hot ingots being taken by giant pincers over to blooming and rolling mills which mold them from massive red rectangles down to thin, gray sheet steel. The Red October plant differed from a Gary, Indiana steel mill chiefly because half its workers were women. They were doing as heavy work as the men.

The tractor plant did not seem quite as efficient as the steel mill, possibly because many men in its assembly line are German and Hungarian prisoners. (The steel mill used four hundred German POWs, but on new construction rather than in the plant.) Director Makoyed explained, "None of them are Stakhanovites, though a few Hungarians are above the norm." Mayor Pigalev said that Stalingrad has "a few thousand prisoners of war" who were "not a decisive force in reconstruction." We saw squads of them everywhere, clearing debris, laying trolley tracks, building factories and apartment houses. None of them were working very hard. Other reporters and I had several chances to talk to POWs without any Russians around. The Germans among them were militantly unreconstructed. It seemed quite appropriate for them to be working in the city they had ruined.

Mayor Pigalev has been given a far lower reconstruction priority than the two factory directors, though Stalingrad as a "hero city" has a far higher priority than most of Russia's war-ravaged areas. (Istra, with only two buildings reconstructed, has a more nearly typical priority.) Though very short of material and skilled builders, Pigalev has made some progress. He said with justified satisfaction: "We have got electricity to almost every room in Stalingrad." On my wanderings about the city I saw wires running down even into dugouts. At night it was eerie to see one or two lights shining from cellars in the midst of acres of desolation.

All Stalingrad and its neighborhood is littered with the wreckage of war. The rusting metal scrap is often piled up over whole acres or strung out for miles along the road. The steel plant will be using this as part of its raw material for several years. Everywhere in and around Stalingrad the roads are rough and rutted. On our way into the city from the airport, twice we nearly tipped over though the bus was going only about five miles an hour. You had to hold on all the time, or you would get pitched off your seat. On our way out to the airport when we left, the bus stuck in the mud; we walked the last mile to our plane.

5

The outskirts of Stalingrad are full of little fifty-by-sixty-foot plots, fenced in with stray pieces of wood and wire. Each has a low, one-room log hut to accommodate a family. Each has a vegetable garden of the neatness that comes only from loving care.

Kids romp in the wide clay streets, while fathers and mothers are off rebuilding the city. Old women hang out the washing on lines stretched over a gooseberry bush from a young peach tree to a young cherry tree.

Even in the middle of Stalingrad, chickens scrabble among the ruins. In one block that seemed a hopeless heap of rubble, several of us saw one evening a wisp of smoke curling upward. We went over to investigate, picked our way down a broken flight of steps, and knocked at a battered wooden door. A woman opened it and urged us to enter. In a room twelve feet by sixteen we found a minor miracle of family planning. Seven people lived, cooked, ate, and slept in this space; its only privacy was a tiny, curtained cubicle behind the big, brick Russian stove, on top of which a boy slept at night. The smoke we had seen was from the fire for their evening meal, which was cabbage soup with a few small scraps of meat and fish. The room was a salvaged bit of cellar with a single small window. They had cut and fitted the window, made the floor, and whitewashed the room all without help from anybody; the city had run in the electricity.

Two sisters, their husbands, a grown daughter, and a boy and girl, both under eight, made up the household. I wondered what they did when one of them was ill or had insomnia. "We didn't always live like this," the sister who had let us in assured us. "Before the war we had three rooms." That was above average then; they are still above average. They even had a small sewing machine carefully tucked away in one corner—a sewing machine is one of the rarest and most prized of Russian possessions. Two different middle-aged Russian women told me mournfully how much easier and cheaper it had been to get a sewing machine before the Revolution, when Singer had a large factory in Russia, than it has been any time in the last quarter-century. Soviet Russia makes relatively few sewing machines; they are expensive and short lived, whereas most of the old Singers are still running. One of the sisters was a seamstress and worked home at her machine each day; she netted $100 a month from it, more than double the $42 Russian average. The other four adults were all employed—one husband as a builder and one as a timber worker on the Volga, the other sister and her grown daughter as janitress and shop assistant. Thanks largely to the seamstress, their total monthly earnings came to $344 a month, which again made them well above the average Russian family. As a result, they had extras: a little loudspeaker plugged into the state's wired radio system which was playing lively music during our call, some small oil paintings for their walls including one delightful primitive of a Volga steamer, and above all occasionally meat and fish at the same meal, a feast by Soviet workers' standards. The room also had two profile plaques, of Lenin and Stalin.

The whole family was very chipper, though one of the husbands said: "We wish we had more room." None of them see any early prospect of that. Like American housewives with unexpected callers, the two sisters kept apologizing for the fact that their home was not neater. It was actually very tidy indeed. Not an inch was wasted. Three double beds, one in the cubicle, served for sleeping and sitting—they had no chairs, and ate their meals standing or perched on the edge of a bed. Their spare clothes, fewer than those the seven had on their backs, hung on four hooks. The three spare pairs of shoes for the seven of them were under one bed. They dipped their water up by the pailful from the muddy Volga, four hundred feet away.

The friendliness of that household was matched wherever we went. If any of us paused, we were soon surrounded by a small crowd of shabby people chattering animatedly with us. The farmers' market for unrationed food, even though some of the Stalingrad prices were higher, was decidedly gayer than those in Moscow, where shoving and bargaining can get rather grim. Mayor Pigalev's city administration has done at least one thing to cheer the people. When we asked the little city architect why the theater where we saw the variety show had been completely rebuilt when housing was so desperately short, he explained: "We wanted our people, who have endured so much, to have some happiness now and a visible pledge of happiness to come." The theater seats about nine hundred. On an average, each Stalingrader could attend one performance there a year. That is a slim pledge of better times. But it is something. The pleasure in the audience the night we were there was deep and real.

From the time we finished breakfast until, exhausted, we fell into our beds at midnight or later, our Soviet guides to Stalingrad kept us on the go. (We ate our luncheon sandwiches in the bus.)

They were very thorough in what they showed us and very attentive as they showed it. Breakfast fortunately was set at 9:30. No Soviet official gets up early if he can help it; he has to work very late. Stalin likes to work until 2 or 3 A.M. and any dictator's habits have a wide influence on his whole country's bureaucracy. (You could never go through any Nazi building without encountering a covey of little black Hitler mustaches.) Since I wanted to see some of Stalingrad by myself, I twice got up at dawn. Both mornings, as I came out into the hotel hall before six, I found the porter sleeping on the couch and the chambermaid sleeping on the floor: the only places for them to sleep in crowded Stalingrad. Soviet sex equality often works out like that.

The second morning I strolled down to take a ferry across the Volga. Small steamers that can cram in a couple of hundred passengers leave every ten minutes and take twenty minutes for about two miles to a pier slightly higher up on the far side. The fare is 8¢. The incoming ferry disgorged a characteristic crowd of commuters to a Soviet city: laborers and office workers on the way to their jobs; peasant women going to market, with cans of milk and baskets of vegetables at either end of their shoulder yokes; teen-aged boys and girls with textbooks under their arms, heading for the higher grades of the city schools; and the usual thick sprinkling of officers and soldiers.

Then I went aboard for an uncrowded return trip to pick up the next morning batch of commuters from the far shore. On our way we met the vehicular ferry, a large, flat tugboat-towed barge on which were four wagons of hay, five trucks with sacks of grain and potatoes, and several smaller vehicles loaded with supplies for Stalingrad from the farms on the east bank of the river, which were untouched by the war. Oil barges from Baku were coming up the river, and barges with timber and raw materials were coming down. Though it was mid-April and much warmer than in Moscow, chunks of ice were still floating in the Volga. But the river was carrying a bigger, steadier stream of traffic than one sees on Russia's roads and railways. The Volga is the great central artery of Russia, as the Mississippi is of America. It plays about the same part in Soviet traffic as the Mississippi did in ours in Mark Twain's day.

Remembering Mark Twain made a lot of things suddenly click.

For as the Volga is like the Mississippi of his pilot days, so these people living along it are like the free-and-easy, friendly midwesterners of his books. Even our boat was wood burning like his. When we got to the east bank, the large village there was strikingly reminiscent of the Hannibal, Missouri, where Mark spent his boyhood.

There were the neat, small, wooden houses with Victorian fretwork along the eaves and around the windows. There were the lace curtains, begonias and geraniums in the windows. A few of the houses were even two storied, like Mark's own home in Hannibal, now a museum. The houses and roads had an unpainted, unpaved frontier look that Mark would have recognized. The wooden fences could have done with Tom Sawyer's or any other system of whitewashing. I even met one lad of about Tom's age, dragging his feet on his way to school the way Tom did. He was not dragging his hands. He had a two-foot birch whittling stick, from which his shiny-bladed penknife was making shavings fly first at one end and then at the other. He was a real Stakhanovite among whittlers. Tom would have been as glad to know him as he was to make friends with Huck Finn.

Even at its most Middle Western, Russia can go suddenly Middle Eastern. Through the village, parallel to the Volga and quarter of a mile from it, runs a wide clay highway. Milling around on it was a herd of livestock that included five camels. Two of the camels were hitched to a hay cutter like the model we use on my farm in New Jersey! The other three camels were loosely yoked together, one with a long-legged, teetery babe suckling her. Two men and three women were sitting by the road while the scragglebearded head man of the party had a cup of tea at a small teahouse. Presently he came out and mounted a horse. One of the other two men mounted the remaining horse, while the second got on the curved iron seat of the hay cutter. The horsemen cracked their whips in the best Cossack fashion (one camel that got a smart lash whinnied in pain, just like a horse), and the whole cavalcade slowly started south, with the women trudging along on foot. This too is typical of Soviet sex equality.

The return ferry was again jammed with commuters, this time mainly shopkeepers, shoppers, and peasant women from more distant collectives who had walked up to fifteen miles that morning to bring their wares to market.

As we headed out into the Volga, I saw the long, narrow sweep of Stalingrad on the Volga's western bluffs. In the clear morning air almost the entire twenty miles it ribbons along the river were visible. Smoke poured from its largely rebuilt factories. Only an occasional apartment house was also abuilding, here and there in that long panorama of ruin. I had seen the contrast firsthand in each of those miles as we had slowly jolted north and south under the escort of our painstaking guides. Here I had it all in one sharp picture. The evidence the long panorama provided of Soviet wartime heroism and Soviet postwar priorities made it a view I can never forget.

Chapter 8. THE FARM

THIRTEEN days before the Communist Revolution of October 1917, Lenin promised: "The Soviet regime will not deprive the peasants of a single kopeck (1/100th of a ruble) of their property." Russia's peasants had got land of their own rather rapidly in the final decades of czarist Russia. They got even more after the democratic Revolution of February 1917.

Thirteen years after Lenin's promise and the Communist seizure of power—the moment the Communists felt strong enough to do it—they took the peasants' land away. One cheap promise bought the Communists the peasant neutrality they vitally needed until they could liquidate their other opponents. Then they liquidated the leading peasants, the kulaks, in what was perhaps their bloodiest single purge (most estimates are above five million), and put the rest of the peasants back into a form of collective serfdom not unlike their existence before Czar Alexander II liberated the serfs in 1861.

The urge to own land, which has been a widespread human desire ever since the first tribe stopped being nomads (it is even to be found in New York advertising men), is still basic among Russian peasants. I have quoted the farm lad of seventeen born in 1930—the year the Kremlin began its swift, harsh collectivizing of Russia's farms—who told me so feelingly how he wanted land of his own. I have quoted Kalinin's admission that peasants still wanted their own land when the Nazis invaded and his boast that the war had changed their minds. Actually, peasants took advantage of the war's confusion to reacquire every piece of land they could. The Kremlin started a sweeping agricultural purge in 1946. It was headed by Politburo member Andrei Andreyev, who in 1947 reported that "2,255,000 cases of misappropriation of collective farm land have already been established, covering 11,-750,000 acres."

Brutally as the Kremlin has treated the peasants, it has treated them more gingerly than any other Russian group. Peasants were over 80 percent of the population in 1917; they still make up more than 60 percent of Russia's people. Without the food they grow, Russia would starve. The Kremlin has had to make certain concessions in dealing with them. From the first, it has squeezed as much out of them as it could. One peasant delegate to a 1920 Soviet congress put it pointedly and timelessly: "The land belongs to us—the bread to you; the water to us—the fish to you; the forest to us—the timber to you."

After the 1930-31 collectivization, the Kremlin found it had actually gone too far for safety. It yielded a bit. It agreed that peasants could have a little piece of ground around their hut for their own. This varies from half an acre to two acres on different collective farms. In 1932 the Kremlin also gave peasants permission to sell vegetables, eggs, meat, milk, etc. grown on their own holdings, and to set up markets where they could do so freely and legally. Peasants who live near enough a town, railway station, or river port to sell there have been getting a regular ruble income from that ever since. They spend it on everything from the small radio I saw in a one-room log cabin where a family of nine was living to bananas at 90¢ apiece. I once saw a group of peasant women buying these in Moscow after they had sold their nontropical farm produce at equally staggering prices to hungry Muscovites. Peasants who saved their rubles in the hope that the cost of consumer goods would eventually fall found nine-tenths of their cash rendered worthless by the Kremlin's devaluation of December 1947—which was largely aimed at peasants.

The collectives are by no means completely Communized. Peasants not only own their huts and small plots of ground but can have livestock—though they must feed it either with what they can grow on their own plot or with grain and hay bought on the expensive open market. I did meet a number of peasants who owned a cow, some who had smaller animals, and quite a few with chickens. One family even had eight chickens, not much in America but spectacular in Russia. Most of the personal peasant holdings I saw were about an acre. It is impossible to grow plenty of vegetables for a family including enough to carry you through a long Russian winter, grow some more to sell at a farmers' market, and also provide summer pasture for a cow and her other feed and hay—all on an acre or so of land. Yet I saw hundreds of peasant women selling milk plus other products in various farmers' markets. Peasants must do some cutting of corners on collectives.

The Kremlin probably realizes the situation, but has decided not to bother about such petty graft when it is profiting from the peasants in so many ways. The Kremlin, remember, requisitions at $5.83 a ton the potatoes that a collective farm grows— and while I was in Moscow a ton of potatoes was selling at $220 in ration stores and $1,430 on the open market where they were 65¢ a pound. The Kremlin has other ways to keep peasants from piling up too many rubles. Devaluation is one. A second is the average 350 percent sales taxes on anything peasants buy. A third is the Kremlin decree forbidding peasants from selling anything not produced by their own family. If twenty families in a collective farm have something to sell the same day, twenty different people must trudge off the long miles to the nearest farmers' market. That puts a ceiling—of the indirect but firm sort the Kremlin loves—on the amount any peasant family can sell and the profit it can accordingly make.

The peasants are the least cowed people in Russia, both in speech and in manner of life. Every peasant house I chanced to enter had its ikon corner where religious pictures hang, something like the shrine in devout Roman Catholic homes. A number of those houses did not have a picture of Stalin, who is the Communist ikon and whose picture hangs in most Russian houses. There are few Communists on farms, a fact that causes the Kremlin much concern. In 1940, less than one collective in twenty out of Russia's 250,000 had a Party cell and there were only 153,000 Party members on farms—an average of less than one per collective. Since the war, the Kremlin has begun doing something about that. It has put thousands of Red Army veterans who are also Party members in charge of collective farms so they can "exert discipline and leadership." Their rank is "brigadier"—the Kremlin uses military titles even on farms. At one collective I visited, in an area undamaged by war, the first new house in over twenty years was being built—for the new brigadier, a Party member and ex-officer of the Red Army who had just been brought in from the outside to run things. He was away for the day, and several villagers openly voiced their resentment at the favoritism being shown him. A number of families had long been doubled up, waiting their chance for the next new house.

The Kremlin also keeps a close check on collectives through the machine tractor stations (MTS) which dot Russia, and which nearly every collective must use for its plowing, sowing, some of its reaping, etc. The MTS have been a Party and secret-police agency ever since the Communists started them. They are centrally located, serving fifteen to fifty farms, and are hence ideal eyries for keeping tabs on the surrounding countryside. They reduce the Kremlin's dependence on the peasants by making the peasants dependent on something the Kremlin controls. Since the terrible slaughter of livestock at the time of collectivization, there have never been enough horses to plow Russia's farms—and the Kremlin sees to it that nearly all Russia's tractors are in the MTS. The MTS are a superlative check on what the peasants at each collective are actually doing, since they know just how many acres were plowed, what crops were sown and (when they help with the reaping) how big the crop was. They are a useful source of Kremlin income, since being a monopoly they can charge high for their plowing and other services.

With its well-established MTS system plus its steadily extending program of putting Party members in as farm brigadiers, the Kremlin has as complete—if not quite as minute—a control over the peasants as it has over the proletariat.

2

The collectives pay the Soviet state a percentage of what they produce. Each one has a "plan" which it must fulfill. If its chickens do not lay enough eggs to meet the state's quota, the collective must sell part of its own share of some other product and use the money to buy the missing eggs from another farm or on the open market—a costly but necessary process. No collective will have any eggs for its members until the state's quota is met.

What with the state's various charges and drains on a collective including what is paid out to the MTS and other state institutions, only about 35 percent of the total annual crop is left for the members of a collective. (The landlord-sharecropper ratio in America, which Communists so often attack, is usually fifty-fifty.) Boys and girls go into full-time farm work at fourteen or earlier. Each worker on a collective gets paid according to the number of "labor days" he or she has worked during the year. Soviet farms have piece rates like Soviet factories. A speedy peasant may get in two or three "labor days" in a calendar day; a slow one will not even keep up with the calendar. The payment is rather small, often only a few pounds of grain per working day, but the peasants do not complain about getting less pay than city workers.

The advantages of being a farm rather than a factory worker in Russia do not lie in wages but in usually having more food than city folk and, even though it is only a log hut on a small plot, a place you can call your own. Farms must deliver their state quotas even if the crop is affected by storms or drought, so food shortages do sometimes hit the farms worse than the cities. The peasant's life is very little duller than that of people in the towns like Istra. Moscow would provide a bit more excitement but for most Russians everywhere there is hardly any public entertainment worth mentioning.

The peasants were serfs for hundreds of years under the czars, until 1861. Now, in a sense, they are serfs again. The two exhibits that struck me most in Moscow's Historical Museum were: a large painting of the Kremlin in czarist days with crowds of people, quite ordinary people, walking around inside (the czars let them; the Communists do not); and the interior of a Russian peasant's hut about 1840 in the days of serfdom. This czarist interior, exhibited in a Communist museum, was as well furnished as any peasant hut I entered in 1947—better than some. Probably it was also better than serfdom's average, but it did show that whatever slight advance—which the kulaks and other peasants managed to make after serfdom ended—has disappeared again under collectivism.

Communists make a good deal of pother over what they have done on collective farms—"electrification," "tractorization," etc. Almost all the collectives I saw near Moscow, Stalingrad and Leningrad were without electricity. Once I drove the last thirty miles into Moscow after dark. I passed hamlet after hamlet with nothing but the occasional glow of a kerosene lamp in the windows. There are quite a few high-tension electric lines around Moscow, bringing power into the city. The road twice passed under such lines. Each time our headlights caught the nearest pylon, a collective village was huddled lightless around its base.

The tractorization is more evident, though Communists never mention the control function of the machine tractor stations. In 1947 Politburo member Andreyev claimed that in 1940 Soviet agriculture "had really become the most mechanized in the world." Andreyev carefully chose 1940 as Russian farming's most mechanized year (the Nazis struck just as the 1941 harvest was starting). Yet even in 1940, a Soviet official spot check announced that farm labor in grain production averaged 4¾ man *days* per acre. America's average is 8¾ man *hours* per acre.

During the war, Germans carried off 190,000 of Russia's 712,000 tractors and combines. Russia's peak annual production of tractors was 115,595 in 1936; by 1940, production had fallen to 31,000 because most tractor plants were making tanks. The 1945 tractor production was only 8,600 and in 1947 it was under 30,000. The 1950 goal is 112,000, or less than 1936, though the tractors will have more horsepower. Most of Russia's present tractors date back to before 1938; a tractor over ten years old is not at the peak of its efficiency.

The bulk of Russia's crops, including a good deal of the grain, is still reaped slowly and arduously by hand. Women do most of it. John L. Strohm, an American farm editor who toured Russia in 1946, states that women did "at least 80 percent of the work on farms I visited." Strohm asked Soviet Minister of Agriculture Benediktov: "How much work will women in the Soviet Union do on farms when things get back to normal, say fifteen to twenty years from now?"

"Only 55 percent," Benediktov answered.

Women were doing about 80 percent of the work on the Russian farms I visited in 1947. Few men, except old ones and middle-teen boys, were in evidence. Farms show the terrible loss of young men Russia suffered during the war; you do not notice it in city crowds except for the unusually high number of cripples. Of course casualties are not the whole story. Many farms are like the one I saw near Stalingrad: some husbands were still in uniform and others were helping rebuild the city. The Kremlin is also deliberately drawing men from farms as fast as it can. It has been doing that since 1917: to get more industrial workers, to build up new cities, towns, and mines in Siberia (many of which, like Alaskan settlements, are largely male—though they are much bigger than those in Alaska), and for recruits to the army and secret police. Most of the Soviet armed forces' 1,500,000 draftees a year (for an average two-year term) come from the farms.

Russian farming, even where somewhat mechanized, is far from efficient. In a study of twenty-one of the world's leading countries, made just before the war, Dr. Ellsworth Huntington of Yale found that Russia ranked nineteenth in agricultural productivity per worker, ahead only of China and India. Sir John Maynard states that Russia averages twelve workers for every hundred acres under cultivation, four times Britain's average of three workers per hundred acres, while the Russian wheat crop averaged only sixteen bushels an acre—less than half Britain's thirty-three-bushel average.

There have been no detailed Soviet agricultural statistics since 1935, when the total grain crop was 90.1 million metric tons. The Kremlin now says that the total 1940 grain crop was 118.8 million tons, a figure which most non-Russian experts on Soviet farming think exaggerated. (At the time, Kalinin announced that the 1940 Russian grain crop had reached an all-time record of 110 million tons.) The 1950 grain goal is 127 million tons. America, with a population about two-thirds that of Russia, produced 108 million metric tons of grain in 1940 and 131.1 million tons in 1945.

3

The vast Russian plain has shaped the Russian character; the people have the plain's extremes and contradictions. Only a generation ago nearly nine-tenths of Russia's people were peasants exposed to the plain every day of their lives. Two-thirds of them still are. Since the Communists exterminated or expelled nearly all of Russia's small ruling, business and middle class, there are today almost no Soviet citizens more than two generations from a peasant's log hut. That has stamped its traits on them all.

The Russian plain is not nature at her gentlest. It would have stunned Wordsworth. The same place the same year can have tropic heat and Arctic cold, twenty feet of snow and parching drought. The peasants of the plain are frantically active at the peaks of the season and then practically hibernate during the cold. The justly famed Russian endurance is more a product of the heat than of the cold. The age-old job of getting in the harvest by hand, working for weeks on end almost round the clock in the long, northern-latitude summer days, with their southern-latitude fierceness of heat calls for almost superhuman stamina. Russians have developed it. They can take an orgy of work as readily as they can take an orgy of anything else. Unlike people from more temperate climates—like most Americans—they can even take an orgy of patience.

If a Russian's endurance comes primarily from the summer, his patience comes from the winter. For six months of the year— winter snow plus spring and autumn mud—Russian peasants can hardly get about their village. Often they lie motionless nearly all day on top of their brick stoves (which double as beds) so as to use less energy, hence have to eat less and thus conserve the scanty store of food that must sustain them to the next harvest. For century after century they have had to learn how to make waiting a real activity, a full-time occupation. Otherwise they would go mad before the snow melted and the mud dried.

I know one American who speaks Russian and spent two years there. Only once did she see Russians show any annoyance over waiting. That was when she was ill and went to a Soviet clinic. She waited, like everybody else. After an hour or so the doctor came. He glanced round the room, saw she was by far the best-dressed person there, knew she must accordingly be the most important, and took her first. At this rank favoritism, some of the Russians—who had been waiting all day—let out a low wail of protest. The doctor turned and stormed at them:

"What do you think you are? What do you mean by this display? You have been waiting all your lives, and it won't hurt you to do some of your waiting here."

Russian peasants knew a collectivism for long centuries before the Kremlin installed the collectives. That was the czarist *mir*, or self-governing communes of peasants. In the *mir*, Russian peasants developed a deep, voluntary desire for unanimity. They thought there could be only one proper decision on any point.

Once a decision was reached, it was truth, it was authority—and they followed it obediently.

One can readily see the advantages to czars and Communists alike in this traditional, firmly rooted conviction held by an overwhelming majority of Russia's population. By letting the collectives remain in many ways like the *mir*, the Kremlin has gradually been able to transfer that peasant respect for truth and authority to itself. The Kremlin, which suspects everybody and everything, suspects the peasants too. But the thoroughness of its control over the peasant, though extorting more from the peasants economically than less supervision could, is not needed politically. The peasants, though they have retained more individuality than the city proletariat, have on the whole accepted the Kremlin's authority. Nearly all of them want more land for themselves. They will grab some any chance they get—as more than two and a quarter million different peasants did during World War II by the Kremlin's own figures. But they are not going to revolt.

This peasant obedience to authority can even extend to a foreigner. If the person to whom you are talking assumes you have some authority, he answers your questions as readily as he would answer the cross-examination of a Russian Orthodox priest at the confessional. This does not happen in Moscow, where even street cleaners are well aware that foreigners not only have no authority but are to be avoided. I experienced it at a war-ruined collective farm. Everybody except one old woman was out working in the fields when I stopped. She answered all my questions as fully and exactly as she could, and showed me everything in which I took the slightest interest. The women on this farm outnumbered the men by nearly three to one. "Very few men returned to this village," she said. Her husband had been killed; her son was still in the Army two years after the war. She herself had evacuated the village's 105 cattle before the Germans arrived, and later had come back to help with its slow restoration. Only forty of the ninety houses had yet been rebuilt. The 105 cows had been left in the region where they had been evacuated; the collective thus far had been able to build up a herd of only fourteen.

At the end, knowing that she would be interrogated by another authority later in the day, she asked me—this strange authority calling at her village—"What shall I tell the farm brigadier about your visit?" Through my interpreter, I told her to tell the brigadier the entire episode and to add that an American, interested in agriculture and in Russia with Foreign Minister Molotov's permission, had wished to see a Russian farm. Since she would also be reporting the shiny new Zis limousine in which I had come, an evidence of authority most impressive to Russians, I knew that this would be enough to satisfy the brigadier that she had acted correctly.

4

Russia's war-ravaged collective farms show the same signs of sternly calculated central planning, more interested in production than in people, as Stalingrad and its 70-60-20 ratio. On the ruined collectives, the top priority went to rebuilding the collective barns (the farm equivalent to Stalingrad's factories) while the people still lived in dugouts. The Kremlin is more concerned with steadily raising each farm's planned output quotas than in restoring prewar living conditions.

The collective farm at Lenino, twenty-six miles northwest of Moscow, was the nearest to the capital that the main Nazi forces came on that particular approach. For twelve bitter days in November 1941, Lenino itself was in the midst of the battle; half the village was occupied by the invaders. Its two rows of facing log huts run up and down a hill on either side of a narrow valley, most of them on the north hill (which the Germans held) but the church and a few other buildings on the south. Villagers who refused the Nazi command to evacuate toward Germany were shot on the spot. Over half of Lenino's 1941 population of two hundred was killed. The village head man (a Party brigadier had not yet been installed here) said, with poignant understatement: "The Germans even killed the toddlers who were taking refuge in the trenches with their mothers." Near the ruined church and birch-dotted graveyard of wooden Orthodox crosses on the south end of the village were three mass graves for the thousand people killed in the battle for Lenino—one for Red Army men, one for the Germans, and one for the villagers.

Every house in Lenino was ruined. Of thirty-eight horses, only three were saved. The farm received four German horses as war reparations, and with a mare bought from village funds (she has since foaled) Lenino now has nine horses. Lenino is very proud of that chestnut foal. The farm's seventy cows were evacuated to the Urals as the Nazis neared. They have been left there, but from young heifers the state later provided, the farm is now back to fifteen cows, fifteen calves—and a milk quota.

During the war only two men, both over fifty, were left in the village: the short, friendly head man and a tall scrawny farmhand who looked like a New Hampshire hired man. These two men and fifteen women rebuilt the collective barns out of the remnants of ruined timbers. The largest is a twenty-five-by-forty-foot building with dirt-floored stalls for cattle and horses, and an open-ended hayloft. It has two electric light bulbs. I praised the electricity. The head man turned his palms upward deprecatingly and said: "Everything is so primitive compared with what we had. We want to build a cultured barn on the site of our old one. You can see the bricks of the old foundation there. But with only women and only these damaged materials, this was the best we could manage." Actually, the barn looked quite as good as most I saw on collectives untouched by the war—and many of these last had no electricity.

Next to the "uncultured" barn was a large, thickly thatched vegetable cellar, half sunk in the ground, which had the forty tons of seed potatoes Lenino was treasuring for the sixty-five acres which, according to plan, it would plant as soon as the weather permitted. I thought again of the $5.83 a ton at which the Kremlin would requisition the potatoes—and the tremendous price at which they would be sold to hungry city folk.

Beyond the vegetable cellar was the third collective building, housing the farm's smaller livestock: a few sheep, four brood sows, and a boar. The two old men with the women and children lived in a couple of dugouts while they were constructing the communal buildings. Afterward, they could begin to build the first house.

"Our plan this year calls for eight brood sows," the head man said. "So we must buy four more. The plan also calls for two hundred chickens this year, which we will buy as baby chicks from a near-by poultry collective this spring. Next year we will have a state quota of eggs to meet."

A few handsome white Leghorns with one ruddy-combed

rooster, all scratching in busily on the steaming manure pile beside the barn, were the only chickens Lenino now possessed. "The feed is such a problem," said the head man. "I am not yet sure how we will feed the two hundred which the plan requires."

"Hens won't lay properly unless they are fed properly," I said.

"That is true," he answered sadly. *"Nichevo."*

Lenino has 345 acres under the plow and 125 acres in pasture and woodland. The two old men and the women had filled in the trenches which had scarred and spoiled the fields. In the spring of 1942, just a few months after the Nazis were driven away, they had set out a small orchard of thirty apple trees. These five-year-old trees were well pruned and in good shape, with neatly whitewashed trunks. They were not yet old enough to bear a state apple quota.

Though there are thirty-four families in the village, only twenty-six of its 127 adults work on the farm. "Some came back from the war invalided and are too weak to work," the head man explained. "Their families look after them. And a great many of the young people prefer to work in the factories. There are brick and textile plants within three miles." That way they can get factory wages but farm food—a rare and fortunate combination in Russia—since each house in Lenino has about an acre for a garden.

I asked about private livestock. "Besides these thirty communal cows and calves," the head man said, "each family has a cow— or if it can't afford a cow at least a goat. Before the war, every family had a cow."

"Any pigs?" I asked, knowing that Russians love pork as much as Moslems despise it. He said, rather regretfully, that there was no privately owned pig in Lenino.

"Will anybody here get any meat from the offspring of those brood sows?"

He looked shocked at the mere idea and said, "They are for the state quota."

Before the war, Lenino had three tractors and two trucks. Now it has one tractor and no trucks. "It has been especially hard," said the head man, "to bring materials to rebuild the village without either of our trucks." But the state has provided some aid, though it has not restored the tractors and trucks it requisitioned. Each family whose house was destroyed got an allotment of $833 for building the usual Russian rural one-room log hut. More important, since money by itself means very little in Russia, each family got a permit to spend the sum on forty cubic meters of lumber (logs, planks, roof beams, etc.) at special low government prices, plus other materials like nails, doorknobs and a few panes of glass. All these materials are unobtainable in Russia without a state permit, which is why the collective previously mentioned is getting its first new house in twenty years—for its new Party brigadier.

"After we have built three more houses," said the head man proudly, "each family in the village will have a home. Widows with four or five children wake up at night now and can't believe they have a roof of their own. We lived in dugouts so long."

The log walls were chinked in the traditional Russian fashion with a kind of plaster made of clay and straw. All had roofs of a rougher thatch than you see in Normandy or Britain. Many of the huts already looked so weathered that I again asked if they were all postwar. "We do not paint farmhouses in Russia," the head man said, "so even one-year-old houses look gray after rain and a winter's snow."

Lenino is an above-average collective; each house in it has electricity. (Eleven of the fourteen collective farms I visited in Russia had no electricity at all.) It still has only the one communal well, a square hole sixty feet deep, lined with logs. A wooden cylinder with a rusty chain wrapped round it went across the well head, with a crank at the side. I watched a woman who, not trusting the chain, brought her own rope along rather than chance losing a pail. She slowly cranked up three buckets of water, wrapped her precious coil of rope around her waist, then started out for her hut, a quarter of a mile away at the other end of the village, carrying a pail at either tip of the wooden yoke over her left shoulder, and the third bucket in her right hand.

The Nazis had used the Lenino schoolhouse as their command post, and destroyed it down to the foundation when they left. The school had been rebuilt and Lenino's children were again getting a seven-year education—as much as they could receive in any village of the Soviet Union.

On leaving Lenino, I drove through the gently rolling Russian landscape with its pleasant pine and birch groves, and stopped at the machine tractor station (MTS) of Aksenovka, a few miles nearer Moscow. A mechanic there told me that the buildings now used by the MTS had once housed 2,500 pigs. In 1941, he explained, "the pigs were evacuated." With the Germans stopped at Lenino, the place had not been damaged by the fighting. Afterward, since the neighborhood MTS had been bombed out and the pigs were not brought back from the Urals, the MTS took it over. It had thirty-one tractors, a couple of combines, and various plows and other farm implements to attach to the tractors. The Aksenovka MTS served nineteen villages within a radius of eleven miles. Lenino was one of them.

I asked if they had any new tractors. "All ours are old ones from before the war," he said. The MTS has two drivers for each tractor "and of course," he continued, "the Soviet brigadier and his staff." The eighty men at this MTS are more than twice as many as would be needed for that machinery in America—but an MTS does have those control functions.

The mechanic was a lean, quiet, leather-faced man of about forty, who showed no emotion of any kind until he got on the subject of the pig farm here before the war. Then his face lit up and he waxed almost lyrical:

"I was the mechanic for the trucks that brought the pig food from Moscow. We got the slop from the best restaurants and hotels. We even got the spoiled candy from candy factories. Those pigs lived well! We got them when they were half grown and had them for three months of fattening before they went to the slaughterhouse. According to the plan, they were to gain eight hundred grams (1.76 pounds) per day while here. But on food like that, they gained 1,200 grams (2.64 pounds) a day! With that many pigs gaining that fast, we could each have a pig for ourselves."

I thought of Lenino and its state pigs, from which it never even gets the crackling, and of the Russian soldier back from the Soviet zone of Germany. When asked what impressed him most there, he had said, with simple, telling conviction: "The pigs." I hoped that every Russian who wanted them could some day have pigs of his own.

Chapter 9. THE QUESTIONS

NO TWO people see exactly the same things. No two reach exactly the same conclusions. But every question about Russia which anyone has asked anywhere since World War II ended has been a direct or indirect question about the possibility of World War III. It is asked in Stalin's speeches, it is asked in Saskatchewan. The character of the Russian people, the nature of the Soviet state, its chances of survival, the Kremlin's methods of consolidating and extending power at home and abroad—all are aspects of that fundamental question.

Americans put it in a range of queries from "Should we appease Russia?" through "Should we be firm with Russia?" to "Should we attack Russia?"

They are serious questions, asked by Americans from Henry Wallace to William Bullitt. They require serious consideration.

2

The Russian people are not likely to revolt against the present Russian regime at any time in the now foreseeable future. The Kremlin guards against that much more brutally than it need. The overwhelming majority of Russians, while not enthusiastic about their government or their living conditions, are not rebellious. The Soviet regime does partly fulfill the needs of the Russian character.

The only likely chance of an early change inside Russia would come through a struggle over Stalin's succession. Since every element in this feud would be Communist, the fight would probably produce a harsher Communist regime than Stalin's, just as his became harsher than Lenin's. The difference would be of degree, not of kind. The chance of any such new regime being non-Communist is almost nil. There might be some confusion and dissension in the world Communist movement while the new Russian equilibrium was being reached. Such an upheaval might provide non-Communist countries with a few years' slight respite. It would be wiser not to count even on that.

The Communist system is very inefficient; its frictional loss is tremendous. Its crude, wasteful engine does generate a formidable power. The emotional forces which fuel that engine are to be found in most human beings. They rise to the surface in unsettled times. A portly Republican congressman on his first visit to Europe, when seeing autumn-1947 conditions in the Ruhr, gasped: "Why if I lived here, I'd be a Communist myself!" The tragedy beneath these emotional forces is that, once a Communist clique makes use of them to grab power, the people are more frustrated than ever. The Communists run the country for power, not for the people. There is no way of voting them out, as you can any American administration.

Russia will scarcely be in a position to provoke major war against major opposition before 1960. Before then, it will rely on capitalist collapse rather than Communist conquest, and try to rush into Europe's power vacuums before America can pump oxygen into them. The Kremlin's greatest single hope is that an American depression will convulse the entire non-Communist world. Lacking that, world Communism will use all the means it can, from open seizure of Czechoslovakia to underground movements in Ecuador. It will use every device at its disposal in America.

The Kremlin will copy still more from capitalism, especially if America stays economically strong. But it will hold firm to the Marxist theory, re-emphasized in Stalin's 1946 speech, that capitalism must sooner or later go to war to solve its own economic problems. The Kremlin will continue to tell the Russian people, as piercingly as possible, that the whole world (America in particular) has warlike designs on the peace-loving Soviet Union. The Russian people will believe at least part of this propaganda.

Russia's backwardness, slow postwar recovery, and low living standards are no cause for American complacency, though they do give America some vitally needed years to restore the rest of the world. Russia has the size, the resources, the man- and woman-power to make great industrial advances even under Communist inefficiency. Some time in the 1960s, Russia may well become a first-rank industrial power, with its industry geared for war to an extent impossible in America. By the 1960s, Russia might also have a few atom bombs. Then, as now, it will have the world's largest army.

Russia will then be ready to use that strength in any way the world situation permits. It will use its strength sooner—much sooner—if America does not pursue a firm, constructive foreign policy. But by the 1960s, if America has consistently helped other nations to help themselves, the non-Communist world will have the moral and physical power to withstand any and every Communist threat.

The one thing the Kremlin respects is power.

3

Should America appease Russia?

You often hear the assertion, especially from Henry Wallace and his school, that America could gain Russia's "trust" by friendly gestures and further concessions. Trust is a human quality. One person can trust another, but no person can trust any institution. That gives the institution too much power.

I love America. I do not trust it. Every person ought always to be watching his country. What a country's government considers good for the country may be very bad for humans. Soviet Russia provides shocking evidence of that. But any country, including America, provides some evidence. When people do not trust their government, they run their country for themselves. By and large, Americans do that—which is the chief source of America's strength and happiness.

A government official can be trusted as a human being. But an official is just that and nothing more while he represents his government. Sir Henry Wotton put it ironically but correctly three centuries ago, when he said, "An ambassador is an honest man, sent abroad to lie for the good of his country."

This principle applies to any government in any century. In Russia's case, other factors limit the personal role still further. The Kremlin does not even trust Communist Party members. Distrust of the individual runs through the whole Soviet regime.

Non-Russians come from a corrupt and hostile world; they are still less to be trusted.

People like Henry Wallace who think that the sparkle of their particular personality and their readiness to meet Russian demands could change the Kremlin's actions at all significantly do not merely ignore these principles. They also impugn the ideology of those who have followed the strictest of Party disciplines all their lives—and seen all who wavered or argued, shot or sent to Siberia.

The importance of ideology in Soviet Russia cannot be underestimated. An authority on this topic has observed:

It may be argued that the Soviet leaders are power-conscious realists whose pretensions to ideology are only a cynical sham. Never forget that ideology is the only positive feature in a regime which has otherwise brought little but harshness, cruelty and physical misery to the human beings who have fallen within the range of its influence. In the name of ideology, it has committed acts which, deprived of any ideological motive, could be classified only with the most stupendous crimes in the history of mankind.

Ideology is the figleaf of Soviet respectability. Tear it away, and the present Russian leaders stand exposed as only the last of the long series of cruel and wasteful rulers who have driven a great people from one military ordeal to another throughout the course of centuries in order to assure the security of their own oppressive regimes. No one is more aware of this than the Soviet leaders themselves; and no one is more conscious than they of the terrible responsibility they bear to Marxism for the acts they have perpetrated in its name.

Can there, then, be no trust of nations in general and Russia in particular? Toward the end of World War II, the governments-in-exile of Czechoslovakia, Poland, and Yugoslavia decided—with American and British encouragement—to appease Russia and show their full trust in the Kremlin by merging their governments with the Kremlin-backed Communist elements in their countries. They did so. Those who tried that appeasement and showed that trust saw the Communists gobble up their countries. Now they themselves are either puppets (in or out of office) like Benes, exiles like Mikolajczyk, or dead like Masaryk.

The best any nation can do in relation to any other nation, is to keep on friendly terms and meanwhile study it as thoroughly as possible. The study should cover every conceivable contingency, like those of a large insurance company. If careful study of a given nation's traits is reassuring, the actuarial estimate will be good. If it is disquieting, the estimate will be bad. Such carefully calculated knowledge is about the most that can be hoped for in any international relationship, even between long associated nations like America and Britain.

America can be that dispassionate in studying Russia, though it is far from easy. It is very doubtful whether the Kremlin can be that dispassionate in studying America. Suspicion is basic in the Soviet Union. Furthermore, the Communist credo declares that the capitalist system is not only decadent and will soon collapse, but that meanwhile it also breeds slavery at home and wars abroad. With such doctrine as Holy Writ, Russians who calculate from any other viewpoint will be up for heresy.

For at least some years, probably longer, this combination of Soviet views will make it impossible for Russia to recognize that America does not intend war and is, in fact, honestly anxious for friendly relations. The period will not be made shorter by American appeasement, which would simply strengthen the worst elements in Soviet thought by confirming their delusions about American slyness and decadence.

Soviet-American relations can be improved only if America shows unhurried understanding and firmness. To abandon the world to Russia, or to appease Russia, would simply encourage the Kremlin's worst traits. It would strengthen all the Kremlin's delusions about America. It would lead the Kremlin to keep overstepping bounds until finally America would have to stop appeasing and take action. It would end any hope of peacefully reaching a durable peace.

4

Should America attack Russia?

Lincoln's statement, "This government cannot endure permanently half slave and half free," is often quoted at you. Then the arguer adds, "Wouldn't Lincoln say that of the world today?" He would. That does not necessarily mean war. Lincoln did not say

America would have to go to war with itself about slavery. He spoke in 1858, and war was very far from his thoughts.

If Americans, north and south, had known in advance the toll of the Civil War (from which the states that started the shooting have never completely recovered), the Civil War would almost certainly never have been fought. Most Americans now know in advance the toll which another war could take. There are many Russians who do not know it because of what the Kremlin hides —on, for example, the atom.

Fear—of Russia, of responsibility, of every tangible and intangible possibility the future may hold—leads some Americans to say "Drop the atom bomb on Russia now." Fear has started a lot of wars. It has never finally settled anything and never will. For America to attack Russia with atom bombs or any other weapon, as Japan attacked us, would be insane. Militarily, it would not be the quick, cheap victory its advocates claim. Morally, it would not solve a single American dilemma—it would simply pose more and worse dilemmas. If America let its fear of Russia lead it into conquering Russia, we would then—by the insane logic of fear—fear ourselves and everything else in the world, just as the scared men in the Kremlin, having conquered the Russian people as much as they can, now fear themselves and everything else in the world.

High-minded people, who want to abolish slavery in Russia and everywhere else, also quote Lincoln's sentence. They usually think the Civil War was fought over slavery. It was not. It was fought over states' rights. When Lincoln became President, some time after several southern states had seceded and formed a Confederacy, he did not advocate the abolition of slavery or suggest that as the cause for going to war. The issue was whether a state which had acceded to the union had the right to secede. Late in 1861, Lincoln removed General Frémont from his command for freeing slaves in Missouri. It was not until January 1, 1863, and only with grave misgivings about the strict constitutionality of his course, that Lincoln issued the Emancipation Proclamation freeing the slaves. Slavery was not settled in the Constitution until three amendments were added between 1865 and 1870. The issue of fair treatment for Negroes in America has still not been settled.

America's favorite fallacy is that you can legislate goodness.

You can't. The Supreme Court has used those three constitutional amendments to justify the constitutionality of many things their drafters never dreamed about, but they have not brought justice for the Negro.

I saw for myself that there is slavery in Russia. I hate any sort of slavery. But you cannot stamp out slavery simply by war and you cannot simply legislate away slavery's aftereffects. People do not change very fast by fiat. The Communists in the Kremlin have as complete a control over people as ever existed. How much have they managed to change the basic Russian character since 1917? How much effect on the German and Japanese character is American occupation now having? If we did heed our extremists' urging and did manage to conquer Russia, how much effect would an American occupation have on people who speak a hundred different languages and number more than the German and Japanese put together?

America should never fight Russia on the issue of slavery, any more than the north went to war with the south on that issue. We have made progress away from slavery in America. We are going to make more. It has been slow progress, even in America dealing with our own fellow citizens. The Russians have a different way of life; real subservience to Russia's leaders has been a part of their character for centuries. American occupation, if that ever should happen, would change these Russian prejudices no faster than Americans have shown themselves capable since 1861 of changing their prejudices about Negroes.

Many Americans think that the woes of the world would be solved if the rest of the world would only imitate "the American way of life"—from ideals to plumbing. Long years spent in many other countries have taught me that what foreigners mean by "American hypocrisy" is that the world really might be better off if we prated less about our ideals and practiced them more. There can also be too much claptrap about bathtubs. Just because other people's bodies sometimes smell a little higher than ours, their actions are not necessarily lower.

In their own fear or folly, the men in the Kremlin may attack America. They are much less likely to do it if America shows strength and consistency in world affairs. Even so they may strike at, say, the Dardanelles which America has in a sense guaranteed by aiding Turkey. If so, the whole world will be in a position rather like America's in 1861. The issue will again be not slavery but states' rights.

South Carolina thought the federal Fort Sumter commanding its great port of Charleston infringed on its own sovereign prerogatives, so it besieged and took Sumter. Soviet Russia thinks the Dardanelles, commanding the largely Russian-held Black Sea, infringes on its own sovereign prerogatives. It too may decide to use violence. The resulting war would be a civil war between the world's two great forces. The states' rights issue would be whether any state, South Carolina or the Soviet Union, had a right to take unilateral action by force. Other states would join in, as they did in 1861, because whenever that issue is raised by force it becomes a very far-reaching and vital issue indeed.

The world is now in the same state of uneasy peace between two great forces as America was in the decade before the Civil War. In Congress, both sides made speeches like Vishinsky's in the United Nations. There were the same vitriolic press attacks on each other, by the abolitionist and slave papers. There were the same occasional physical incidents, as when a southerner came up behind the seated Senator Sumner of Massachusetts and nearly killed him by beating him over the head with a cane, or when John Brown and his band of fanatics raided Harper's Ferry. It was in those unsettled years that Lincoln said, "This government cannot endure permanently half slave and half free."

What did he mean? He did not mean war. He suggested peaceful means of settlement. Time and the hotheads were against him. Before he could take the presidential oath, the south had seceded. The firing on Fort Sumter soon followed. Lincoln was a man of peace, but no man can lie down to a Sumter. Thus Lincoln took his stand on the states' rights issue that South Carolina had tried to twist into an issue of self-defense, claiming it had taken Sumter because Sumter had threatened South Carolina. In 1939, Russia made a claim of similar proportions about Finland's threat to the Soviet Union.

What followed in 1861 is still, in many mays, America's most terrible war. What followed the victory of 1865 was, in its way, equally terrible. Even had Lincoln lived, he could probably have done little to lessen its bitterness and injustice. Men's passions, once aroused, do not die down easily. When I hear some Americans talk about the aftermath of a possible war with Russia, I wonder if the "reconstruction period" following this new civil war would be any more constructive than the one after 1865.

If the Civil War had never been fought, the pressure of the free north and west plus the south's own dawning realization that slavery was uneconomic would eventually have brought a peaceful solution, probably the federal government's buying the slaves from their owners and setting them free. That would have cost America money but less money (not to mention blood) than it spent on the war—a parallel to the solution America now hopes to attain by financing the Economic Co-operation Administration and other international projects. We are preparing for a serious Soviet threat by bolstering the non-Communist world to meet it. Our ultimate, peaceful hope is to build up the pressure of an increasingly free world upon Soviet borders and gradually across them. The final emancipation of the Russian people depends on perfecting our own American freedom at home and bringing its actual example to bear abroad. That is the one way we can make our talk of "freedom" convincing. To clean up our own house has more than propaganda value: it shows our maturity, our awareness that nothing we can give others will have any lasting value until we have created it with faith and sweat inside ourselves. The more America develops that inner strength, the greater will be our strength abroad, the more we can moderate Communist expansion, and the sooner we can cause Russia to change its present inhuman system.

Far more vividly than was possible in 1858 or 1861 we can see in 1948 what a world civil war would mean. The world is part slave and part free. But there is no human means, including the most total American military victory, which could *quickly* make it free. Freedom is a slow development. We should encourage its development by every peaceful means we can. We should be ready to fight for it if we must. But if we really believe that democratic capitalist freedom holds more hope for the world than Soviet Communist slavery, we should not be afraid of a peaceful trial of strength between the two systems.

Any American who finds this course a very slow way to end the

evils of slavery should contemplate human history and—in particular—American history since 1861.

5

I began this look at Russia with two people on the Russo-
Finnish border, the woman in the Soviet security police and
myself. I have tried to follow her counsel and "write with the
heart."

Any human issue, however global or cosmic, begins with people.
It ends with them. In Russia, I often found myself contrasting
two men of the opposing systems: Lenin and Lincoln.

Lenin's tomb symbolizes Soviet Russia in its capital Moscow, as
the Lincoln Memorial symbolizes democratic America in our
capital Washington.

Lenin's waxlike figure is the center of one, as the brooding stone
statue of Lincoln is of the other. There are no quotations from
Lenin's work on the walls of his monument; though he was a
notable writer, he produced nothing so superb as the Gettysburg
Address or the Second Inaugural. But in both monuments you
find the people of the country.

To visit Lincoln, you climb a flight of steps, your eyes on the
figure who looks out in grave and kindly welcome. Only after you
are in his presence do you turn to look where you then see he is
looking: at the grass, trees and water, the Washington Monument
and the Capitol. There is no pride in his look as he surveys all
this and the people coming up the steps. There is wisdom, sorrow, and faith. You see that look before you begin to read the
speech on either side of him. When you have read, you draw a
deep breath. Then you walk round the colonnade, looking at the
placid Potomac and the quiet beauty of Lee's Arlington. You
linger and ponder.

In Lenin's tomb you go underground. There are armed soldiers
outside, inside, and on the steps leading down. Thirty feet below
the surface you turn into a rectangular vaulted chamber with
indirect lights gleaming on the polished walls of black and red
granite. Lenin lies in his glass coffin as though asleep, a coverlet
drawn about him. Only his head and hands are showing. The

mighty brow, the slight sardonic pucker of the lips, the slim-fingered expressive hands are strangely thrilling.

You have less than half a minute in the chamber. Entering on the east, you walk round two sides and round the foot of the coffin with a guard rail keeping you out of reach, and leave on the west. You must keep moving. One of the five times I visited Lenin I was the only person except the dozen armed soldiers always there. Even then one cannot pause. Every time I tried to stop, or even slow down, the nearest soldier started toward me, his hand tightening a little on his rifle.

I never once saw a Russian in any part of Lenin's tomb show the open emotions so often seen in Americans at the Lincoln Memorial. There is no time to show emotion and the atmosphere scarcely encourages it.

If the Lincoln Memorial sees more trust, leisure, and affection, it is not only because it has wide vistas on all sides and the one aging attendant leaves you to your thoughts, while in Lenin's tomb you are hemmed in by walls and kept moving by armed guards.

It is because of the two men and their beliefs. They personify their systems. Both were great leaders, thinkers, pioneers, artists of expression.

Lincoln said: "God must have loved the common people, he made so many of them."

Lenin said: "One would like to caress the people, but one cannot; they bite."

PART III

On the Edge of Russia

◉

Chapter 10. SCARED SCANDINAVIA

THE four Scandinavian nations are scared. They have cause. In the last war, three of them were invaded by big neighbors. Only Sweden, which has no land fronting on a big power, has managed to stay neutral in every war since 1809. Finland was a province of czarist Russia for over a century before winning independence in 1917, was invaded by Soviet Russia in 1939, and in 1948 was reluctantly forced into an alliance with the Kremlin. Norway was overrun by the Nazis in 1940 and is now subject to direct pressure along the common frontier Russia has had with Norway since it took northern Finland in 1944. The Kremlin has demanded bases in the Norwegian island of Spitsbergen, with the logical argument that this would merely balance America's postwar retention of bases in the Danish island of Greenland. Denmark is well acquainted with German aggression: Bismarck seized Schleswig-Holstein in 1864 and Hitler grabbed the whole country in 1940.

The four are among the most civilized and cultivated countries in the world. They simply want to live and let live. Instead, they expect to be crushed between America and Russia if there is another war. As one Dane said to me, unhappily, of America's refusal to quit Greenland and Russia's designs on Spitsbergen, Scandinavia is *"en lus mellem to negle*—a louse between two nails."

Scandinavians are acutely aware of Russo-American rivalry. They prefer America. Norway, Denmark, and Sweden have joined the Economic Co-operation Administration. Finland would too if Russia had not forbidden. That is not because the four Scandinavian countries are capitalist; the Socialists are the strongest single party. But these Socialists know the dangers of Communism and think that American policy offers much more hope of world reconstruction than does Soviet policy.

Denmark, Norway and Sweden can benefit greatly from the Economic Co-operation Administration even though America will not directly give them very much under it. All three produce export surpluses which are vitally needed elsewhere among the sixteen European nations co-operating—and all three are suffering from the universal dollar shortage because America exports so much more than it imports. Under ECA, Denmark can sell its meat and milk products, Norway its fish and ships, Sweden its manufactured goods to the ECA participants which need them and be paid in ECA dollars. The Scandinavians can in turn spend these dollars in America or elsewhere for the raw materials and machinery which they need for their own production and reconstruction.

2

The people of Scandinavia, like their cousins in Minnesota, believe in hard work, personal initiative, and individual freedom. This belief is instantly apparent as one crosses from Russia to Finland. In the last miles of war ravage on the Soviet side of the border I saw ruined, largely unrestored towns, villages, and farms. Except for the smartly uniformed security police, people were in rags. They lived in dugouts and log houses. Few of the fields were plowed. Everything seemed static.

Just over the border was a big Finnish lumber yard, the first going concern our train from Leningrad had passed since dawn. The Russian passengers on my train watched raptly as a small birch-burning engine shunted up and down the sidings. After collecting seventeen loaded cars of lumber, it chuffed off into Russia with the latest installment of Finnish reparations to the Soviet Union. This new lumber yard would have done credit to Seattle. Directly beyond it, though the war raged through this area in 1944, we passed neat fresh Finnish towns and well-kept farms with handsome new buildings. The people were well dressed and happy-faced. Farmhouses and barns were built not of logs but of planks. They were painted. I saw no paint on Russian farms, in or out of the war-torn areas.

On both sides of the present border old trenches and earth-filled log revetments bore witness to the bitter fighting. Just past the lumber yard the Finns had had an antitank barrier of roughly shaped granite rocks zigzagging up a hill. Now a sturdy, towheaded Finn behind a brown horse was plowing between the boulders in the few places where there was room. Near the crest of the hill stood his neat new house, with its bright red tile roof, and his new big red barn. Here was a man who had started again from scratch on the battlefield.

In relative terms, Finland suffered almost as heavily as Russia from World War II. Of its entire population 6.5 percent were military casualties, compared to 7.8 percent of Russia's population. At the war's end, Finnish industry and agriculture had both dropped still lower, compared with prewar, than the Russian. Finland lost 12 percent of its territory to Russia, including some of its very best; Russia gained in area. Per capita, Finns were assessed eleven times the reparations of Italians.

Finland lacks Russia's natural wealth. It has no vast fertile plains, no coal, oil, iron, or other vital raw materials. Forests are the only natural resource in which it is relatively as rich as Russia. Its fields are small patches chopped out of those forests. It does not have Russia's subtropic and temperate expanses; only one tiny tip of Finland lies south of 60 degrees. Since it lost Petsamo to Russia, it has no ice-free port. Helsinki's harbor is frozen nearly five months a year.

Above all, Finland—like Soviet Russia—was until 1917 under the yoke of the czars. Both got their present system of government that same year. In no year since then has Communist dialectical materialism given as much materially to the ordinary Russian as democracy has given the ordinary Finn. Crossing from the Soviet Union to Finland a generation after 1917 was very instructive. The Russians on the train also found it very instructive. I watched their faces as they saw fresh mile after mile of the non-Russian world.

3

Finns have freedom of speech—even about Russia. One said to me as we were having a glass of the weak beer that saves grain for Finland's tightly rationed bread: "It's really too bad that we don't get along better with the Russians. We have many things in common. We both like to drink. We even have the same proverb about the best way to settle things being over a drink. And Russians are often such fine people individually. But get them in a mass and they go crazy."

There is no crazy Russian mass in Finland. The Finns have a hard row to hoe but know how lucky they are to be the only defeated country of World War II which was not occupied. Except for Soviet troops on the Porkkala base (only ten miles from Helsinki; Finns consider it a dagger pointed at their capital), there are scarcely two hundred Russians in Finland. The Soviet Union interferes very little with Finnish internal affairs, but in effect shapes its foreign policy. Finland's aged President Juho Paasikivi (born 1870), a banker and anything but a Communist, says flatly: "Finland must get along with Russia. It has been on the losing side in every war against Russia for the last 250 years and suffered grievously in consequence." Paasikivi accordingly reasons that Finland must not go counter to the main lines of Soviet foreign policy, though remaining unmistakably Finnish at home.

This is not a recent Paasikivi precept. He has been saying it for decades and Stalin respects him. On this basis, Paasikivi negotiated the 1940 and 1944 armistices at the Kremlin; Finns are convinced that no one else could have got them such good terms. Paasikivi was prime minister from 1944 to 1946, when he succeeded Field Marshal Carl Gustav Mannerheim as president. It was on Paasikivi's insistence that the Finns reluctantly agreed to negotiate a Russo-Finnish "friendship and mutual aid" treaty when Stalin asked for it. On April 6, 1948, this was signed in the Kremlin. The treaty's preamble "takes into account Finland's desire to stand aside from contradictions between the interests of great powers"—a clear statement that Finland does not intend to serve as a springboard for Soviet attacks westward. The rest of the treaty leaves Finland much freer than Soviet satellites from Poland to Albania.

After the pact was signed, Paasikivi made a broadcast supporting it—and added: "Elections will be held as scheduled. Any attempt to overthrow Finland's parliamentary and democratic institutions would be doomed to failure." It is this stiff-necked self-reliance (the Finns also showed it while fighting alongside the Germans in 1941-44), which caused an American who knows them well to tell me in Helsinki: "It's wrong to call Finland a satellite. These people are nobody's satellites. They're Finns!"

After two doses of Finnish fighting in the last war, the Russians refrained from trying to occupy this land of forests. Even in czarist days, Finns often took to the woods and defied the authorities. A Finn explained to me, smiling: "We call them 'forest rangers.'"

The Kremlin may also have decided that it could net more in reparations from Finland peacefully than through an expensive and bloody occupation. Finns pay their obligations. When I observed to Ilomari Harki of their Reparations Commission that Finland was known for being honest, he answered with a wry smile, "Yes. But it's a pity it costs so much to be honest."

Honesty has indeed cost the Finns a great deal. The $300,000,000 worth of goods (at 1938 prices; about $500,000,000 now) that they must turn over to Russia are the highest per-capita reparations any loser of World War II has been required to pay. Reparations took one-fourth of Finland's 1946 industrial production and more than one-eighth of its entire national income. Yet even the Russians say that Finns have kept to schedule with minor exceptions.

Lauri Kivinen, president of the Reparations Commission, explained even these exceptions: "90 percent of the delays have been due to slow deliveries from abroad of machinery which we ordered there because we do not make it ourselves. If we are delayed in turning over only two out of two hundred machines in some new factory we must deliver as part of reparations, the Russians list the whole factory as being late and refuse to count it until all machines are in. That means we are penalized 5 percent a month for delay. Sometimes the Russians are not so strict—but often they are." In June 1948, trying to influence the forthcoming Finnish elections, the Russians cut reparations by $75,000,000—but penalties may make up for this.

Machinery and ships comprise two-thirds of the reparations. The other third is in wood products. The wood part is easy enough.

But the Finns never manufactured much machinery or built many ships before 1939 and this part has been difficult. Large capital investments were necessary—in one case they had to construct a whole series of plants to make a prefabricated house factory the Russians demanded. This has a bright side. When reparations are finished in 1952, Finland should have a much larger national income and more industrial self-sufficiency than in 1939.

4

Reparations are costing the Finns some things they value more than money. Like Britons, they normally look on their home or apartment as their castle. Like Americans, they normally cherish the sanctity of private property. But the necessity of keeping all Finns alive and fairly happy, and at the same time meeting their annual reparations so that Russia will have no excuse to interfere, has forced them to take some drastic steps.

For on top of their other problems, the Finns must somehow, somewhere house and employ 450,000 Karelians—over one-tenth of Finland's 4,100,000 population—who emigrated en masse from the chief province Finland lost to Russia. The highest estimate I got of the number of Karelians who stayed in Karelia was "forty." One Finnish leftist told me: "Not even the Communists stayed."

So Finland has had to requisition living space ruthlessly. Every person over ten years of age is allowed one room (two children under ten count as one adult). Kitchens and bathrooms over a certain small size count as separate rooms. No family can have more rooms, including living rooms and the like, than it has members over ten years of age or their equivalent in children. One person living alone rates one room only. Families have to double or triple up in one house, depending on its size. The same goes for apartments. I saw one apartment with name cards of three new families under the brass name plate of the original occupant.

I asked a man whether Finns liked this room requisitioning. He said: "Of course we don't and we won't continue it one minute longer than we can help. But until we finish paying off our reparations, we will not have much left for new houses." Even so, Helsinki has more new buildings going up than does still more crowded Moscow.

Farmland is being requisitioned even more sternly to provide arable land for many Karelian farmers. I met one Finn who had had to sell fifteen acres of his thirty-five-acre country place to a refugee Karelian family who are building their house right next to his. He had wanted to keep his entire place, but as his wife said: "After all, I didn't lose a son in the war so this is my war sacrifice." Actually he is lucky. Under the resettlement regulations people with jobs and a home in town plus a farm must either give up their town job and home, and move out to—and work on— their farm, or give up the farm. Even where they chose the farm they had to sell some of it to refugees. This man told me frankly, "I made the place over to my son so we would not lose it all. He will work on it as a farmer and so we could keep part." North of Helsinki I saw a 550-acre model farm that the government had entirely expropriated from a Helsinki factory owner named Komulainen.

It is easy to see what slicing up of big efficient farms like this into small units—so small, Finnish farm experts say, that many of them are economically impractical—will mean to Finland's farming efficiency for at least the next five years. It helps to explain why Finnish agricultural output in 1946 was only 60 percent of the prewar total while industrial output had recovered to 86 percent. But something did have to be done for refugee Karelian farmers—and American pioneers found that you cannot carve fresh farms very fast out of forests.

War has also brought in its wake inflation and lower living standards. The Finn mark is officially valued at about one-fifth of what it was before the war. It is really worth about one-tenth. A top official told me: "The working class here had relatively small savings and did not have capital assets or goods which it could change to money values. People simply have to lower their standard of living. I personally know of many workers and white-collar employees, especially government workers and those with growing children, who have had to sell furniture to keep going. Others solve the problem by holding down two jobs." He added, deadpan: "The second job preferably one on which they will not have to pay taxes."

Finnish taxes are high. By official government statistics they stood at 779 in 1947 compared to 100 in 1935. In the American meaning of the word practically all Finns are "workers." The whole country has only six people who are millionaires in American dollars. It has exactly one hundred with an annual income of one million Finn marks, $7,350 at the official rate of exchange. The tax on this size income is 60 percent.

The cost of living in 1947 was officially 546 as compared to 100 in 1935. A Finnish housewife in a family that entertained me more lavishly than it should have on ersatz coffee and sugarless cake had a bitter comment on the high cost of living. "Food prices are much worse even than they appear on that index," she said, "for it does not include black-market prices. It is based on rationed items alone and you must buy more than rations to live." She cited butter. It cost twenty-eight Finn marks a kilo in 1939 and thirty-six in 1941 and is now officially 152 on the ration cards. "But actually butter can be bought only in the black market at prices that lately have ranged from eight hundred to one thousand marks a kilo. Yesterday I did get good butter for only six hundred Finn marks a kilo." Then she paused, smiled sadly and added, "And I say 'only six hundred' when it was twenty-eight in 1939."

This makes Finland sound like a far grimmer country than it is. Actually Finns are cheerful, quite well dressed, and unless reasonably well fed, the men, women, and children could not exercise half so violently as they all do on their numerous beaches and playgrounds. The spring school vacation is known as "ski vacation" because in April the skiing all over Finland is so good. They do have their freedom. To people whose personal fiber is almost as tough as the granite ledges that crop out all over their country, even in their fields, that means a lot. The Finns kept their individual character and language for centuries under the Swedes and for more than a century under the czars. They are keeping it now.

5

Communists are a distinct minority in Finland. In the July 1948 elections, they dropped from forty-nine to thirty-eight seats in a Parliament of two hundred. The Party membership is 45,000. Finland's present program is far from communization or even socialization. Finns of all political shades assured me that nothing had been nationalized since before the war and that little or nothing would be taken over by the government in the foreseeable future. Less than one-fifth of Finland's land and industry has been nationalized, a much lower percentage than in many European countries.

One extreme left winger told me crossly: "Finnish Socialists prefer to make small reforms in the existing capitalist system rather than change it for a new system." Less than an hour later, I heard K. W. Varho, who directs a chlorine factory for the Finnish Chemicals Company (a branch of Britain's Imperial Chemical Industries, as capitalistic an outfit as you could find anywhere) and who could qualify on all counts for membership in the National Association of Manufacturers, say: "Our Finnish Socialists are really very sound fellows. They are in the difficult position of having to talk a lot of socialization to attract the masses without actually doing any real socialization at all."

Finland's leading Communist is the stocky, blue-eyed, graying Yrjo Leino (born 1897), whom the non-Communists in the cabinet ousted from the Ministry of the Interior in May 1948 because he was packing both the regular and the secret police with Communists. The Interior is a far more important cabinet post in Europe than in America, because of this control over a country's police and also because most Interior ministries in Europe keep a dossier on every citizen of any importance—which permits a minister of Interior who so desires to practice every conceivable sort of blackmail and pressure. In Finland's 1947 cabinet crisis, the Socialists offered to accept a Communist premier if they could replace Leino with a Socialist. The Communists refused. One of the few signs of Soviet internal interference is the press censorship that Leino conducted by informing newspapers ("on little slips of paper," one editor said) what they could not print. The chief taboo is criticism of Russia. However, the press covers Western news accurately—which is not the case in the satellites.

When Leino was dismissed, the Communists called a general strike, hoping to paralyze Finland and thus force their opponents to yield. The strike was only half-successful; not quite 40 percent of the workers walked out. Leino proclaimed, "We shall not surrender the post to any other party!" A compromise was finally arranged whereby a Communist fellow traveller, Eino Kilpi, was made minister of Interior and Leino's wife, Hertta Kuusinen was appointed minister without portfolio. A Helsinki observer commented: "The Communists tried out their machinery and found it wasn't oiled. But they'll try again."

Hertta Kuusinen (born 1904), who uses her maiden name, is the Number 2 Communist in Finland. This brown-eyed, good-looking, well-dressed daughter of Otto Kuusinen, a longtime Comintern leader now president of the Karelo-Finnish Soviet Socialist Republic (which took over southeastern Finland after the 1939-40 war), heads the Communist bloc in Parliament. After the 1948 Czech coup, she told a Communist rally: "Finland must follow the same road as Czechoslovakia."

That same week a top Finnish Socialist said: "We aren't Czechs!" The Finns are not; they will fight, even against hopeless odds, if a coup is pulled on them. And their Communists are not one-fourth as strong as the Czech Communists were. For example, they do not control the courts, which would be essential to a coup. Russian and Finnish Communists both know that any attempt at a coup like the Czech one would almost certainly produce a struggle to the bitter end in Finland that would cost Russia a lot of men and time to put down—and might start a far bigger war.

In fact, Finnish Communists are reduced to the kind of shrewd but indirect tactics I saw when motoring in western Finland. I passed what looked like the large wooden ground floor of some new building and asked my driver what it was. "It's a Communist dance floor," he said. It was at a crossroads intersection, handy to several villages. The Communists sponsor three dances a week there all summer, which is the best available amusement for the young folk of those parts. I asked my driver, a Socialist, whether young Finns like the Communists. He said: "I don't think they really do, but they like a chance to dance." I asked him what Socialists had as counterattractions. He said glumly: "All we have are workers' halls."

The joke I heard most often was inspired by the nude family on Finland's large, lavender thousand-mark note. This bill depicts a group of women and childen of various sizes and shapes —all naked—holding a large mooring rope as they face out to sea. Any number of Finns told me that this "symbolizes Finland in 1952 gazing at the last shipload of reparations leaving for Russia."

The Finns don't really expect to be stripped bare. They know they now have more clothes, food, and freedom than their Russian neighbors. They know that "if the world remains stable"—a phrase you hear a lot there—and they can continue to go their

own sturdy gait, the end of reparations in 1952 will see them even
further ahead of ordinary Russians.

6

Sweden is the most scared country in Scandinavia. The Swedes
long avoidance of war gives them an extra terror of it—and the
have a lot to lose. By hard work and carefully calculated neutrality
the Swedes have developed an exceedingly pleasant form of exist
ence. They concentrate on the material rather than the ideal
Sweden may well be the least spiritual nation on earth. It is fa
harder to find a person worried about his soul in Sweden than i
Russia or America. Swedes are even more concerned with comfor
than Americans. They are solid, stolid, towheaded Nordics in lov
with their possessions and scared half to death that they will los
them all to gangsters. So they did business with Hitler—and jus
missed being swallowed by him. They now do business with
Russia.

Sweden is something rare in Europe: it looks as it did in 1938
At least, Sweden and the Swedes are much the same—foreigner
there look and act very different from 1938. Sweden has as man
visitors as can somehow locate the foreign exchange to come. Th
visitors' attitudes have changed. Take the British. Before 193
they traveled around Europe with casual, tweedy ease, sometime
almost arrogance, that made Europeans think they were all lords
Now they are shabby and somehow pathetic, often ill at ease, try
ing to make their precious little stock of currency stretch to bu
a few things to take home—often British goods they cannot ge
in Britain.

Europe's products also flock to Sweden. The Swedes have th
most varied and abundant food on the whole ravaged continent
Cheese is an example. In Sweden I sampled top-notch Englisl
Stilton, French Roquefort, Italian Gorgonzola, Dutch Edam an
Danish blue—each better than I was able to get in its own country
These nations are short of food including cheese, but they are stil
shorter of what is needed for recovery and reconstruction. So, tak
ing another notch in their belts, they send some of their best an
often most tightly rationed products to Sweden in exchange fo

he high-quality Swedish industrial exports that during the war vent mainly to Germany.

Swedes usually attribute their material blessings to "the middle vay." Sweden is still in the middle, but as an official said to me: 'The world has moved further left, so of course Sweden has moved vith it."

With one short interlude, Sweden's Socialists have held power ince 1932 with a majority in Parliament. They have therefore had free hand long enough to make their regime a fair test of ocialism—a much fairer test than Britain, where Socialists have)een in power only since 1945, amid all sorts of postwar complicaions. Sweden shows both the attractions and drawbacks of ocialism.

Sweden is also an example of how most parties in Europe, even hose which call themselves conservative, lean toward socialistic neasures. The bourgeois parties complain of excessive controls, vhich the all-Socialist government has multiplied since 1939. They riticize many details and methods of administration. They do iot fundamentally attack the Socialist regime's policies. They riticize few basic principles.

The political platforms of Sweden's five parties which, reading eft to right, are Communist, Socialist, Agrarian, Liberal, and Conervative, do actually have more similarities than differences. A iwedish independent said to me disgustedly, "You can scarcely ell them apart." The Socialists have a majority in both houses)f Parliament with Conservatives the next biggest and Comnunists the smallest. In the 1944 Parliamentary election, Comnunists won fifteen out of 150 seats in the lower house. In foreign)olicy Swedish Communists invariably follow the Kremlin. In lomestic policy they generally tag along with the other Swedish)arties, who all refuse to collaborate with Communists.

The only major postwar government measure vigorously op->osed by the bourgeois parties was an income and inheritance tax)ill which the Socialists openly admitted aimed at leveling out ncomes and breaking up Swedish fortunes. Finance Minister Ernst Nigforss said it was designed to lower or cancel the taxes on more han a million workers (from whom the Socialists draw nearly all heir voting support) while taxing the middle-income groups more ieavily and putting what in some instances are confiscatory taxes on the rich. Wigforss does not plan to socialize any more Swedish industries since the taxes levied on them already give so large a part of their profits to the government. Bertil Ohlin, leader of the Liberal Party, says of the Wigforss program: "He wants to oblit erate the individual's power, independence, and freedom of action We call that a serious threat to the efficiency of our productive system. Without a decentralized building-up of capital, we will not get sufficient initiative and enterprise."

This leftward turn of Sweden's middle way is mostly at the ex pense of the middle class. It is an effort to raise the standards of the workers slightly by lowering those of everyone else. Owing to earlier high taxation, Sweden has only 870 people (about one in eight thousand of its 6,750,000 population) who own as much a $250,000 worth of property. The burden of providing the tax revenue that relieves the workers thus falls almost entirely on the middle and upper-middle wage groups. One professional man told me: "The janitor in my apartment house has such low taxes that he can afford a motorboat. I can't even afford a bicycle." A Socialist official said: "Our chief labor problem is middle-class slackness and absenteeism." Sweden certainly has few incentive for the ambitious: anyone earning more than $4,000 a year i heavily taxed and it is no longer possible to leave any large sum to one's family. This helps explain the Swedes' emphasis on living as pleasantly as possible in the present. It helps account for the low birth rate and the fact that almost everybody lives in a small apart ment. (Stockholm has very few private houses.) Practically no one can afford servants; so, the smaller one's family and living space the easier one's existence. The average Swede would much rather own a boat or a vacation cabin than a house. It is more fun and less care.

Judging from Sweden, Socialism's emphasis is on equal distribu tion of the sum total of assets already in a country rather than on trying to increase the total or to provide exceptional rewards for exceptional work. The result is uninspiring. But at least it should not cause Americans to be terrified of democratic Socialism. Our own system of democratic capitalism can provide so much more abundantly that we are unlikely to choose the Socialist way.

Some Americans look on Socialism as a disease only a little less dangerous than Communism, and fear we will be "infected" by it if we aid countries with Socialist governments or strong Socialist minorities—i.e., most of the sixteen nations enrolled in our European recovery program. Except for extreme left-wing Socialists like the Nenni group in Italy, they differ markedly from Communists. Like Sweden's Socialists, they have been chosen in free elections and believe firmly in the democratic process, in the fundamental freedoms of speech, press, worship, and assembly, and in the rights and dignity of the individual.

The overwhelming majority of Europe's Socialists know all the dangers of Communism and are trying to stabilize Europe against it. We Americans should accept the Socialists of Sweden and other countries as fellow workers in the effort to build a Europe healthy enough to withstand Communism. We can legitimately require two things in Sweden or any other country we aid: (1) that its government redress the just grievances of its citizens (2) that it use true democratic methods. The first is necessary to insure that any nation we aid can provide enough for its citizens so that they will not have to heed the alluring promises of Communism. (If, for instance, the Italian regime elected in April 1948 cannot right the wrongs from which many Italians suffer, the Communists may yet win Italy.) The second will insure that whatever has been democratically voted in can be democratically voted out if people change their mind—that is a fundamental difference between a Communist country and a democratic Socialist or a capitalist country.

What we cannot require, in Sweden or elsewhere, is that the majority agree with American capitalism. If we believe in the democratic system, we must believe in its eventual good results. The basis on which the non-Communist world co-operates is not the common sharing of any one "ism"—capitalism, Socialism or whatever—but the sharing of democracy, majority rule and minority safeguards. America can aid any country, including Sweden, which practices these and be reasonably certain that such assistance will help build a peaceful, non-Communist world.

Sweden too is trying to help other countries, though it has its own problems. The low Swedish birth rate between the two world wars has produced a serious labor shortage. Though the world wants Swedish goods, its heavy industry is producing at only 80 percent capacity. The shortage is not of materials, machines, or

money but of men. A Swedish leader told me: "We need 90,00
more skilled workers. We want to import only skilled men. Ther
are two million unemployed in Italy alone. Unfortunately most o
them do not have the particular skills we need. We now have com
mittees arranging to import skilled labor from Italy, Austria
Hungary, and Poland. We also hope for some of the Sudete
Germans whom the Czechs expelled to the American zone o
Germany."

"Are you trying to import any Germans?" I asked.

"No," he said firmly.

This shortage recalls France in the 30s with its declining birt
rate and need to import labor. No country that has to begi
doing that can look on its future with entire equanimity—an
Swedish morale in 1948 is as uncertain as that of France i
1938. The Finns have much better morale than the Swedes, eve
though they are open to much more direct pressure from Russia

Swedish terror of Russia stems partly from the summer of 194
when the Russians fired hundreds of rockets and pilotless weapon
from German experimental bases over Sweden (instead of merel
firing them out over the Baltic), to frazzle Swedish nerves. Swede
figures that next time these weapons might be loaded with ex
plosives and aimed at Stockholm. The Swedes, who look on thei
country as far more important to the world than Finland, als
consider that the Soviet pressure on the Finns is really directed a
them. The Finns, who do not think Stockholm is the hub of th
universe (as Vermonters do not think that of Boston), are sardoni
about the Swedes' self-importance. When Russia demanded
Finnish alliance early in 1948, Sweden was much more frightene
than Finland. Said one amused Finn: "Oh, the poor Swedes!
don't know how they can bear this!"

Sweden faces a still greater problem than its labor shortage
"After all," Swedes kept telling me, "we are in Europe and mus
keep on living in Europe. We have to get on in a difficult Euro
pean situation, and above all, we must help our neighbors."
During the war, Sweden tried to salve its conscience for tradin
with Germany and allowing Nazi troops to travel via Swede
to Norway; it did Red Cross work all over Europe, aided refugee
from the Nazis, etc. Since the war it has not only bought Europea
cheeses but extended credits totaling over half a billion dollar

Russia, Britain, Finland, Norway, and other ravaged countries. To equal that sum per capita, America would have to extend post-war credits of over $10 billion.

The biggest single credit, as well as the most controversial one, is $280 million for five years to Russia. One reason the Swedes gave this credit was to try to keep Russia in a good humor, as they used to propitiate Nazi Germany. They have since quietly cut down the amount and increased their trade with non-Communist neighbors on the ground that they could not produce anything like as much technical equipment as Russia wanted.

I was in Sweden in late Spring. Swedes thronged their parks, where almost all the benches in this far-northern country face south. There they sat in their lunch hours and long evenings looking south toward Europe, starting to soak up their brief but glorious summer sun. Around them in the tidy parks of cities that have never known bombs were blooming the beautiful Dutch tulips which a grateful Holland gave Sweden as thanks for aid during and after the war. It was a simple, stirring, heartwarming sight. It was a small sign, not much but something amid the chaos and gloom of a continent, that Europeans can pull together and that Europe will bloom again.

7

Denmark made me realize more strongly than ever before the appalling number and variety of the tragedies Hitler caused. Denmark was Hitler's "show window," the "model protectorate" for his new World Order but its scars are still apparent.

"The Nazis killed my uncle," a Danish girl told me. "He had done nothing. He was just rounded up as one of their hostages and then shot."

An official said quietly of his son who was in the Resistance and jailed for several months by the Nazis: "It was not good to have them holding my only child. They were torturing and killing many. Every morning as I woke, my first thought was, 'What have they done to him during the night?'"

Denmark's finance minister put it from another angle when telling me of the tremendous occupation costs which Germany charged Denmark for the privilege of playing unwilling host—

more than seven times the prewar national debt. He cited th
massive concrete forts, shelters and pillboxes the Nazis made th
Danes build all through Denmark: "They were very expensiv
to build. We now find them very expensive to destroy."

The Danes know they were lucky to suffer no worse than the
did. One official told me: "In a sense our postwar problems ar
too little. We would pull together better if they were bigger.
They seem to be pulling pretty well anyway, though they al
agree that labor is not as efficient as it was before the war. Dane
often say when they meet each other or see somebody putterin
along: "*Saa du har travlt*—so you are busy?" It is said with a sligh
sneer and only a slight smile.

Danish industry and agriculture are still well below prewa
output. The labor slow-down is only part of the trouble. Ther
are also postwar supply difficulties. Russia cannot for some tim
supply the oil cake it used to provide for Danish cattle. Argentina
the other big prewar supplier, wants dollars, of which the Dane
have few. Denmark can get little coal, an import equally vital t
its economy, from its two prewar suppliers, Britain and Germany
It buys what coal it can from America, but the cost and trans
portation come high.

Politically Denmark is fairly stable, with a minority Socialist
government ("Increase Production" is its slogan; it is not under
taking any Socialist experiments), a vigorous Liberal Party, and
a dwindling Communist Party that lost half its seats in Parliamen
and won only 7 percent of the popular vote in the October 1947
national election.

Economically Denmark is slowly but steadily recovering. It is
still one of the world's biggest exporters of bacon, butter, and
dairy products. If there is a stable world in which it can trade,
Denmark has a brighter future than most European countries. Its
high-quality food products have always been in demand and its
production costs have been kept relatively low.

Danish youth are not entirely satisfied. Many want to emigrate.
"Denmark is such a poky country," one told me. Another said:
"I was in the Danish Resistance but I am not really a Danish
patriot. I want to spend my life elsewhere." This postwar pessimism
is not so wide as in many European countries, for example Britain

and Germany, and does not seem deep or fierce enough seriously to endanger Denmark's future.

The Danes eat fairly well, since they are a food-producing nation, but are very strictly rationed on clothes. Unlike the Swedes, they import no consumer goods, saving their foreign exchange for materials needed in their factories, farms, and reconstruction. From Sweden, I brought some Danish friends the first bananas they had seen since 1939. Next morning the two-year-old daughter of the house had the first banana of her life. Sitting in her grandmother's lap, she gazed very dubiously at this strange object and took the merest taste. Her eyes widened with surprise and pleasure at the exotic new flavor. She took a larger bite, then a huge third bite, and quickly ate the whole banana. The skin had been dropped in a wastebasket on the other side of the room. As soon as she finished, the little girl slid down from her grandmother's lap, made a dash for the waste-basket and tried to eat the skin too!

The Danes are now debating whether they want to demand back South Schleswig, which Germany took in 1864. Though it undoubtedly has a small Danish minority, many Germans there now claim to be Danes in the hope of escaping Germany's war punishment. In ten years or so, they would doubtless agitate to have the province go "home to the Reich." Danish opinion is somewhat divided, but most people want the border kept where it is.

Danish opinion is not at all divided on the problem of German refugees. In the closing months of the war, Germany poured over two hundred thousand refugees into Denmark—more than 5 percent of the total Danish population. It is as though America were suddenly inundated with over seven million refugees from a country which had occupied us for five brutal years. The Danes have treated the Germans much better than they were treated. They have put them in model camps, fed them 2,270 calories daily of food they would rather have exported to help pay for Danish recovery, tried to teach them some democracy, brought their health up to the high Danish level, and spent over $100,000,-000 for which they will never be repaid—on top of all their other German occupation costs.

More than half of these German refugees are still in Denmark, not because they or the Danes want it but because the four great powers occupying Germany have still refused to let them back into Germany. The Danes have to keep on feeding and caring for the families of their aggressors. One German wife after another at the biggest camp, Oksbol in Jutland, told me tearfully: "My husband who was a prisoner of war has now been allowed to go back to Germany. He has work and a home for me and our children. He writes that he cannot understand why civilians like us cannot go back to Germany if prisoners of war can."

The argument is unanswerable. The great powers delay because nearly all those refugees are unemployable—women, old men, and small children—who would be a burden on any government. Of course these same women told me in almost the same breath: "We hated Hitler. We never realized what he was doing." At least some of them were lying. Not one of them showed the slightest sign of remorse for what Germany did. They were too busy complaining, not about their present living conditions, but about not getting exactly what they wanted. Afterward I asked the camp commandant: "Do these refugees realize Germany lost the war?"

"Yes," he said, "but they don't know why."

The Danes would like to be friendly with both Russia and America. Greenland has them in a dilemma. America occupied Greenland in 1941, to protect it "against the present dangers for the American continent." We still occupy four bases there, with a temporary wartime agreement our only justification. Russia wants all American troops to leave Greenland. The Danes say: "It is our island, and the world is supposed to be at peace now." America's military strategists answer that the world has not yet really returned to peace, that they do not believe the Danes can protect Greenland, and that American forces will not leave until Russia has at least agreed on a peace treaty for Germany.

"The Diary of a Day Off"

Visby, on the Baltic island of Gotland, calls itself "the city of ruins and roses." The mile-square island of Stora Karlsö near by is a sanctuary for the seafowl that come to nest on the hospitable ledges of its weathered limestone cliffs, so unlike the hard low granite shoreline of a great part of Scandinavia. Henry Page and

had narrowly missed visiting both islands during a prewar stay
in Sweden. Nine Junes and an era later, my plane from Stockholm
circled low over Visby's sharp-gabled red roofs, girded by gray
limestone walls and towers, with the sea surging in alongside. I
found that the regular boat run to Stora Karlsö had been canceled because waves were breaking over the pier there, but that
I could charter a smaller boat and try to land in a sheltered cove.
That worked, after we edged in under cliffs where thousands of
gulls and guillemots were nesting, while thousands bobbed like
corks in the sea and thousands more wheeled and screamed overhead.

Stora Karlsö has been a bird and flower sanctuary for over
sixty years. Only jack rabbits, which look even bigger than the
Kansas jacks, can be killed there. A few select hunters have a brief
season for these after the birds have left in August, to keep the
rabbits down to a number that will not starve on so small an
island. Not long ago it was necessary to have one unscheduled
hunting season. A pair of foxes crossed to the island on ice in
winter (when seven miles of open salt water freeze solid, you are
pretty far north), bred, and then with their young feasted on birds
and eggs. It took more than a year to track down and kill all
nine foxes. Only now is the bird census returning to normal after
the havoc of this invasion.

The waves had kept off all other visitors that day. The island's
few inhabitants—lighthouse keepers and bird guards—greeted my
guide and me and then left us alone. The springy grass uplands
were strewn with rare and beautiful flowers. Great golden cups of
the adonis flower nodded above its feathery green foliage. There
was a lovely white patch of the large wild anenome, with slender
stems a foot high and roselike blooms three inches across. Wild
orchids were myriad: the squat purple and yellow spikes of "Adam
and Eve"; the taller, slenderer pink and lilac spikes of *orchis
mascula;* the fragrant little red and white balls of *orchis odoratis-
sima.* In some sheltered swales these were as thickly sprinkled as
stars in the Milky Way. I lay among them, gazing up at the blue
bowl of sky, and watched the skylarks rise and fall with the
throbbing intensity of their song.

We found an eider duck on a nest well hidden by high grasses
and slowly tiptoed within a few feet while she watched anxiously

with black beady eyes. We clambered along the cliffs, seeing the
gulls' nests, each with its brown eggs splotched with black. The
guillemots were on yet higher, narrower ledges, where they hatch
their light green, black-spattered eggs on the bare rock. I climbed
to one tiny shelf, scaring three mother guillemots temporarily
away from their eggs, one of which I rolled round on the rock
to prove what I had heard but never quite believed: they are so
blunt shaped that they roll round but not off, no matter how
narrow the ledge or how high the wind.

Even a bird and flower sanctuary, where a little world war has
exterminated the foxes, is not all sweetness and light. The gulls
prey on the guillemots, the guillemots on the fish. We lay on one
grass-thatched bit of overhang where we could look straight down
at the sea, and across a few yards and down 150 feet at a whole
sunlit cliff where hundreds of guillemots (they resemble penguins
with their stubby wings and black-and-white livery) clustered
along the ledges. The much bigger gulls soared and wheeled
overhead. Suddenly they would dive at the ledges. The guillemots
would screech and huddle together. The gulls pounced on eggs
thus exposed and flew triumphantly away. The grass around us
was littered with shells from previous forays.

"A little later, when the baby guillemots have hatched," my
guide said, "I have watched here and clenched my fists while the
gulls swooped down to grab the babies in their beaks. They fly to
those rocks by the waves and dash them to death. Then they
swallow them whole. You can see the little bodies going down their
throat by jerks, the way a snake swallows something. You hate gulls
then."

The waves on our return voyage were slightly less spectacular.
Motoring back to Visby, we zigzagged twenty miles through
pleasant farms past several little villages with big old stone
churches. Farmers were cutting asparagus and tending their fields
of vegetables. Their wives and daughters in buttercup-strewn
meadows moved their stools and milk pails from cow to cow.
Amid these pastoral scenes two different companies of soldiers
briskly maneuvered.

I dined that evening with Mr. Beer, tourist director for the
island, and his pretty daughter Marie Louise, just back from six

months of perfecting her French in Paris. Mr. Beer conscientiously pumped me full of Gotland data as the orchestra played American jazz and a succession of men came up to our table, clicking their heels and bowing for parental permission before they invited Marie Louise to dance.

"Our Gotland population is only fifty-seven thousand," Mr. Beer told me, "and last summer we had fifty-three thousand tourists. You can see what that means on a small island. We even get many foreign tourists. Before the war American cruises sometimes stopped here."

He smiled in recollection. "Once I remember," he said, "Visby was their last port of call before Leningrad and Russia. A Soviet official came here with a black list of people on the ship who could not go to Russia. One was Marc Connelly, your American playwright of *Green Pastures*. He was very puzzled and said 'I am sure there is some mistake.' But the Russians would not let him or the other black listed people go on. They were unloaded here at the height of the season, and I somehow had to find rooms for them and get them to Stockholm where they could meet the ship on its return. Later the Russians wired that it *was* a mistake about Mr. Connelly. They had thought he was someone else, someone dangerous. But by then it was too late."

"What do you think of Russia?" I asked.

"You should ask that in Stockholm. What do we quiet people on Gotland, out of touch with the great world, know about Russia?"

"You must have some opinion."

He turned serious. "Well," he said, "we all want to get on with Russia as best we can."

Later, while Marie Louise was again dancing, he said, "We have imported many things from America. Most of them I like. But I honestly do not care for your jazz." Just then the orchestra shifted into a fast, bouncy version of *Open the Door, Richard,* with a tenor singing the American words. Swedes all over the dance floor started jitterbugging. Marie Louise had been asked to dance that time by a third different Swedish officer stationed in the neighborhood.

"Why are there so many troops on a quiet resort island?" I asked.

"If you had been here during the war you would not have

found it so quiet," said Mr. Beer. "This island would be the perfect springboard for attacking Stockholm. It is at the strategic center of the Baltic. There were barbed-wire entanglements and tank traps all over the island. We had six large Swedish detachments here—not only the Navy, but air, antiaircraft, infantry, artillery and coast artillery units. For a long time no visitors at all were allowed. We knew the Germans wanted to take Sweden if they could do it without too much trouble. This was the way they well might have come."

"That still does not explain why you have so many troops here now."

"Many remain," he answered. He did not elaborate. I remembered Swedish dread of Russia, and the leader who had said to me in Stockholm: "We cannot help knowing we have a very big neighbor."

Mr. Beer discreetly shifted to Gotland's history. He told how Visby had been a great port on the east-west and north-south trade routes of Europe and Asia for over a thousand years. "In the old days we were a free island, a free port. We were great traders. Men from Gotland sailed down the Vistula and the Rhine. They went to Novgorod and along the Volga to the Crimea and the Caucasus. They bartered furs and amber for pearls and spices with the caravans coming from the Orient. In the fifth century there was already a Gotland colony in Constantinople."

He continued, with pride in his little city's long history: "In the 1300s, Visby was a city of twenty thousand when Stockholm had only three thousand. Then Visby ranked fifth among all the commercial cities of Europe—after Hamburg, London, Antwerp and Bruges. There was a song sung through Scandinavia about Visby, 'the city so rich that its girls spin with golden thread and its pigs eat from silver troughs.' A Danish king, Valdemar Atterdag, thought he would like so rich a city. He came and took us in the year 1361. We were not so rich after that, though we still prospered somewhat. Then in 1525 men from Lübeck, in Germany, crept ashore through the mist one night and sacked Visby. They burned the whole city, even sixteen of our seventeen beautiful churches. That is why we have so many ruins and have never fully recovered. In 1671 the Swedes took us from the Danes. But Gotlanders keep some of their old independent feeling. When

Gotlander takes the boat he does not say 'I am going to Stockholm.' He still says 'I am going to Sweden.' "

With a flourish the band finished *Open the Door, Richard*. The jitterbuggers drifted back to their tables. My thoughts were a blend of the jazz and this postwar Europe so changed and yet so like prewar Europe. I thought of the Visby ruins I had seen and wondered whether, in the twenty-third century, any ruins of the last war will seem romantic. I thought of how the Lübeck Germans had wantonly ruined Visby and its beautiful churches, as Hitler's Germans wantonly ruined peaceful Russian towns like Istra with its lovely old churches. I recalled Lübeck itself, that great Hanseatic port that throve on to modern times while retaining some of the medieval charm I saw there before the war. Now Lübeck too knows ruin, and a retribution no less terrible for being more than four centuries coming.

I thought of the friend with whom I had almost visited Gotland that prewar June. He was killed off another island—Okinawa, on the other side of the earth. I thought how close America is to both.

Chapter 11. THE SATELLITES

SEVEN countries in Europe are Soviet satellites: Albania, Bulgaria, Czechoslovakia, Hungary, Poland, Rumania, and Yugoslavia. The Baltic countries—Esthonia, Latvia, and Lithuania —lost all semblance of independence in 1940 and became three of the U.S.S.R.'s sixteen Soviet Socialist republics. There are recurrent rumors that these seven may also be incorporated in the U.S.S.R., but thus far they retain their own constitutions and regimes. They are Soviet satellites because their foreign affairs are run at Russia's behest and their domestic affairs by Communists in a way that brings them ever closer to Russia.

Finland escapes the satellite category, though its foreign policy is largely Soviet dictated, because its domestic policy is distinctly Finnish and not Communist. Russia has tried to make satellites of its zones of occupation in Germany and Austria and has fallen short of success, handicapped by the fact that neither Germans nor Austrians wish that fate, and draw enough stamina from the presence of the Western occupying powers to resist it. Italy would have become a satellite had the Communists won the April 1948 election, nor is this danger over. The Kremlin has high hopes of other European countries becoming satellites—notably Greece and France, where Communism is powerful. Russia has concentrated on France, Italy, and Greece because if it can win either or both of the first two any effective partnership of western Europe will be thoroughly disrupted, and if it can win either or both of the last two the Mediterranean will be subject to its control.

The seven satellites are undoubtedly a major Russian asset. They have an area of 446,730 square miles and a total population of 84,796,040. In extending the Soviet sphere to the Stettin-Trieste line they have brought Russian dominance farther west into Europe than ever before. But the importance of the satellite

214

should not be overestimated. They are not Europe, or even the bulk of it.

The six countries that would form the core of any western European partnership (Belgium, Britain, France, Holland, Italy, and Luxemburg) are slightly larger in area (455,276 square miles) and have nearly twice the population (152,357,928). This does not count Scandinavia or the World War II neutrals like Ireland, Portugal, Spain, and Switzerland, whose sympathies are on the side of the West. Nearly three-fourths of Germany's industry and population (48,000,000 out of 66,000,000) are located in the three western zones.

The part of Europe that supports the Marshall Plan is bigger, much more populous, and far better industrialized than the part which supports the Molotov Plan. Only in food is it less self-sufficient, and even there its deficit is not unmanageable in normal times. As Eugen Varga (Russia's top economist until his disgrace early in 1948) told the Kremlin, the Soviet sphere of Europe is small potatoes in total European recovery. By and large, the satellites share Russia's own economic weaknesses: their greatest shortages are in heavy industry and mechanical know-how of all sorts. To repair war damage and expand their economies according to their Soviet-style plans, they need the steel, coal, and oil, the machine tools, railway, chemical and electrical equipment of which Russia is critically short itself. That is why the satellites were eager to join the Marshall Plan. When Moscow took down the strap, they all stayed home. Now they are getting virtually no industrial products from either Russia or the West.

While the satellites are normally a food-surplus area (before 1939, Poland and Rumania were especially large exporters of food), the war has disrupted even that. Russia, short as it was of bread at home, had to send a million tons of grain to its satellites during the 1947-48 crop season—400,000 tons to Czechoslovakia, 300,000 to Poland, 150,000 each to Bulgaria and Rumania. Without bread, the local Communists might not have been able to keep their followers in line. In another year or two, the seven countries should again be agriculturally self sufficient. After 1950 they may have a little surplus food to barter for manufactured goods. But they face an even slower recovery than that which western Europe should make through economic co-operation bolstered by American aid.

2

What is it like to be a satellite?

The essence of Russian treatment of satellites is to be found in a policy Stalin developed originally for the Soviet Union and Trotsky sourly termed Stalin's only contribution to Soviet theory. After the October Revolution, Stalin was assigned the "nationalities question," i.e., how to handle Russia's many national, racial, and linguistic minorities. The human beings in these various groups had no more use either for Communism or for Moscow control than does the average citizen of the seven satellites. Something had to be devised to make it palatable for them.

With Lenin's approval, Stalin set up an "autonomous" republic for each separate nationality, thus allowing the Tajiks, Uzbeks, Turkmens, Khirghizians, Moldavians, Kazaks, Tannu-Tuvinians and other peoples of the Soviet Union to preserve some part of their individual languages and culture. (Marxist mental rigidity is shown by the fact that American Communists copied Stalin and long urged that the Negro question be solved by carving an autonomous Negro republic out of the deep South. Communists made few converts among American Negroes, largely because of their stubborn advocacy of this Jim Crow republic which practically no Negroes want.)

Various minorities in the Soviet Union gagged at "autonomy." They wanted independence. The Red Army was sent to show them the light. Leaders who put local interests ahead of the Kremlin were killed, jailed, or exiled. It developed that what Stalin had meant was not even autonomy—but local color.

Once the members of any given minority had accepted their fate, they were allowed to wear their national costumes, preserve their music and ballads, continue their cookery, perform their folk dances and celebrate their own holidays. (If the holidays are too numerous, they are amalgamated.) Behind this screen of local customs and set of safety valves for local pride, the Kremlin grasps all the real power. The local dialect is taught in all the schools and pupils learn appropriate passages from its epics and folklore— Russian is taught too, and bright pupils soon realize which language will get them ahead. The district government has a façade of local worthies—but the key posts in administration, Party, and secret police are held by outsiders sent from Moscow. In a recent list of awards for meritorious service in "autonomous" Tannu-Tuva, thirty of the thirty-two names were Russian.

The seven satellites also retain their own folk dances and cookery (just as Georgia, if Russia ever takes over America, will be allowed to have corn pone and pot likker). They still are freer than the Soviet minorities but fear that this would not last spurred a nationalist Communist like Tito to oppose Russia in June 1948.

The Red Army has been used in several satellites and looms just over the horizon in all seven. Its pressure broke up Hungary's Small Landowners Party, which had won a 57 percent majority in a free election, and installed a Communist regime. In Rumania, when the Big Three sent Andrei Vishinsky, Averell Harriman and Sir Archibald Clark-Kerr (now Lord Inverchapel) in January 1946 to arrange for free elections, Harriman asked Vishinsky, who is utterly cynical, how many votes the Communists would get in a ' free election. "If the election was *really* free we might get 40 percent," said Vishinsky, adding with a grin, "but with just a little pressure we would win 90 percent." (Vishinsky had presents waiting for his two colleagues when they boarded the Moscow-Bucharest train for the Rumanian negotiations—chess sets. It was a not-too-subtle Soviet hint that they had better play chess and leave the work to Vishinsky.) After the trio left Rumania, Red Army pressure was increased, opposition leaders like Julius Maniu were railroaded to jail, and the Communist front eventually got 92 percent of the vote in a rigged election.

The Bulgarian Communists staged a reign of terror in seizing power, and executed nine thousand opponents, including the Peasant Party leader Nikola Petkov.

The men Moscow has picked to hold the vital posts in the seven satellite regimes are not Russians, like those sent to control the "autonomous" Soviet republics, because that would be too glaring an affront to nations so recently independent. But they have had long Soviet training in Russia and know Soviet methods by heart. The Kremlin also tested them thoroughly and knows them by heart. Josip Tito in Yugoslavia, Clement Gottwald in Czechoslovakia, Georgi Dimitrov in Bulgaria, Enver Hoxha in Albania,

Anna Pauker in Rumania, Boleslaw Bierut in Poland, Matyas Rakosi in Hungary—and most of their vital subordinates—have had years of indoctrination in Moscow. Tito is the only one of them who has yet managed to fool the Kremlin.

These local leaders have given Moscow whatever it wants. To give a small sample list, the economic treaties they engineered have handed over to Russia control of: Rumania's oil (the largest field in Europe outside Russia), Hungary's bauxite (one of the world's biggest sources of aluminum), all Bulgarian, Rumanian, and Hungarian air transport, and all Danube shipping. Russia's favorite economic pincers is the "joint company"—a fifty-fifty ownership by Russia and the satellite involved, with 100-percent administration by Soviet-picked executives. The chief function of the joint companies is to keep goods flowing into Russia. In 1947 Russia took nearly all of Poland's 15,000,000 tons of export coal and all 203,000 tons of lumber which Rumania exported. As one ruefully resigned Rumanian observed: "It is more blessed for us to give than to receive." One reason Tito rebelled was weariness at being on the giving end. He decided charity began at home.

The non-Communist majority in the seven satellites (the top vote Communists have ever received in a free national election anywhere in the world was 38 percent in Czechoslovakia in 1946) has been almost completely cowed into submission. People still tell jokes against the regime, especially in Budapest, where one tale is of two dogs—a fat Hungarian mastiff that met a shivering little Austrian dachshund at the border and begged for entry.

"Are you crazy?" asked the dachshund. "Look how thin I am. It's cold here and there's no food."

"At least," said the mastiff, "I'll be able to bark."

Joking aside, the Communists have an iron grip on all seven countries. Two of them may be taken as typical of the Communist tactics: Poland and Czechoslovakia.

It is often asked why these two *have* become complete satellites while Finland, with a much smaller population, has not. In the former Nazi satellites of Hungary, Bulgaria, and Rumania, the Kremlin could work its will; the Red Army was the occupying power in them for three years before the peace treaties went into effect in September 1947, by which time Communist regimes were firmly entrenched in all three. In Yugoslavia and Albania, local Communists were in control from the moment the Germans retreated, so the Red Army did not have to appear in force, though picked groups of Soviet officers and political advisers were used to consolidate the Communist hold in both countries. But why has Finland held out when Poland and Czechoslovakia succumbed?

The Red Army is one of the several reasons. It liberated all of Poland and most of Czechoslovakia from the Germans, and stayed in those countries for some time after liberation, the vital period during which their regimes were being established.

A second reason is that the Finnish government never had to leave Helsinki during World War II. Both the Polish and Czech regimes had to flee their country and become governments-in-exile for almost the entire period of the war. The psychological difference was enormous, and so was the physical difference. In order to get back into their countries at all, the Polish government-in-exile had to make terms with the Moscow-backed Lublin Committee of National Liberation while the Czech government-in-exile had to reach an agreement with the Moscow-backed Czech Communists headed by Clement Gottwald. This had Trojan-horse results in both countries.

A third reason is that Finland is in a better geographical position for independence than either Poland or Czechoslovakia. It is not in the midst of Europe, like these two, but on the fringe. Forests cover most of Finland and are an aid both to defense and—in case of Soviet occupation—to partisan activity that would be a costly drain on the occupying power. Poland and Czechoslovakia have fewer forests and natural defenses; it is easier for an invader to roll over the country and then for an occupation army to stamp out the embers of resistance.

A fourth reason is the difference in national temperaments. Finns are more rugged individualists. Though their cause was almost hopeless, the Finns fought their invaders in 1939; the Czechs and Slovaks, who also knew their cause was almost hopeless, did not fight partition in 1938, occupation in 1939, or the coup in 1948. One could put it another way: the Czechs and Slovaks are more practical, the Finns more pigheaded. The Poles, like the Finns, have a fighting temperament; the other reasons are enough to account for different outcomes in Finland and Poland.

In 1945 the non-Communist leader in each of the three countries—Paasikivi in Finland, Mikolajczyk in Poland, Benes in Czechoslovakia—publicly proclaimed that his country must get along with Russia's policy but could and should run its internal affairs without Soviet interference. This is a quite understandable course for any small Soviet neighbor to follow.

Paasikivi still leads Finland along this line. Mikolajczyk, for two years of extreme difficulty and danger to himself, tried to observe this policy while the Communist-controlled government bloc gave Russia everything it wanted. Before 1947 was out, he had to flee for his life.

Benes also made an honest effort to follow this course—and after the Czech Communist coup became a mere figurehead of a president. In June 1948, he refused to accept either the new Communist constitution or the one-ticket election results. The Communists allowed Benes to "resign"—but not to leave the country.

The one satellite that has openly dared oppose the Kremlin since the war is Yugoslavia. In June 1948 the Cominform ("information" bureau of European Communists, which actually has a political function) denounced Tito and other Yugoslav Communist leaders for their "hateful attitude toward Russia." Communists the world over dutifully took up the cry. Yugoslav Communists had merely refused to be 100 percent obedient to the Kremlin. Tito, for example, had wanted a Balkan federation of Yugoslavia, Bulgaria and Albania, in which he would be the leading force; Russia wanted to run the three nations individually. The significance of the split could be exaggerated—Yugoslavia was still a dictatorship and its ideology was still Communist. But it showed how far Russia is from complete intellectual and physical domination of its satellites—and certain weaknesses in the Soviet position there. Basic differences exist between the "international" Communism entirely run by Russia and "national" Communisms which stress their own autonomy and development. These differences will continue to grow. Tito, for instance, called on "nationalist and patriotic Yugoslav sentiment" for support. Similar colonial problems may well crop up within the next few years in other parts of the Soviet empire.

3

Peter Zaremba is a Communist and the mayor of Szczecin, as Poles call once-German Stettin. When his city's new hospital was dedicated, he and I were next to each other in the front row of a large open-air congregation attending Roman Catholic Mass. All through the service this Communist led the congregation in the right responses.

"Most Poles are Catholics," he told me afterward. "It is the Polish custom to start a dedication with a Mass. It has been so for centuries. It would be silly to upset so old a tradition."

Polish Communists are not so silly. They voted to keep the words "So help me God" in the governmental oath of office. When they nationalized Poland's large estates, they exempted all Church property. But they say privately: "The last fight will be with the Church."

The small, smart, efficient high command of Poland's Communists, which one observer told me was "Tammany Hall with tommy guns," plans to fight its battles one at a time, though occasionally these overlap. The projected seven-point program of absorption: (1) the wartime London government (2) the underground (3) the Socialists (Communism's prisoner in the government bloc) (4) the schools (5) the middle class (6) the peasants (7) the Church.

The country's top Communists are in Warsaw, like President Boleslaw Bierut, Party Secretary Wladyslaw Gomulka, Cabinet Secretary Jakob Berman and Minister of Industry Hilary Minc. But wherever you go you find them in the key posts, working longer and harder hours than almost anybody else in Poland to make up in energy what they lack in numbers. In "the recovered lands," as Poles call the large slice of Germany which the Potsdam Conference turned over to Poland to administer, the two biggest cities have Communist mayors: Zaremba at Szczecin and Bronislaw Kupczynski at Wroclaw (once Breslau).

These two, who were boyhood chums in Poznan, personify Communist use of both brain and brawn. Balding, professorial Zaremba speaks six languages and worked as a clerk with the Nazi occupation force to spy for the Resistance. Stocky, genial Kupczynski who looks like a Bowery tough when he stops smiling, won Poland's highest medal for valor, as a fighter in the Resistance.

Such leaders look after their followers as thoroughly as Tammany Hall ever did. Instead of Christmas baskets and summer clambakes, the 7,500,000 workers and intellectuals among

Poland's 24,000,000 population whom the Party wants to cultivate receive food and housing well above the low Polish average—and the better jobs. Nearly a third of the state budget goes into sub-sidies for this new elite.

A Polish painter in a blitzed Warsaw suburb told me that each of the arts—painting, music, theater, writing, etc.—was run by a government trade union committee. If an artist wants privileges he must join the union. "Writers must be very careful to follow the correct lines," he said, "but we other creative artists have not been so much disturbed."

"Then you can paint anything you like?"

"Well, not exactly, for our union committee of course has ideas. For instance, it told us lately that there was too much neglect of still lifes, and that we should concentrate our chief effort on them for a time."

"What do landscape and portrait painters think of that?"

"They are not very happy," he said.

The tommy gun has become a feature of the Polish landscape. Every railway platform I saw in Poland was patrolled by a man with a gun. Poles, who jostled familiarly with the many soldiers on all such platforms, edged gingerly away from the patrols. Every government building I visited was guarded by men with tommy guns. On one two hundred-mile stretch of highway in central Poland, I passed nine armed control points where other men with tommy guns inspected traffic.

The first two of Communism's seven battles are almost won. Typical terror tactics have eliminated all independent-minded members of the London government who, like Stanislaw Mikol-ajczyk, tried to return. No organized opposition remains. Every party now represented in Parliament is a Communist tool. The underground has been almost eliminated by the 1947 amnesty. The government's promise not to prosecute those who surrendered with their arms brought 59,576 fighters out of hiding. The regime kept this promise. It is easier to stay in power with at least some popular support than by force alone. The amnesty was a very popular move.

Poland's Communists do put Polish interests high, though they put Russian interests first. A sardonic Socialist told me: "Our trade treaty with Moscow provides that Russia gets our coal, and in return we give them our textiles." The trade is not that lopsided, though Russia pays only $2 a ton for the coal. While 80 percent of Poland's 1946 foreign trade was with Russia (the prewar average was 1 percent), this fell to 55 percent in 1947. Polish Communists are trying to increase their trade with the West because it, and not Russia, can provide the machinery Poland desperately needs for its recovery. Poland was the first nation to accept the Marshall Plan "in principle" and the Communists, like other Poles, were disappointed when the Kremlin told them to decline.

Ships flying the flags of fourteen nations were in Gdynia the day I landed. But even Poland's ports are not entirely her own. The former German Swinemunde, now Swinoujscie, has thousands of Red Fleet sailors. One of the few Polish sailors I saw there said bitterly: "This is a Soviet base." Swinoujscie's ice-cream shop had the Russian word for "ice cream," *morojne*, before the Polish word, *lody*.

When I asked Mayor Zaremba about Szczecin harbor, he said: "The Russians have any section of the port they want. Sometimes they move from one section to another."

The Communists won their third battle, against their own allies the Socialists, in the spring of 1948 when the Socialists, after years of mounting pressure and frightened by the Communist coup in Czechoslovakia, finally agreed to merge the two parties and lose their identity. As one Socialist MP told me: "We provide nearly all the government's support, but the Communists have all the power." The Socialists do have six cabinet ministers, including Premier Josef Cyrankiewicz, in a system where the premier has almost no authority. The Communists have the ministries that matter. They control the army, the secret police, education, military courts (where the important—i.e., political—trials are held), foreign trade, and Poland's entire economic life.

The Communists are now fighting their fourth and fifth battles, for control of the schools and the middle class. "We can never win the old people," a Communist frankly told me, "so we must educate the youth our way." They are writing new textbooks and hand-picking students and teachers. They even have a "Social Commission" to control all exams and make sure that every pupil is "correct" in his social thinking before he can pass, no matter how high his scholastic grades.

The pitchfork to prod the middle class has three prongs. One is a Communist-dominated commission to fix taxes for towns-people; your rate of tax depends on your rate of co-operation. The second prong compels all small businessmen (big business has been nationalized) to get permission for every product they make and every price they charge from the Communist minister of Industry—Poland's biggest producer and their own chief competitor. The third prong is strict supervision of small shop-keepers, with taxes up to 90 percent on their profits. Most Poles believe that within three years all Polish shops will be state owned.

The sixth and seventh battles, against the peasants and the Church, will not come until the Communists have consolidated their other victories. Since the Poles are as stubbornly Catholic as the Irish, the fight with the Church may never occur—if only the Church will pay lip service to the regime. Communist President Bierut has stated that the question of whether the present religious freedom will be continued "depends on the attitude of the clergy; on whether they will accept the state of things existing in Poland."

The struggle with the peasants will almost certainly come before that with the Church, not only because the Communists have to depend on them for food and hate the feeling of dependence, but also because it is the one class in Poland that has a physical basis for resistance. Shopkeepers can be squeezed, intellectuals intimidated, businessmen nationalized, and factory workers fired—but farmers who grow their own crops are basically self sufficient.

The Communists have won almost no support among the peasants, who are two-thirds of the population, and fear them more than anybody else in Poland. In dividing big estates (82 percent of Polish land was in small holdings even before the war), Communists have made nearly all the plots too small to support a family, so that later they can justify collectivizing them on the Soviet model. They have already taken some steps toward collectivization by keeping many large properties intact as "state farms" worked by hired hands, and by pooling the nation's tractors into a State Tractor Organization with 247 substations like Russia's machine tractor stations. Poland has only 7 percent of its prewar horses, so this gives the regime a real hold over farmers who want their fields plowed.

Any attempt to collectivize the farms would start a struggle that would rock Poland to its foundations, as in 1931 it rocked Russia.

To build up strength for that eventual struggle, the regime is meanwhile weakening every other class in Poland. A scientist put it this way to me: "All our life is being lowered to the Russian level by the law of connected vessels." (When a pipe connects liquids standing at different heights in two vessels, the liquids level out.) A prime factor in this lowering process is the secret police, which had its 1947 budget of $170 million upped to $230 million for 1948. Other Polish controls have also taken on a Soviet severity. In Poznan, railway workers who had protested that their ration cards were not being met were sentenced to ten years as "saboteurs against the state." Three factory hands in Gdansk (formerly the German Danzig) received long jail terms for "spreading rumors."

Every time I mailed a letter from Poland to a foreign address, I had to take it to a post office and hand it in unsealed for inspection —"to prevent currency smuggling." But a woman who had stood next to me in one of the lines said: "They want to look at those of us who still dare to send letters abroad. I will keep in touch with the outside as long as I can."

I saw another sign of satellite Poland when I went to call on a quite ordinary Pole in Warsaw. His street address led me to a large building with several entries. Since I had no apartment number for him, I asked a man for directions.

"She is the one who knows," he said, pointing to a woman in black seated on the far side of the courtyard where she commanded a view of every entry. A girl halfway across the court said the same thing. When I got to the woman and asked, she promptly told me.

On my way out an hour later, she waved me over and said: "You were up there quite a while. Is there anyone else along the block whose address you want?"

The last time I had met that sort of block supervisor was in Soviet Russia. The time before was in Nazi Germany.

4

Except for Stalingrad, I have seen no city to match the ruins of Warsaw. The Nazis nearly killed it, but hard work has already restored a good deal of the city's life. Men of all parties took pride in showing me buildings that had been hollow shells six months earlier. The gaps between such structures are still wide. Scattered through the rubble are little shrines and graves of Poles who died fighting for liberty. On walks through Warsaw, I saw on many walls rows of fading photographs of these thin-faced, burning-eyed young men, the name and date under each. As they pass the photographs, men take off their hats.

On one such stroll I stood for more than two hours opposite the massive iron gates of Mokotow Prison, where most of the capital's political prisoners are held. Several times a day the gates open to release some man or woman in whom the secret police have at least temporarily lost interest. Relatives often wait there all day, on the chance their loved ones may be released. A woman keeping patient vigil said her husband had been in Mokotow for sixteen months, simply because he was arrested to serve as witness in a court-martial that ended five months ago.

Poland is on a gently rolling, nearly defenseless plain which has been alternately overrun by Russians and Germans for centuries. After World War II, the Poles had to yield seventy thousand square miles of their country to Russia on the east. In return, the Big Three at Potsdam awarded them forty thousand square miles of Germany to administer—economically a far richer area than the one they had lost—with the inference that a large part of it would be given to them permanently at the peace settlement. The Poles demand it all, and to strengthen their claim have expelled over five million Germans from this territory, keeping only those who can be useful to them. In the town of Miedzyzdroje (formerly the German Misdroy) a German doctor and nurse delivered a Polish baby in the room just under the one where I was trying to sleep. They were the only medical attendants in this town, which has been completely resettled with Poles. The two of them will not be sent back to Germany until others can be trained to replace the Polish doctors and nurses the Nazis murdered.

An understandable though unhappy result of Poland's exposed position between great powers is that throughout its history there have been many Poles willing to serve the interests of the then-dominant power. Every important Polish family has done this to preserve its lands and titles—or to win more lands and titles. The Radziwills are an outstanding example. There'll always be a Radziwill, even if he has to turn Communist.

The most revealing interview I had in Poland, as illuminating as my afternoon at the Writers Club in Moscow, was with ex-Prince Christopher Radziwill, who in the days of Poland's extreme-right Pilsudski dictatorship supported Pilsudski and now actively supports the Communists. He shed a lot of light on the way so many intellectuals in so many countries now react to Communism, "the new reality." In Europe during the 30s I often used to hear almost the same phrases and arguments advanced to support the new orders in Germany, Italy, and Spain.

"You have come to the right person for contrasts," Radziwill began when I asked his views on Poland. "I have belonged to three different Polish privileged classes. Before the war I was in the privileged class as a landowner and aristocrat; I am the fifty-first Radziwill named Christopher. During the war I was again in a Polish privileged class; the Germans kept me for years in Maidenek and Buchenwald in a group that included our present Socialist premier, Josef Cyrankiewicz, who became my good friend. Now I am a member of the new Polish privileged class: the intelligentsia. The Government treats the intelligentsia who co-operate with it even better than its top civil servants. It pays us far better. When I headed a section of the Foreign Office, I got 15,000 zlotys ($150) a month. Now, as political editor of *Kurier Codzienny* (Daily Courier) I get 40,000. As in Russia, we are the new elite."

Prince Radziwill then made it clear that he was now known as Mr. Radziwill. "That is more in accord with the new Polish reality. But I am the only man in the present Polish Parliament who also sat in the Senate under Pilsudski. I even sit for the same electoral district I did then—Radom, near Kielce, south of Warsaw."

"What sort of opposition did you have in the last elections?"

"The same sort of opposition there was under Pilsudski," he

said. "The Mikolajczyk peasants." [Mikolajczyk fled soon afterward and the Communists seized his party.]

"What causes the opposition?"

"That is our great problem. We in the government must somehow make all Poles understand the need of friendship with
Russia—because not only the rightists but many leftists are hostile
to Russia. There are even leftist cabinet ministers here who
hate Russia. I agree with Napoleon, who said: 'It is impossible
to make history against geography.' Poland has tried to do that—
unsuccessfully—for 150 years. It is time Poland realized that its
only chance to exist is with Russian evolution, which is not Russian revolution."

"Is that the Democratic Party program?" I asked. The Democrats are one of the stooge parties in the Communist bloc. Radziwill sits in Parliament for the Democrats, as well as being political
editor of their party paper.

"In the broad sense, yes," he said. "Ours is the party for the
working intelligentsia—like lawyers and doctors—and the thinking workers. Before the war the intelligentsia was less than 5
percent of the Polish population. The Nazis cut it to 2 percent.
In concentration camp I often saw the Nazis pick out Poles with
glasses and shoot them, reasoning that anybody with glasses must
be educated. They wanted to exterminate all educated Poles as
part of the process of turning us into one of their slave states."

"Then the Democratic Party and the government bloc do contain most of the remainder of Poland's intelligentsia?"

"No," Radziwill admitted. "Most of the intelligentsia opposes
the government or at best is neutral 'against' it."

"You say that the Polish intelligentsia is much smaller after the
war and that few of them belong to the Democrats," I observed.
"And nearly all the Polish workers I have met are either Socialists, Communists or sympathetic to Mikolajczyk. So what is the
Democratic Party's mass base?"

Radziwill very charmingly let the cat right out of the bag. "The
Democrats do not possess a mass base," he said. "We got our forty-
two deputies in Parliament only by going along with the two
Marxist parties and the government peasants. Of all four parties
in the government bloc, we are the most loyal to the bloc. For

we Democrats know that without the bloc we would not exist as a party at all."

"What is the difference between Polish Communists and Socialists?"

"Nearly all the best Socialists were killed in one way or another during the war," Radziwill said. "They have few good new men, and most of the survivors are second rate. The Communists are quite new men, but very strong and very able. I think the ablest Communist is Gomulka—a good Pole and a very strong man. But we Democrats do not have as difficult a position as the peasants in the government bloc. They have nothing to offer the peasants."

"Surely they have land to offer them."

"Not even much of that. Foreigners have a greatly exaggerated idea of Polish land reform. Less than 20 percent of Polish land was in very large estates—a much lower percentage than in Hungary or East Prussia. We have confiscated the property of seven thousand land-owning families and given it to four hundred thousand peasants—which still leaves over two million Polish peasant families with no land and no real change in status. Poland had an agricultural surplus population of nearly eight million before the war. We still have a huge one. All that peasants want in any country is some land that is really their own, and fair prices for their products. Polish peasants who have land distrust the government because they fear it will take their land as it already has from large owners. Even if the government did confiscate some more land, it could never get enough to satisfy all the landless. And the present government's program is not and cannot be one that would actually appeal to peasants. It is impossible to rebuild Poland and strengthen the industrial workers and at the same time do much for peasants. The peasants know it. They know the low fixed prices the government has set for farm products—and how little they can buy in return. They do not like the government. And after all, Poland is still more than 60 percent peasant."

"Then what did the land reform accomplish?"

"Probably the best thing it did," said Radziwill, "was to bring the peasants much closer to reality. Take my own estate. I had 5,000 hectares (12,500 acres). Four thousand of that was in forests, and the new Poland has nationalized all woodlands. No peasant got any of that. Of about 900 under cultivation, 750 were divided among landless peasants and the other 150 among peasants who previously had only two or three acres of their own. Most of the farm workers living on my former estate got no land at all. Now until my property was actually distributed, even jobless peasants there would not go elsewhere to look for work because they said to themselves, 'Someday somebody will kick Radziwill out and then we'll have this land for ourselves.' That hope, plus what I and the working peasants did for them, kept them alive and going. Now they do not even have that hope. The land has all been divided. That is forcing them to realize they will have to go somewhere else and work. And our government will increasingly see to it that they go where they are needed and do what they are told—either in factories or on the land we have recovered from Germany in the west."

"Is Polish rural overpopulation really that bad?"

"It is," said Radziwill fervently. "We have twenty-three million hectares of agricultural land and sixteen million peasants. It's terrible; it's like China."

"You sound pretty pessimistic."

"I am not pessimistic," Radziwill assured me. "You just have to face realities. Poland has more reason to be optimistic now than she had in 1920. It is much fairer to compare 1947 with 1920, each two years after an armistice, than to compare 1947 with 1939. Of course, we were not nearly so devastated after the last war. But in 1920 we had no place to put our rural overpopulation. Now we have better farmland in the west than the larger area we returned to Russia in the east. And we have great new industries and mines in the west which can use most, if not all, our unemployed peasants. Before 1939 Poland had an agricultural surplus, but very little industry. When we have built the new Poland, we will have a much better balanced economy. Our national income will be higher, with far fewer people among whom to distribute it. In 1939 we had a population of about thirty-five million. Now with the six million war dead—and remember, only about sixty thousand died in battle; the Germans killed nearly all the rest in cold blood—the Ukrainians and others returned to Russia, and the Germans in our newly restored western areas returned to Germany, we will have about twenty-four million people."

"Then what," I asked, "have the peasants and intellectuals got against a new Poland that can give them a bit better land and a higher standard of living?"

"Polish peasants are very stubborn, religious, conservative people," said Radziwill. "They despise Communist Russia. When I last toured my electoral district, many peasants came up to me and still tried to offer the toast 'Death to the Mongol.' They do not understand Russia. And the Russians do not understand them. One of the greatest Soviet mistakes here was the way they made their war graves. They put their cemeteries all over Poland, most of them in the center of our town and village squares. None of those mass monuments or individual markers has a cross. They are all topped with the red star. Every time a religious Pole sees one, he naturally thinks to himself: 'Russia is atheistic and Communistic.' To a religious Pole, a grave without a cross is a grave for a dog.

"As for Polish intellectuals, they are very stubborn too. The government has a rather difficult situation in the universities. Most of the professors are in the opposition, and not as many students are from the worker and peasant classes as there should be. Few of the students are even from families of the old intelligentsia. Most of the present ones come from a rather awful class of newly rich. Their fathers are self-made men who profited during and after the war because they had no morality. The students come from such homes because those are the ones with money. A new university bill which the government recently put through Parliament will change all this. The bill provides scholarships for workers' and peasants' children so that they will furnish most of the students and be the bulk of the new Polish intelligentsia."

"I have heard about this new bill," I said. "Is it not the same bill which provides new teachers to train this new intelligentsia the right way? Does it not specify that all new university teachers will be appointed by a government commission, instead of by each university itself?"

"You do not quite appreciate the bill," said Radziwill. "Most of the professors in most of the universities oppose the government. So it would not be possible to get professors favorable to the government by leaving further appointments up to the individual faculties. We face the problem of putting the government's will into effect without putting the professors down. The special commission will solve the problem. It is composed of picked men from several universities. It will appoint all new teachers. No one is going to be dismissed, no matter what his views are, because Nazi murder means we already have far too few professors. But quite soon after the law has begun operating, most of the professors will have been chosen by the commission."

"I think I understand the bill very well," I said.

"In any case you must try to understand Poland's position," said Radziwill. "Poland is in eastern Europe. But Poles want to stay western as well as go along with Russia. We are an eastern outpost of Western culture. We want to remain Western in our culture, outlook, and contacts. But we must also go along with Russia, even if Polish friendship for Russia is more with the brain than from the heart."

Then Radziwill turned to the subject of anti-Semitism in Poland: "Before the war, Poland had some 3,500,000 Jews or one-tenth our population—about the same percentage as Negroes in your population. There was strong anti-Semitic feeling here, largely for economic reasons. The children of peasants and workers and the poorer intelligentsia did not have much opportunity, partly because the Jews had all the small shops and many of the small key positions. So all these groups were strong against the Jews. The landowners were not; we helped the Jews because they often helped us. Landowners, including myself, had a sort of unwritten alliance with them.

"The mass Nazi killing of Jews had a very bad effect in Poland. Poles hated the Jews but they would never have dreamed of killing them in that fashion. But once Poles knew it was that easy to kill Jews the tendency and temptation is sometimes there—as the Kielce pogrom proved. I will never forget the day that the Nazis killed seventeen thousand Jews at Maidenek while I was in another part of the concentration camp—not only because of the mass murder but because that evening many of my Polish fellow prisoners got drunk to celebrate. That's terrible. But it's true.

"Of course nearly all Poland's Jews were slaughtered. Their little shops and businesses stood empty. A new Polish bourgeoisie took over. Now, when an occasional Jew does come back from concentration camp or other exile and takes his place back, his successor hates him. And every other member of the new Polish bourgeoisie fears that by some chance *his* predecessor might return as from the grave. So they also hate these stray returning survivors. That too is terrible, though perhaps it is human nature, especially when you remember that nearly all the poorer Poles never had very much. When the Jews disappeared this new bourgeoisie had a little more opportunity than they had before.

"Poland now has only about 100,000 Jews, or at most 150,000. But many Russian Jews of Polish extraction have come as part of our population transfers with Russia. They think Poland is better than Russia. The ignorant Polish feeling is against them, both as Jews and as Russians. You hear ordinary, not well-educated Poles speak of them contemptuously as 'Jewish Communists.'

"Of course that is very unfair. Actually they are almost all little capitalists; nearly every one of them is setting up as a small shopkeeper. I don't know any class more capitalistically inclined than small shopkeepers. And these Jews must have disliked Soviet Russia or they would not have left; they had their free choice and could have stayed. So it is equally unfair for Poles to have an anti-Russian feeling against them, especially when they have all proved their Polish extraction.

"Now we thinking Poles very well understand that Polish anti-Semitism is not only bad in itself but bad propaganda for us in Western countries. But some of that ignorant mass prejudice is still there. We are trying to counter it. The Kielce pogrom was by oppositional partisans; my parliamentary seat is in Kielce province, and I know quite a bit about that affair. The government really had nothing to do with it. But I must also tell you that when the government sent militia there to save the Jews, the militia, instead of saving them, fell in and helped to kill them. But that was not the government's fault—and the government certainly did not make the rumors that started the pogrom.

"About two hundred thousand surviving Polish Jews have already gone away to the West from Poland. Few if any of those who had the choice of going to Russia or of staying in the areas that were to become Russia, did do that. Polish Jews have instead gone to America, Palestine, or anywhere else they could—even to Germany. Poland will give the remaining 100,000 to 150,000 their passports to any country that will grant them entrance visas.

Nearly all of them will eventually emigrate from Poland if they can. Perhaps that will be the end of the Jewish problem for Poland."

Poles have never been fair to Jews. The existence of a huge ghetto in the Warsaw of 1939 speaks volumes on that.

5

When the Nazis completed their grab of Czechoslovakia in March 1939, the world knew it faced war. When the Communists completed their grab of Czechoslovakia in February 1948, the parallels were ominous. But Russia, bled by World War II, does not possess the overwhelming military advantage that Germany built up in the years before it struck. Stalin is a more cautious man than Hitler, and the Western world is more alert. Czechoslovakia is once again an example and a warning. It is not necessarily another prologue to a fearful drama of war.

Czechoslovakia was turned into a complete satellite partly for defensive reasons. Russia had wanted to maintain it as an attractive mannequin, modeling a New Look style of government between Communist dictatorship and democratic freedom. When the possibility of western European recovery increased, and Czechoslovakia showed real interest in the Marshall Plan, Russia feared that its model might find other nations' styles more attractive than they found Czechoslovakia's. It feared that such desires would then spread further into its sphere and that Czechoslovakia might even become a country through which Western styles would enter the East, instead of the opposite.

Russia did not dare risk losing Czechoslovakia, not only because of its strategic importance (Bismarck said, "He who rules Bohemia rules Europe," and the country is shaped like a dagger that points both ways) but also because of its industrial importance. It is the only one of the seven satellites where a majority of the population is not engaged in agriculture. Bohemia, the country's chief province, was the industrial heart of the old Austro-Hungarian Empire. Czechoslovakia, with its 14,800,000 people, inherited this area in 1919 and increased its output considerably. Hitler, in the years he ruled it, built many plants there and upped production about 40 percent. Czechoslovakia's present Communist rulers have this accumulated heritage, plus a fair-sized force of skilled labor even after the loss of three million Sudeten Germans whom the Czechs have expelled from their western border areas since 1945, thus cutting their population to about twelve million.

The Russo-Czech trade pact is the most important single economic agreement in the Soviet sphere. It covers goods worth a billion dollars and dovetails most of Czechoslovakia's foreign trade into the swap system of the Molotov Plan operating in eastern Europe. It makes Czechoslovakia the workshop for the largely rural Soviet security sphere which can no longer get manufactured goods from the West because Russia blocked that trade and cannot get the goods from Russia (which itself needs more of them than it makes).

Czech Communists, led by President Clement Gottwald, have launched a Five Year Plan inspired by Russia. They want a 200 percent increase in heavy machinery, an 80 percent increase in metals, a doubling of the chemical industry, and a transformation of the famed Czech glass and pottery industry "toward the production of technical needs," i.e., away from luxury goods toward industrial glass, electric bulbs, terra-cotta pipes instead of china, etc. The raw materials Czechoslovakia needs will come from the Soviet sphere—coal from Poland, copper from Yugoslavia, cotton and wool from Russia—and the manufactured goods will funnel back there. Czechoslovakia used to have two-thirds of its trade with the West, and the changeover will be difficult. The Czech blast furnaces, for example, are built to consume high-quality iron ore that used to be imported from France, Germany, and Sweden. The Russians now supply low-quality, high-sulphur-content ore which has badly damaged some of the furnaces.

The Jachymov mines supply Russia with uranium for possible atom bombs. The Skoda arms plant, already one of the biggest in the world, is being enlarged. Russia takes most of the Skoda output, but it is also an arsenal for the international Communist underground. The Belgian police recently seized 117 boxes of Skoda-made guns consigned to a Communist in Peru; they were labeled "ironware" and discovered only when one box broke open while being loaded on the ship.

If they had a free choice, the great majority of Czechs would line up with America and the West. But America has been inept in Czechoslovakia ever since the closing days of the war. American troops could have liberated Prague and the western half of the country, where the German troops were eager to surrender to them; instead, they were ordered to halt just beyond the border, which let the Red Army gain all the credit for liberation and gave Communists a stronger voice in the Czech government than they would otherwise have had. Then America showed little interest in buying Czech products, which forced Prague to trade elsewhere and gradually become enmeshed in the Soviet economic net. In 1947, when we were spending over two billion dollars to help Europe, we made little effort to aid the Czechs, who were then hanging in the balance. In the spring of 1947 Congress slashed our information budget there to a minuscule $31,000, so for a year before the coup, the average Czech got only a distorted Communist version of America's intentions. Most Czechs I met said that we had no interest in their country. At the World Festival of Democratic Youth held in Prague while I was there, the small American delegation was Communist led and its one jerry-built display emphasized our lynching of Negroes. Russia sent five hundred colorfully costumed boys and girls with a symphony orchestra, two ballets, and a troupe of Mongol dancers who stole the show.

The Kremlin moved when the Czech Government accepted an invitation to the July 1947 conference in Paris on the Marshall Plan. It was a unanimous acceptance. Even the Communist cabinet members agreed; they knew Czechoslovakia needed trade with the West. Stalin summoned Gottwald to Moscow and gave him a personal lecture. Threatened with rupture of the Russo-Czech alliance, the cabinet unanimously voted to reverse its earlier unanimous decision. The episode showed the Czechs how completely they were under Soviet control. More significantly, it showed Russia that Czechoslovakia—even its Communists—still had illusions of independence. Gottwald was ordered to end such nonsense and bring his country to heel.

Gottwald can be genial or tough. Born in 1896, he joined the Party in 1921 and became its leader in Czechoslovakia in 1929. After Munich he fled to Moscow, returning with the Red Army at the end of 1944. In his first speech as a member of the Czech Parliament in 1929, he had said: "You, gentlemen, are asking me what we are here for. My answer is simple. We are here to break your necks." But in 1943 he offered to co-operate with President Eduard Benes' government-in-exile. Benes eagerly accepted the offer and went to Moscow to sign a Czecho-Russian pact based on it. Afterward Benes said to Stalin in Gottwald's presence: "Mr. Stalin, I have complete confidence. We have signed an agreement for non-intervention in domestic affairs, and I know you will keep it." Stalin and Gottwald beamed assent.

For the next four years, Gottwald showed his genial side and Czechs of good will like Benes and Jan Masaryk let themselves think that their necks would never be broken. Guests arriving for dinner would find Gottwald on all fours on his living-room carpet playing "horsie" with his granddaughter. He clinked glasses with all comers. When the evening was rolling along he would bring out his violin. Soon everybody would be singing the folk songs of Gottwald's Moravian childhood.

Even after the 1947 Moscow reprimand and reversal, Gottwald at first moved quietly. He agreed to the informal summer truce which all Czech political parties took—and the Communists outwardly observed it. That July one high Czech official paused long enough in packing for his holiday to tell me: "This summer has even more crises than last. But we have had no real rest for years, all of us in every party are exhausted and it's the hottest summer anybody can remember. So we decided to postpone our disagreements until cooler weather. That's reasonable—and Czechoslovakia is still a reasonable country." (This man was one of the first officials the Communists ousted after the coup.)

Gottwald, like any trained Communist, did not bat an eye in switching from toughness to geniality and back to toughness as the Party ordered—just as Andrei Zhdanov successively starved the Leningraders, charmed the Finns, and purged the Russian intellectuals. In the fall Gottwald abruptly broke the truce by announcing that the Communists intended to win an absolute majority in the May 1948 elections. He moved to annex the Socialists by making an agreement of "co-operation" with Zdenek Fierlinger, their fellow-traveling leader. The Communist press took up the "with us or against us" line which had been the prelude to the Communist steamroller in each Balkan satellite.

Czechoslovakia's four non-Communist parties closed their ranks.

In November the Socialists held a party conference, got a back-stiffening message from Benes, voted out Fierlinger and his Communist fusion policy by 283 votes to 182, and replaced him with Bohumil Lausman, a middle-of-the-road Socialist. Gottwald knew he had to strike. Two of his subordinates already held the keys to any coup: General Ludvik Svoboda commanded the army and Minister of the Interior Vaclav Nosek commanded the police. Both began putting Communists in all positions of control. Early in February, Nosek ousted the chiefs of Prague's four main police districts and replaced them with Communists. The four non-Communist parties forced a cabinet showdown. By a strict party vote the cabinet ruled that the ousted police chiefs be reinstated at once. When Nosek refused to reinstate them, the fifteen non-Communist cabinet ministers laid the crisis in President Benes' lap by resigning. It was a brave gesture, but Gottwald was ready for it. Nosek's Communist policemen, armed with tommy guns and rifles, surrounded Prague's radio station and government offices. Communists seized the radio and announced that no Czech could leave the country except with a newly stamped police visa. General Svoboda told the army, "We must seek a stronger brotherhood with the Soviet Union," and the police began arresting non-Communist leaders. Communists broke up counterdemonstrations with gunfire.

Even a Latin American revolution comes with intrigues inside the cabinet, gaining control of the army, then seizure of radio stations, government offices, and the key members of the opposition. The memorable thing about every Communist revolution since the one Lenin led in October 1917 is the way the organization is set up in advance throughout the mass nerve centers, by first making undercover preparations which seem quite innocuous.

The Czech affair was a striking example of how a Communist revolution operates. It takes more than parties and political leaders to forestall such coups; every non-Communist citizen in a country must be aware of what is going on and help oppose it.

When the Communists start to take over a country, they take advantage of any social or economic unrest by stirring up the people with whatever catch phrase will appeal to them most. Communists do not hesitate to say diametrically opposed things to different groups. While I was in France, for instance, *L'Humanité* (the Communist newspaper for city workers) and *La Terre* (the Communist paper for farmers) said *in the same week* exactly the opposite thing about food prices. City workers were told: "In April, the Communists were in the government, and butter cost 255 francs a pound. Today the Communists are no longer in the government, and butter costs 370 francs a pound. Now do you understand why you are hungry?" Farm workers were told: "We are happy to note an appreciable increase in the price of milk, which rises from 9.75 to 15 francs a liter, and of butter, which is increased by 60 percent. Thus the authorities seem to have lent an ear to the claims we advanced on behalf of French farmers. . . . Let us hope that the new price level will become generalized for all farm products."

After the Communists have gained some strength by these tactics, they try to join a coalition government. Once in the regime —in position to pull an "inside job"—they aim at taking one key post after another until they are ready to grab the whole works. In elections, they vote solidly and split the opposition by threats, propaganda, and physical intimidation. Where they have local control, they rig the voting. They plant Communists and fellow-travelers in every party. They infiltrate labor unions, churches, and all other organizations. While they are softening up these groups, they attempt to get four cabinet posts: Interior (control of the police and opportunities for arrests, beatings, and blackmail), Justice (so they can sentence their foes and protect their friends), Information (to run the press, radio, and all opinion-forming agencies), and War (to use the armed forces to complete their conquest of a country). Czechoslovakia's Communists had been steadily softening up their country for three years before the coup.

Benes, frail and aging, begged Gottwald to reopen negotiations with the other parties. Gottwald refused. Instead, he handed Benes the list of a new Communist-approved cabinet and told him he must accept it at once. Otherwise, he warned, there would be a general strike and bloodshed.

"You are talking to me like Hitler!" Benes shouted. Two hours later his will broke and he signed the list. The next day Benes swore in the new cabinet, which included one famous non-Communist holdover: Foreign Minister Jan Masaryk, son of Thomas Masaryk, the democratic founder of modern Czechoslovakia, its first President and its patron saint since his death in 1935. Like Benes, Jan Masaryk had often proclaimed that Czechoslovakia would be the "bridge" between Communism and democracy.

After the swearing-in, Gottwald announced: "If anybody thinks that an exchange of leaders is enough, and otherwise everything may remain as before, he is mistaken." There was a Communist purge of "negatively disposed" judges, teachers, journalists, politicians, civil servants, and businessmen. The new minister of Education ordered Stalin's picture hung in every classroom and declared: "This is not merely a matter of a picture, but a conception of national life." Czechs by the thousands tried to flee across the border into the American zone of Germany; one said, "I never thought that Czechs would turn to Germany for refuge." The Ministry of Social Welfare sent all who were purged to work in quarries, mines, and lumber camps. The new "people's democracy" had arrived at Soviet-style slave labor in less than two weeks. Soon afterward it had reached the Soviet one-party election slate— all other parties were suppressed or merged with the Communists. By June the Communists gleefully announced that less than 5 per cent of Czech industry remained in private hands. Communist Premier Antonin Zapotocky proclaimed that the country's entire industrial and agricultural system would be reconstructed "to eliminate every vestige of the capitalistic system."

After the coup, Jan Masaryk avoided people, though he had always been most friendly and approachable. The ninety-eighth anniversary of Thomas Masaryk's birth occurred the following week. Clement Gottwald and his cohorts gathered at the grave of Czechoslovakia's founder for a propaganda field day. Gottwald said: "If Thomas Masaryk were alive he would approve us." Jan Masaryk's presence in the cabinet gave the claim some justification.

Later in the day Jan Masaryk came to the grave alone. He stared at it, then started to weep. He sobbed for nearly an hour.

Three mornings later his bruised body—its neck broken—was found in the stone-paved courtyard of Czernin Palace, sixty feet below an open window in his apartment. The evidence pointed to suicide, though many suspected murder. The Communists cynically hailed him as a martyr to their cause and had another propaganda field day, complete with a state funeral and burial beside his father. In the funeral oration, Gottwald asserted: "I can prove to you that Jan Masaryk clearly and without compromise agreed with the action program of the new government."

Jan Masaryk did not agree with the Communists, though he spent the last years of his life trying to compromise with them. He was an easy-going man who believed he could make concessions indefinitely. An effervescent and charming companion, he was a humorist who could sometimes be serious, an epicurean with a stoic streak hidden deep inside him, a son who revered his father. When he did finally realize he had compromised with Communism beyond the point where compromise is possible, he also realized that death had a certain dignity.

Chapter 12. PRESSURE IN THE MEDITERRANEAN

SINCE 1945, America has become the leading power in the Mediterranean. As Britain's weakness became evident there after V-E Day, America had the choice of replacing British influence or permitting Russian domination. The challenge came as early as the Potsdam Conference in July 1945, when Russia demanded bases at the Dardanelles and trusteeship of Italy's African colony at Tripolitania—which meant Russia would control Turkey and be right athwart the Mediterranean trade routes and the Arab world that stretches from Morocco to the Persian Gulf. This prospect was not encouraging for Turkish sovereignty, Arab independence, or world trade, all of which America desired. The Soviet demands were rejected—Hitler had rejected Molotov's rather similar demands at Berlin in November 1940 for control of Turkey and the Middle East "to the shores of the Indian Ocean." Hitler said no because he wanted to control that area himself; we said no because we want it to be independent.

In August, 1946, Russia told Turkey that it must not only have bases at the Dardanelles but Turkey's two eastern provinces, Kars and Ardahan. When the Turks appealed to the other powers, America again backed Turkish sovereignty. The past year had made it clear that more than words were needed to stop Russia. A naval detachment was sent to the Mediterranean and Secretary James Forrestal announced that it would stay to support American aims and policies there.

America now has the greatest naval force in the Mediterranean. Many nations have tried to make it their lake since the Phoenicians three thousand years ago. America is the first to make a strong bid without holding a single base in it, let alone any stretch of its shoreline. The amazing development in naval-supply methods made in the Pacific during World War II renders this feat possible. We keep one of our three Atlantic task forces in the

Mediterranean: a 45,000-ton aircraft carrier with 130 planes, three cruisers, ten destroyers, and the necessary maintenance ships. The three forces rotate every four months. Since their seagoing machine shops can make most repairs, major overhaul can be delayed until they return to a base in America. They visit Mediterranean ports only on invitation and, while they buy fresh provisions at them, could be completely supplied from home if necessary. They can refuel from tankers at sea. Not even the British, who controlled the Mediterranean's waters for over a century and still have bases from Gibraltar to Cyprus, maintain as strong a naval force there.

American ships are in the Mediterranean as a counterweight to the Russian land forces pressing down on this highly strategic area. Soviet pressure, notably on Greece and Turkey but also on Italy, France, and the entire Arab world, would be much greater if our fleet stayed home. Indirectly, these ships even help to stabilize Russian land forces along the Stettin-Trieste line in central Europe by providing the threat of an outflanking counterattack if the Russians struck westward. One Russian fear is that, if it began a war, America and Britain might retaliate by sending their far stronger navies through the Dardanelles into the Black Sea and using Turkey as a base for amphibious and air attack.

Even before World War II ended, America had largely taken over British responsibility in Italy. America has since replaced Britain in Greece, Turkey, and Saudi Arabia. The British are withdrawing their troops from Egypt, the Suez, and Palestine. The Mediterranean area, which has been vital to the world since men started keeping records, is undergoing one of its great historic changes. We are trying to hold things steady enough for the change to be smooth—and away from imperialisms instead of to another imperialism. This has required a co-operation with the British of which few Americans are fully aware.

The British Mediterranean system is still a smoothly operating administrative machine with an influence through the whole region based on long experience, trade contacts, cultural relations, traditional commitments, and political skill. It is the most unifying force in the Mediterranean, and there would be no quick or easy substitute for it. Its accumulated know-how helped to operate such wartime organizations as the Anglo-American joint Middle

East Supply Council, which had an economic control approaching dictatorship over most of the Mediterranean area. American postwar policy there still needs this British system just as British policy needs the Americans, for neither country can do the job alone.

Unless the two co-operate, it would be impossible to restore Italy, end the Greek civil war and start Greece on the road to reconstruction, guarantee Turkey, locate some solution for the heartbreaking problem of Palestine, develop the oil of the Middle East, and find the economic basis for a healthier Arab political existence.

America's Mediterranean policy is not identical with the British and cannot be. If the two were identical, America would be blamed for British mistakes and tyranny, past and present. America, for example, wants the Arab countries to have freedom more quickly than do the British. The Mediterranean means more to the structure and communications of the British empire—in the oil and trade of the Middle East, and in the lifeline to India, Singapore, and Australia—than it does to America. But the similarities in policy are much more important than the differences.

Taken altogether, the pools of oil scattered through the eastern end of the Mediterranean area are the biggest oil reserves in the world. Russia runs the Rumanian fields and of course has its own great fields around Baku. The rest are controlled by American and British concerns, with Dutch and French participation in some of the companies. The largest of the ten British and American fields are those of the Anglo-Iranian Oil Company in southern Persia, the Iraq Petroleum Company around Kirkuk, and the Aramco developments in Saudi Arabia. Britain and all western Europe now get most of their oil from the Mediterranean; after the tremendous drain on America's wells since 1939, Washington planners consider these Middle Eastern fields of prime importance to America's future oil needs either in peace or possible war. The political and strategic importance of Middle Eastern oil is one of the chief factors shaping both American and British policy in the Mediterranean. For one thing, it has helped to make the American attitude in Palestine less pro-Jewish than it would otherwise be—though Washington could not in any case completely ignore Palestine's Arab majority.

The Arab world's wealth and privileges have long been monopolized by a few big landowners and merchants, with nearly everyone else in dire poverty, yet bearing the burden of the heavy indirect taxes that support the regime. The fact that this parallels the Soviet class and tax system is not known to the Arab masses, to whom Communism sounds very attractive. Their feeling is quite understandable in Egypt, for example, where sixteen million peasants go hungry and fourteen hundred rich men (none of them paying an income tax) control nearly half the land irrigated by the Nile.

The old British method of ruling each country through a fraction of its privileged fraction is not good arithmetic. During the war a million Arabs working for the Allies in half a dozen countries got better pay, food, and consumer goods than they had ever known before. The mere realization that a better life is possible gives ordinary Arabs a powerful impetus toward the unknown blessings of Communism when they see no other way to improve their lot. British Foreign Secretary Ernest Bevin, no defender of outworn imperialism, proposed a "People, instead of Pashas" program to raise Arab living standards by Euphrates River irrigation works, a Jordan Valley Authority (partly modeled on the Tennessee Valley Authority), and other projects. Britain has no money to put such schemes into operation, but America could provide the loans and the technicians that would let the major crossroads of Europe, Asia, and Africa change its present near-feudal system not to Communism but to democratic capitalism. Certainly the Arab world will not stay feudal.

2

In the spring of 1948, after one year and $300 million of American aid, Greece was worse off than it had been in the spring of 1947. No more than 25,000 of the country's 7,450,000 population were Communist-led guerrillas in the mountains. These 25,000 men had driven 520,000 farmers and villagers to refuge in the cities, and had given Greece a total of 1,400,000 unemployed by half-paralyzing what transport and industry remained after the Nazi's great wartime destruction. Because almost all Greece is mountainous—less than one-fifth of its land can be cultivated—

and the Greek army of 132,000 men could not be everywhere at once, this relative handful of guerrillas had disorganized the whole country. By night they raided villages and towns, even those near Athens. They burned houses, took the scanty food supplies, and, to replace their casualties, abducted youths by threatening to shoot them and their families if they did not come.

When the Greek government tried to flush the guerrillas out of a given district, most of them escaped to some neighboring range of mountains or skipped over the border into friendly, Communist-controlled Albania, Yugoslavia, and Bulgaria, where the Greek Army could not follow. There they rested and re-equipped before returning for fresh raids. Via Albania and Bulgaria they could count on receiving Russian arms and aid.

The guerrillas, under the leadership of wiry, blue-eyed, Stalin-mustached General Markos Vafiades (born 1906) who proclaimed himself premier of the "Provisional Democratic Government of Greece" on Christmas Eve 1947, see to it that their destruction far outruns American reconstruction. They not only blow up more bridges than can be rebuilt and more locomotives than can be shipped from America; they have even halved the inadequate Greek food production by scaring the peasants away from their fields. The resultant human misery is terrible. When I was in Athens, nearly two million people were crowded into a city which, because of German wartime destruction, had fewer houses than the Athens of 750,000 I visited in 1938. They had fled there because it was the one place in Greece that everybody considered safe.

Early in 1948 the Greek and American governments agreed that economic reconstruction could not possibly be carried out until internal security was restored—which meant ending the civil war. In March the Greek Army, re-equipped with American arms and accompanied by a few picked American advisers, began its effort to seal off the northern border and systematically wipe out every guerrilla stronghold south of it. But one cannot seal completely a boundary that stretches for five hundred mountainous miles, and rounding up guerrillas is a slow process at best— as America discovered in the long years it took to pacify the Philippine guerrillas after the Spanish-American War.

It is always possible that Russia may signal its Albanian and

Bulgarian jackals to help Markos win Greece. If the troops of these two Soviet satellites were beaten, they could fall back over the border without damaging Russia's own prestige; if they won, Russia and Communists everywhere would reap the benefits. The knowledge that at least some American troops, including the battle-equipped marines who are part of America's Mediterranean naval force, would fight alongside the Greeks will doubtless keep Russia from using the Red Army itself—such a direct Soviet-American clash could well start the world war for which Russia is not really ready.

More probably, Russia will simply continue to send aid to General Markos, hoping that he can withstand any armies sent against him, that the Americans will finally decide they are pouring money down a rat hole, that the inefficient Greek government will bumble itself into even greater difficulties, and that the weary Greek people, who have not really known peace since 1940, will then turn to the Communists in despair. But Greeks are industrious when they get a chance. If their army can eliminate the guerrillas or even restrict them to a few remote mountains, American aid could soon put the country on the road to recovery.

The American mission to Greece, headed by ex-Governor Dwight Griswold of Nebraska, is always energetic, often efficient but too rarely tactful. Its lack of tact is most regrettable, since four hundred years of Turkish occupation have given the modern Greeks certain oriental characteristics that Pericles might not have recognized. "Face" is one. Griswold tended to make the first public announcement of the Greek government's economic plans. The ramshackle coalition led by the aged liberal Themistocles Sophoulis (born in 1860, he is by far the oldest premier in the world) naturally lost "face" with the Greeks. Nobody in any country works well with an outsider who comes in and arrogantly takes over. Griswold also had the habit of nagging at the Greek leaders in public, instead of exhorting them in private. Their reaction was, "If Griswold is that eager to get things done, why doesn't he do them himself?" The truth of the axiom that you can lead a Greek but you can't push him has gradually dawned on Dwight Griswold.

While the members of the American mission are able technicians, most of them knew nothing of Greece and many still have an awesome ignorance of the political side of their job. One top American military man there assured me, "I almost never read the news. It might distract me from my work." They are men of essential good will, experts with no ax to grind. They may strengthen democracy in Greece which, although it originated the idea, word, and practice of democracy, has seen it rarely in the last 2,300 years. (Even so, racked as it is by civil war, Greece still has more democracy and civil liberties than any country in the Soviet sphere.) But the mission as a whole vividly illustrates America's need for a big well-trained corps of men and women to carry out our steadily enlarging international responsibilities. In the long run, all the dollars in the world can never make up for inadequate brains, background, humanity, and solid politico-economic skills.

It would also help if American officials abroad had George C. Marshall's sense of history. In his first speech as Secretary of State, Marshall said: "I doubt seriously whether a man can think with full wisdom and with deep conviction regarding certain of the basic international issues today who has not at least reviewed in his mind the period of the Peloponnesian War and the fall of Athens."

Athenian democracy was exhausted in the struggle with the hard and sterile tyranny of Sparta. But this occurred only after the Athenians alienated the other Greek states by their arrogance, having abandoned many of their original democratic principles. One Sunday in Athens, I asked two members of the American mission to accompany me up to the Acropolis, that glorious symbol of democracy's start. Both declined.

One said: "We've been too busy to visit the Acropolis. I don't believe any of us have gone there yet."

The other agreed and added: "There's nothing but some old ruins up there anyway. But I guess that hill does give you a good view of Athens."

3

The Turks find the present situation frighteningly like Europe of the 30s. They look on the Greek civil war as a second Spanish civil war and wonder if Turkey will be the second Poland. The Turks have kept an army of seven hundred thousand men on war footing ever since 1940; first for fear of Germany which overran the Balkans to their European border, and now for fear of Russia which squeezes them between Bulgaria on the west and the Caucasus on the east. Military preparedness has bled them white, for 90 percent of the nineteen million Turks are peasants and the country has little industrial or mineral wealth. Three-fourths of Turkey's budget goes to the army.

Until early 1947, only Britain's economic and political aid enabled the Turks to maintain their costly, nerve-racking resistance against Russian demands on the Dardanelles, Kars, and Ardahan. When Britain's financial crisis forced it to withdraw, America began a $100 million annual subsidy to keep Turkey from cracking up under the cost of continued mobilization.

A glance at a map shows why Russia wants to control the Dardanelles, in fact all Turkey. If Russia struck at western Europe without holding the Dardanelles and Turkey, a hostile fleet could pass through the Straits and across the Black Sea to attack the soft underbelly of the Soviet Union, while all Soviet and Rumanian oil fields and most of Russia's industry could be blasted from Turkish air bases. The American military aid program to Turkey includes a string of airports big enough to handle B-29s. In this air and atom age, they are probably the nearest bases that America could use if Russia went to war—nearer to Moscow than the Pacific island bases were to Tokyo and Hiroshima. Washington strategists often speak of "the problem of delivery," a phrase with chilling implications when atom bombs (or any bombs) are involved. The position of Turkey looms large in these discussions. So American aid to Turkey is a powerful check on the expansionists in the Kremlin.

The Turks are no longer terrible, but they are still tough. Even if they had no outside aid, they would resist a Russian invasion as long as they could. But American planes and guns unloaded at Istanbul and American warships visiting Turkish ports are a steady reminder to Russia of all that invasion would imply.

Under Turkey's great modernizing leader Kamal Ataturk, the remotest Anatolian villages got schools, radios, the Gregorian calendar, a Westernized alphabet and at least a weekly mail complete with newspapers. Turks say that Ataturk "thumbed through a mail-order catalogue of Western civilization and ordered some of everything." Even adults were told to educate themselves, and illiteracy dropped from 90 to 25 percent. Since Ataturk's death in 1938, the regime has been carried on by his old cronies, headed by Ismet Inonu who is now serving his fourth term as president. Hardening of the reform arteries (from old age and long grip on power) has turned it into a reactionary regime, and after 1940 the Ataturk social measures were virtually canceled because the army needed all the money. In the 1946 elections the Ataturk-Inonu People's Party had its first real opposition since the republic was established after World War I. The Democrat Party might have won on its plank of renewed reform if Inonu's henchmen had not faked many of the returns. Inonu has since promised that the next election will be completely honest. If it is, the Democrats will probably win. Both parties are firm in their resistance to Russian pressure.

The Turkish peasant is far from satisfied with his life today. He knows that the *Moskoff*, as he calls the Russians, are the reason his sons or brothers are in the army for three and four year periods, so that there are fewer family hands in the fields. The army requisitions his horse, quarters troops in his house, takes over his crops, and uses the consumer goods he needs—all because of the *Moskoff*. He has fought the *Moskoff* thirteen times in the last five centuries and will do it again if he must—but he hates to see all that Ataturk did for him being undone.

Russia has the resources to keep its armies mobilized and to make an occasional reconnaissance in force across the border. Turkey cannot afford mobilization—but neither does it dare demobilize and run the risk that the next reconnaissance might be an invasion. Russia may never attack but meanwhile it is steadily strangling its neighbor's economy. Yet the Turks will not release any troops until they are certain past doubt that the Truman Doctrine will be consistent American policy, and are also certain past doubt that the Russians understand that America will back them against Soviet aggression. They prefer independence to modernization until they can again enjoy both.

4

The world often forgets that capitalism can be much more revolutionary than Communism. In technical equipment, a capitalist oil field or automobile factory runs revolutionary rings around its Communist counterpart. In human society, a well-imagined, well-run capitalist enterprise can produce the most revolutionary changes. Saudi Arabia is a case in point. It is the only country I have ever been where (according to all the people who should know) there is not a single Communist. This in itself shows that it is the least advanced (in the Western senses of literacy, industrialization, its people's political activity, etc.) country in the not especially advanced Arab League. Yet in the last few years American capitalism, in the shape of both private enterprise and the American government, has made an impact on Saudi Arabia that can only be described as revolutionary.

From King Ibn Saud down, the Arabs find American capitalism helpful and constructive. They want more. Their desire is a bracing reminder to Americans that our capitalist system will be welcomed by other countries as useful and beneficial if it is not introduced as a means of exploitation. Properly presented, capitalism can far outweigh the appeal of Communism. Success depends on the people and the approach. In Greece, Americans do not seem especially effective in carrying out either public American policy or private American interests. In Saudi Arabia, they seem to be effectively executing both.

The American people and American business have concerns in Greece quite similar to those they have in Saudi Arabia. Why the difference in effectiveness? Apparently the Americans in Arabia know what they are basically supposed to be doing, and are right in there doing it. The Americans in Greece lack any clear basic notion of what they are up to; their drive is seldom connected to any conveyor belt.

It is imperative for American government and American capitalism alike to be sure their conveyor belts are hitched up. Each must decide what its job is in a given foreign country and then send the right men to do the job.

This is what Lieutenant Colonel Dale E. Seeds and Mr. James MacPherson are doing in Saudi Arabia. Lieutenant Colonel Seeds, a shrewd young graduate of the University of Washington, operates the U.S. Army Air Force Base at Dhahran. A combat aviator during the war, he got his present rank in 1944. MacPherson is a hard-bitten, plain-spoken sixtyish Scot who says that the proudest moment of his life, as a naturalized American, came when he was summoned to Washington as wartime aide to Donald Nelson. In 1943 he took over the vice-presidency in local charge of Aramco, the Arabian American Oil Company—which is the biggest single American commercial interest in the Middle East.

5

The American-built airport on the Persian Gulf at Dhahran in Saudi Arabia, with its long runways and modern air-conditioned buildings, is the best base between Egypt and India. A key stop on commercial plane flights around the globe, it is also the only airport run by the U.S. Army Air Forces within a radius of two thousand miles. Lieutenant Colonel Seeds is well aware of its significance.

"Just look at a map and see where you are," he said. "America has interests in the Middle East. And this airport is right on top of one of the world's biggest oil pools."

"How do the Arabs feel about the combination?"

"They know that every great power is interested in airplanes and oil," said Seeds. "They'd rather trust us Americans than anybody else. King Ibn Saud gave the Arabian oil concession to American operators because he said they were the most likely to develop it into a paying proposition and the least likely to try to run Arabia. That was in 1933. Lately the king said that almost everything which has happened since has confirmed his original judgment.

"I guess the king had something of the same idea in mind when he agreed to let America build this base. He wants to modernize Arabia without changing its old customs. He knew that some day Arabia would need good airports and the knowledge to run them. So he let us build this fine big base which we then thought we'd need to ferry troops to the Pacific when the war in Europe ended —and wrote a clause into the agreement that after the war America would use it to train Arabs in the different phases of airport management. It's not child's play learning to run radio beams and such. The king probably figured this was a good way to get instructors."

"Can the Arabs learn everything about airplanes?"

"We don't know," said Seeds frankly. "Over in Jidda we taught aircraft recognition to Arabs who wouldn't even have recognized a train. Arabia has no railroads. But this is a hell of a lot more complicated than aircraft recognition. It's the first time in history anyone has taken camel drivers and tried to turn them into airplane drivers. The first class of Arab trainees is due here next month. And Washington hasn't even provided me any textbooks or Arabic-speaking instructors. We may have to write our own texts and train our own teachers as we go along. Perhaps that's the best way in a brand-new program like this.

"They'll have to be taught communications, the control tower, and minor maintenance like servicing, refueling, and putting air in tires. I don't know how long it will take them to master things like major engine overhauls or fuselage repairs or handling the really intricate machines. Doing that kind of work is like learning to build a big, complicated airplane in the first place. I expect Americans or some other foreigners will have to be here for quite a few years teaching the Arabs all that."

"How long will the air force stay?"

"The agreement lets us stay until 1949," said Seeds. "If this is to continue a big commercial airport, used as it is now, the Arabs can hardly take over all phases of its management until some time after that. But the question of what will happen after 1949 has not yet been raised."

"What if the Russians raise it?"

"What would they have to raise?" asked Seeds. "We're here under an agreement and the only way we could stay would be under an agreement. The American Air Force personnel at this base is exactly ninety-four. How could they hurt anybody? All we have besides that are some Arab and Italian laborers. We're much more likely to have trouble from Washington. Half the time the guys in Washington forget this base exists. The other half they preach economy and threaten to abolish it. As long as the Arabs want to have us, it seems like pretty poor economy to abandon the one airport America operates in the whole Middle East."

"Would it save much?"

"Not the way they talk millions and billions in Washington," said Seeds. "Dhahran costs America $700,000 a year including the airport training program we promised to give the Arabs when we signed the agreement. If we had even $800,000, we could boost our efficiency a lot. And we should have an absolute minimum of $100,000 for new construction this year, though we really need $250,000. It seems cheap enough, considering.

"But it's hard getting anything at all from Washington. The GIs here call it the end of the line. It is. You couldn't get much farther than this from any part of America. We're over seven thousand miles airline from New York and over nine thousand from my home town of Seattle. They scarcely bother to send us our mail. They won't even give us a post exchange. We have a hard time rustling rations. And there's damn little to offer the men for recreation. The thermometer goes up to 140 degrees and stays there. You already know what the *simoon* is like."

"Yes," I said. The afternoon before, Mrs. Seeds had run a finger over a chair in her living room. "It's been dusted three times today," she told me. "And it's gritty again already." Then she showed me the screened-in porch at the back of the house. "It was swept clean this morning," she said. Already over a hundred pounds of sand had silted down over it again. The *simoon* had been blowing ever since.

"At that, you're lucky," Seeds continued. "A little later the wind will be blowing off the Persian Gulf, instead of from inland. It will be just as hot as this, almost as dusty—and terribly humid."

Seeds does not even have enough air-conditioning equipment for all his base buildings, and what he has is too old to be reliable. Most nights men have to set up their cots in the air-conditioned post theater—which is available because there are no movies. The base recently acquired a band, by recruiting some Italian laborers from Eritrea who are also musicians. During the day the band's vocalist drives the post garbage truck. The base had a contest to name the band, and after Seeds rejected names like "Arabian Knights" and "The Sheiks of Araby" for fear of possible international complications, a corporal won the prize of a bottle of bourbon by suggesting "The Desert Troubadours."

"How do you get on with the Arabs?" I asked.

"I'm satisfied," Seeds said, "and they seem to be. Their ways aren't always our ways, but they play ball, better than they would strictly have to. The other day a sergeant got drunk, ran off with a base car, and raised cain in an Arab town up the coast. They could have done plenty to him and been well within their rights. But they simply put him in the local jail to sober up. Next morning they sent him back with a note, 'We know that Colonel Seeds will see that justice is done.' When they show trust like that, you have to respond. I took away the guy's stripes and shipped him out.

"When you have an Arab's word, you have something. We may have our misunderstandings occasionally, but even if we do, I'm sure we'll both be able to settle them."

Arab ways are not always American ways. The next morning, there was a hand-cutting near the base. Arabian pickpockets are still punished by having their right hand cut off in full early-Moslem fashion—with certain modern scientific refinements. A doctor from the local Aramco hospital is now present to numb the forearm with novocain, before the official chopper hacks off the culprit's hand, and to dress it afterward. Thus today's Arab pickpocket feels no pain in the first half-hour, is far less likely to die of blood poisoning, and in due course has a much handsomer stump than the pickpocket of a thousand years ago.

6

"Aramco's oil concessions," MacPherson told me, "run to the year 2005. Actually they're good only as long as we get on with the Arabs. I was with Standard's oil operations in Mexico. Our company got along well with the Mexicans and did fairly by them. But we had to pay the penalty for the Dohenys and others who were just concerned with getting as much oil as they could and to hell with any Mexicans that got in their way.

"The last thing we want here is another Mexico. We're dealing squarely with the Arabs, and they with us. Ibn Saud has never broken his word to us in the fourteen years we've had this concession. He speaks of us as his partners in developing Arabia. He means it. And it is a partnership. His big objective is to better his people's lot. He's the greatest man and character I've ever known in my life. He's a great statesman, a good diplomat, and he's a proved warrior. How many men now alive are all three?

"We've sunk well over $100 million in Aramco so far, and will put in $400 million in this area by 1952. We've already borrowed $102 million for installations right here and another $125 million to start a pipe-line to the Mediterranean that will easily cost $200 million more with the facilities needed to go with it. Aramco has plowed back into expansion every cent it's earned. We'll do that for at least another five years to get things going. Counting expenses here, pipelines, tankers and all the rest, Aramco's four parent companies will have sunk $1.3 billion by 1953 without having got a cent from it. That will be twenty straight years of investment in this concern without returns, since Aramco got its first concession in 1933. Of course, we expect a pretty quick turn-around after 1953. Meanwhile the king, who *is* Arabia like Louis XIV was France, gets a twenty-one cent royalty on every barrel. So Arabia is making profits a damn sight faster than we are."

"With Mexico in mind, isn't it a risk for any oil company to sink much money in foreign concessions?" I asked.

"Naturally there's a risk," said MacPherson. "We're taking it. Calculated risks are what built capitalism. Capitalism won't run unless you keep taking them. We're capitalists and not ashamed of it. No other group of oil companies in the world could finance or swing as big and long-range an investment as this before getting any returns. The only other two that could even conceivably swing it are Shell and Anglo-Iranian Oil; they're both British, which means their sources of supply are so limited that they could never get the material in time. Even with dollars, we can't get material anywhere near as fast as we need it.

"Four years ago we were producing only 10,000 barrels a day. Last week we had a new peak day of 265,500. In six more months it will be 325,000. [It was.] It's the quickest development of any major oil field in history. Arabia is already the fifth biggest oil-producing country in the world. The Arabs are getting over $20 million a year in royalties. Soon it will be twice as much, plus the money that Aramco spends locally in dollar exchange. That's the money that will let Arabia develop whatever modern things it decides to have.

"There are two big things I stress to the 1,400 Americans Aramco has here now—and we'll have many times that number before we stop expanding. Of course, we'll always have five to ten times as many Arab employees as we have American. The first thing I stress to American employees is our relations with Saudi Arabia and our getting on with this country. That's plain horse sense. If a man can't get on with the Arabs, we don't want him. If he strikes an Arab, he's through.

"The second thing, naturally, is production. We've got to keep it moving up. We're sitting on top of at least six billion barrels of proved reserves, about a third those of the whole United States. God knows how much more there may be. If we don't keep upping production, that huge investment can never pay off—for Arabia, us, or anybody else. After the way the war lowered American reserves, we must develop the Middle East. Some day we may need this oil even more than we do now."

"What else is Aramco doing?" I asked.

"We're teaching Arabia something practical and useful about Western methods," MacPherson said. "The whole Middle East has never had a middle class. Without a middle class and entrepreneurs it's almost impossible to have any kind of free enterprise. The Arabs are not only learning a lot about trade from us, but about machinery and manufactures.

"Do you know, there had never been a brick kiln in Arabia until we came? The Arabs know how to make good bricks, but they just baked them in the sun like the old Egyptians. That sort of brick does not last too long. The same brick, kiln baked, lasts forever. We want to use all the local materials we can. It saves terrific shipping costs, and we can get the stuff a lot faster. We started the first brick plant in Arabia by a clay deposit a few miles east. This administration building is made of those bricks, and they're good. Now the Arabs are pretty much running that plant themselves. We're using the native gypsum and stone. Some of our Italian laborers have taught the Arabs how to cut stone and build fine walls and buildings. Did you see the stone walls over by the tennis courts and swimming pool?

"When Aramco came, this part of Arabia had only a couple of cars and practically no modern machinery of any sort. About the only wheels were those on pulleys getting water out of wells. Now there are hundreds of Arab-owned cars in this area, as well as our own. Our first Arab workers scarcely knew what any machine was for. Now they not only handle quite a few kinds of machines, but they're buying more machinery for themselves every year.

"We're deliberately encouraging an Arab middle class and entrepreneurs. King Ibn Saud heartily approves. Putting Arabs on their own whom Aramco has helped train builds up the resources and know-how of this area—and all Arabia. In the long run it supports Aramco's own operation. We've not only given this area its first schools and first hospitals. We're developing a big training program in many different lines. Not just the brick factory. Aramco's electric lines are now strung by Arabs under Arab supervision. An Arab contractor, Mohammed Sahrawi, whom we helped put in business, has his own crew of twenty Arab welders and does the preliminary welding for our oil pipe lines as well as final welding for our water lines and flow lines. Two Arabs who got all their automobile training with Aramco have set up their own garages near here in the last few months.

"The Arabs are much better off doing all those things for themselves instead of depending on us. We're helping them to realize it. Two years ago Aramco had four Arab contractors working for us. Now we have fifty-five—and they employ 4,150 Arabs on their own. We backed them and helped them get equipment. Now they're on their own. They take other contracts. The man who built Prince Feisal's new palace in Jidda was trained by us. We want them to branch out like that because it spreads the risks. And we'll keep right on encouraging Arabs that started with us to strike out for themselves.

"If everybody is on the Aramco pay roll, every headache comes straight to us. Contractors not only get some of the opportunities, but some of the headaches. By taking other jobs, they not only supply the increasing Arabian demand for such services, but hedge against any eventual Aramco cutbacks in construction or other operations. Aramco loses a good workman every time an Arab with us branches out on his own. But the Arab community gets something we previously had to supply and another candidate for the middle class it needs. These Arabs are making good. They're training other Arabs. They're like American businessmen who had no college education, but know how to grow once they get a chance.

"And Arab kids lap up education the way a cat laps cream. Have you seen those Bedouin boys over at Jebel School?"

"Yes," I said. "They've got sharp eyes and sharp noses. The

teachers told me that a lot of them stay up most of the night to study. They try to cram six or eight years of education into two or three."

"That's Arabia in a way," said MacPherson. "This country never had much money for developments until we struck oil here. We made our first tanker load shipment in May 1939. Then the war came along to disrupt things. Now Arabia can really start going places and squeeze a lot of progress into a pretty short time.

"It will stay a strict Moslem country, but there are plenty of modern ideas that don't conflict with the Koran. Arabia has a great new period coming up. Think of the electricity and sanitation systems, the ports and air conditioning this country could use. It's never grown enough food to be self-sufficient. But there's a lot of water as well as a lot of oil underground in Arabia. With pumping and proper irrigation, this country could grow several times what it does now. Take the experimental farm over at Al-Kharj. That was started right out in the desert near some limestone water pits. I'm proud to say Aramco helped start it. Aramco men are still running the deep-water pumps that make it possible. It already has three thousand desert acres blossoming like the rose, with American agricultural experts to give advice. The king is right behind it; he wants to develop Arabian agriculture. It is showing Arab farmers and nomads what Arabia can grow. In one Al-Kharj test section they're getting sixty tons of alfalfa a year— eighteen cuttings, with all that water, warmth, and year-round growing weather. There are quite a few places in Arabia where that could be done. They're not all as difficult mechanically as Al-Kharj to supply water for irrigation.

"I'm a businessman. I want Aramco to make money, good money. In due course we should. God knows we're putting in enough money meanwhile without any immediate return. Once we do start getting decent returns, sometime in the 50s, it will take twenty or thirty years just to recover our original investment. I'll never live to see that—though I certainly hope you will.

"But there's something else I've seen Aramco put into Arabia. That's some American know-how and philosophy and way of life. Arabians have their own traditional way of life, but from the king on down, they know they can add some Americanism to it without hurting themselves. There's another ism that will come into Arabia—and the whole Middle East—if ours doesn't.

But if Americanism comes the right way, that's the one the Arabs want."

MacPherson represents what *Pravda* calls "capitalist oppression." He is a hard driver. His language can be as blistering as it is eloquent. He keeps everybody in Aramco jumping to boost production. His subordinates fear him, as well as respect and admire him. But they are not oppressed as they would be in Russia. Their fear of the boss is far less than the fear you find among Soviet underlings—and their efficiency of operation is far greater. When you compare the way capitalist Aramco plans an almost incredible increase in oil output, and then overfulfills its plan with the way Communist Russia keeps having to cut down its plans for oil production, you know why Stalin tries to copy capitalism.

Both Seeds and MacPherson represent the American interests in Saudi Arabia, which *Pravda* calls "an American satellite." If *Pravda* is right, this American "satellite" presents a happy contrast to the Soviet type of satellite. King Ibn Saud freely entered into his agreements about Dhahran airport and the Aramco concessions. Arabia is a sovereign state and if it canceled those agreements at any time, the Americans would have to withdraw—as the American oil operators had to leave Mexico. Russia's satellites are forced into their agreements with the Kremlin, and any man in those countries who tried to cancel such an agreement would meet an unhappy fate. The Russians in those countries talk like the lords and masters they know they are—they never dream of saying, much less practicing, MacPherson's precept of conduct in a foreign land: "If a man can't get on with the Arabs, we don't want him. If he strikes an Arab, he's through."

The difference between the capitalist and Communist systems in their respect for the rights of other people and in their efficiency of operation shows why we Americans can slowly but surely achieve the free world we want—if we will be American.

Chapter 13. THE DEFEATED

GERMANY and Austria are still under Big Four occupation. No peace treaties have yet been negotiated for them, and none are likely soon. Germany is the center of Europe and the crux of the peace. If the Big Four could compose their differences there, they could do it anywhere. Instead, they sponsor separate Germanys and the split is widening.

Germany collapsed so utterly in defeat in May 1945 that there has since been no central German administration of any sort. The central Allied administration, paralyzed almost from the start by the fact that any one power could halt its proceedings by veto, fell into sheer frustration in March 1948 when the Russians refused to call a scheduled meeting of the Allied Control Council. The Russians then showed a great eagerness for the Americans, British, and French to leave their three sectors of Berlin, which is a hundred miles inside the Soviet zone of occupation. In June the Russians closed all road, rail and water approaches from Trizonia to Berlin, hoping to starve the Allies out. America and Britain responded with a great air armada to fly in food.

The Germany that existed before Hitler seized Austria and Czechoslovakia, and started World War II, is now in three fragments and a splinter.

The splinter is the 738-square-mile Saar Basin, rich in coal, which was administered by the League of Nations from 1920 until a plebiscite returned it to Germany in 1935. Again separated from Germany, it is now administered by France. The Saarlanders voted overwhelmingly in October 1947 for economic union with France, and both America and Britain have announced that they are willing to have the Saar awarded to France by the peace treaty. For all practical purposes, it is already part of France.

The three fragments are the 95,000 square miles of Trizonia (the American, British and French zones of occupation), the 46,400 square miles of the Soviet zone of occupation including Berlin, and the 40,000 square miles of eastern Germany which the Potsdam Conference gave Poland to administer and which the Poles will claim at the peace settlement. Trizonia has most of the people and industry; the two eastern fragments have 48 percent of the land and 55 percent of the prewar German food production. A third of the nine million Germans in the Polish area had fled westward before the advancing Red Army in 1945; the Poles have expelled almost all the remaining six million, who are now scattered round the rest of Germany. Trizonia has forty-eight million (72 percent) of the sixty-six million Germans and the Soviet zone only eighteen million (28 percent).

Stalin has said that coal, steel and oil are the three industrial essentials of a country. Germany has no oil wells, but most of its synthetic oil plants are in Trizonia. An overwhelming percentage of Germany's 1938 coal and steel production also came from Trizonia: 80 percent of the coal and 86 percent of the steel, compared to a mere 3 percent of each from the present Soviet zone. The rest of the 1938 German production, 17 percent of the coal and 11 percent of the steel, came from the Silesian area Poland administers.

The complete failure of the Council of Foreign Ministers to reach a German peace settlement either at Moscow in the spring of 1947 or at London that autumn sprang from Russia's unyielding insistence on two points: $10 billion in reparations, and an equal voice in the control of the Ruhr. The three Western powers maintained that Germany could not possibly pay such reparations; America emphasized that it was pouring in over $500 million a year just to keep Germans from starving and could not let Russia siphon off more than that sum every year. As for having Russia in the Ruhr, the others refused to grant that, after Moscow had consistently refused to implement the German economic unity agreed on at Potsdam. Russia has kept its zone entirely in its own control. Why should Russia expect a voice in—and veto power over—the Ruhr, which is the most important area in Trizonia?

Though the Council of Foreign Ministers may have met for the last time, and no over-all German peace treaty is likely to be worked out for years, the Western powers have wisely resisted the temptation to sign a separate peace with their rump of Germany. They have simply taken the best temporary alternative of bringing their three zones into a fairly close partnership, open for the Soviet zone to join whenever the Russians allow. Having the great bulk of Germany's population and industry, Trizonia makes more political and economic sense than three separate zones would. But it must be part of a larger and more self-sufficient unit ever to survive, let alone thrive. If Russia cuts it off from eastern Germany, it must have the close co-operation of western Europe or perish.

At present the two Germanys are going in the opposite directions of their respective masters. Eastern Germany is run through the Communist-dominated Socialist Unity Party (SED), western Germany through the Christian Democrats and Social Democrats with the Communists averaging only 8 percent. (Though democratically elected governments have been set up in the various states of Trizonia, they can be overruled even in minor matters by the military government authorities.) Eastern Germany has socialized most of its industry and trade; western Germany has avoided socialization. Eastern Germany is being economically linked to the Soviet sphere; western Germany is being drawn into the European recovery program.

Trizonia, especially the Ruhr, is vital to western European recovery. Before the war, Ruhr mines produced 440,000 tons a day —the largest coal production of any single area in Europe. Ruhr-produced coal costs $10 a ton; American coal, delivered to Europe, $22 a ton. Because Ruhr production averaged less than 225,-000 tons a day for most of 1947, European countries spent $600,-000,000 on American coal—and almost the entire sum came from American loans and gifts. This is economic madness. If America had fed the hungry Ruhr miners and their families an extra $50,-000,000 worth of food, it could have saved $550,000,000. When the miners got a slightly higher ration late in 1947, following the merger of the British zone with the American, daily output soon rose to 300,000 tons.

The Ruhr was also Europe's largest single prewar producer of steel. Much of it was made from high-grade French ore. Now the French argue that German coal should come to French ore and be made into steel in France, so that the German power based on steel can never again overwhelm France. One can appreciate the French fear, but this arrangement is also economic madness. It requires far more coal than iron ore to make a ton of steel; to take the coal to the ore makes the steel far more expensive. The iron ore of the Mesabi range in northern Minnesota is shipped to Pittsburgh because of Pennsylvania coal; no one would dream of building a steel plant at the Mesabi and shipping coal there.

The French fear can be quieted by other, better measures. The French have a much surer guarantee from America and Britain that Germany will not again be allowed to overrun France than they were able to obtain after World War I—when Wilson did give Clemenceau a pledge that the Senate refused to ratify. Not only are Americans and British far more aware of the threat, but the divided Germany of 1948 is far weaker than German in 1919. Trizonia has a slightly larger population than France but it grows less than half its own food. Until it is reunited with the agricultural east, it must depend on foreign sources for what it eats. This fact (1) curbs any aggressive tendency which Germans in Trizonia might have, and (2) brings home to them the vital necessity for true international co-operation. The present plan is to put the Ruhr's economy under the control of a permanent international board composed of America, Britain, France *and Germany* —plus three small neighbors who were 1940 victims of Germany, Belgium, Holland, and Luxemburg. This will not penalize the Ruhr but make it part of a healthily functioning western European economy instead of what it now is, a stagnating region of confusion and misery.

The six powers, with no German representatives present, debated for most of the spring of 1948 in London's mausoleum-like India House. They agreed to:

(1) Create a federal German government for the three western zones, which the Soviet zone could join "as soon as circumstances permit." A German constituent assembly would meet in September to draw up a constitution for the government, which would take office early in 1949. The regime would not be strongly centralized, but loosely federalized, to prevent it from becoming too strong.

(2) Establish the seven-power board for the Ruhr, which would allocate the region's coal, coke and steel so as to fulfill Trizonia's

role in ECA. America, Britain, France, the Benelux group and Germany would have three votes each on the board.

(3) Provide for military occupation of Trizonia until "the peace of Europe is secured." As an extra guarantee for the French, "Germany must not again be permitted to become an aggressive power." Also, "key areas" like the Rhineland and Ruhr will have military occupation even after the full-scale occupation of Trizonia ends. There will be a "system of inspection" to keep the Germans disarmed.

The Germans in Trizonia complained bitterly about the London agreement. The Socialists called it "a one-sided foreign decision which lies beyond any German responsibility." Germans of all parties declared that only Germans could run the Ruhr efficiently enough to make it "contribute properly to European recovery" and that the regime planned was not nearly strong enough— which showed the renaissance of German nationalism. General Lucius D. Clay, the American military governor, said soothingly, "Our desire is to have a government responsible for German affairs as soon as possible," and emphasized the amount of responsibility Germans would have in planning the new state. General Sir Brian Robertson, the British military governor, announced that Britons had now accepted the Germans as "Christian and civilized people," to be treated accordingly. The Allies and Germans alike agreed that the western zones of Germany were part of Western Europe and ECA.

Trizonia's stake in western European co-operation is more food and raw materials, and a bigger slice of its own production (as it increases output) to use for its recovery. Secretary George Marshall has defined American policy: "The economic restoration of Germany, the heart of Europe's economic life, is essential to European recovery. German restoration must proceed simultaneously with that of the rest of Europe."

Unfortunately these are words, not yet deeds. While most of western Europe is back to its prewar industrial production (though not to its prewar strength since so much still needs to be renovated and rebuilt), Trizonia's output is only two-fifths of 1938. Caught between American free enterprise and British socialism, the western German economy is at dead center. Thus far its labor has had no incentive to work and business has had none to produce.

Many Trizonians favor Western Union, and nearly all of them believe that Germany must be allowed to play its part in whatever plan is finally worked out to restore Europe and halt the Communist advance. "If you want to build the best possible orchestra," says a Frankfort doctor named Lutz Walz, "you've just got to include the German fiddle." In the long run, security and prosperity for all Europe will have to be based on some form of European federation. Even in the framework of a European customs union, if no more can be achieved at first, the Ruhr and other Trizonian resources could be a major factor in a sound economic co-operation that would do more than a dozen high-minded resolutions to hasten Europe's integration.

The mention of Germany in connection with such a broad, constructive program simply highlights the failure of the Big Four there to date. The Soviet zone is being bled for the reparations that Molotov could not get at the Council of Foreign Ministers. The western zones have not even reached the low output levels to which the moribund Allied Control Council agreed. Hunger, inflation so bad that mere money has lost its power to spur effort, lack of clothes and transport and housing, failure to re-educate and de-Nazify, when combined with French revenge, American impatience, British casualness and Russian calculation, has made Germany, as one American there told me, "a combination of insoluble problems inextricably intertwined."

2

The elegant oak-paneled office had paintings and a Persian rug. I congratulated the high German official of the Soviet zone on the handsomest surroundings I had seen in ruined Dresden.

"Yes," he said. "This was a Luftwaffe headquarters before we took it over for the Saxon state administration. Goering looked well after his own."

Germans have always looked after their own, with little regard for others. To travel round postwar Germany is to realize how strongly, even fiercely, that trait is re-emerging. Very few Germans have any real remorse for 1939-45.

"That was war," they say, and wave their hand to dismiss even the atrocities. They flock to Berchtesgaden by the thousand for pilgrimage climbs over Hitler's favorite mountain. You meet them even on the slopes—marked *verboten* to Germans—around his chalet and eagle's nest eyrie. They turn stony faces to foreigners on the mountain as though the latter's mere presence on the holy soil was sacrilege.

Elsewhere, the German attitude toward outsiders is a curious combination of bitterness and complacency. German after German told me solemnly that Hitler's only mistake lay in trying to do the right things the wrong way. They actually believe that nobody ever suffered as they have suffered. They want to tell their troubles and, like a girl I met in Munich, are not interested in hearing the troubles of others. This girl had lamented at length over Munich's overcrowding.

"What are the most crowded living conditions you know here?" I asked.

"Some people have to live four and five in a room," she replied.

"In Stalingrad and Warsaw, cities which the Germans destroyed, I often saw eight and ten people living in a single small room."

"*Ach,*" she said, with an impatient toss of her head. "Slavs will tell you any lie that suits them."

The self-pitying complaints that Germans stilled under Hitler, for fear of the Gestapo, are again pouring forth in a flood of frankness such as they have not enjoyed since the Weimar Republic. Even in the Russian zone, Germans of all political creeds say they have more freedom of speech—and complaint—than they had in Nazi times. They do not hesitate to blame the Allies for all their present troubles.

The Dresden official, a member of the Communist-controlled SED which administers the zone under careful Soviet supervision, himself swung into a criticism of his masters so sharp as to be quite inconceivable in Russia itself.

"We must refer the smallest things to the Russians for approval," he said. "We have no powers of control and very few of supervision, even over local supplies. The Russians take what they want. So we have little food, less consumer goods, and almost no coal or wood. Perhaps you will say Germans are bad and need punishment. But you cannot say Germans are lazy. Our economy would not run down if we were given half a chance. Take away the barriers between the four zones, let us have our own materials and food, and we will have the means to work and the strength to work with. Soon there would be more for everybody, the Russians and the Germans too. There would also be more for the other nations to whom Germany must pay reparations. Before long you Americans could stop sending us food and materials, which cost you much money."

"What keeps the four zones from unity?"

"The Russians say it is America and Britain," he answered. "We do not see your newspapers, but we can listen to your radio —and the BBC says it is Russia. For us here in Saxony, it is hard to know. One thing we do know; we badly need coal and iron from the Ruhr."

"Did Saxony get its coal and iron from the Ruhr before the war?"

"No," he said, "we got it from Silesia, which Poland now has and wants to keep."

"Was it America and Britain that turned Silesia over to Poland and so cut Saxony off from its source of supply?"

"Russia and Poland did it," he admitted. "But at Potsdam, America and Britain agreed to it. Germany cannot survive without at least part of Silesia."

"America and Britain agreed to it as a temporary administrative measure," I reminded him. "It was part of the price they paid at Potsdam for what they thought was to be economic unity for the rest of Germany. Then they did not even get that. America has repeatedly proposed revising the boundary."

"We know that the trouble over returning any of Silesia to Germany comes from Poland backed by Russia," he said unhappily. "We all hope that America will hold firm and not yield to Russia there."

"Then I hope you also understand why America must also hold firm on matters like the Ruhr until there is economic unity," I said. "If the West makes all the concessions, that will not bring peace."

"The Russians say America will not agree to a peace settlement because America wants to control Germany itself," he answered.

"Do you believe that?"

"Goebbels," he said, "often found it useful to accuse other nations, as loudly as possible, of wanting what the Nazis wanted themselves. Under Hitler and Goebbels, thinking Germans learned *swischen den zeilen lesen*, to read between the lines."

On V-E Day the Allies seemed almost united. The Germans, humbly incoherent, thought the conquerors would impose their will and that this would be a German democracy. The vanquished were ready to submit. In each zone, however, the occupying power tried to set up a German administration in its own image. None of them succeeded, because that is a slow process at best and they were all in too much of a hurry. They were further handicapped because most Germans with administrative experience had to be de-Nazified.

Even the happy-go-luckiest people in the world would have become disgusted and contemptuous at the administrative muddle and chaos in which the Allies soon landed. The Germans, far from being happy-go-lucky, are the most methodical and efficient people on earth. In no country could it be more important for occupying powers to be businesslike and thorough. Nowhere did they make such a mess of things. The Dresden official had a point. So did the anti-Nazi German who complained to me: "The Nazis were horrible, but at least you knew where you stood when they ran Germany. If you needed any sort of permit, you could get a yes or no from the Nazis very quickly. Now it seems you can get no answer at all—ever."

The Big Four's administrative mistakes became that much worse when, after they began to deadlock in the Control Council, their next move was to attack each other in front of the defeated. Once the Germans saw Allied disagreements and shortcomings, they regained their own peculiar arrogance. When the British used twenty-five tons of TNT to blow up a big concrete antiaircraft emplacement in Berlin—and it was only chipped—Germans who were watching cheered wildly. That night, under cover of darkness, they painted the inscription "Made in Germany" on the structure.

Germans chuckle over the story of a Russian who asked: "Why must you Germans always talk about food? Why not talk about music and culture, as we do?" A German answered: "I suppose everybody talks about what he hasn't got."

Germans show an attitude of tolerant contempt toward Americans who, they say, "care more about being liked than being respected."

From Aachen to the Erz Gebirge, Germans are now growing ever more definitely German in their concerns. Despite all difficulties and zonal barriers, Germans talk and think remarkably alike. Throughout Germany, they share somewhat similar conditions.

They have a common shortage of food and fuel. The daily ration hovers around 1,600 calories in Anglo-American Bizonia, and is even lower in the once food-surplus Soviet zone. Nobody is starving as such, but there is much malnutrition. Disease then takes a high toll among the enfeebled. The Soviet occupation forces live off the land and ship food to Russia; the Americans and British have spent over $2 billion feeding western Germans enough to keep alive.

They have a common shortage of goods. In all zones, most window displays of clothing, leather goods, etc. have the telltale trademark of postwar German economy. This is a little sign that reads: "We make high quality articles from our own models with your materials." Few Germans have the materials.

In some senses, Germans are discouraged and drifting. Nearly all of them dread the thought of another war, though a few are stupid enough to hope Germany can benefit by it. But in many senses, Germans are again pulling purposefully in tandem. They are not running Germany, though a lot of the lesser administration is already in their hands. But the occupying forces feel the growing power naturally wielded by sixty-six million stubborn, resilient people set in the heart of Europe. This power will keep on growing with the slow, steady force of a rising tide. Britain's financial crisis cut the British control staff from sixteen thousand to five thousand, which has given the Germans more responsibility in key areas including the Ruhr. Even Russia has withdrawn one hundred thousand dependents of the Soviet occupation force. Their continued exposure to a country so materially advanced even in defeat was undermining Russian morale.

Germans are quite willing to use either East or West to their own advantage. "If America has true culture, it will fight Russia and rid the world of Communism," a winegrower in the French zone told me. "We will help and then you in turn can help rid us of these French swine who take all my hock at their absurdly low fixed prices. In the good old days I got a much better price."

3

Four-sectored Berlin has no real life of its own. Its center is bomb shattered and the Allied headquarters are located in outlying parts miles from each other. The city's only unity is a frantic buzzing of intelligence officers, informers, planners, propagandists, and black marketeers. Most Americans lead a life much like Iowa's with bingo, baseball, dog shows, jukeboxes and a Skyrider Ballroom to keep them from wondering too hard whether and how the Russians will try to push them out. Most Germans live in patched-up ruins, get their fuel by pushing a baby carriage to a park on the outskirts and chopping branches from a fallen tree, and wonder about the next day's food. Thousands of anti-Communist Germans have disappeared, many of them traced to Soviet secret-police headquarters and no farther. The German reaction to such Russian pressure was shown in the October 1946 Berlin elections, when the Social Democrats got 48.8 percent of the votes cast, the Christian Democrats 22.2 percent, and the Russian-backed SED only 19.7 percent.

Berlin is a huge pile of rubble where the four occupying powers squabble. Russia wants all Berlin as its first step toward winning all Germany—and because it fears Trizonia will succeed, making the three western sectors of the city a focus of infection for the whole Soviet zone. But the heart of the German problem is not in Berlin; one must go to the four zones to get at it.

Outside Berlin, each zone is clearly German but has taken its tone from its occupying power. Most interesting is the Soviet zone, which on a smaller and less severe scale reminded me of Russia. Despite the most consciously thorough indoctrination methods of any power in Germany, the Soviet authorities have had little success in converting their zone to Marxism.

The Russians have had more success in introducing Soviet living standards. A Meissen baker said bitterly when I asked what he thought of Germany's future: "If this goes on, we'll have Russian conditions, won't we? They are lowering us to the Russian level. They want workers here to have only 150 marks a month and to own just one suit of clothes, as in Russia. Germans are used to better than that." A Meissen housewife asked about her city's famous china put it still more succinctly: "You can't buy any."

An SED trade-union official in the textile town of Oschatz told me: "Our mills started up again last fall with raw wool from Russia. All the cloth ever since has been sent back to Russia." In Leipzig, still Germany's greatest book-manufacturing city, a printer said that "at least half" the printing was now in Russian for export to Russia.

The Russians are stripping their zone of everything, from jet planes to bathtubs. Most industries must send 90 to 100 percent of their output to Russia. On V-E Day the zone had eleven thousand miles of railroad line. Now it has but 4,300 miles, which almost cripples its transport. Only one of the twenty-six tracks that led into Leipzig's main railway station is still there. I myself saw four trainloads of railroad tracks and ties (with the tie plates still attached), and three trainloads of used automobiles, moving eastward to Russia. Since the zone's entire output of synthetic rubber is requisitioned, most of the automobiles and trucks that remain are stalled for lack of tires.

The Russians also skimmed the cream of Dresden's world-famed art collection: 1,695 paintings that included Raphael's Sistine Madonna, seventeen Rembrandts, twenty-four Van Dycks, seventeen Rubenses and seven Poussins, as well as paintings by Velasquez, Vermeer, Correggio, Van Eyck, Holbein, Monet, Manet, Renoir, Degas, and Van Gogh. "Perhaps the paintings will bring the Russians culture," said one sardonic Dresdener. "God knows they need it. They wash in water closets."

Another Soviet export is skilled German labor for Russian factories. Unskilled laborers are forcibly sent to the Saxon and Czech uranium mines that Russia is frantically exploiting. Both to avoid such drafts and for fear of the Russians, many Germans flee to the western zones. The month of August 1947 alone brought one hundred thousand such refugees.

Prewar, the Soviet zone was always a food-surplus area, which the three western zones were not. But steady Russian drains on

German agricultural output mean that, far from having a surplus, Germans there get even less to eat than in the hungry west. The wife of a Dresden factory worker, who herself works to get a bit more food for their two small children, told me that her whole family was "hungry all the time." Near Bitterfeld, townsfolk were using their Sunday off to glean the few stray wheat stalks left in the stubble of a wheat field. They grind the grain by hand and make a sort of bread. Some, unable to wait, were eagerly breaking the stalk heads open and eating as they gleaned. It left a grayish paste of kernel shell around their lips.

The one German I met in the Soviet zone who ate his fill was a farmer with thirty acres and two horses. "My family has enough to eat," he said. "But smaller farmers and villagers do not—and I cannot see how city folk live."

In the spring of 1947 grain collections from farmers in the American zone were only 32 percent of quota. The enforcement machinery was quite inadequate, and the farmers naturally preferred to sell on the black market. The Russians, who know how to exact food from Soviet collective farms, have used their time-tried techniques much more successfully. At Schlepkow, for instance, they gave a farm to German refugee Fritz Schmidt from East Prussia, had him join the SED, and then made him their local watchdog. He kept a card index on his neighbors for the Russians. When farmers lagged in their deliveries, he called a Soviet control officer who released some with warnings and took others to jail. As a German but a newcomer to the region, and as a recipient of land the Russians could always take back again, Schmidt was an ideal Soviet agent. The pressure of fear on the farmers he watched was enough to be effective without being enough to cause violent reaction.

At the village of Mildensee near Dessau a lad of sixteen, so small that he looked only ten, told me: "The Russians take 80 percent of our food." His father interrupted: "No, no, they take only half or a little more—that is, a ton and a half from each hectare [2.47 acres] of grain. They have all the grain brought to a central place, so they can measure it and be sure they get their share."

Another Mildensee farmer said: "If a cow dies, I still have to deliver her quota of milk. We are fined if we do not. My neighbor had a poor harvest last year and drought this season. He did not have feed or pasture enough for his cows. So he killed one. The Russians fined him six thousand marks. Four peasants in this village have been fined—but none have yet been put in jail. If you lack money to pay the fine, then you must pay in animals. In villages near here some peasants last year were jailed for up to six months for not meeting their grain delivery quotas in full. But we in Mildensee, luckily, were able to meet our quotas. So they gave us bigger quotas this year."

In the Soviet zone, unlike the three to the west, a German cannot take even a ten-mile train ride without a permit. The permission is not easy to get. City dwellers in western Germany regularly take trains out to the country to barter for food with anything they may have, from spare clothes to their wedding ring. But the police in the Soviet zone, if they find you leaving a train with food, take it away from you. In the Dresden railroad station I saw a notice signed by Saxony's minister of Internal Affairs, Dr. Fischer, and the minister for Food and Trade, Dr. Knabe, warning travelers that "farm produce and barter products you have collected or carry with you will be confiscated."

In Leipzig I met a man who discussed this ruling with the grim sadness I also heard from other Germans:

"I am the only person in my family young and strong enough to buy vegetables in the country, so I try to go out once a week. I take a train about twenty-five miles in different directions, and then walk several miles into the country. You need a special permit from the government to take even the shortest trip, so every time I must think up a reason. Often they do not believe my reason, and refuse me the permit. Everyone else has the same troubles. But we keep trying, for we need vegetables so badly. Very often, even when we succeed in making a trip and finding some vegetables to buy, the police take them away as we return. Most people lose their package at least half the time. I have been a little luckier than that; you have to keep your ears open and try to hear at what station the police are confiscating that day, and then get off at the station before. Often that means a long walk—but I still have my vegetables. It is always very nerve-racking. The government says it does this to stop the black market. But they do not try to stop the real black market. People like me bring back only what they can carry, what their families need for eating."

Nothing is more characteristic of postwar Germany than the little plantings of tobacco that run to the tens of thousands. Amateurs grow it everywhere, even in bombed-out shells of buildings. In Nuremberg, a German lawyer told me he spent his spare moments cultivating a small garden among the ruins. I asked if it had tobacco. "But naturally," he said. "Not very good tobacco, but at least much better than the weeds I must otherwise use as substitute." Germans cure the tobacco themselves, chop it up, and make cigarettes or a pipe mixture from it. The craving for tobacco is still tremendous in the land of the meerschaum, and the shortage as great as at any time since the war. A package of American cigarettes cost 110 marks in Berlin, half a workman's monthly wages.

No one, of course, lives simply on his wages. Everybody barters, scavenges, and does little deals on the side. A standard German joke is for one person to ask another, "How's your job nowadays?"

"Job?" says the second. "Don't be silly. I can't be bothered with a job. I have a family to support."

4

The American zone has far fewer Americans than the Soviet zone has Russians. Most of the Americans, though not the most important ones, are downy-cheeked GIs in their late teens. They have no real notion of why they are there. At Passau, in Bavaria, one of their officers told me: "We aren't making any impression on the Germans that I can see. There are only three hundred Americans in this whole area of some seven hundred thousand Germans. Our number is being further cut. Very few of us are interested in Germany, and still fewer know the language. So the Germans pretty much run things themselves. De-Nazification here is almost a farce. The Germans handle it; fines are the only penalty they ever hand out. Paying a fine doesn't exactly re-educate a Nazi. So far as I've been able to find out, this area has no program whatever for German re-education or democratization."

The Americans have the poorest educational program of the

four zones. Less than a third of one percent of our German occupation budget is spent on education. The Russians have printed twelve new textbooks per child in their zone, the French seven, and the British five. We Americans have printed only two textbooks per child. Communist books, periodicals, and literature of all sorts are printed in huge quantities in the Soviet zone and sold at a low price in all four zones. America allots so little paper in Germany for democratic books and magazines that only a few thousand copies of any one book or periodical can be printed for sale among sixty-six million people. Nazi restrictions kept Germans from access to democratic literature printed in other countries; our mail and currency restrictions now produce the same result.

A top American official in Germany was fairly hopeful: "Economically we have made little progress, but at least in our zone we have created a sense of freedom in a people unaccustomed to it. There is no fear of arbitrary police action. This is not true in the Soviet zone." An official nearly as important was more pessimistic: "I've been working on policy matters here since July 1945, and I still don't know what American policy on Germany is."

A British observer was still sharper: "Germans in the American zone now understand that, by and large, their first and only duty is to cause no trouble, feed themselves without a riot, and get on with the business of living any way they can. The other term for that is, I suppose, 'the American way of life.'"

American economic policy on Germany, though more specific than the platitudes of its political policy, has suffered from a basic contradiction. In the American zone, Germans have been given no real opportunity for the free enterprise which is the essence of the American system. We are not showing the Germans what the American-type economy is like, or removing barriers so they could learn its advantages for themselves. We have largely kept the old Nazi totalitarian methods of economic controls and checkups.

The American zone has central economic planning—and we do not even administer it as well as the Nazis did. (Whatever else the Nazis were, they were usually efficient.) Our authorities drew up a zonal plan for allocation, supply, and production. Then they allowed so many exceptions that scores of individual, unrelated factories make products not called for in the original plan, using a lot of hard-to-get, expensive raw materials. This leaves little foreign exchange to buy the imports which the central plan called for. The central plan has now largely collapsed.

The British zone is in some ways as British as Weston super Mare. Approaching the medieval city gate of Lübeck, one can scarcely see the gate for the sign on it: TO THE SQUASH COURTS. The Atlantic Hotel in Hamburg serves a more British—and much more ample—meal than you can get in London. The British aimed at a sort of liberal social democracy in their zone, and have not attained it.

Their lesser achievements, and their willingness to draw on their own slim dollar reserves as long as they could to help finance Germany, have been overshadowed by their great failure: to bring Ruhr production anywhere near the prewar peak. Besides the failure in coal, steel production is less than 20 percent of the 1938 output of nineteen million tons. The shortage of these two has resulted in one of the world's most vicious circles. You cannot mine coal without steel and you cannot make steel without coal, you cannot do either without adequate food, and you cannot expand other industry without all three.

The French zone is the smallest and worst-run of the four. The French have half-wrecked the zone's economy and engendered a hatred among its 5,500,000 inhabitants that will last a long time. "The French have cut more wood in two years than the Germans cut in fifty," said a German forester. A businessman in Coblentz told me: "The French had a wonderful opportunity here. We had had our noses full of Hitler. They wanted the Rhineland, and we wanted something different from what we had. They could have won us. But their tactics have lost us completely. Their military government is like Hitler. One does not expect full justice from an occupation force, but one would think the French could at least obey their own rules. They don't. We are at the mercy of any local French commandant, and have no means of appeal."

5

It is clear that none of the four occupying powers has succeeded in convincing the Germans that its program is entirely right. The Americans, British, and French have failed in their various ways.

But Trizonia can still be salvaged. If not just food but a large stock of raw materials is sent there, so that both work and rewards for work will be available to its great number of skilled Germans, the atomization of German society can be stopped, reconstruction can be enormously encouraged, and Trizonia can both aid and be aided by the rest of western Europe. A top American in Germany even brought in the balance of power. "Much of the margin between a weak economy and a strong economy in Western Europe," he declared, "lies in the potential of western Germany. If Western Europe is to become a group of nations strong enough to balance politically and economically the strength of Russia and its satellites, western Germany must be a part of the group— giving freely of its resources and receiving freely in return."

Military occupation must continue until: (1) a real accord is reached with the Russians and (2) the Germans have shown the world that they can be as friendly and peaceful as the world already knows they are able and hard working. There are not enough American forces in Germany to stop the Red Army very long if it pushes west, but General Lucius D. Clay, the American military governor, is content with a "thin screen of American troops," which is enough to warn the Russians that invasion means war. Just as one of the navy's top combat commanders, Vice Admiral Forrest Sherman, commands the American warships in the Mediterranean, so Lieutenant General Curtis E. Le-May the air force's best long-range-bombing strategist, commands our small but skilled air unit in Germany. As long as we keep commanders of the caliber of Clay, Sherman, and LeMay in Europe, the Kremlin knows that we will fight there if we must.

Though keeping a sharp eye on the development of German national spirit, the Allied military government must give the Germans a freer hand than it has yet done. Unreasonable restrictions only encourage nationalistic resurgence. For instance, it is ridiculous that Germans are forbidden North Sea fishing boats with which they could bring in seafood to increase the nation's scanty diet. German officials should be given more responsibility in running German affairs. We must certainly cut the maze of red tape with which we have swathed German trade and industry.

It is silly for Americans to hope that Germans can become good practicing democrats in less than a full human generation—if that oon. Germans are all too apt to say, as several did to me, "Indeed, we need democracy. Above all, we need a strong leader to turn us into a democracy." This political problem, coupled with the problem of physical reconstruction, poses a gigantic task for us in Germany. We cannot be impatient or try to ignore the mess. We must make up our minds that the job will take a long, long time to do—but must be done. The best non-Nazi spirits perished in the concentration camps. Those who survived are mostly mediocre. We must not expect any very shining German political initiative overnight, or even in our lifetime. A whole new German generation must learn a whole new way of life.

Germany's present politicians are second rate. Probably the best of them is Kurt Schumacher, head of the Socialists, who was a top sergeant in World War I, where he lost his right arm. Twelve years in a Hitler concentration camp wrecked his health. He has the sick eyes of a sick man; they dominate a taut, bony, lined and eloquently mobile face. He is a fiery German nationalist; his program has been described as "not National Socialism but rather a sort of socialist nationalism."

Wilhelm Pieck, Germany's leading Communist, is an aging (born 1876), opportunistic party wheelhorse who fled to Moscow when Hitler seized power. He returned with the Red Army. Now he is co-chairman of the Socialist Unity Party (SED), which the Russians organized by forcing the Socialists in their zone to merge with the Communists. The other co-chairman is an ex-Socialist stooge, Otto Grotewohl. Pieck has welcomed thousands of Nazi small fry into his party: "We call on all the little members of the former Nazi party, who committed no crimes, to join us." He proclaims that "German youth is free of all political guilt." Copying Hitler, who made huge busts of himself available to all patriotic Germans at low prices, Pieck has allowed five mass-produced busts of himself to be placed on sale—from a 530-mark model in gilded bronze to a terra cotta "People's Model" at eighteen marks.

The best-known Christian Democrat leader is bald, incisive Jakob Kaiser, who headed that party in the Soviet zone for two and a half years before the Russians ousted him in December 1947. Kaiser is an old-line union leader and a man of real personal courage. He helped stage the July 1944 plot on Hitler's life. But he is not a very effective politician or administrator. And the Christian

Democrats have probably enrolled more ex-Nazis than the Communists themselves. Even in conservative Bavaria they have slumped from 35.1 percent of the municipal vote in 1946 to 18.5 percent in 1948.

In their way, the Russians have failed even worse than the Americans in Germany. They have extracted a lot of reparations, but they have injected relatively little Communism. They do not even have a complete grip on their chosen instrument, the SED— and at best it is not a very effective instrument. Almost certainly, there are fewer convinced Communists in all of Germany than there are in either Italy or France.

Chaos and then Communism are almost sure to come if Trizonia continues to stagnate as at present. But if western Germany becomes a working partner in the Economic Co-operation Administration, we will all benefit thereby. If this help-yourself help does bring German recovery, the not-too-pressing threat of German Communism will subside and Germans will eventually have a fair chance to choose, as sooner or later every people must, their own form of government.

By education and good example (though never by mere preaching at them), the German people may eventually be led to become as politically beneficial to the world as they have been harmful. They have made great contributions, from string quartets to the development of new industrial processes.

Perhaps the havoc Germany has wrought in the last two wars (not unassisted by the woeful policies of many other nations, including America) far outweighs all the contributions that Germans have made to world science and culture. To tour Europe, from Stalingrad to Coventry, makes one think so. But back home one thinks again of the Americans, from Carl Schurz to Albert Einstein, who came to us from Germany, and of the contributions which those of German stock have made to our nation's progress. The German people are worth saving. No effort we make to save them would be too great. Besides these positive reasons, we have a terrifying negative reason, namely, the prospect of what would face the world if German efficiency, organizing genius, inventiveness, tenacity and fanaticism were combined with the might, still so vastly latent, of Russia and Russian Communism's technique and ideology.

It should encourage us in our struggle that many Germans in all four zones are trying to steer their country into peaceful, constructive paths. I recall an earnest, cheerful intellectual I met in the Soviet zone. She wore a neat white, tweedlike suit she had made for herself from flour sacks.

"Germans must work," she said. "That is their only hope of salvation. Those who work and fight for life, who struggle to rebuild, will come through. Those Germans who now relax are lost. Nowadays it is all a horrible struggle for life. You never dare stop to think 'I am tired' or you might not go on.

"It is now very hard for Germans to say or judge what is right or wrong. We have come through so many political and economic changes that we can hardly decide that yet. But there should be a standard of right and wrong, even above nations. To be moderate in everything and to respect the political opinion of everybody and to see that everyone is protected in his rights. A middle way must somehow be found."

"Do you think any other Germans share your desire for moderation and some middle way?"

With quiet fervency, she replied: "I am sure that very many Germans feel as I do on this."

6

Austria was a part of the Nazi empire from Hitler's seizure of it in March 1938 until its liberation in the spring of 1945. The first specific postwar aim on which the Big Three agreed (at the initial meeting of the Foreign Ministers at Moscow in October 1943) was that Austria should be "free and independent with political and economic security." This pledge is one more memorial to the breakdown of big-power co-operation.

The Austrian peace treaty has been kicked around even longer and harder than the German one—and is a little nearer the goal post. In fact, if the other three powers would bow to Russia's insistence that the Austrian province of Carinthia (less than 5 percent Yugoslav) be awarded to Yugoslavia, and would agree to the Soviet definition of German property in Austria, under which Russia takes title to everything the Nazis stole from Austria after they grabbed their little neighbor, the treaty could be quickly signed. The Kremlin would then control nearly all the Austrian economy. Political domination would soon follow, so the other three powers refuse. At the Potsdam Conference, Russia demanded $250 million in reparations from Austria, which America and Britain refused. The Russians have since taken at least $225 million in goods and equipment from their zone, and in March 1948, just before the meeting of the Big Four deputy foreign ministers on the Austrian peace treaty broke down in London, demanded $175 million in cash from Austria within two years, two-thirds of Austria's oil production for fifty years, and control of all Austrian shipping on the Danube.

Since the Czech coup, Austrians have been in no hurry for their treaty. Once it is signed and the occupation troops withdraw, they fear that Russia would take them over as it took the Czechs. Their fears are not quieted by the continued Russian refusal, in the Allied Control Council at Vienna, to let Austrian police have anything but small arms. The Russians themselves have heavily armed thousands of picked Austrian "factory guards" for the plants they took as German assets. These well-drilled, uniformed "guards" could out-gun the Austrian police in any fight.

The Austrians have stood up to the Russians. Stating that his country's small police force had "only one rifle and ten rounds of ammunition for every three men," while the Communists had "twenty thousand armed 'factory guards,' " Foreign Minister Karl Gruber has repeatedly asked the Big Four to let Austria begin recruiting the army of 55,000 which its unfinished treaty specifies. The Russians always veto this request. Gruber has not hesitated to criticize Soviet occupation policies and to declare that "Russia is trying to strip Austria naked." Austria is poverty stricken, as shown by the tale of a Council of Foreign Ministers session on Austria. When the statesmen successively emerged from the conference chamber, the attendant called: "Mr. Bevin's Rolls-Royce," "Comrade Molotov's Zis," "General Marshall's Cadillac," "Herr Gruber's galoshes."

The Russians cordially detest Gruber. When he came to the Moscow Conference to present Austria's case, they assigned him a small, dark room up under the eaves of a second rate hotel, while his rival, Foreign Minister Edvard Kardelj of Yugoslavia (an ardent Communist), was given a luxurious suite at the best hotel.

Kardelj could have a box at the ballet whenever he desired; Gruber could not even get a third-balcony ticket, though kind-hearted Americans occasionally bought him a seat. The contrast in the between-the-acts promenade was striking. Gruber strolled about alone and ignored, while Kardelj strutted down from his box surrounded by a swarm of underlings and four secret-police guards.

Austria has more strategic importance than any of Russia's satellites; it is the keystone in the arch of middle Europe. It thrusts squarely into the Soviet sphere between satellites Yugoslavia and Czechoslovakia; its frontier on satellite Hungary is the main gateway to the Balkans. The Danube runs through Austria past Vienna and is a traditional boundary; East has met West there before. The Huns, Magyars, and Turks all tried to break into Europe through the country which Charlemagne called his Ostmark (eastern frontier) 1,200 years ago. Now legions from the East are again at the Danube, waging battle for a bridgehead to western Europe. A Communist Austria would run border to border with Italy's Communist-inclined north, close the Communist gap between Czechoslovakia and Yugoslavia, put a Communist state next to Switzerland, and completely outflank the American zone in Germany. From airports in the Austrian plain east of Vienna, bombers could reach any part of Europe.

As in the days of Charlemagne, Austria is the eastern frontier of the West in Europe. It is just as important to the West, politically and strategically, as it is to Russia. The Kremlin will never allow Austria to stay Western if it can help. Ernst Fischer, the lanky, long-haired Communist leader in Austria, says smilingly, "After all, the Danube flows east." However, the Communists have less popular support than in almost any European country; in the 1945 elections they won only 5 percent of the vote while the Catholic People's Party received almost exactly half and the Socialists 45 percent. The Communists were assigned only one minor cabinet post, Power and Electricity, and its holder resigned in November 1947 because the government would not follow the Soviet line.

The Communists have had little success in trying to infiltrate Austrian organizations. In May 1948 their one officer in the Austrian Federation of Trade Unions was defeated for re-election.

Not long before, at the Student Council elections in which 18,300 Austrian university students throughout the country participated, the Communists had polled only 575 votes.

White-bearded President Karl Renner, a Socialist elder statesman (born 1870) and black-mustached Chancellor (Premier) Leopold Figl, leader of the People's Party, represent the working partnership of Austria's two strongest forces—Socialism and Catholicism. Before Hitler the two forces were bitter opponents. The Socialists held power in the 20s; the Catholics replaced them in the 30s. During the party strife in 1934 the Socialists barricaded themselves in the fortresslike blocks of apartments for workers built during their regime and Catholic Chancellor Dollfuss shelled them into submission.

Nazi fire gutted the great Gothic Cathedral of St. Stephen, but its five-hundred-year-old spire still soars above the city in slender majesty and still moves the Viennese to write songs. The apartment houses got a worse battering than Dollfuss gave them but remain essentially intact. The co-operation of these two sturdy European forces, Catholicism and Socialism, gives Austria's 6,-500,000 weary people some hope that the Ostmark can once more be held against the East.

Austria and the Austrians, especially the Viennese, look even shabbier than when I first saw them in December 1935. They had plenty to be bleak about then, for the gay and gilded center of an empire had become the outsized capital of a bankrupt, rump republic which was still heading downhill. They have more to be bleak about now, when the baroque grandeur of their buildings is a backdrop for rubble and they have even lost their beloved opera house, where in a single week I once heard Toscanini, Weingartner and Furtwangler conduct. But the Austrians carry even disaster with an air. Vienna is rebuilding itself much faster than Berlin, the music both in Vienna and Salzburg sounds as good as ever, and the Austrians, though shabbier, seem less downcast than in 1935. Then they saw little left to live for; now, at least, they know what they do not want to live under. They are working hard to reconstruct their own kind of country. If Communism comes to Austria, it will have to come from the outside.

The Russians have shipped away much of Austria's industrial equipment. They take all but a dribble of the production of the

Zisterdorf oil fields (which is in their zone). They have a firm grip on Danube shipping. They live off the land—their zone grows most of the food in a nation that has never been agriculturally self-sufficient since World War I—and let the Austrians go hungry. The Americans, on the other hand, ship in through ECA two-thirds of the food which Austrians eat. America also pays its own occupation costs; the other three powers charge the Austrian government.

A major ECA project is the Austrian share of the Alpine hydro-electric scheme, which will provide a large part of Austria, Switzerland, northern Italy and southeastern France with electricity. Only if Austria is included, politically and economically, in some sort of Western Union, can it hope to be reasonably self-sufficient when ECA aid comes to an end. Clothes and all consumer goods are very scarce.

As I drove into Vienna, I stopped at an information post for directions to the press hostel. The man at the desk did not know, and asked an elderly, distinguished-looking Austrian sitting near him in a well-tailored ensemble topped with a Homburg hat fit for Anthony Eden. Then he introduced, "Herr Direktor Biewald of the Victoria Company, who is going that direction and will be glad to show you the way." When we got there, I thanked the Herr Direktor and asked whether I could not drive him to his destination, now that I knew how to locate the hostel. "No thank you," he said, climbing over his side of the jeep, "I can walk the rest." He stood expectantly on the sidewalk as I tried to think what to offer a prosperous-looking company director. He solved my dilemma.

"Please," he said, in his clipped, precise English, "could I have one American cigarette?" When I gave him two, he was almost overcome. Later I checked the cigarettes' value (they are a better gauge than currency to the economic health of most European countries) and found I had given him the Austrian equivalent of a day and a half's wages.

You see the Russians all round Vienna. They have taken over the old Imperial Palace and use part of it as a military hospital, part as an officers' club. One evening I strolled through the former palace gardens and discovered that its greenhouses had been turned into a bar-buffet where Soviet officers were solemnly playing American-made slot machines.

Earlier in the evening I had visited the Soviet-requisitioned Grand Hotel. The Red Army sentry let me in. The interior was a far cry from the gleaming marble decorum of the British headquarters in the Hotel Bristol a block away. The entrance hall and circular main lobby were dusty and unkempt, the furniture had seen much better days. The bar on one side and the restaurant at the far end were jammed with Russians and their wives. The small private dining room off the third side of the lobby, which had a dozen tables for four, was occupied only by two Soviet generals, each dining in solitary state several tables away from the other. Each, dazzling in white summer dress uniform that glittered with orders and medals, was being served by his own two waiters.

Most memorable of all were the occupants of the main lobby itself—six Russian kids, from a girl of twelve to a boy of seven. One boy wore nothing but bathing trunks. They were playing the most hilarious game of tag, all screaming at the top of their lungs as they chased wildly around the lobby. The oldest boy, about ten, was especially active in leap-frogging over chairs, jumping up on sofas, shoving tables between himself and his pursuers, caroming off colonels and their buxom wives who quite unconcernedly passed in and out of the restaurant. Their bare feet thudded merrily on the cool, dirt-streaked marble floor, while six scuffed little pairs of shoes stood primly in a row along one wall.

I had seen the less engaging side of the Soviet occupation as I motored through Austria to Vienna. I first drove 107 kilometers in the American zone, then 166 kilometers (104 miles) in the Russian zone, both drives through exactly the same sort of rolling, village-dotted countryside. Geese and chickens were so surprisingly numerous after I crossed from Germany to the American zone of Austria that I started a rural census. In the 107 kilometers I passed twenty-six tractors, 112 separate flocks of geese and so many flocks of chickens that I stopped counting. In the 166 kilometers of the Soviet zone before the outskirts of Vienna, I passed one tractor, not one goose and three individual chickens about twenty miles apart.

When I told these contrasting figures for the two zones to an official in Vienna, he smiled sadly. "Yes," he said, "Our eastern-zone tractors, like our eastern-zone watches, have gone yet farther east. Many of the geese are still here, but not where passing eyes can see them. You know, the Russians will pluck a goose—any goose at all."

PART IV

The Western Marches

⊙

Chapter 14: WESTERN UNION, FRANCE

THE areas covered by Western Union, western Europe, the Economic Co-operation Administration and what the Moscow radio calls "the Western bloc of aggressors," overlap but are not identical. The Soviet term is the biggest and vaguest; by it, the Moscow radio means practically the whole non-Communist world. The other three, which have a somewhat more real geographical existence, have their center somewhere around the Rhine. They are a twentieth century equivalent to the medieval marches or border districts which in various European countries were responsible for keeping on the alert against enemy forays.

Western Union still has only its five founding members: France, Britain and the Benelux countries (Belgium, the Netherlands, Luxemburg).

Western Europe has no formal organization or status, but its present definition also includes northern, southern, and a bit of eastern Europe; it extends from Norway, Sweden, and Denmark through Trizonia Germany to Italy, Greece, and Turkey.

The Economic Co-operation Administration has seventeen European clients: the twelve just listed plus Eire (Ireland), Iceland, Portugal, Switzerland, and Austria. Russia, its satellites, and Finland refused to accept invitations to the Marshall Plan conference that laid the groundwork for ECA. Franco Spain was not invited.

In discussing western Europe and any blocs or organizations based on it, two facts are all important. First, no grouping of its nations would ever be effective without American backing and aid. Second, no grouping of its nations would ever have started without Russian threats and aggression.

After World War II, for example, France refused even to consider a network of alliances in western Europe; it had a pact with Russia which De Gaulle had negotiated, and saw no need for anything else. After all, did not France's old friends and allies, Poland and Czechoslovakia, have similar friendship pacts with Russia?

Britain likewise opposed any western alliances; it had the twenty-year treaty with Russia which Churchill had negotiated, and surely that was enough. Besides, U.N. could settle eventual disputes.

America had avoided entangling alliances ever since the advice of George Washington, and simply wanted to pull out of Europe.

What happened? In less than three years, America had waded into European affairs up to its neck. France, Britain, and Benelux had formed the closest military alliance any of them had ever entered. Even economic and political union had come closer, in a year or two, by a generation or two.

Fear was Europe's catalyst—fear of Russia. U.N. had not worked out the way the West expected. Russia had used it to veto anything and everything it disliked. In U.N. and elsewhere, Russia had also thundered that a western European bloc would be a hostile act toward Russia and contrary to the high principles of U.N. Under the cover of these thunderings, Russia organized an eastern European bloc, riveted to itself, by methods that reached a terrifying peak in the Czech coup of February 1948.

The actual splitting of Europe into an east and west came in July 1947. Russia broke the continent in two. When America, belatedly realizing that UNRRA would not be enough to restore the war-ravaged continent, offered economic aid to *all Europe* through Secretary of State Marshall's speech at Harvard in June 1947, Foreign Minister Molotov went to Paris to consult with Foreign Ministers Bevin and Bidault. Then Russia, without even asking the terms, rejected the aid and forced every other nation it could to do likewise. Andrei Zhdanov, a leading member of Russia's Politburo, told the September 1947 meeting of Communist leaders from eight countries that organized the Cominform: "The Soviet Union will employ all its resources to prevent the success of the Marshall Plan"—i.e., Russia would try to ruin the seventeen European countries that had accepted American aid. In November 1947, Moscow ordered the Communists of France and Italy, its two strongest parties in the west, to disrupt these nations by strikes and riots before they could benefit from American efforts to promote their recovery.

Such Russian tactics stirred western Europe to a unity that would have seemed incredible in 1945 or 1946. But the rape of Rumania, Bulgaria, Hungary, Poland and Czechoslovakia, and the attempted rape of Finland, Germany, Austria, Greece, and Turkey, made it clear what Russia wanted and which nations stood next in its way. Defense was urgent, and these nations turned to the U.N. Charter which, far from having barred regional blocs as Russia asserted, specifically endorsed regional organizations such as the Pan-American Union. In January 1948, Ernest Bevin formally proposed a Western Union. France and the Benelux countries promptly agreed.

After the Czech coup the five nations hastily added a defense pact. Signing this pact, Belgian Premier Paul-Henri Spaak put his finger on what Europe really needed for recovery: "The best treaty in the world is worth only what its execution is worth. A diplomatic formula is not hard to find. A military agreement is not hard to make. But economic collaboration between people—that is the obstacle which must be surmounted."

2

It is difficult to realize how many obstacles there are to simple "economic collaboration between people." An American business executive I met on his return from France did manage to convey the obstacles. He said: "I was over there selling 20,000 tractors at $1,500 each. That's $30 million. France wants and needs them, but it hasn't the dollars. America needs bauxite for aluminum and France has fine bauxite. So we buy the bauxite, ship it back fairly cheap in ships that take American coal to France and would otherwise just return in ballast, import the bauxite into America in bond, make aluminum, then take the aluminum out and get back our bond, sell the aluminum to Argentina and Greece for dollars—and then at last have dollars to pay for the tractors! It's hard to make a straight sale in foreign trade these days. You have to use barter methods, and go round Robin Hood's barn."

The rest of the world has this tremendous dollar shortage because America exports so much more than it imports. Apart from loans and gifts, other countries can get the dollars to pay for these American exports only by giving gold, goods, or services in return. Between World Wars I and II, America took almost all the gold in the world in such payment, so that method is out. America has never bought enough abroad to close the gap. Nor are foreign services rendered to Americans, whether by an Italian gondolier taking a Nebraska couple around Venice or by a British ship carrying tin from Malaya to Manhattan, now enough to close the gap.

If there is ever to be an international economic balance, America will have to buy more goods and services abroad. But such a balance cannot even be imagined until the war-torn parts of the world, especially those in Europe, have had a chance to recover.

Europe's seventeen countries in ECA are, in normal times, a powerful economic group. In 1938 these seventeen produced more coal, steel, aluminum, electricity, potatoes, wheat and dairy products than America did—though they also had 110 million more people. Their over-all standard of living, if lower than America's, was far above the world average. Their chief deficit was in bread and feed grains for people and livestock—they imported, from outside Europe, forty million tons a year (compared to only six million tons from the eastern and southeastern parts of Europe now in the Soviet sphere). Exports of manufactured goods more than paid for their food imports—and with better co-ordination the seventeen could have had a much bigger production and much better living standards.

Since the war, the seventeen have ranged from near-starvation in Greece through belt-tightening in Britain to relative comfort in Belgium and Switzerland. Their food deficit is greater than ever and their industrial production is not enough for their own daily needs plus reconstruction—let alone for necessary import payments. ECA help, added to their own self-help and co-ordination, reduces their plight from the desperate to the very difficult.

From both the American and European viewpoint, the prime emphasis of ECA is economic. It has political and strategic overtones: to stop Communism's westward thrust and to strengthen non-Communist Europe. But ECA's indispensable objective is the economic recovery of Europe. If we Americans merely try to buy allies for a possible war with Russia, we may get the allies—weak ones—and will certainly get the war. If we want peace and a strong, healthy Europe, we must put economic recovery first. ECA's fundamental aim is quite simple. To the tune of $5.3 billion in its first year, and $18 billion through 1952, ECA is making dollars—and the manufactures, raw materials and food that can be bought with dollars in any country—available to seventeen nations which are very short of dollars. It is not a relief but a recovery program. It is meant to have steadily decreasing deficits over a period of several years.

During these years, the seventeen nations will be rebuilding their ruins, restoring their agricultural and industrial production, raising their skimpy standards of living, stabilizing their currencies, and gradually getting their foreign trade back to normal. When ECA succeeds, there will be no more need for ridiculously roundabout barter deals involving American tractors, French bauxite, and aluminum for Argentina. In a stable, co-ordinated seventeen-nation European economy, each country can produce, export, and import enough to attain a better standard of living than it had in 1938.

By 1951 the seventeen ECA nations hope to surpass their 1938 production of coal, steel, electric power and bread grains. Coal is scheduled to rise from 551.2 million tons in 1938 to 582 in 1951 (1947 production: 441); steel from 33.8 to 43.9 million tons (1947: 23.7); electricity from 121.4 to 236 billion kilowatt hours (1947: 170); bread grains from 35.5 to 36 million tons (1947: 30.2). Each country will also concentrate on upping the output of certain special products for mutual benefit. Thus Greece will try to increase its production of dried fruit, while Britain is to double its output of tractors and supply most of Europe.

Even if all this works out, it will not bring as high a standard of living as in 1938. For a long time, much of this production must go for reconstruction. Despite its war casualties, Europe has twelve million more bellies to feed and bodies to clothe than in 1938. Before the war, a third of Europe's imports were paid for by income from overseas investments and services—these have almost vanished, which means that when ECA ends Europe will have to pay for this third of its imports by additional exports, thus having less to consume at home.

As Spaak said, the hardest single obstacle that faces the seventeen is to get real economic co-operation. The practical difficulties can only gradually be overcome. The Benelux customs union, for example, took five years to negotiate. Belgium and little Luxemburg—999 square miles, 285,000 population, rocking along placidly under Grand Duchess Charlotte—have had an economic union since 1922. But the Dutch and Belgian economic union bristles with difficulties. A Belgian brewer moaned to me that the better Dutch beer would ruin him. Dutch glassmakers complain that the Belgian glass industry will put them out of business.

Actually, it will be years before glass, beer or anything moves freely from one country into the other. The first stage of Benelux, which went into effect on January 1, 1948 (having been haggled over since 1942), merely provides for the same customs duties in both countries. It does *not* allow Dutch and Belgian goods to pass freely through the two countries; a careful quota system has been established, to be lowered over several years. Not before 1953 do the three countries expect to have full economic union, with no internal customs barriers and with similar labor laws, social legislation, currency, and taxes. Even at this leisurely schedule, the Dutch state that the Benelux economic union can never be completed unless at least $300 million of ECA aid is earmarked for their purchases in Belgium, to bring them up to the more prosperous Belgian level.

When three small, closely linked neighbors have to advance this slowly toward full economic union, seventeen more widely differing states will find it still slower and harder. The will for economic unity is there and the eventual benefits are obvious. But the specific steps are very painful. It may be necessary for America to prod the recalcitrant by making ECA aid dependent on specific progress toward economic union. This could be done both by the leverage of stimulating each country's self-interest through a series of rewards and penalties, and by allotting some ECA funds for definite projects of an international nature, such as a European power grid.

France and Italy have had a joint committee studying customs union since September 1947 "in order to hasten the reconstruction of Europe." It has made some progress. Italy has a labor surplus and France needs labor, so they are arranging a labor migration. The two countries plan to mesh their economies into a more efficient machine by having one joint commission buy their essential imports and another find more markets for both nations' exports. Marseille and Genoa have long been bitter rivals, especially for the trade to and from landlocked Switzerland; a committee is now studying means to share the trade between the two ports. But the textile manufacturers of France and Italy have the same chill suspicion of customs union that American textile manufacturers show toward lower tariffs. French building unions are enraged at the thought of skilled but cheaper Italian labor undercutting them. Italy's Fiat auto plants fear the competition of French Renaults and Citroens.

In small but significant ways the seventeen ECA nations are making specific progress toward greater economic unity. Recently they agreed to a co-operative allocation of all their coke which, along with substituting other grades of American and German coal for coke wherever possible, promises an extra, vital 1,500,000 tons of European steel production in 1948. ECA has cut international traffic barriers. Busses and trucks can now move across European borders without the old welter of permits for each trip and necessity to halt, unload, and transship at many borders. Refrigerator cars have been pooled for free international movement, in an effort to make Italy "the California of Europe" for fruit exports. (Since the war, few countries in Europe have dared to send freight cars abroad; they are all so short of cars that strays are seldom returned.) Many ECA nations have helpful bilateral agreements; thus Italy has provided laborers for Belgian coal mines in return for guaranteed exports of Belgian coal to Italy.

All this is a start—but only a start. Unless America puts whatever legitimate pressure it can on the seventeen countries for economic union among themselves as one of their repayments for the billions of ECA aid, the year 1953 may see almost as many customs barriers in Europe as there are now. That would be a tragedy, most of all for Europe.

The heart of the world's heartland is still Western Europe. But unless its various politico-economic pieces can be fitted together, none of its people will thrive. The seventeen ECA nations must become a free-trade area—as America's forty-eight states are a free-trade area. In the House of Commons debate on Western Union, Premier Clement Attlee of Britain referred wistfully to the eventual possibility of such a European customs union on the analogy of American states. So did other speakers, reflecting the deep European envy of our vast internal area of free trade. To many thoughtful Europeans, this explains why we are so prosperous and they are so poor. But doing anything much about it seems beyond Europe's slaves of sovereignty. Attlee himself went on to mention "the immense complexities of those problems"—and merely suggested "continuing studies of them."

Only the speedy removal of barriers to Western European trade can make possible the development there of a modern, large-scale, continent-wide industrial system. ECA provides the best opportunity in history for such a development. The fact that European industry was severely shaken by the war and clearly needs to be reintegrated in a more sensible pattern, plus the fact that the lure of our ECA billions can temporarily outweigh the fears of Belgian brewers, French bricklayers and Italian textile manufacturers, makes Europe's otherwise almost impossible economic union at least a possibility. If we miss the opportunity of ECA, an opportunity limited to only a few years, the end of the program will inevitably see Europe's national governments reverting to their normal selfish ways—because their constituents will put them under the same shortsighted domestic pressure for "protection" as Congressmen are under from our shortsighted manufacturers, labor unions and farmers.

Except for the small, leisurely example of Benelux, no Western European nation has yet taken a single step away from economic sovereignty which it could not retrace the instant "normalcy" appears on the horizon. "Economic collaboration between people" has its obstacles! Yet, down in their hearts, many key Europeans long for us to prod their nations into a bold, farsighted attempt to build an all-European economy. From Oslo to Athens, a steadily growing number of men and women believe that during the years of ECA we Americans have our greatest—and probably our final —opportunity to bring Europeans into an economic union of

themselves so strong and beneficial that none of them will later
want to break it.

3

Lacking economic unity, Western political and military union
can be carried only so far. But common danger has forged a common will, and the urge for integration may be strong enough to
achieve all three. In the spate of meetings, speeches, and resolutions for unity during the first six months of 1948, the single most
significant resolution was one signed by 190 members of all parties
in the British House of Commons, "Mother of Parliaments."
Britain had long been the most cautious country of all when it
came to solid moves toward European union. Now even hyper-
cautious Premier Clement Attlee admitted, "Europe must federate
or perish."

The key parts of this widely supported resolution read:

Steps should now be taken ... to create in Western Europe a political
union strong enough to save European democracy and the values of
western civilization; and a trading area large enough, with the colonial
territories, to enable its component parts to achieve economic recovery
and stability

.   .   .

There should be an emergency policy designed to secure immediate
and effective cooperation between the countries of Western Europe;
and a long-term policy designed to bring into being a federation of
Europe.

The emergency policy should establish forthwith a Council of
Western Europe consisting of representatives of the governments of the
sixteen participating countries in the European Recovery Plan, and
Western Germany, to lay down the broad lines of common action. The
council should have power to set up permanent international staffs
to coordinate the social, economic and defense policies.

The first and most important test of the economic staff would be to
frame concrete proposals for the stabilization of the currencies of
Western Europe; for the development of trade; for the execution of
the European Recovery Plan; for a comprehensive production plan,
including agriculture and the heavy industries; and for colonial
development.

.   .   .

The long-term policy should be to create a democratic federation of Europe, with a constitution based on the principles of common citizenship, political freedom, and representative government; including a charter of human rights. Such a federation should have defined powers with respect to such matters as external affairs, defense, currency, customs; and the planning of production, trade, power and transport. To achieve this objective, the governments of the states of Western Europe should take steps to convene, as soon as practicable, a constituent assembly composed of representatives chosen by the parliaments of the participating states, to frame a constitution for such a federation.

How soon is "as soon as practicable?"

(1) In the economic field, it will be years before most of the seventeen are at all eager to entrust to a federation any very sweeping "defined powers" over "currency, customs; and the planning of production, trade, power and transport." Control of the purse strings is the key economic power in a family, federation, or empire—and the resolution nowhere gives the proposed federation any power to tax.

(2) In the military field, the nucleus is already there. Britain, France, and the Benelux trio have established a joint, permanent general staff and assigned as its first tasks "common defense problems" and "such questions as standardization of armaments and equipment of the naval, military and air forces, and the joint use of air and sea bases." Italy will soon join the defense group; Greece, Turkey, and the Scandinavian countries will doubtless enter in due course. America, which is already furnishing military equipment to France, Greece, and Turkey, was informally asked to provide all its members with arms and to guarantee the alliance (i.e., agree to fight if any of its members are attacked).

Washington answered that since American occupation troops in Germany stand between Russia and the West, any Soviet attack would automatically involve America without a guarantee. On armaments, Secretary Marshall announced that America might grant military lend-lease. American enactment of a peacetime draft spoke volumes to western Europe—and points east—on American readiness to fight if any part of the West were attacked.

(3) In the political field, at least a limited union will be organized. It may be a long, long time before it has any more power

over its member nations than America's almost powerless Confederation had over the thirteen original states between its ratification in 1781 and its replacement by the far stronger federal government in 1789.

No organization of western Europe can have real force unless America supports it, and in effect belongs to it. Russians, western Europeans and Americans all speak of the proposed Western Union only in terms of countries belonging to the ECA. That simply underlines the fact that America is its one essential member. When he proposed Western Union, British Foreign Secretary Bevin put this unmistakably. He said: "The most important development that brought all this to a head and caused the whole issue of Europe to be focused was the proposal by Mr. Marshall of the European Recovery Program."

The profound revolution in American foreign policy since 1941 is summed up in the Vandenberg resolution, approved by a unanimous bipartisan vote of the Senate Foreign Relations Committee in May 1948. Senator Vandenberg, an isolationist until Pearl Harbor and not a proclaimed internationalist until January 1945, now called for a revision of the U.N. veto power and meanwhile provided a method for America to extend collective security within the U.N. framework. He proposed the formation and development of a Western regional arrangement "based on self-help and mutual aid" under Article 51 of the U.N. Charter and pledged America's "association" with it. Vandenberg added that his resolution "applies to security the same formula we have applied to economic recovery."

America's 150-year avoidance of entangling alliances was over. What the Vandenberg resolution quietly but firmly stated was that America, for the first time in its peacetime history, has made itself a part of western Europe for mutual defense.

4

Several countries which are geographically part of western Europe are not handled in any detail in this book.

Switzerland is too happy to have much recent history. Its watches are as accurate, its scenery as superb, its people as worthily dull as ever.

Andorra, Liechtenstein, Monaco, and San Marino continue their miniature existence.

Spain still has its detestable dictator Franco, who managed to seize power because the Western nations (including America) failed to recognize the danger of Fascists as clearly during the 1936-39 Spanish civil war as they did later. In World War II he strengthened his grip on the Spanish people because the Western nations (including America) aided him in return for his neutrality and a few belated, reluctant gestures toward the Allied cause. Since the war, he has stayed in power because the Western nations (including America) have not yet been able to figure out what they could properly do about him.

Portugal still has its dim dictator Salazar, and still owns the Azores, those mid-Atlantic islands so useful in an air age. Salazar recently extended to 1953 the right for American military planes to land in the Azores.

Eire (Ireland) continues to live in a little world all its own, an agreeable world to which the austerity-stricken British escape whenever possible for eggs, steaks, and good cheer. Eire's firm conviction that the rest of creation scarcely matters is exemplified by the announcements at Shannon, the world's most international airport. These announcements are always given first in Gaelic, a language understood by few Irishmen and not one in ten thousand of Shannon's foreign clientele.

5

Three men personify the main forces of postwar France: Charles de Gaulle, Maurice Thorez and Robert Schuman.

General de Gaulle (born 1890) believes that only a strong, rightist government, headed by himself, can be firm and forceful enough to take the measures—all of them politically unpopular—needed to restore French stability and bring about the nation's recovery. He claims that his "Rally of the French People" (RPF) is not a party but a "movement." In any case, it is the biggest political force in France and rolled up six million votes in the October 1947 municipal elections while the Communists dropped from 5,500,000 to 4,700,000 votes. (They would get under 4,000,000 now.)

Until De Gaulle emerged from his voluntary retirement at the Communist threat, Thorez (born 1900) had successfully built the Communists into the country's largest party by following his own dictum: "France is a bourgeois country, and unless and until we control the police and the army, only bourgeois methods will succeed here." A month after being put in second place by the Gaullists in the municipal elections, the Communists got a worse body blow from Moscow itself. The Kremlin ordered them to stop ECA by paralyzing France with a general strike. For four weeks, the Communist-controlled labor unions dutifully tried to oblige —and damaged French Communism more than they did France.

Schuman (born 1886) is a mild bachelor from Lorraine who broke the Communists' strike by refusing their demands and mobilizing the force to back up his refusal. Supposedly a mere stopgap premier from the discredited Popular Republicans (the heaviest losers in the October elections), his handling of the strike was the first dramatic action of Schuman's life. It so bucked his self-confidence that he has steered a reasonably successful and constructive course as premier ever since, confounding the Gaullists and the Communists but encouraging the ordinary Frenchmen who would love to avoid both extremes.

Of the four western European countries that were major powers in 1939, the French now have the least difficult reconstruction problem. Theirs is infinitely easier than that of the Germans, and definitely easier than that of the British or Italians. France is the only one of the four nations that is normally almost self-sufficient in food, which in hungry Europe is something to cheer about. The disastrous 1947 drought (France's wheat harvest, for instance, was only 3,400,000 tons instead of the usual 7,000,000 tons), cut average rations to 2,400 calories a day until the 1948 harvest was gathered, but even then the French ate decidedly better than the Russians, Germans, or Italians and have every prospect of continuing to do so.

French industry was not so damaged as the German or Italian, and has nothing like the tremendous export burden which British industry must meet if Britons are even to eat. With the help of ECA (which has allotted it $1.13 billion for 1948) and its own resources and skills, France should recover sooner than Britain, Italy, or Germany possibly can.

The French task is still a heavy one. Repair of war damage, capital investment to modernize antiquated industries, maintenance to make up for a decade of neglect, extra manufacture to make up for a decade's similar neglect of consumer goods, the needs of the army (including an expensive war still raging in French Indo-China) and expanded social services, in sum, have put a load on the French that could not be carried without ECA help.

Prices are fourteen times higher than in 1938, while wages have risen only six times. For the cost of two eggs now, the French housewife could have bought a whole chicken in 1938; for a glass of wine, a whole bottle of Burgundy; for two boxes of shoe polish, a pair of shoes. Every further bit of inflation hits the hard-pressed workers and their families in the pit of the stomach. (The farmers, who sell plenty of food on the black market, are better off than they were in the 30s.) It was ostensibly for higher wages to meet increased prices that the Communists called their general strike. If Schuman and the other moderates in his coalition cabinet (of Popular Republicans, Socialists and Radicals, each party smaller than the Gaullists on the right and the Communists on the left) fail in their efforts to halt inflation, middle-of-the-road Parliamentary government may be finished in France. For the apparent alternative is a showdown between De Gaulle and Thorez.

De Gaulle does not call Thorez and his followers Communists. He contemptuously terms them "Separatists" and the "agents of a foreign power." The Communists, in turn, accuse De Gaulle of planning to be a dictator, and many other Frenchmen agree. But if they had to choose between one or the other, the two-thirds majority of non-Communist Frenchmen would practically all plump for De Gaulle instead of Thorez. They are like Henri Millet, a Parisian who operates an electric saw in a children's toy plant. He said: "I don't think De Gaulle wants to be a dictator—surely he could have seized power long ago if he had wanted." In fact, De Gaulle probably could have done so when he returned with the liberating armies in 1944, or even when he withdrew from the premiership in January 1946.

Having once been head of state and left it of his own accord, De Gaulle is certainly not a combination of bravado, bluster, persecution mania, and inferiority complex like Hitler or Mussolini.

As befits the son of a philosophy professor, his views are not too specific. He wants a head of state with powers at least as strong as an American president, fewer bureaucrats, a small but well-equipped army, and a larger industry. His economic views are even vaguer, but he has publicly backed one experiment now being practiced in 1,100 French factories, some with as many as a thousand workers, where wages above the basic rate are fixed every month by a joint management-worker board according to the factory's total turnover. It is something of a mixture between the bonus system and co-operatives, and has usually upped both production and wages where tried. The non-Communist labor unions are willing to try it widely, and since four-fifths of France's factories are relatively small, it might have a major success. De Gaulle's endorsement of it shows that any regime he headed, however conservative, might be enlivened by a few new social experiments.

In his remarkably prophetic military book, *The Army of The Future,* published in 1934 (it outlined the *blitzkrieg* tactics of massed tank formations supported by airplanes; the Nazis, unfortunately, were far more impressed by it than the French General Staff), De Gaulle wrote an unconsciously revealing sketch of himself:

"The depth, the singularity, the self-sufficiency of a man made for great deeds is not popular except at critical times. He is seldom liked, though anyone in contact with him is conscious of a superiority which compels respect. Moreover, his faculties, shaped for heroic feats, despise the pliability, the intrigues and the parade through which most brilliant careers are achieved in peacetime. Thus he would be condemned to emasculation or corruption, if he lacked the grim impulse of ambition to spur him on. It is not the passion for rank and honors, which is only careerism, that possesses him; it is beyond doubt the hope of playing a great role in great events!"

Churchill could have written these words and Churchill is no dictator. De Gaulle at least knows the dangers of dictatorship—he has written of them: "Dictatorship can at first assume a dynamic aspect which contrasts agreeably with the anarchy which preceded it. But it is the fate of dictatorship to exaggerate. The nation becomes a machine which the master progressively and frantically accelerates. In the end the spring breaks and the grandiose edifice crumbles in sorrow and blood."

However unpredictable De Gaulle may be, Thorez is all too predictable a Communist. He violently opposed France's entering the war in 1939 (Russia was then allied with Germany) and when his age group was drafted he fled to Russia, where he sat out the war. At first De Gaulle refused to let him come back, on the grounds he had been a wartime traitor. But other Communists' heroism as partisans—after Hitler invaded Russia in 1941—gave the Party a prestige that far outweighed this political handicap.

After liberation, this partisan prestige gave the Communists an initial impetus which Thorez followed up by skillful organizing (all ninety departments of France have active Communist sections, each with hundreds of cells) and a shrewd mixture of French nationalism with pro-Russian policies. Until the French Communists' compulsion to tag after Russia became too glaring, they did very well indeed. They still serve Russia's interests well. The twenty-eight-day general strike cost France 4,000,000 tons of coal, 400,000 tons of iron and steel, and an estimated half the total national income for three weeks—in all, the equivalent of three months of ECA assistance.

What the strikes cost the Communists was much of their control of French labor. Under hard-boiled Benoit Frachon, their union expert, they had jockeyed aging Socialist Leon Jouhaux out of the leadership of the General Confederation of Workers (CGT) he had held since 1909. Though only one out of every seven union members was a Communist, Frachon had packed 85 percent of France's industrial unions with trusted agents. These key Communists got their unions to walk out but when the workers realized what was happening, they walked back. After the strike collapsed, an anti-Communist movement started in the CGT, and a third of its six million members seceded to form a new general union, the *Force Ouvrière*. Leon Jouhaux seceded too; the leaders of the shrunken CGT were left with the knowledge that it would shrink again if they tried to use it further as a Communist stalking horse.

"Schuman is a shy man," says one of the French premier's friends, "and he can be pushed up to a point. But once you reach his limit, you cannot budge him." The Communists, who did not realize this at the time they struck, were stunned when Schuman presented the French Assembly with a strike-control bill (1) mobilizing an extra eighty thousand troops to guard workers who wanted to return to work, and (2) providing heavy fines and imprisonment up to five years "of all those who by violence, distribution of false news, threats or other fraudulent means, seek to incite a strike."

The Assembly Communists screamed: "Bismarck! Tyrant! Dictator! Boche!" They tried to block the passage of the law by every Parliamentary device in the book. They proposed 250 amendments, and insisted on a roll-call vote on each. The Assembly wrangling went on for two straight days without adjournment. When they had failed with all other means, the Communists sent an intermediary to Schuman at his home.

"If you will so authorize me," said the envoy, "I can get the CGT to issue orders for everyone to go back to work tomorrow morning."

"What are the conditions?"

"Certain wage increases, less than they have been asking."

"That I can accept, within reason."

"Also withdrawal of your bill."

"No," said Schuman. "If the government does that, it admits that nothing can be done in France without Communist consent. It would mean wrecking of our foreign policy. It would not only mean that I might as well go back to planting beans in Lorraine— to which I have no objection—but also that the recovery of France would be indefinitely postponed."

The envoy kept arguing. After a few minutes, Schuman said firmly: "If you will excuse me, I have not shaved for two days. I would like to shave now."

The Assembly passed Schuman's bill 408 to 184, with only the Communists opposing. Within a week the strike collapsed.

France faces plenty of other problems. There was the absurdly high valuation of the franc at 119 to the dollar, on which De Gaulle had insisted for reasons of prestige but which meant a growing black market in foreign exchange in France, impossibly high prices for French exports abroad, and less tourist revenue. Schuman devalued the official franc to 214.4 to the dollar, and provided a legal free market for certain exchanges at a still lower value. The French economy promptly improved.

To crimp the inflation that plagued every French wage-earner and forced city people to spend practically all they earn on food, Schuman sent convoys of military trucks through the country-side, buying food direct from the farmers and cutting out exorbitant middleman costs. The traders had to cut their profiteering, as potatoes, carrots, beef and veal fell 10 to 20 percent in markets all over France. Schuman's secretary rushed excitedly in with the tidings: "Mr. Premier, Mr. Premier, vegetables are coming down!"

"Let us not be excited," answered Schuman. "The vegetables are not."

When the Communists attacked his government for getting its munitions and armaments from America, Schuman retorted, "Did Russia refuse American arms?" and called for a vote of confidence in which he again got every non-Communist vote cast.

The ticklish course which Schuman—and all moderate Frenchmen—must steer between the extremes of Gaullism and Communism is aimed at having France acquire what Schuman calls *"le climate psychologique de la baisse,"* which can be translated as "the art of sinking." His task is not only to deflate prices but to deflate the bitterness, hysteria, and frustration which Frenchmen derived from their not-too-glorious role in World War II, and on which both De Gaulle and the Communists flourish. The French are flighty in their postwar wounded pride. Schuman would like to persuade them to sink gently, down to the reassuring reality of the good French earth. If he can do this, France may yet avoid the extremes.

6

French fear of their old enemy Germany and chagrin at their reduced world role fizzed up afresh in June 1948 when they were faced with the necessity of approving the western German state which America and Britain wanted—and French representatives had finally, reluctantly accepted out of necessity and impotence. Foreign Minister Bidault had tried to detach the Ruhr from the rest of Germany, had argued for a much looser federation of German provinces instead of a centralized regime, had sought much firmer guarantees for French security than either London or Washington would give. Having failed on every major point, Bidault then had to accept the Anglo-American pattern or see France isolated. A French refusal might mean the loss of German coal, American aid and what military guarantees had been given.

Frenchmen were bitter. De Gaulle denounced the agreement and proclaimed his readiness to form a new government. Thorez called it "a national disaster." The moderates were also hostile, but after a lashing debate gave the Schuman cabinet a vote of confidence by an eyelash margin of 297 to 289. They all felt like the Parisian to whom I had suggested that France's one real hope of ever again being a major nation was to cut the cackle of being "a great power" for at least ten years—and concentrate on recovery.

"You mean," he retorted, "to be like Denmark? It was a great power once. Now it is content to be a little country and live quietly, as well as it can. We French have our pride. We aren't bovine, like Sweden or Switzerland. We have to have color and pomp and panoply. It's part of our nature. We have to feel we're somebody."

In fact, the French still have their unique blend of panoply and practicality. In a Chartres hotel, *madame la patronne*—buxom, bourgeois, middle aged—spoke with the rolling eloquence of a Racine about the atom bomb, her city's medieval stained glass, and her conviction that civilization was rapidly coming to an end. "Ah, yes, monsieur," she said in the next breath, "but even so you must eat your lunch. The Chateaubriand is excellent today."

France is a country of 41,500,000 people, who know they cannot stand alone but hate to admit it. In return for American aid, without which they could not recover, the French have entered a Western orbit in which they are an important but secondary unit. Their feelings toward America are as friendly as could be expected under the circumstances. In largely ruined Lisieux, I asked a carpenter who had done the damage. "Your American planes," he answered sourly. "A bad souvenir, monsieur, a bad souvenir." But in Yvetot, another American-bombed town, I saw a parade of well-dressed people with placards protesting their lack of housing —the protests were not against the bombing but against the French government for failing to build new homes.

On Omaha Beach, still littered with its wreckage of the American landing, I encountered a lad of seventeen working on a dike. With glowing eyes he described D-Day as he had seen it from a near-by bluff: "It was a marvelous sight to us, as you can imagine, to look out on those big beautiful American ships." The mistress of the Château de Vierville, on the headlands behind the beach, told how the G.I.'s stormed up quickly enough to keep the Germans from burning the château, which had been used by them as headquarters. The windows on one side of her drawing room opened on a fine view of the Channel and part of the beach. She led me to a window on the other side and pointed at the wood beyond her smooth green lawn. "The Boche fought fiercely for that wood," she said. "Many of your soldiers were killed there. I think of them often."

The greatest crowd I saw in France was in the vast, dusty bowl of the Vincennes race track on the eastern edge of Paris. Over 250,000 Parisians, nearly all of them middle class, thronged there on a warm autumn Sunday to hear De Gaulle. The staging was a little reminiscent of a Nazi congress at Nuremberg: the high white balcony like a ship's prow from which De Gaulle spoke, the loud-speakers everywhere, the row of thirty-six flagpoles on either side of him with white pennons bearing the blood-red Cross of Lorraine that dangled limply in the windless air, the stern-faced young Gaullists who controlled the crowds, girls who gazed upward at De Gaulle with rapt expression. Some of the girls never moved till the long speech was over, then began to cry. As at Nuremberg, the anti-Communist passages in the speech were the most violently applauded. But De Gaulle spoke in a slow, strong, convinced voice that contrasted with Hitler's ranting; he used moderation, irony —and flashes of humor—in a way Hitler never could.

The crowd itself was no more German than the Eiffel Tower. The grave-faced men were in frayed but neat Sunday suits, tightly buttoned; the women were also soberly dressed, many in widows' weeds, though some girls wore gay-colored frocks. As the afternoon grew hotter, many made cocked hats out of newspapers. The passions of a Nazi rally were notably lacking, with the crowd listening silently and only occasionally giving a burst of applause, which De Gaulle quieted with a soothing gesture.

Except for the guards and the political bobby-soxers, here were men and women come not to an emotional extravaganza like Nuremberg but to a meeting which would help them make up their minds. The mood was neither parade nor picnic. These were individuals, not automatons. They lived in a country of real political differences; the Communists were conducting a cross-country walking race through the forest of Vincennes as De Gaulle spoke and—more significantly—had sabotaged the power on the nearest subway line two hours before the speech. Scores of thousands had had to walk for miles on dusty roads to get there. They did it with Gallic verve, jeering at the cars that crawled past in a traffic jam worse than that at a big American football game.

France is as charming and individual as ever. The Bretons take pride in being different from the Basques; the dark, suspicious Auvergnats seem of another race than the smiling, sunny people of Provence. The rich red earth of Burgundy differs from the sandy loam of Bordeaux as much as the men and wine of these two ancient provinces. Normandy has its massive, round-arched churches; the Loire its lavish Renaissance châteaux.

Local color retains a more real meaning in France than in the "autonomous" republics of Russia. French regional differences contribute their separate tangs to the zest of a country which to know is to love. What the French, like the other peoples of Western Europe, have not yet fully realized is that everybody can still "feel we're somebody" in a larger federal union. In this free federation, there will be much more than the folk dancing, regional cookery and symbolic shreds of autonomy which is all that the Kremlin allows the various people under its thumb.

Paul Reynaud, who was premier when France fell in 1940, expressed this in the most effective speech of the June 1948 debate on western Germany. He knew what another French defeat could mean, and thus was able to rise above mere fear of the Germans. "We have already said no to the East," he said. "If we now say no to Britain, America, and Benelux, what good will our isolation be? France must work for the organization of Europe in the interests of safeguarding peace and for the integration of western Germany in that framework." Reynaud's speech was the only one in the whole bitter debate that drew applause from the entire National Assembly—except the Communists.

When the free men of Europe form a federation as politically and economically united as France, with each country as individual as the different parts of France, they can finally have peace and prosperity.

Chapter 15. BELGIUM, HOLLAND, ITALY

PERHAPS the thing that is least thoroughly reported in postwar Europe," a keen observer told me in Belgium, "is what Europe's conservatives are doing." Since it is already the most socialized continent in history and the trend still seems to be that way, reports on Europe have concentrated on Communism and Socialism—from Moscow, to the Manchester whose cotton mills used to be the ultimate in liberal *laissez-faire* and are now planned down to the last bobbin.

Here and there, conservatives are accomplishing something in Europe. Nowhere is the right operating more interestingly—or more constructively—than in Belgium. It is not old-line conservatism. But it is something that conservatives and rightists anywhere would recognize and understand. It depends on some fairly basic human principles, certainly not copyrighted by conservativism but which are present whenever conservativism is successful. These principles include incentives, room for individualism, hard work, common sense, and planning that resembles an informal family budget rather than doctrinaire degree—the sort of planning that allows a spring hat for mother, circus for the kids, and even a car for dad. Belgium has more big new American cars than any other country in Europe. There is butter on Belgium's bread. It has shops more crowded with foreign and domestic goods than the Sweden which thrived on neutrality. Belgium makes every other war-ravaged country in Europe look drab in comparison.

Yet the German occupation left Belgium's cupboard very bare. How has Belgium managed to get some strength through abundance, when other countries failed to manage strength through austerity? One answer is that it *was* lucky and another is that it squeezed every ounce of advantage out of its luck.

Compared to its neighbor Holland, Belgium did have a quick,

easy liberation. Most of it was freed at lightning speed in September 1944, though Antwerp later got a lot of buzz-bombs, the German counteroffensive Battle of the Bulge was largely fought in Belgium, and parts of the country were not liberated until February 1945. But most of Holland had one last terrible winter under the Germans until freed in April 1945. All through the war, the Belgian Congo, one of the world's richest sources of copper, uranium, and tropical products, was piling up profits for Belgium's government-in-exile and it has continued to do so peacefully ever since. Holland's even richer Netherlands East Indies were overrun by the Japanese. Since the war, the East Indians have been waging a fight for freedom from the Dutch; this has meant not only bloodshed, bad publicity for the Dutch and sundry other disadvantages, but also a steady drain on Holland's treasury instead of a handsome income. Four-fifths of the Dutch army of 150,000 is now in the Indies, attempting to win back these rich islands.

When the Belgian government returned to Brussels from London in September 1944, it carried out a sharp, swift financial reform, and then offered the benefits of free enterprise. Under the Nazis, the country had been flooded with 188 billion paper francs, four times the prewar amount. The government temporarily froze 90 percent of this, allowing no one more than two thousand francs in currency, and promised to release the rest gradually—"as production increased." As a result, Belgium largely escaped the postwar inflation that hit the rest of Europe. At the same time, the government imported every kind of consumer goods from potatoes to nail polish. Any worker could buy what he wanted with his wages. With this incentive, Belgians began to work like billy-o. By the spring of 1948, Belgium had regained its prewar standard of living and its prewar industrial output—the first war-affected country in Europe to do so.

The biggest party in Belgium is the conservative Social Christian Party (called the Catholic Party before World War II), which got almost half the seats in Parliament in the 1946 elections—an amazing feat in a postwar Europe that was going further left than ever. The premier in the coalition government is a bulky, genial, moderate Socialist, Paul-Henri Spaak (born 1899), who is one of the ablest statesmen in Europe and may well be the first head of any western European federation. But the Catholics have most of the cabinet posts, shape Belgium's middle-of-the-road policy, and have definitely barred any socialization. The Communists got 12.7 percent of the votes in the 1946 election, but have since lost ground. Their leader, Jean Terfve, complains: "Belgians are a peculiar people. They always grumble, but fundamentally they are satisfied."

In their mildly stubborn way, the Belgians are as individualistic as the Finns. "The Belgian is a born smuggler and law-dodger," one of them told me proudly. "So the laws have to stay fairly sensible, and be the laws he wants, or they will be ignored. For two thousand years before 1830, we Belgians were successively ruled by the Romans, Franks, Spaniards, Austrians, French, and Dutch; we learned how to break unpopular laws and dodge the consequences." The Belgians are also practical; Catholic Monsignor Honore van Waeyenbergh, head of Louvain University who was jailed by the Germans for refusal to collaborate, told me: "I used the black market under the Nazis; you had to do it to live."

Belgians think their abundance a wiser policy than Britain's austerity. A high official told me: "To start restrictions is like throwing a pebble into a pond. You never know how far the ripples will spread. We'll go on with free enterprise in Belgium as long as we can. Everybody here, from the royal family down, is in business one way or another, and we all have a practical business approach."

The royal family gave Belgium a postwar headache; the Socialists bitterly opposed King Leopold III's return because of his wartime dealings with the Germans. The Catholics wanted him back, but compromised on a regency under Leopold's colorless and uncontroversial brother Prince Charles. Leopold may abdicate in favor of his son, Prince Baudouin. The royal family has had wide business interests ever since King Leopold II founded companies to exploit the Belgian Congo. The Congo is now one of the world's largest sources of uranium; by agreement with Belgium, the American government has a monopoly on buying it. Despite rumors to the contrary, this is not a large Belgian source of income; America pays only $200 a ton (the peak year: about 11,000 tons) for the raw ore which after extensive treatment in

America yields from 2 to 48 percent pure uranium. Only a tiny fraction of the uranium is the chain-reacting U-235. Copper is the biggest single source of the Congo's annual revenue of approximately $110 million.

The chief Belgian problem, except for its fear of another war (Belgians over thirty years old have lived nearly nine years under German wartime occupation, and as one of them wryly remarked to me, "Any time anybody starts playing war, he plays it in Belgium"), is how to stay prosperous when the neighboring countries are not. Belgium depends on foreign trade; this little land of 8,400,000 inhabitants is the most densely populated nation in the world, with 710 people per square mile. It normally imports half or more of its food and pays by exports. If Belgium lowers wages, its people will not prosper at home; if it keeps high wages, its products will be undersold by other countries' competition when the present sellers' market ends. Belgian locomotives, for instance, are already being undersold in Latin America. Belgium is now trying to solve the problem by upping industrial efficiency. It will also have to cut prices. In June 1948 Greece cancelled a sizable order for Belgian steel when the Belgians asked $110 a ton compared to an American price of around $55 a ton. This was partly because the Belgians were trying to charge what the traffic would bear; their domestic price for steel is about $60 a ton and they sell to Britain for $75 a ton.

Another Belgian problem, shortage of dollars (most of its exports are sold in the British sterling area) will be eased for a few years by ECA providing other nations with dollars they can use to buy Belgian goods—and which Belgium will then spend on goods in America. In 1947, Belgium bought $515 million worth of products in America—and America bought only $62 million worth in Belgium.

Rather than fall to their neighbors' level, the Belgians would naturally prefer seeing their neighbors rise to Belgian standards. They are very active workers for Western Union. Premier Spaak says, "There is no other solution for Europe."

2

The Dutch, who also have a conservative government, chose the austerity means of recovery and are living close to the subsistence level. They scrape along on rations that barely feed and clothe them. By 1952, if Dutch calculations are correct, the Netherlands will be somewhere near its comfortable prewar standards. Meanwhile, the Dutch lack Belgian incentives—and are not working so hard.

Holland is slowly recovering. The Nazis flooded one-tenth of its fields with salt water and nearly all of these have already been put back into cultivation. Railways were back to normal by early 1948, and shipping should be restored by 1950. But agriculture and industry are both well below prewar levels.

The Dutch are still a shining example of Toynbee's principle of the-greater-the-challenge-(within limits)-the-greater-the-response. All Dutch are orderly, but all parts of the Netherlands are not equally orderly. The lower a village lies below sea level, the more clean and orderly it is likely to be. On higher ground, you often find a relatively disordered village.

The fact that a quarter of Holland's 15,764 square miles lie below sea level has been of the utmost importance in forming the Dutch character. As one Dutch leader says: "While others learn political theory as they grow up and read books, while others educate themselves more or less slowly to the necessity of co-operation, every child here learns almost as soon as he learns to speak the lesson of social co-operation, because of the danger of the sea. He learns that he has a personal responsibility for maintaining the great engineering works which make it possible for him to live. If something begins to go wrong with the waterworks, it can be an inconvenience in ten minutes, and soon may be a calamity. All of us understand that all must work together to fix it. We have lived for centuries in the shadow of calamity. This has influenced our attitude toward religion, politics, and everyday life.

"So we have a people whose unity goes deeper than the unity of other European nations, not in spite of—but because—we take our differences of opinion very seriously. Ours is not the superficial tolerance of indifference. Our sense of order brought about by fear of the sea is so strong that we can live together although we disagree on what we consider the most fundamental things. In Holland a high degree of government planning exists side by side with a great degree of personal liberty. This is not surprising. A country whose existence depends on social effort will understand the need of government planning. A country where life depends on personal responsibility will understand liberty."

Holland's sixteenth and seventeenth century religious wars were among the most bitter in history. But when the Dutch Protestants finally won their freedom from Spain's Catholics, they did not take away the Dutch Catholics' freedom. That sea-instilled sense of the need for national order and cohesion outweighed the religious cleavage. The strength of the Dutch royal house is that ever since the religious wars it has understood the people. A basic political fact in Holland is that 30 percent of the people are Catholics and will remain Catholics. If any Dutch government happened to forget this, the House of Orange never did. So the Dutch Catholics feel as deeply attached to the intensely Protestant House of Orange as do the Protestants themselves. The present Dutch Premier, Louis J. M. Beel, is a Catholic, even though Holland is heavily Protestant.

Europe still has seven monarchies, a system that must have some harmony with human nature since it started early in history and is still going fairly strong. In a country of two languages like Belgium, or in a complex commonwealth like the British Empire, a monarch is often the only unifying symbol and a quite useful one. In Belgium, where the present king is a somewhat discredited exile, almost everybody believes in the monarchy as an institution and the Belgian Communists to whom I talked claimed the same eagerness to see it continued which the Socialists and Catholics both claim and believe.

A proper monarchy is above pettiness or party strifes, and can therefore personify the country in times of joy and sorrow and provide a continuing, stabilizing influence at all times. Princess Elizabeth's marriage brightened the harassed Britain of 1947; the late King Christian X's daily horseback ride through Nazi-occupied Copenhagen reminded the Danes that royalty was setting an example of resistance; Gustav V was a good king when Sweden was capitalist and is still a good king now that Sweden is Socialist. A wise monarch like Victor Emmanuel I, aided by a statesman like Cavour, can be the rallying point to unite a dismembered country like the Italy of 1859. A silly monarch, like Victor Emmanuel III, can let in a mountebank like Mussolini and get some tarnished grandeur before having to abdicate. Mussolini made

Victor the emperor of Abyssinia and king of Albania, but an Italian coffeehouse rhyme had the right angle:

> When our Victor was plain King
> Coffee was a common thing.
> When an Emperor he was made
> Coffee to a smell did fade.
> Now he has Albania's throne
> Coffee's very smell has flown.

The House of Orange led the struggle to liberate Holland; its head has been Holland's first citizen for four hundred years. In May 1948, Queen Wilhelmina announced that because of her failing health she would abdicate in September 1948, the week of the golden jubilee of her coronation, in favor of her only child, Crown Princess Juliana. Not long before, one of Wilhelmina's cabinet ministers had been asked: "Would you say the queen was politically astute?" His answer showed what a good monarchy can mean.

"I would not," he said. "Political astuteness means nothing to her. Since 1890 she has been on the throne—eight years under the regency and the rest alone. In that time she has transacted public business every day with this aim in view: 'Make no move that the Dutch people will not approve.' What matters to her are the beliefs and prejudices of the people, whether she agrees with those beliefs and prejudices or not. Only a very stupid person could do that for half a century without acquiring a wonderful sensitivity to the character of the Dutch people—and Queen Wilhelmina is very far from being stupid. All of us look upon the queen as knowing more about the Dutch people than we do."

3

On April 18, 1948, 94 percent of the Italian voting population went to the polls and by a more than two-thirds majority rejected Communism. Italy was ECA's first great political victory; had it not been for the prospect of further American aid and the western European co-operation which that aid makes possible, the Italian Communists would either have won the election or become a minority so big as to make majority rule unworkable. Decisive as the victory was (less than a month before, some Western observers had feared defeat), it did not permanently eliminate the Communist threat. It merely gave non-Communists a chance to restore Italy. If they muff their chance, the Communists will sooner or later take over the country.

Italy is, therefore, not only ECA's first real victory but a typical test of what ECA must accomplish long range if it is not to end in failure. Nowhere does ECA face a quick, easy triumph. Europe's problems are too wide and deep for that.

In Italy, for example, forty-six million people inhabit an area smaller than New Mexico (which has only 530,000 people). Italy is as poor in natural resources as it is rich in history. Little of the land is fertile and not even Mussolini's desperate Battle of the Grain made it self-sufficient in food. Now it has three million more mouths to feed than it had ten years ago, and less than 70 percent as much to feed them with. Nor does Italy possess raw materials to trade for food; it has few ores of any sort, less coal, and almost no oil. Not even Britain depends more on imports to make the export goods to buy further imports.

Italy's one great resource is its people, who work harder for less than any other people in western Europe. But the destruction of war, the red tape inherited from Fascist bureaucracy, and post-war shortages and dislocations have visited upon Italy the twin tragedies of nearly two million government employees (more than twice as high a percentage of the population as in America) and over two million unemployed.

There is no speedy solution to that set of problems.

Italy is also handicapped by the fact that, although Italians love liberty, they have never actually known a democracy in the modern western sense. Until World War I, Italy could be accurately described as "a country of thirty million ruled by three thousand for the benefit of three thousand." (Italy still has glaring contrasts between rich and poor, made worse because its privileged classes, unlike those of Britain, show no sense of responsibility toward their fellow countrymen.) In the unrest after World War I, the Fascists headed by Mussolini took over the country and stamped out what little democracy it had. In the unrest after World War II, it is only surprising that Communism did not reap a full harvest.

An Italian pessimist told me in Rome: "Not two of us in a hundred really understand what democracy means. All that any government has taught the rest of us is to be out for what we can get." Many, disgusted with all politics, are like the man who told me: "What we want is just a chance to work and to live a little better." About that time, Foreign Minister Count Carlo Sforza was set upon by a crowd that surrounded his car. He cried: "I know you want bread! I work sixteen hours a day so you'll get it." The crowd's bitter reply: "You work—but we can't."

In those circumstances, between 1944 and 1948, Italy developed the biggest Communist Party in the world outside of Russia. Its enrollment of 2,250,000 meant one Communist in every twenty Italians, while Russia's 6,000,000 members meant only one Communist in every thirty Russians. The Party is led by Palmiro Togliatti, who has been called "the ablest Communist since Lenin." Not even Lenin was a shrewder strategist.

The son of a pious, low-paid government bookkeeper in Genoa, Togliatti was named Palmiro because he was born on Palm Sunday, in 1893. He still quotes the Bible to good effect in his speeches and in 99-percent Catholic Italy he poses as a champion of the Church. Under his leadership, Communist deputies voted against divorce and for the Lateran Pact which reaffirmed the Vatican's right to intervene in certain Italian secular matters. His entire program has this seeming moderation.

Togliatti is a veteran in Moscow's service. A Socialist in World War I, he helped found the Communist Party of Italy in 1921. When Mussolini broke up the Party and arrested every Communist he could lay his hands on, Togliatti fled to France and then to Russia. A top agent of the Comintern, he was used for trouble spots like strikes in the Ruhr and the civil war in Spain. In 1943, as head of the Comintern's Mediterranean division, he was one of the seventeen who signed the decree abolishing the Comintern. (The others who made that propaganda gesture of "dissolving" the Comintern now hold key posts in many countries. They include President Otto Kuusinen of the Karelo-Finnish Soviet Socialist Republic, President Clement Gottwald of Czechoslovakia, President Georgi Dimitrov of Bulgaria, and Communist Leaders Maurice Thorez of France, Anna Pauker of Rumania, Wilhelm Pieck of Germany and Matyas Rakosi of Hungary.)

In March 1944, after an absence of eighteen years, Togliatti returned to Naples under the personal sponsorship of Andrei Vishinsky, who was then the Soviet member of the Allied Control Council for Italy. Looking like a professor, in his horn-rimmed spectacles and neat, double-breasted blue suit, Togliatti immediately restrained the revolutionary ardor of his Communist associates. He forbade antiroyalist agitation, rolled up the Red flag in favor of the national green, white and red emblem, got Moscow to recognize Marshal Pietro Badoglio's royalist regime, and entered it himself as the first Communist cabinet minister in Italian history.

His masterly moderation soon began to pay off. The Communist program called for bigger rations, "democratic schools," civil service reform, jobs for veterans, "encouragement of industry," "higher wages but lower production costs," increased exports, broad social services, and monetary stabilization to assure "the recovery of business." While the Communists wanted to distribute Italy's "feudal estates to landless peasants," they promised "full respect for holdings of one hundred hectares [247 acres] or less." "That is a good-sized farm," Togliatti explained, with sweet reasonableness, and never mentioned the horrid phrase "collective farming."

Practically all Italians could subscribe to this fine-sounding program. They did, by the hundreds of thousands, from poor peasants and unemployed city workers to the debutante in Milan who chirped, "Communism doesn't prevent you from listening to music, sipping tea, or eating pastry." The Communists were the smoothest-operating and best-led party in Italy. Togliatti took advantage not only of hunger and postwar confusion, but of the prestige which Communists had earned by their perennial resistance to Mussolini and their courageous partisan activity against the Germans. In an Italy where Mussolini had left a mass of graft and corruption, the Communist leaders were relatively honest and efficient. They blackmailed manufacturers to swell the Party funds, but they provided good government for the people in any town that voted for them.

Soon they were voted into control of many of Italy's most famous cities—Milan, Genoa, Florence, Mantua, Ferrara, Venice, Pisa, Leghorn, Parma, Turin, Bologna, La Spezia, and Siena. Pietro

Secchia, the Party's chief organizer, put the objective clearly: "A Communist section for every church tower in Italy." By 1948, this was nearly achieved.

Togliatti's program persuaded millions to believe that the Communists were Italian before they were Communist. The personal background of the Communist leaders has quite naturally made them many friends and followers. Gaetano Invernizzi, the Communist labor leader for northern Italy, is typical. The story of his life which Invernizzi told Emmet Hughes of *Time* can be told with minor variations by thousands of key Communists all over Europe. The zeal and discipline symbolized by his story go far to explain the power that Communism derives, both from the hold it has on its members and the attraction which their long personal record of hardihood and self-sacrifice can exert on nonmembers.

"Before the First World War," said Invernizzi, "I was like any other son of a workman's family, without any special political ideas. I worked in a factory that made cloth dyes—that's where I got these scars on my wrists. I volunteered for the army when the war came, then after Caporetto my ideas began to change. When the war was over and the Italians had won nothing, I saw that only the rich had gained. I became a Socialist, but not a very militant one and I still went to Mass. Then the Fascists came, and anyone in a labor union had to fight for his life. Socialists weren't very effective, and I found more and more of the people whose ideas I sympathized with were Communists. I began to lose my faith. 'God?' I thought, 'if you really exist, I can't see that praying to you does much good in times like these.'

"In 1922 I became a member of the Party and the same year my wife and I had to flee to France. I worked making covers for chairs. In 1930 the French police ordered me out of the country for my Communist activities. I went to Belgium. The Belgians threw me out. I went to Luxemburg. They let me stay, but there was no work. I took an assumed name, got back to France and became head of the Italian Communists in Lyons. Then in 1932 the Party ordered me and my wife back to Italy. We had to go all through the north, organizing the Party's underground. That year there were fifty of us doing this work. The Fascists caught forty-seven.

"Just to save us, the Party sent us to Russia. Then in 1935 we were sent back to Italy again to help organize opposition to the war in Abyssinia. This time we were caught. I spent the next eight years in the Castelfranco Emilia prison near Modena. I had plenty of good Communist company there. Even when Mussolini fell, the Badoglio government refused at first to free us. We began a hunger strike, and some of us managed to escape. I was lucky. Those who didn't were found by the Germans. They were all shot.

"My wife and I fled to the mountains. We organized the first Partisan units in Italy, the ones that cleaned up the Germans around Lake Como. But my wife's brother died in Malthausen. I spent nineteen years without seeing my mother and father. But there were thousands of others who suffered much more."

Now Invernizzi says with some pride: "I work hard and the workers here know that I do. Even though I'm uneducated, every day important people come to this office—doctors, engineers, all sorts of professional people, too—to discuss labor problems. They all know I honestly represent the workers' interests. A lot of people I know don't trust the Communist Party—but they trust me."

There are many Italian Communists like Invernizzi and they do evoke confidence in a confused, corrupt country.

Until the fall of 1947, Italy's Communists did stay fairly Italian in their interests. For example, they opposed Russia's efforts to award Trieste to Yugoslavia—though not as violently as Italy's other parties did. Their popular support continued to grow, especially since they were in the opposition and could attack the government's do-nothing policy. Meanwhile, they riveted their control on almost every labor union in the country (so they could cripple Italy by calling a general strike), and kept their wartime underground army of two hundred thousand well drilled—the Communist partisans never surrendered the firearms with which they fought the Germans, and so could start a civil war if they wanted to.

In the fall of 1947, Togliatti completed a political maneuver as brilliant as his strategic use of moderation. He persuaded the great bulk of Italy's Socialist Party, led by the Communists' picked man Pietro Nenni, to join the Communists in a formidable Popular Front. The combined parties controlled nearly two-fifths of

Italy's votes—more than any other single party including the Christian Democrats who were the base of the government. Since the Christian Democrats' policy of inaction had been losing them ground, it seemed probable that the Popular Front could win the 1948 election.

4

Moscow chose that crucial moment to demonstrate that Togliatti and his followers were Communists first and Italians second. Like the French Communists, they were told to riot against the Marshall Plan. Only the $2 billion of American aid since 1943 has kept Italy from complete breakdown; only America could continue to supply the economic aid that Italy had to have for reconstruction. Togliatti himself, like the Polish and Czech Communists, had earlier supported the Marshall Plan. All this made no difference. In September, Togliatti had helped establish the Cominform—successor to the Comintern he had helped "dissolve" in 1943. In November the Cominform sent word to stop the Marshall Plan in Italy before it got started.

Togliatti struck—as unsuccessfully as Thorez. Every key city in Italy had its Communist strikes and riots. Togliatti and his generals staged an armed reconnaissance, a rehearsal for a possible revolution. They had to know how their rank and file would act when they faced rifles and armored cars—and they had to know where the government had concentrated its armaments. The government was ready. From the Alps to Sicily, it had forces wherever the Communists rioted—and those forces kept amazingly steady. The Italian police showed they could maintain order without giving provocation; not once did they fire into a crowd. The test of ordinary Communists' combative spirit must also have disappointed Togliatti; in Naples, two police volleys into the air emptied the main square of rioters in less than an hour. Even the strikes were not completely successful and the Communists soon called them off.

For non-Communist Italians, the results were immediately favorable. The government, surprised at its own strength, finally had the nerve at the end of November to stabilize the lira at a realistic 589 to the dollar compared to the previous highly artificial 350 to the dollar. By one bold stroke, Italy almost ended its black market in currency, boosted the exports and tourist trade which are its two main sources of foreign exchange, and so greatly increased Italians' confidence in the lira that the cost of living actually fell. The basic economic recovery which the Communists had hoped the government would never achieve (since economic failure would hasten their coming to power) was thus indirectly aided by the Communists' own abortive riots!

The political results were as disastrous to the Communists as the economic outcome. By mid-December, Premier Alcide de Gasperi was able to build a much broader coalition government than before. Two small but vital Italian left-wing parties finally agreed to join the cabinet. One was the Republican Party, led by Randolfo Pacciardi, brilliant commander of the Garibaldi Brigade in the Spanish civil war, who had previously been an ardent believer in the possibility of co-operating harmoniously with the Communists. "Until now," said Pacciardi grimly, "we have made attempts of mediation and pacification toward all Republican forces [i.e., including the Communists]. But we cannot continue merely reciting prayers in a world of wolves."

The other and still more important party was the right-wing Socialist group, led by Giuseppe Saragat, which had split from Nenni's Socialists when the latter merged with the Communists in the Popular Front. The addition of five cabinet ministers from these two parties gave the government a far firmer base than it had possessed before Togliatti followed Moscow's orders and ruptured his policy of moderation.

Premier Alcide de Gasperi, head of the Christian Democratic Party, was born near Trento in 1881. Like Togliatti, he was the son of a low-paid government official. An Austrian subject, the first half of his life—Italy did not acquire this Italian-speaking area until after World War I—he was active in the Italian nationalist movement as a student at the universities of Innsbruck and Vienna. In 1919 he joined the Popular Party (now the Christian Democrats) founded by a Sicilian priest, Don Luigi Sturzo, which was designed to implement Christianity by social and political action. He became head of the party when Mussolini drove Sturzo into exile. Later Mussolini banned the Christian Democrats and twice jailed de Gasperi. In 1929 he got an $80-a-month position in the Vatican Library. The furniture in the modest apartment he still keeps as premier was bought on the installment plan while he was working in the Vatican; in that period, one of his four daughters married a butcher in Milan and another became a nun.

During World War II, de Gasperi reorganized his party and joined the underground in its guerrilla war against the Germans. In the postwar elections, the Christian Democrats polled eight million votes and became the biggest party in Italy; a lot of Italians agreed with its program of social reform. But until the November 1947 crisis, it had largely let its promises lapse. Since the party's financial backing came from rich industrialists and landowners, it had stalled on its pledges of effective taxation and land reform. The one major measure that de Gasperi had enacted was a law boosting the sharecroppers' share in their harvest. By the fall of 1947, the Christian Democrats had in effect become a minority regime; its popularity was ebbing and the Communist-led Popular Front was a larger party.

Even the government revival that was inspired by stopping the Communist riots, succeeding with financial reform, and getting the Republicans and right-wing Socialists into the cabinet, did not bring easy sailing. The Popular Front went all out to win the 1948 election. Early in February the city of Pescara had an election, and the incumbent Christian Democrats were swept out of office by the Popular Front. A little later, the Czech Communist coup redoubled the Italian Communist efforts. With a reported $15 million from Moscow for "election expenses," and promises of something for everybody—including the social measures that the Christian Democrats had promised in 1946 and then not performed—the Popular Front made a very effective campaign.

The Roman Catholic Church also took an active part in the election. From the Pope to the lay workers of Catholic Action, the Church denounced the Popular Front. Pius XII, who administered the Vatican's foreign affairs before his election to the papacy in 1939, by no means believes in the Church staying aloof from politics. Though the State of Vatican City is physically the world's smallest (108.7 acres), its influence is far-reaching. The Vatican generally endorses American foreign policy and violently attacks that of Russia. In May 1948 the Pope instructed the archbishop of Prague to forbid Czechoslovak priests (notably Father Josef Plojhar, minister of Health in Gottwald's cabinet) from co-operating with the Communists. The same month, the Pope had Cardinal Mindszenty, the primate of Hungary, denounce the Red regime there for nationalizing schools and "installing an atheistic curriculum in them." The Polish hierarchy issued a similar pastoral letter, repeating its determination not to abandon Catholic schools and urging Polish youth "to let no one force the materialistic point of view upon you."

America, Britain, and France put the Popular Front and Russia on the spot by demanding that the Italian-speaking Free Territory of Trieste be returned to Italy and that Italy be admitted to the United Nations. The ordinary Italian wanted both—but the Popular Front had to string along with Russia when it refused both. Nor did the average Italian want to lose American aid.

When balloting day came, almost 70 percent of the Italian electorate voted for their church, for Trieste, for U.N., for American aid—and for at least one more free election. The Christian Democrats got 12,751,841 votes, or 48.7 percent of the total, with a clear majority of 307 of the 574 seats in the Chamber of Deputies, and smaller non-Communist parties got 20.6 percent of the total vote, with 85 seats. The Popular Front won only 8,025,990 votes, or 30.7 percent, with 182 seats.

Even so commanding a victory may not last beyond the next election unless Italy's evils are remedied. Millions of the Christian Democrat votes came from people who fear Communism more than they love progress. These voters are now trying to block reform. A far greater number of Italians voted against Communism, but also against their present unhappy conditions. If they are again disappointed, as they were after the 1946 elections, they will listen to the Communist promises next time. Understanding this danger, Premier de Gasperi declared after victory: "We are not reactionaries. Every social reform which has been promised will be made." He followed this up with a policy address pledging to: (1) distribute big estates (2) drain marshes to provide more farm land (3) increase relief allowances for the unemployed (4) collect taxes more strictly by introducing a "tax morality" hitherto notably lacking because Italians have dodged payment or bribed the tax collector.

Togliatti, undaunted, has again begun to preach land reform, better housing, and full employment to Italy's millions of landless, homeless, and unemployed. He knows how tremendous is the task ahead, and how impatient Italians can get before much progress has been made. Meanwhile, there will be the unrest on which Communism feeds. In the country, it is vital not only to break up feudal estates but to increase irrigation, modernize farming methods, and improve crop yields. In the cities, not only must work be found for over two million jobless but reconstruction, industrial expansion and balancing of the budget must all be energetically tackled.

Both the de Gasperi government and the Economic Co-operation Administration face a searching test in Italy. In only occasional years since 1870 has the country exported enough goods to pay for its imports. It has had to close the annual gap with such "invisible exports" as shipping revenues, tourists' outlay in Italy (which rose to $150 million in 1925), and money sent home by Italian immigrants in America, Argentina, and elsewhere. In its first year of operation, for example, ECA will have to pay for nine-tenths of Italy's wheat imports, three-fourths of its oil and coal, and half its copper.

In 1945-46, Italy had its lowest living standard since the nation's unification in 1870. The war did not damage it to the extent Greece and Russia were damaged, but Italy lost about a third of its invested capital including 30 percent of its power plants, half its railway engines, and 85 percent of its shipping. While it has recovered somewhat, its 46 million people are still producing only about two-thirds as much as 43 million did in 1938. The added population (there will be 50 million by 1960) means that Italy cannot merely return to 1938; it must increase production— i.e., more food must be imported to eat, more raw materials imported to manufacture, and more goods exported to pay for the imports.

The growing number of people in Italy is part of the whole world's population problem. For the last three centuries, mankind has been engaged on what zoologists term "a breeding storm." Between 1630 and 1830, the earth's population doubled: 400 million to 800 million. By 1900 it had doubled again. Now it is 2.2 billion. Despite World War II's havoc, the earth has 200 million more people than in 1938. Secretary General Dennis A. FitzGerald of the International Emergency Food Council calls it "adding another North America to the claimants for the world's food supply." Yet the earth has only 93 percent of the food it had in 1938. The human race cannot increase forever at the present rate without reaching the starvation point, as India has done already and Italy threatens to do.

Italy's basic economic problem is finding productive work for its increased population—including the two and a half million now unemployed. Emigration might take care of a few hundred thousand. But the major solution, from the viewpoint of both economic and political stability, is to develop more industry and to reorganize agriculture. Italy now has nine million farm laborers and six million industrial workers. The figure should be reversed.

Agriculturally, Italy has too many people on too little land— especially in the south, where the rolling beauty of the landscape conceals the peasants' fierce, unending struggle with barren land scorched by arid winds from Africa. There, in particular, Italian children go to work instead of to school, and peasants scratch out a bare subsistence with primitive tools. Italy wastes a lot of man labor growing wheat that can be grown much more efficiently elsewhere. If it concentrated on the products it can raise efficiently —fruit, vegetables, dairy products, olives, wine—and used modern methods to decrease man hours and increase production, it would have more for itself and more exports too, and could release several million farm workers for industry.

Over a ten-year period, it would cost up to $20 billion to transfer these peasants to the cities, train them, and develop the expanded industry that could employ them. This would mean a capital expansion of $2 billion a year for a decade, and Italy has never saved more than $1 billion a year. Foreign loans, public or private, must partly finance the changeover. ECA could help at the start; its provisional 1948 allocation of $703,000,000 to Italy will cover some industrial, machine, and electrical-equipment items, as well as food and raw materials. Once Italian industry is back on its feet, and can show its ability to service loans, Italy can seek foreign investments to develop industries to service further loans, etc.

Italy's largest single source of the foreign exchange it so desperately needs should be its tourist trade. It is a picturesque and hospitable country, with culture, climate, scenery, and entertainment galore. Proper promotion and fuller development of its facilities could bring $300 million a year from foreign tourists. Orvieto's wine, which unluckily does not travel well, is still the mellowest in the world when drunk in its own city. The master works of Michelangelo are still in Florence and Rome. The Bay of Naples is beautiful as ever and you can no longer have an April dawn there spoiled, as one was for me in 1938 when I rose early to get the view from a hillside terrace, by seeing fifty-three submarines suddenly emerge from its limpid waters and practice the maneuvers by which Mussolini hoped to impress Hitler during his state visit.

The main industrial hope lies in the lighter industries. They need more factories and machinery, and credits for imported raw materials, before they can export finished products. Italy must certainly find a better solution than the 1947 one for coal—it needs fourteen million tons a year and in 1947 paid up to $24 a ton for American coal. When Italy can again send fruit, olive oil, and textiles to Germany (its best prewar customer) and again get Ruhr coal in exchange, ECA co-operation will make more sense—and America can stop subsidizing Italy's $24-a-ton coal.

Albert Kohler, a Swiss textile importer, summed up the present absurd situation. He said: "Before the war, trainload after trainload of Italian goods rolled through the Saint Gotthard and Simplon tunnels to Germany, Austria and Czechoslovakia. Each year German coal miners and steel workers received almost half a million tons of Italian lemons, oranges, pears, apples, wheat flour, rice, olive oil. Italy's textile shipments reached an annual value of more than 2.5 billion lire. In return, Germany sent to Italy between twelve and fifteen million tons of coal and more than half a million tons of iron and steel products.

"Today this exchange is disrupted. German coal miners in the Ruhr produce less because they get less food. Italy's fruit and wheat would go a long way toward boosting the morale of Ruhr miners and raising their output. On the other side, German coal and steel would do a lot to improve northern Italy's industrial production.

"Instead, we have a crazy situation whereby the U.S. must send food to Germany and coal to Italy. It's like trying to cure a sick woman by smearing a coat of make-up on her face. American aid must be directed to the root of Europe's trouble; equip European industry with the tools, and production will take care of itself."

Italian textiles already include the only large silk production in Europe, plus high-quality woolen, cotton and rayon goods. Textile output has recovered to 80 percent of the prewar peak, and should be expanded to 150 percent of prewar. The Italian flair for engineering and mechanical design could mean a profitable enlargement of its mechanical-engineering industry: instruments, automobiles, chemicals, and special machinery of all sorts. Italy should also further develop its synthetics, light metals, plywood, hardware, leather work, and shoe industries.

Little of this long-range but vital program can be done without ECA or other American aid. But if it is not well started in the next few years, Italy will not even regain 1938 living standards for its increased population, who want more than they had in 1938 and are willing to work for it. If they cannot get it by reasonably free enterprise in an economically co-operative western Europe, Italian Communists will always be ready to lure them with shiny promises into the Russian orbit.

What can America ask of Italy in return for its aid? Without interfering with Italian sovereignty, it can legitimately make certain economic requirements: that the lira stay stabilized at a sane level, that government expenses be cut to a point somewhere near income, that graft be reduced and efficiency increased, that the Italian regime's own program of middle-of-the-road economic reform be executed, and above all, that Italy genuinely work toward customs union and other co-operation with the countries of western Europe.

Italy means a great deal more to America culturally, historically, and genealogically than it does economically. Nearly ten million Americans or their ancestors came from Italy and all of us have profited, from acquiring Toscanini and the atom bomb's Enrico Fermi to learning the savor of tomato pies. Strategically, the long Italian peninsula stretches from mid-Europe to mid-Mediterranean; Turin is closer to London than it is to Brindisi, and Brindisi is closer to Constantinople than to Turin.

ECA does not take such factors directly into account, in Italy or elsewhere. It cannot even directly consider such political factors as the self-evident one that "democracy" in the American sense has very shallow roots among the Italian people, whose rulers have for centuries given it little chance to grow. ECA as its title indicates, concentrates on a nation's economic life, assuming that until people have economic stability and opportunity they can hardly steer a good course politically. But by encouraging recovery, ECA does encourage freedom.

That the Italian people voted as they did, even before ECA went into full effect, testifies to the great moral and political overtones of America's program for economic aid. Each victory helps all along the line, and makes the complex, distant, final triumph a little more certain. But a Togliatti who has endured a quarter of a century of defeat, exile, and frustration is more patient than an ordinary American or Italian. In Europe alone, Communism has millions of men and women as patient and disciplined as Togliatti and Invernizzi. These Communists know how long and slow will be the struggle to restore Europe's health. Their deepest hope is that we Americans will grow weary before we realize that, by properly using our economic, political, and moral weapons we can win—in Italy and elsewhere—the greatest political battle in history without firing our military weapons.

Chapter 16. GREAT BRITAIN

THE United Kingdom of Great Britain and Northern Ireland is composed of England, Scotland, Wales and Northern Ireland (Ulster), with a combined area of 94,279 square miles and population of about forty-nine million.

Britain, as this area is commonly known, is the heart of the loose-knit British Commonwealth of Nations, which extends to every continent and ocean, covering 13,000,000 square miles with a total population of over 500,000,000.

From the end of the Napoleonic Wars in 1815 to the start of World War I in 1914, Britain was the greatest power on earth—and incomparably the greatest on the sea. The Empire, as the Commonwealth was then called, steadily expanded. The Industrial Revolution, which started in England in the 1760s, made the British Isles the workshop of the world. Food and raw materials were imported cheaply from all over the globe; manufactured goods were exported. The cargoes came and went in British ships, guarded by British bases controlling the world's key trade routes.

By 1800 London had finally wrested banking supremacy from Amsterdam. After 1815 it was the undisputed financial and insurance center of the world. Despite a powerful opposition bid from Paris in mid-century and growing competition from New York after 1880, London managed to maintain its leadership in international finance until New York overtook it in the 1920s. The profits which piled up from all this trading, manufacturing, and financing not only made Britain prosperous at home but were used in great developments elsewhere—railways in Europe, India, America, Canada, and Argentina, gold mines in South Africa, rubber in Malaya, lumber in the Pacific Northwest.

World War I shook Britain, though it expanded the Empire by putting most of Germany's African colonies and Turkey's

Arab dependencies in the Middle East under British control. But on balance, it accelerated the British decline which had actually begun long before 1914. From 1875 onward, American and German industry were taking steadily larger shares of world trade; Britain increasingly had to pay for its imports not only by exports but also by income from those earlier foreign investments. The cost of World War I forced the selling of many such investments.

During World War I, Britain lost most of its South American markets to America and many of its Far Eastern markets (notably China, then India) to America and Japan. This wartime interruption in normal trade relations led to a permanent loss of traditional British markets. After 1918, Britain temporarily took back many of Germany's foreign markets. Between the two world wars, Britain also had the advantage that the food and raw materials it imported could then be bought at relatively low prices, while the manufactures it exported could then be sold at relatively high prices. But on the whole, Britain's decline continued. By 1938 it had an annual trade deficit of $350 million. While part of this was covered by income from foreign investments, the small trade gap that remained now had to be filled by selling some of the investments. Britain was beginning to live on its capital. The accumulated wealth from more than a century of conquest and industrial expansion was steadily being eaten away.

World War II brought Britain disaster. Bombs ruined cities and factories (4,500,000 houses were destroyed or damaged); half the merchant marine was sunk; overdue modernization plans were delayed, and Britain's already old-fashioned industrial plant further deteriorated from overuse and lack of maintenance. Most of the remaining foreign investments had to be sold to help pay for the war. In all, World War II cost Britain one-fourth of its entire capital.

The cost in human terms, over and above war casualties, was also tremendous. Six years of struggle, blackout, blitz and war work on meager rations left the British tired and jaded. They were victors who had no sweets of victory.

Even the terms of trade, which had helped Britain after World War I, now handicapped it. Food and raw materials, instead of being cheap, were now expensive; the price of the manufactures Britain exported in return had not risen nearly so much. If world prices in 1938 had been what they were in 1947, Britain's 1938 trade deficit would not have been an embarrassing $350 million but a staggering $1.6 billion. This reversal of the terms of trade, plus failure to regain the prewar output of such vital British exports as coal and textiles (textile exports had been falling since 1914), the destruction of war, and the need for extra imports to prime the pump of recovery, meant that Britain had an astronomical trade deficit of $2.8 billion in 1947. Britain was bankrupt. It was no longer the great creditor nation of the world but the great debtor nation.

"Before 1914," the Conservative Party's Industrial Charter stated in 1947, "the people of this country were owed by the rest of the world a debt equal to £100 [$400] each. Today each one of us in Britain owes the rest of the world £100."

The London magazine *Horizon* described the result:

"The advantages which position, coal, skill, and enterprise won for us in the nineteenth century have been liquidated, . . . [leaving us] a barren, humid, raw, but densely overpopulated group of islands with an obsolete industrial plant, hideous and inadequate housing, a variety of unhealthy jungle possessions, vast international commitments, a falling birthrate. . . . Most of us are not men or women but members of a vast, seedy, overworked, overlegislated, neuter class, with our drab clothes, our ration books and murder stories, our envious, stricken, old-world apathies—a careworn people."

With economic collapse came political and military deterioration. This too had started decades before. When Ernest Bevin was born in 1881, Britain was able to make more armaments than all the rest of the world put together. When he became foreign secretary in 1945, Britain could not make a tenth of the world's output of weapons. In his lifetime, Britain had declined from the world's first industrial and military power to a position of strategic dependence on America.

Between the two world wars, the British Empire recognized these changes by altering its form. Ireland gained its virtual independence. In 1931 the Dominions officially became autonomous, formalizing the status they had started to attain with Canada in 1867. The India Act of 1935 foreshadowed British withdrawal there. After World War II, the slow dirge of change was accelerated. In 1946 British troops left Egypt; in 1947 India became two self-governing Dominions, and Burma was declared independent; in 1948 Ceylon became a Dominion and Britain ended its mandate over Palestine. Britain no longer ruled the seven seas. In October 1947, the British Home Fleet was cut to the mere token of one cruiser and four destroyers on active duty.

Airplanes, rockets and the atom bomb have turned what was long Britain's added security of an ocean moat into an actual handicap. In case of war, Britain is now more vulnerable than any other great nation to isolation, starvation, and destruction.

Some pessimists say that all this means the end of Britain. It does not.

The British, though downcast, are far from despair. Unlike France, Italy, and Germany, Britain is as stable internally now as prewar—and gives every prospect of staying so. The Commonwealth's ties to Britain are still firm, though voluntary. Except for Canada, the Commonwealth belongs to the sterling bloc and shares London's desire to work the pound back to normal. Next to America itself, Britain is the most indispensable member of Western Union, which got nowhere until the British government came out in favor of it. If Western Union does become a politico-economic reality, it will not only be a bastion of democracy but a great area for the trade which is Britain's lifeblood. For Britain, America, and all others involved, a group of seventeen closely integrated nations offers larger markets, higher levels of consumption and surer trade conditions than seventeen separate, unstable countries ever could.

In the past, Britain's trade with the Commonwealth has been more than twice as big as that with the other European nations in the Economic Co-operation Administration. In 1938, Britain imported $690 million from the ECA countries and $1.37 billion from the Commonwealth; the corresponding figures in 1947 were $1.03 and $3.19 billion. In 1938, Britain exported $402 million to the ECA countries and $865 million to the Commonwealth; the corresponding figures in 1947 were $1.12 and $2.37 billion. If Britons can raise their trade volume with the ECA countries in a Western Union to the level of their trade with the Commonwealth, Britain's economic future will be far more secure—though it must also increase its trade with the rest of the world.

Quite apart from the Dominions, Britain still has the world's biggest colonial empire—2,300,000 square miles with a population of more than sixty million. Burma's independence, and the autonomy which India, Pakistan, and Ceylon now possess, underlines British sincerity in stating that its policy for all colonies is a steady education in self-government, culminating in independence. A British White Paper on "Colonial Developments and Welfare," which the Conservative government issued in February 1940, is now being followed by the Socialist government. The aim is "to promote the prosperity and happiness" of the colonies and make them "partners, not dependencies."

Despite its own financial woes, Britain has appropriated $480 million for colonial education and welfare. It has also started new developments of their resources designed to aid both the natives and Britain, since no colony could be considered fit for independence before it had more economic development and at least some technical knowledge. The native Nigerian transportation magnate Ojukwu, an advocate of independence, admits: "If the British were to leave tomorrow, I would be the first one down on the docks asking them to leave their shoes and clothes behind. We don't know how to make anything and we haven't got the facilities."

(The Nigerians do know how to operate newspapers. In Lagos, the chief leader in their campaign for independence, Nnamdi Azikwe [known as "Zik"], owns and edits the *West African Pilot*, which combines flaming anti-British editorials with a heart-throb column more flaming than Dorothy Dix. Recently, a Nigerian youth wrote in to ask which of the four girls he was living with he should marry.)

One promising new economic development in the colonies is the East African peanut scheme, financed by $92 million from the British government, which from 1949 onward is supposed to yield an annual 150,000 tons of oil, almost equal to the prewar British consumption of edible fats. Since 1939, fats of any kind have been desperately short (in 1938 Britain imported 137,600 tons; in 1946 only 51,000), which has driven British cooking to a new and dreary low of boiled meat (each Briton has a ration of twenty cents' worth of meat a week, about enough for one good meal), boiled fish, boiled cabbage, boiled potatoes, boiled Brussels sprouts and boiled desserts. Until the peanut oil arrives (in 1947 only 13,000 of a scheduled 150,000 acres were cleared; eventually there are to be 3,000,000 acres), Britons must continue to do their cooking with a tiny dab of fat made from vegetable, palm kernel, and whale oils which, as Food Minister John Strachey admitted in the House of Commons, turns blue in the pan and spits out at the harassed housewife.

American reaction to the British Empire has frequently been a smug, total condemnation, though our own twentieth century experience with Guam, Puerto Rico, the Philippines, and the Virgin Islands should have taught us that even a colony which looks like paradise can pose plenty of problems. Britain has certainly profited from its Empire, but any impartial investigator also discovers that the Empire has certainly profited from Britain. Why else do distant dominions like Australia—or South Africa with its Boer majority and memories of the Boer War—keep their bonds with Britain? Why else do India and Pakistan refuse to cut their links with London?

For the century of its heyday, Britain was not an empire held together by brute force like that of Hitler, Napoleon, or Genghis Khan. It was an empire bound by trade, communications and equal justice, like that of Rome. The Roman law, the Roman road, and the arch of the Roman bridge meant as much on the Rhine, Thames, Euphrates, and a thousand lesser streams as they did on the Tiber. British justice, British finance, and British trade routes meant a world free from piracy and free to prosper. One could no more bribe a judge in Burma, Borneo, or Bechuanaland than one could bribe a judge in Britain itself. The Bank of England was as important for the rest of the world as for the Empire. The Roman legion and the British warship were always at their stations because some sort of policeman must back any rule of law. But the relatively small tax that sustained the legion and the warship was repaid many times over, both in the Roman and the British empires, by the general increase in safety, convenience, and welfare.

To every empire comes a time of which it can be said: "The

leadership now passed to other hands." That time came with utter finality to Britain in February 1947. Coal had made Britain great. It had been the basis of the Industrial Revolution. When Britain's coal crisis showed that, at least temporarily, it no longer had even the power to operate its own machines or to heat and light its own homes, the whole world knew that the decline had reached the Empire's heart.

While the coal crisis was still at its peak, Britain asked America to take over the British backstopping of Greece and Turkey against Russian aggression. By a political law as inevitable as physical law, some other force (in this case, either America or Russia) would rush to fill any vacuum left by British withdrawal. America accepted, after fully debating the Truman Doctrine, because the overwhelming majority of Americans realized that the principles on which Britain had administered its imperial commitments— including aid to Greece and Turkey—were sound, just principles.

During the coal crisis, a British premier taught an American president one of the precepts that must govern the conduct of a nation which hopes to hold world responsibility for any length of time. Truman offered to send Britain coal. Attlee declined, pointing out that continental Europe needed the American coal more than Britain.

This sort of enlightened objectivity, this ability to consider factors right round the world and then to reach a decision that does not give all the breaks to pressure groups at home, is what made the British Empire last as long and fruitfully as it did.

It has been asserted that the British tried to dominate Europe as completely as Soviet Russia now tries to do. The difference is very great. For centuries, Britain saw to it that no power dominated Europe—Spain, France of Louis XIV and Napoleon, Germany of the Kaiser and Hitler. Britain never tried to dominate Europe itself, as Russia does try. The period of Britain's greatest power—approximately 1800 to 1930—was precisely the period when most countries in Europe and elsewhere in the world took their longest strides toward national liberty.

In executing its policy to prevent domination of Europe, Britain was often faced with the sort of dilemma that now faces America in Greece, Turkey, and Persia: having to support a regime far from the ideal because the regime of the aggressor nation is far worse. The Poland of 1939 which Britain backed against the Nazi invasion was, for example, something of a dictatorship—though not as totalitarian as Nazi Germany or the Poland of 1948.

When time permitted, Britain usually attempted to raise the legal, educational, and political standards of any nation associated with it. Even where it was most unjust, as in Ireland, Britain eventually admitted its errors. Ireland is more important to the defense of Britain than Poland is to the defense of Russia. Yet Britain did not demand a "friendly government" in Ireland, as Russia demanded a "friendly government" in Poland and every other country along its European border. The difference between an Eamon de Valera and a Boleslaw Bierut or Clement Gottwald is the difference between British and Soviet imperialism.

It is a difference which we Americans should note because, whether we like it or not, we have had such wide international responsibilities thrust upon us that they can only be described as imperial commitments. We can escape them only at the cost of losing what we have already attained at home. We have found ourselves handling our new imperial commitments in a way much more like Britain than Russia, because we have developed our own American version of the British democratic tradition that goes back to a Magna Charta signed long before Columbus.

No country's international leadership lasts forever. Some day, soon or late, America's will end. When that time comes, still later Americans can well be proud if our country's imperial record stands favorable comparison with that of Britain. For all the British faults, history does not record an empire—except possibly for Rome—which brought the world more prosperity, good government and progress than did Britain in its days of imperial greatness.

2

Britain's survival in anything like its present form depends on its economic recovery. At present it has some 49,000,000 people crowded into an area smaller than Oregon with its 1,100,000 people. Before the war, Britain grew less than 30 percent of its own food. Within its limited boundaries, it could never grow more than half the food to keep forty-nine million people from starving.

This is not because of British agricultural inefficiency. Its production per farmer is remarkable. Before World War II, British farm production, both in value of output and number of people employed, was larger than any one British dominion—including Canada. Britain's area is not quite as big as the two top-notch farm states of Iowa and Indiana, but Britain's prewar farm output was bigger than Indiana and Iowa put together. Britain had more cattle than Texas, a cow country nearly three times as big.

In 1938, Britain had half as many sheep as all of America. It produced more wool than Texas and Wyoming, our top two wool states, put together. The British produced more milk than the dairy state of Wisconsin, more vegetables than our top vegetable state California, more sugar beets than our top two states (California and Colorado) combined—and twice as many potatoes as Maine and Idaho, our two leading potato states.

Since 1938, Britain has increased its agricultural output by two-thirds. It is using over half of its densely populated area for farm land, and using it effectively. In 1942, for example, we Americans set a new wheat record for ourselves, with a nation-wide average of nearly twenty bushels to the acre. That same year, Britain's average wheat yield per acre was thirty-seven bushels.

British farm production cannot be raised much higher. It is less than half of what forty-nine million people need to eat. If Britons cannot manufacture—and sell abroad—enough to pay for the extra food and all their other necessary imports, Britain's population must soon drop to under thirty million, perhaps to under twenty million. There is no alternative. Nobody, including America, can go on helping Britain's present forty-nine million for more than a few years if it becomes clear that their import deficit can never be closed.

With British foreign investments largely gone, many factories destroyed by enemy bombs and a large number of the rest obsolete by modern standards, it is easy to see why the odds on Britain's survival are in some ways longer than they are on defeated countries like Germany and Italy.

Many Britons feel this themselves. Opinion polls have shown that up to 42 percent of the population would emigrate if they could—most of them to the various dominions, with America the second choice. Such British emigration colonized much of the world in earlier days. Then it was movement from strength. Now it is flight from weakness. Actually, less than half a million Britons have left their native land since the end of World War II. Transportation is one bottleneck. Two bigger bottlenecks are: (1) because of the pound's weakness, emigrants must have the British government's permission to take their money with them, and (2) hindrances at the far end. The dominions want Britons, but none is geared to take very many at a time. The difficulties in meeting the technicalities of America's immigration restrictions are, of course, notorious.

Under the circumstances, almost all the forty-nine million will be in Britain during the next few years, which will be the period of the great battle for economic survival. Britons are fond of saying that they lose every battle but the last. This is a last-ditch battle. If it is won, most of the would-be emigrants will be glad to stay home. If it is lost, one of the great migrations of history will take place.

What will be the outcome of the battle? Nobody can be sure. I myself believe that things may get worse in Britain before they get better, but that in five or six years Britain may again be breaking even, and that in ten or fifteen years it can *perhaps* have an over-all standard of living equal to that of 1939.

Britain's era of supremacy can no more return than can the set of nineteenth-century conditions which made the era possible. But even in its present weakness, Britain is one of the world's great nations. If the last-ditch battle is victorious, Britain will certainly continue to play a vital role.

Politically, Britain is Europe's only populous country not seriously infected with Communism and is thus the key country in any Western Union. Economically, Britain's need for huge imports is a strength as well as a weakness—every nation that wants to export (including America) knows that a healthy Britain will be one of its two or three best markets. Industrially, Britain remains of prime importance. America is the only country in the world with a greater number of skilled industrial workers; as Russia reveals, such skills are not acquired in a day or even a decade. In coal, steel and oil—Stalin's three industrial essentials

—Britain at present produces more than half of Western Europe's coal and steel, and British-operated wells in the Middle East provide two-thirds of Western Europe's oil. These tangible and intangible assets mean that it would be a great mistake to write Britain off.

Britain desperately needs our aid, but none of us should jump to the conclusion that the Anglo-American relationship is entirely one sided. If Britain had not held against the Nazis in 1940, Russia could not have held in 1941-42—and America would now face a world in which Germany and Japan controlled everything from South Africa to the North Cape, and from the Azores to New Zealand. Britain is now America's best single ally in keeping the same vast area from going Communist. To put Britain back on its feet will cost only a small fraction of what we would have to spend to keep the non-Communist world free if Britain were a broken reed—not just badly bent. Any American who begrudges aid to Britain should ask himself where we would be if Britain either collapsed or went Communist.

To win its battle, Britain must have substantial American aid tapering off for five or six years, a stable and economically unified Western Europe in active operation by the end of this time, and a period of world peace and prosperity lasting until at least 1960. These are formidable conditions, but no realistic Briton would lower them. If they prevail, Britain should greatly expand its trade with the Empire, Western Europe and America. This, plus improved industrial efficiency, more tourist money spent in Britain, earnings from shipping and insurance services, and income from the remnants of overseas investments, should provide the sum needed annually for imports.

Until the sterling-currency countries including Britain can regain their economic balance, American dollar help will be necessary. Britain can scarcely make the pound sterling freely convertible before 1952 or 1953, because of its dollar shortage. Americans must also realize that when ECA dollar aid ends, America must buy at least as much abroad as it sells abroad or there will soon be another hopeless dollar shortage. Britain's basic problem of increasing production is difficult enough. Its second problem, selling enough exports to pay for its imports, will be even more difficult than the production increase once the present sellers' market ends. But Britain has at least some hope of solving both these problems by its own efforts. Neither Britain nor any other country can solve the problem of the dollar shortage—or prevent another world-wide economic depression—if America will not take payment for American exports in foreign goods and services.

Sir Stafford Cripps, who is both minister for Economic Affairs and chancellor of the Exchequer (finance minister) in Britain's Socialist cabinet, has described "the descending spiral" which would be Britain's only alternative:

"If we could neither sell enough goods to the dollar countries nor finance our purchases from them by any other means, we should then be driven to cut still further our dollar imports. We should thus enter a descending spiral of depression, the consequences of which would not be confined to Great Britain alone. Other countries would suffer as world trade was increasingly forced into bilateral channels. Each country would be forced, as we ourselves should be, to balance its accounts at lower and lower levels by buying only where it could sell and selling only where it could buy."

Meanwhile, without America's 1948-52 ECA aid, Britons would quite literally starve before they could recover. Cripps has cut the British diet from 2,870 to 2,700 calories a day (the American average is 3,560). Standing as far as possible from Marie Antoinette, Cripps said: "The public must expect many fewer and much less attractive cakes and buns." He slashed Britain's last two "luxury imports," American tobacco and movies, almost to nothing and taxed each pack of twenty cigarettes sixty-four cents. He frankly told the ill-housed, threadbare Britons that even to maintain 2,700 calories, "which though highly unpleasant should not be disastrous," they would have practically no new houses or clothes, because the materials and textiles that would otherwise go into them must be exported. Britain, for instance, is selling abroad five out of every six cars it makes.

All this austerity, Cripps warned, plus somehow raising Britain's industry to standards that would allow exports 164 per cent of prewar by the end of 1948, would still leave Britain a trade deficit of $1 billion in 1948! Observers thought that 164 percent was overoptimistic, and that British industry would do remarkably well to reach 140 percent of prewar exports by the close of 1948. In April

Cripps did cut his year-end goal to 150 percent of prewar. This meant a year's deficit of around $1.4 billion, i.e., half the 1947 deficit of $2.8 billion. If the gap can be narrowed this much in one year, there is still hope that Britain's break-even point can be reached by the time ECA aid is scheduled to end in 1952. By then, America will have given Britain over $8 billion since the end of the war—and will be well repaid if Britain does win its last-ditch battle. The 1948 ECA allotment to Britain is $1.24 billion.

Although its industrial plant is ancient and war battered, Britain has surpassed its prewar production—except for the key industries of coal and cotton textiles. With about 5 percent more people working, Britain's 1947 output was about 15 percent more, by volume, than in 1937 or 1938. Coal was only 83 percent (199.7 million tons compared to 240 million) and cotton only 55 percent. But steel was at 126 percent (running at the end of 1947 at a record annual rate of over 14 million tons and by May 1948 at an annual rate of 15.2 million tons), electricity was at 167, gas 145, cement 96, tractors 290, passenger cars 100, trucks 175, and merchant shipbuilding 180 per cent of prewar.

The fearfully narrow margin on which Britain operates was shown by the 1947 coal crisis, when another two million tons properly distributed would have kept industry from being completely disorganized for weeks. It was again shown by a power breakdown on May 23, 1948, which paralyzed the whole southeastern corner of England for several hours. This breakdown shut off all the electricity for London's 8,200,000 people and put the British radio off the air, among its other effects, because one power line broke down from overloading and the rest then successively broke down at the extra load put on them.

British industry has seen the Socialist government nationalize coal mines, railways, airlines, electricity, overseas communication and the Bank of England, with more nationalization measures (notably iron and steel) coming up. Industrial management's morale is understandably shaken, but its opposition to socialization by shouting "Free Enterprise Forever!" has been undermined by its own widespread use of cartels, monopolies, market sharing and price fixing. Such restrictive devices scarcely encourage vigorous production or salesmanship.

The problem is not simply mass production in place of Britain's old, slow, high-quality output. It is more complicated. Mass production is not economical unless a plant operates at close to capacity, which requires a large, *constant* market. A big domestic market (such as America's) provides this, and the extra can be sold abroad. A foreign market is much more uncertain, so what is efficient for America may not necessarily be efficient for Britain. However, some change in British mechanization methods is clearly needed. The change will take years, but without considerable modernization—especially in textiles, automobiles and coal—British industry will never win its vital sector of the battle of survival.

A British coal miner, for example, produces less than a third as much as an American coal miner, largely because he uses older methods and machinery. It took 716,000 men to dig less than 200 million tons of coal in 1947. A top American authority declares that by 1954, if there has been reorganization and proper mechanization, five hundred thousand Britons could produce 250 million tons of coal a year. The Labor government has socialized the mines, but because of delay in getting machinery and workers' pressure it has not yet made the mines any more efficient. The National Coal Board has an unwieldy bureaucratic setup, overburdened with parallel lines of ill-defined authority between national, regional, and area managers on one side and union representatives on the other. The price of coal has actually risen since socialization! In the summer of 1947 the Coal Board ordered the Trime Thorpe pit in Yorkshire to make certain changes. The pit workers refused—and most of Yorkshire's miners went out on sympathy strike. The Coal Board finally backed down, the hundred miners at Trime Thorpe won their point—and 570,000 tons of coal were lost. In May 1948 the Coal Board made another move for efficiency by closing a high-cost mine in Yorkshire and merging it with near-by low-cost mines. The workers at the first pit staged a "staydown strike," refusing to come to the surface for ten days. The board was unable to prevent another sympathy strike from spreading through Yorkshire, and held up its program for shutting down over a hundred small, expensive mines around Britain. Sir Charles Reid, the board's top production specialist, resigned in disgust in the board's inability to operate effectively. In 1947, the first full year the mines were nationalized, the Coal Board lost over $100 million—partly because of the high-cost mines (which in recent years had also lost money in private hands) and partly because of increased wages.

Britain's Labor government gets the bulk of its votes from workers and has cushioned them against the nation's crisis as long as it could. Workers are the only class in Britain better off in terms of money, both absolutely and relative to other classes, compared with prewar. The rich are much poorer and enjoy far fewer privileges than formerly. The white collar and professional classes have lost most of their comforts and received only an average 30 percent increase in pay while the cost of living has gone up over 60 percent. Workers' wages are over 75 percent higher than prewar.

Analysis of the distribution of real income in Britain shows that 1946 had the following percentages compared to 1938: rent 43 percent, profits and interest 81, salaries 90, wages 111, pay of the armed forces 454, health and old age benefits 184, and government income 194 percent. The first three, which were drastically reduced, mainly made up middle- and upper-class incomes. The next three, which were greatly increased, went mainly to the working class. The last item, government income, also greatly increased, was chiefly paid by the upper and middle classes—who were already sharply reduced in real income.

With a Labor government in power, British laborers have—for the first time—escaped bearing the brunt of an economic crisis. They relished Socialist Cabinet Minister Emanuel Shinwell's assertion, "The organized workers of the country are our friends. As for the rest, they don't matter a tinker's cuss." They expected "their" government to get them still higher pay and shorter hours. For the first two and a half years Labor was in power, the government never dared tell the workers frankly that Britain could never win through without a great increase in output per man hour. British labor unions have long gone in for feather-bedding procedures like those of American railway workers. They ardently defend these restrictive practices and do not yet fully understand that Britain cannot possibly recover unless people work longer and harder, and allow efficiency measures that will raise the man-hour rates.

With a working population of 18,500,000 (not counting the armed forces, police and firemen), Britain now averages 225,000 unemployed, compared with 1,270,000 jobless in 1939 just before the war. This is barely over 1 percent. So there is no manpower pool on which to draw. The only two ways to increase production are through greater efficiency or overtime. Britain's workers have shown little enthusiasm for either. Their normal wages are ample for rent, their rationed food and clothes, and for more amusements than they could afford in the 30s. Overtime generally puts them into a higher wage bracket, where 45 percent goes as income tax—and there is little to buy with the rest of the money.

With a labor shortage and such full employment that a man who loses a job can at once find another, there is no incentive to sweat, especially since the government has increased unemployment pay and allowances. The natural tendency is to slide along, and relax a little after the strains of war.

In February 1948 the Labor government finally talked turkey to the workers. Premier Clement Attlee called for a voluntary wage freeze, and Britain's union leaders agreed "in principle." Whether the workers would continue to agree was another matter. But Attlee spoke some blunt words; he warned that failure to peg wages and prices would quickly price British exports out of the world market, meaning "mass unemployment and real desperate hunger."

Britain's world position was founded on low-cost, low-wage manufacture. Since the war, by competitive standards, Britain has become a high-cost, high-wage country. Cripps added his warning: "Many of our products are now beginning to meet competition. Hitherto we have been inclined to suppose that production was all that mattered, irrespective of costs. This could ruin our trade." The cost of coal at the mine head, for instance, had gone up from $3.25 a ton in 1938 to $9 a ton in 1947.

A coal miner I met near Cardiff got terrifyingly close to the heart of Britain's problem, which is that Britons won't get more of the things they want until they produce more, and won't produce more until they get more of the things they want. He was one of the absentees whom the government eloquently exhorts to stay on the job. I asked him why Britain's prewar coal production of 240 million tons had fallen below 200 million.

"It's absenteeism," he said. "The pit's cold in winter, and I'll see little sun even when I'm out of the pit. This warm weather decided me to take another 'oliday and get a bit of sun while I can."

"Will they penalize you?"

"Not with the shortage. They'll be right glad to 'ave me back —if I go back. My cousin in Bristol, 'e's doing demolition work. I might take that on myself."

"What about the coal you could be digging?"

"Any bloke wot complains can dig it 'imself," he answered. "Wot if I have laid off? Those government buggers talk a lot—but I notice they don't come near the bloody pit face. Scared maybe.

"We need more food and more pay—and more to buy with the pay—before we'll dig more coal. Even with wot you earn, there's little to buy in the shops, that's worth buying, that is. Everything good goes for export. Well, they'd better send some of it to mine towns, if they want us to send coal to them. That's the export drive I want to see."

"But Britain needs more coal before it can make more goods," I said.

"If we're that important," he answered, "why don't they treat us more important? We've always got the short end of the stick. Before the war we 'ad to dance the owners' tune, and they laid us off when they pleased. Now there's engineering and other workers make more than we do, without 'alf the danger or dirt. My brother lost an eye down the pits. It could 'ave been saved. But there wasn't proper care, and the cut got infected. My brother's fair bitter about it. You can't blame 'im. And 'e's still down the pits. Wot other trade 'as 'e got? 'E and I both went down the mines at fourteen."

"Aren't conditions better now?" I asked.

"Not so's you'd notice," he said. "They talk about putting baths at the pit 'ead, so we could change before we go down the shaft, 'ave a 'ot bath when we come up, and then go 'ome in street clothes. But few mines 'ave it yet. Mine 'asn't. We still track the coal dust 'ome. You should hear my wife about that.

"There was many a week before the war when I was lucky to earn thirty bob [then $7.50] a week—when I was working. And the dole. It was seventeen bob. That was worse. When it's too long a man doesn't work, 'e rots. Then that bloody Tory government did the means test on us. They took any savings we 'ad, stripped us down to bare bones and the rags we stood and slept in, before they'd even give us the dole. That finished the Tories for us."

"What about nationalization of the mines?"

"It 'asn't changed things much," he answered. "There's still the bloody boss. With the old owners you at least knew where you stood. They were out to get the biggest slice they could, and to 'ell with us miners. But this government can't seem to make up its mind and it interferes the wrong places. You should see some of the red tape and regulations clerks that never saw a pit face can dream up."

3

In the July 1945 general election, the Labor party (which is Socialist) won 393 seats out of 640 in the House of Commons. The Conservative party, which had held a majority since 1931 and wielded power through a series of coalition governments, fell to 189 seats though minor parties affiliated with the Conservatives won twenty-four more. The Liberals, who were the great British party from their passage of the Reform Bill in 1832 through the days of Gladstone until the ouster of Lloyd George in 1922, fell to twelve seats—which practically ended them as a party. Twenty independents of various parties were elected, and two Communists. The total Communist vote in a poll of nearly 25,000,000 was 102,780.

It was the first time in British history that the Labor party had won a clear majority in the House of Commons, which means effective rule of Britain. The king has only an advisory role and the country has no Supreme Court that passes on the constitutionality of legislation. Britain has no formal written Constitution, just a body of laws and precedents that Parliament can revise any time it pleases. The House of Lords has a delaying but not a veto power; in 1948, Labor clipped the Lords' wings still more by reducing from two years to one the length of time that the House of Lords can hold up a law that the House of Commons passes.

Labor got its 61 percent of the seats in Commons with only

48.5 percent of the popular vote. The combined opposition was often divided enough to let the Laborite in. So the socialization which the Labor government has since carried out was never approved by a majority of the British voters. For at least the first two years, however, the government had wide popular support. It held twenty-three successive seats in by-elections, an unprecedented record in British Parliamentary history.

The only serious political reversal Labor has yet suffered came in the municipal elections of November 1947, when the Conservatives made a net gain of 621 seats on town councils, while Labor had a net loss of 652. What happened in city after city like Manchester, Birmingham, Reading, and Rugby was that former Liberal votes went Conservative. In 1945, Labor got twelve million votes, the Conservatives almost ten million and the Liberals two and a quarter million. The Liberal vote can thus represent the vital margin between victory and defeat for the other two parties. Labor party organizers privately admit that the Conservatives will get at least four-fifths of the Liberal vote when the Liberal party finally disintegrates.

Labor can never win a general election on working-class votes alone. The British middle class is so big that Labor must pick up at least a third of its votes there. Labor won about this many in 1945 because the Conservative record before the war had been uninspired, to say the least, and because, while all Britons had a tremendous admiration for Winston Churchill as a war leader, few people thought he would be so good in peace. Britons were in the mood for a new broom after World War II; they have not yet definitely decided whether they like the way Labor sweeps. There need not be another general election before July 1950, so their decision may not come until then.

No British party is conservative in the American sense. The Conservatives themselves are at least as far left of center as the Roosevelt New Deal; most observers would say farther. While they have fought each of the Labor government's nationalization measures in Commons, they have formally announced that they will not attempt to repeal any of them if they win the next election. Because of Britain's economic position, any government, including a Conservative one, would have to operate under a much more planned economy and with much wider regimentation than America has ever experienced. Only once since the war has the House of Commons heard a full-dress defense of free enterprise. In the fall of 1947, Churchill attacked Socialist planning. He said:

"I do not believe in the capacity of the state to plan and enforce an active high-grade economic productivity upon its members. . . . I am sure that this policy of equalizing misery and organizing scarcity, instead of allowing diligence, self-interest and ingenuity to produce abundance, has only to be prolonged to kill this British Island stone dead. . . . Here is the policy: establish a basic standard for life and labor and provide the necessary basic foods for all. Once that is done, set the people free—get out of the way and let them all make the best of themselves, and win whatever prizes they can for their families and for their country."

The Labor side of Commons laughed derisively. Anthony Eden, who is the Conservative party's second in command, flushed as Churchill spoke—and did not applaud. Eden and other Conservative leaders have sponsored a quasi-Socialist "Industrial Charter" and campaign chiefly on the claim that they could manage controls better than Labor could.

The Liberal Party was a lineal ancestor of the Roosevelt New Deal; the Lloyd George social measures of 1908-11 were more radical than the New Deal's social security. Lloyd George's favorite slogan during the fight for these measures was "Ninepence for Fourpence," which was his appeal for the poorer half of the voters to back him, since they would receive ninepence in benefits for every fourpence they paid, the difference coming from higher taxes on the upper classes. The Liberal Party was killed by its 1908-11 success, though World War I obscured its fate until 1922; having passed these measures it had nothing new to offer the voters that could be labeled Liberal. Labor simply took up where the Liberals left off.

The British state's concern in social security goes back as far as the Poor Law of 1536. In Tudor England, the government had already admitted that, ultimately, society as a whole was responsible for the welfare of the individual. The law did not work very well, as Dickens and others have testified, but it did contain this fundamental social philosophy. It was temporarily reversed in 1834, when Liberals of the Manchester *laissez-faire* school passed the Poor Law Amendment Act, which declared in effect that the individual's welfare depended on himself and that the state should intervene only to stop actual starvation. This doctrine broke down in the "hungry 40s" and was tacitly changed in practice, though the 1834 law stayed on the statute books. In 1833 came a parallel act in education, the first government grants for schools, which merely gave money to voluntary bodies (Church of England and nonconformist schools) since Parliament did not think that the state itself should ever directly run education. This attitude also, inevitably, changed in practice. In 1870 Parliament set up government boards all over Britain to build and operate schools, though the aid to voluntary schools was continued and state schools were built only where voluntary effort was inadequate.

The change in the last century from this attitude that everything depended on private effort, to the present British attitude, with its state-sponsored "cradle-to-grave" social security (popularly known as "womb-to-tomb") and its compulsory schools (with the state providing free secondary education for anyone and university education for the brighter children), is a change that has set its mark on every political party and all British thinking.

Britons often pretend to despise brains. There is really far more respect for intellectuals in Britain than America. One of the important differences between the two countries is that, politically, "professor" is an epithet here and a term of prestige there. The New Deal "brain trust" was soon driven out of public life. British governments frequently pick professors for the highest posts (Sir Oliver Franks, the present ambassador to Washington, was head of Queens College, Oxford, at the time of his appointment) and nobody objects. Intellectuals actually influence British opinion— even British politicians.

Striking instances of this are Lord Keynes and Lord Beveridge, men who held key government positions, influenced more British legislation than any other two men of their times, and were given peerages—all because of their brains.

Keynes had a tremendous impact on international economic policy from the time he quit the British delegation to the Versailles Conference in disgust at the impossible reparations assigned Germany, and wrote his devastating *Economic Consequences of the Peace.* He taught at Cambridge and saw his influence widen until the government had to call him back; his influence has continued to widen since his death in 1946.

Beveridge retired about the time Keynes died; his influence is also still spreading. He was born in India, of a deeply moral British couple who had made a practical religion of public service. His father never rose far because he repeatedly announced that the British should leave India as quickly as possible; his mother, said Bernard Shaw, was "perhaps the cleverest lady and the wickedest in her opinions that I have ever met." Their example burned itself into their son. After a brilliant record at Oxford, Beveridge began to study social security and in 1909, when only thirty, published *Unemployment: A Problem of Industry.*

This work was so basic and revolutionary that it was the foundation for the Liberal reforms before World War I. Seldom, if ever, has a learned work so quickly become legislation. In 1919 Beveridge became head of the London School of Economics and between the wars made it possibly the most notable school in the world both for economics and social studies. On the side, he continued to be a great economic investigator. His study of unemployment in the 30s made him realize that his original doctrines were incomplete; his revised publications spurred the Conservative government to set up a Beveridge-headed committee which issued the Beveridge Report in 1942.

The Beveridge thesis, further expanded in his 1944 book, *Full Employment in a Free Society,* is summed up in three words quoted from Charlotte Brontë: "Misery generates hate." He believes that unemployment's greatest evil is not physical but moral —not the want it causes, but the fear and hatred it breeds. The distress, he states, has two beginnings. First, interruption of earnings through unemployment, illness or old age. Second, the fact that a man's wage is not related to the size of his family so that large families in themselves may be a cause of want.

From these premises, Beveridge concluded that any satisfactory system of social security must provide: (1) state insurance to cover sickness, unemployment, old age and widowhood (2) adjustment of family income to family needs by means of family allowances. The Conservatives began a legislative study of Beveridge during the war; the Socialists continued it and have put practically all his recommendations into law.

From Lloyd George Liberals in the first decade of the century to Attlee Socialists in the fifth decade, Beveridge has been behind every major piece of British social legislation. He influenced even the Conservatives—their Industrial Charter has been called "Beveridge and water."

Some of the results are: $1 a week for every British child after the first (a duchess or a dairymaid can draw it for her second child), paid until the child is sixteen if it stays in school until then; greatly increased social-insurance benefits of all kinds; a National Health Act that is virtually socialized medicine and to which every wage earner compulsorily contributes about $50 a year.

Beveridge states that it may not be the individual's fault if he is unemployed, and that unemployment is therefore not the responsibility of the individual but the state. He says that the level of demand maintains employment, and that if the level falls off because of the mistakes or wrong policies of private enterprise, the state should step in and create employment. He adds that socialization itself is irrelevant to his policies, since they could be followed in either a capitalist or socialist state. His aim is always to have slightly more jobs than workers, so that labor always has a sellers' market and no fear of unemployment.

The Beveridge solution poses a fresh set of problems. Formerly there was some sort of balance between employers trying to get more and more work out of men for less and less wages, and unions trying to get more and more wages for less and less work. Once the state promises full employment, it takes the fundamental decision about industry out of the employers' hands. Soon this cramps the unions' style too, for unless labor voluntarily accepts a wage policy that limits its demands, a country possessing both full employment and aggressive union tactics would head straight for inflation. The alternative is for the state to enforce a compulsory wage-price policy that limits both workers and employers.

Does Beveridge's type of "full employment" actually bring a "free society"? Or does it merely produce more regulations and a less free society than before?

Whatever the answer, the politicians of every British party have accepted the professor's prescription. The statutes, often drawn almost word for word from Beveridge, are on the books. He has changed the whole climate of argument in Britain. Any discussion of social matters there starts from his assumptions, whether you agree with them or not.

Neither the Liberals nor Labor have ever developed a real policy about the relationship between organized labor and the state. The Labor government has still not tried to answer the question of the role of trade unions in the British industries it has nationalized. Can they strike against "the bloody boss" when the state is boss? Can collective bargaining work at all in a part-socialist or largely-socialist economy? If not, who determines wage rates? And how? What freedom for labor, if any, can a Labor government actually afford?

Russia has answered these questions by making labor unions a tame adjunct of the state, responsible for workers' lavatories, clubs, and vacation hostels, but with no power to strike or even to request a wage raise. Attlee and Cripps hinted at a similar answer, though not so brutal a one, when they called for a freeze on workers' wages in February 1948. British labor leaders, both in the government and in the unions, are aware of three possibilities they find highly unpleasant: (1) there is no reason for a vast union setup if wage-setting is taken out of the various unions' hands (2) this would lose a lot of very comfortable jobs for the union leaders (3) British Communists would jump at this chance to accuse right-wing union leaders of "betraying the workers" and thus increasing Communist strength in the unions. The question of what a Labor government can do for—or with—labor may well become the toughest politico-economic question in modern British history.

The Labor Party has small use for British Communists, and at recent party congresses has rejected motions for affiliation with the Communists by votes of six and eight to one. Britain's Communist Party has a membership of only forty-two thousand. It is much more dangerous industrially than it is politically. About thirty thousand of its members belong to unions, and by their untiring activity have won key positions and exert influence out of all proportion to their numbers. The 1947 meeting of Britain's Trade Unions Congress had an estimated seventy Communists among the 833 delegates—or one out of every twelve, though the Communists have only one in every 250 of TUC's total 7,500,000 membership. Harry Pollitt, leader of Britain's Communists, has defined the Party line on union activity: "We must rouse the workers to a consciousness of the dangers that face them. Make them indignant at the one-sided character of the government policy; develop the mood to resist cuts and shortages, the mood to demand wage advances to meet the rising cost of living, and for the fulfillment of their demands." Britain's Communists, of course, oppose ECA aid.

The most important British Communist is not Pollitt but Arthur Horner, secretary of the National Union of Mineworkers and the uncrowned king of British coal. Horner was born in Wales in 1894, started work in a barbershop at twelve, went down the mines at eighteen, and later organized the miners at the Welsh town of Maerdy. In World War I he refused to bear arms in what he called "an imperialist and anti-working-class war." He was jailed. Afterward, he went back to Maerdy, which soon became known as "Little Moscow." In the coal strike of 1921, Horner led a procession to the Maerdy pit heads and demanded the withdrawal of the safety men. Without the pumps being manned, the mines flooded and all their machinery was ruined. That was the death of Maerdy. Not until seven years later were any of the mines reopened, and then they soon went into bankruptcy. Now not a pit wheel turns in the town.

Horner admires John L. Lewis: "He is a very clever trade union leader who has done a lot for the miners of America." He admires Lenin more. There is a white porcelain head of Lenin in Horner's office, and he says: "I look at Lenin a lot when I have a hard decision to make. He's the man who said, 'When you have a steep hill to climb, it's sometimes better to go zigzag instead of straight up.'" Horner has put Communists in key positions throughout his union and is trying to pull other unions into his own.

Will Horner try to do to all Britain what he did to Maerdy? He has said: "If there were a possibility of war with Russia, the coal fields would stop." Since 1945, Horner has not only been the union's secretary but its national production officer, which makes him responsible for production throughout the British coal fields —a key position for activities of all kinds. This dual job signifies so much to him that he recently refused a $20,000 post on the

National Coal Board—though his present salary and allowances total only $4,000. His friends say: "That's like Arthur; he never will be bribed." Others say: "He'd rather have power than money."

But so far the Socialists, not Communists, hold power in Britain. Their leader, and Britain's premier, is Clement Attlee (born 1883). The first time I ever saw Attlee was in a corridor of the Houses of Parliament in 1935; the Conservative member of Parliament who was with me twitched my sleeve and said: "Do you see that insignificant little pipsqueak? *He's* the Leader of His Majesty's Loyal Opposition!" And he laughed. Others have laughed at Attlee's seeming insignificance. They are wrong. In his own party, Attlee is a figure of some stature and decision. An Oxford graduate and distinguished officer of World War I, he became interested in London social work early in the 1900s and thence gravitated into the Labor Party, Attlee stands at the crucial midpoint in the Labor Party. For Labor is really two parties: union men, who provide most of the votes, and intellectuals, who provide most of the doctrine and a lot of the direction. Ernest Bevin (born 1881) and Herbert Morrison (born 1888) are two top Laborites who have come up through the unions; Sir Stafford Cripps (born 1889) and Dr. Hugh Dalton (born 1887) are two of the top intellectuals. Attlee is the quiet man in the middle, around whom all the conflicting forces in the party can rally. Men of the two groups often clash violently in cabinet meetings, where Britain's policies are really decided. Firsthand observers of cabinet sessions have often reported that Attlee is much more than a mere moderator. He listens, makes decisions, and silences anyone who then objects.

Foreign Secretary Ernest Bevin is a man of ponderous weight and pithy wit. At ten he went to work as a farm laborer at sixpence a week, later took night courses at a Socialist free school, helped organize a dock workers' union in Bristol, and in due course became head of the Transport and General Workers' Union, with 1,250,000 members. In Churchill's wartime coalition cabinet, he was minister of Labor. He was criticized at the start for slowness in employing women. "Give me time, give me time," he rumbled. "Do you expect me to get two million women in labor all at once?" Bevin knew relatively little about foreign affairs when Attlee assigned him that portfolio after the Socialist victory in 1945. He learned fast. After Bevin's first policy statement in Commons, a friend drily remarked: "He's picked up all of Eden's principles and dropped nothing but his aspirates." (Bevin does still occasionally drop his aitches; his wartime slogan to workers was "Give 'itler 'ell!"). Actually, British foreign policy is about as bipartisan as American foreign policy—for about the same reasons. Bevin told some Socialists who wanted a "new" policy: "What you forget is that facts don't change." When asked the aim of his foreign policy, Bevin said: "To go down to Victoria Station, get a railway ticket and go where the 'ell I like without a passport or anything else." He hopes to do that with Western Union.

Home Secretary Herbert Morrison is the son of a London bobby. He ran London's police and all its other civic workers when he led the London County Council from 1934 to 1940. He early became a Socialist worker and later commented: "I observed that the party talked a great deal about the universe but knew little about its own ward." Morrison never neglected the wards, and is largely responsible for Labor's decisive control of London. "Maybe I wasn't born to rule," he says, "but I've got used to it."

Labor's nationalization strategy was largely worked out by Morrison, and as the party's leader in Commons he has driven it firmly, even brusquely, through Parliament. Some people have charged that Morrison wants to be a policeman "like his father." Morrison has an answer for those who think Socialists want to be totalitarian. When he was head of the London County Council he had a sign put up in all classrooms expressing a most antitotalitarian sentiment: "The teacher may be wrong. Think for yourself."

Scholarly Hugh Dalton was chancellor of the Exchequer, traditionally the No. 2 cabinet post, until November 1947, when he indiscreetly told a journalist some of the taxes in his new budget a few minutes before he rose from the government front bench in Commons to tell them to Parliament. No one profited financially from this advance leak, but cabinet secrecy is so sacred in Britain that Attlee immediately dismissed Dalton. After a period of penance, he was reappointed to the cabinet in May 1948 with a trouble-shooting assignment. Dalton's performance at the Exchequer got both praise and blame. His greatest single boner there was his failure to realize there would be such a run on sterling when it became convertible to dollars on July 15, 1947. He was let down by his civil-servant assistants, who failed to devise a watertight system of separating current sterling transactions (convertible into dollars) and sterling balances (inconvertible). In the month before Dalton and his assistants woke to reality and finally suspended convertibility, their miscalculation cost Britain more than a third of its $3.75 billion loan from America. (It would be more accurate to say "cost America," since this loan must now be considered a gift.)

Sir Stafford Cripps, a vegetarian with a strong Christian conscience, is the best brain and ablest administrator in the Labor government. When he was appointed minister for Economic Affairs in September 1947, after the sterling convertibility crisis, even Churchill conceded: "At least we have one first-class intelligence now brooding upon our affairs." In November, after Dalton's budget leak, he was also appointed chancellor of the Exchequer, and so supervises Britain's entire economy. The ninth of his line to sit in Commons, Cripps' brilliant mind first led him to research chemistry and then to law, where he earned up to $150,000 a year as an outstanding barrister. He joined the Labor Party in 1929, and during the 30s led its left wing in an effort to ally Labor with the Communists in a Popular Front. Labor expelled him, and he concentrated on the law until Churchill sent him as British ambassador to Moscow. The Labor Party welcomed him back to its ranks after the war; he is now one of the top two or three men in its government.

To make the wage freeze on the working class more palatable to them, Cripps slapped a capital levy on Britain's dwindling wealthy class in his April 1948 budget. He cut taxes on small incomes by $400 million, then levied an equal amount by a "capital contribution" from everyone making over $8,000 a year who has an income from investments of over $1,000. This, on top of regular income taxes that range up to 92 percent, meant that a man with a $200,-000 income from investments, already paying $181,000 in taxes, would have to pay $96,500 more—that is pay $77,500 more than his actual income! The middle classes, whom Labor is now starting to woo, knowing that the next election is not far off, got some benefits. A married man with two children and earning $2,500 a year had his tax cut from $250 to $175.

Austere Sir Stafford, with his love of cold baths and raw carrots, has led Britain into its increasing austerity. Some people suspect a connection between the personal and the national; the London *Economist* has observed: "However right Sir Stafford is at present, it is difficult to suppress the suspicion that he is right because he is in his element, because he positively prefers an austere, restricted, controlled economy, because, like the tympanist in an orchestra, his instinct, when he has nothing else to do, is to go around tightening up all the screws."

Cripps is, however, definitely a democrat before he is a Socialist. So are most British Socialists, including Clement Attlee and Ernest Bevin. About fifty Labor members of Parliament are Socialists before they are democrats. They want the Labor Party to move much farther left. At least some of the fifty would like to abolish Parliament as it now functions. They are a definite minority both in the Labor Party and in Britain, and like the Communists—toward whom they are not especially friendly—will never get in power unless all Britain grows more radical than now seems likely.

In the last generation, Parliament has changed considerably. Some nonleftist authorities, as well as the left Socialists, consider it out of date. The change started long before the present Labor government.

Parliament is a more rubber-stamp body than America's Congress. On every important vote, for example, every member of the House of Commons must vote as his party decides. Otherwise, he risks expulsion from the party. Ordinary members of Parliament have far less influence than formerly, and almost never see a bill of theirs become law.

Not even a strong American president, like Theodore or Franklin Roosevelt, can count on having his party invariably support him in Congress. A British premier can count on party support, as a matter of course, as long as he is considered fit to hold office. The premier and his cabinet shape policy, not the party. While the cabinet belongs to, and is responsible to, Parliament, it knows that its decisions will become law.

In World War I, the need for central planning and controls

put a great deal of extra power in the hands of Premier Lloyd George and key members of the cabinet. This has not been relinquished; it has extended. The British civil service, which is responsible more directly to the cabinet than to Parliament, has also become steadily more powerful as the scope of bureaucratic administration grew. In the last ten years, the practice of ruling through administrative "Orders in Council," most of them never debated in Parliament, has become a leading and evidently permanent part of British government.

Winston Churchill (born 1873) still leads the Conservative opposition to the Labor government—though many Conservatives wish he would retire. He spends relatively little of his time in the House of Commons, and while there pursues his own line, rather than the official Conservative course. His tongue is as pungent as ever. He called Premier Attlee "a nice, modest little man, with a good deal to be modest about." But after Attlee one day in the House dealt with him rather effectively, Churchill muttered, "Feed a grub on royal jelly and it may turn out a queen." One of his barbs at the government was: "The inherent vice of capitalism is the unequal sharing of blessings, the inherent virtue of Socialism is the equal sharing of miseries."

The Conservatives suffer from the fact they have no clear policy, and gain from the fact that many middle-class voters who were attracted to the Laborites in the last general election will apparently turn from them in disappointment next time. Few Britons speak of the Conservatives with glowing enthusiasm. Fewer think of Churchill as anything but a Grand Old Man. It is no secret that Churchill himself would like to win the next election and be premier once more—for a few months, before turning the mantle over to younger Conservatives and departing in a blaze of glory. Asked if he would like to be premier again, he answered: "I never believe in leaving a pub before closing time." Churchill enjoys reminding Anthony Eden that Gladstone formed his last cabinet at the age of eighty-two.

Eden (born 1897), the perennial "bright young man" of British politics, is clearly the Conservative heir apparent. As he waits for his long-delayed inheritance, Eden has grown gray and tired. Britons still tend to think of him as a promising, handsome young man—but they don't see him close up. He is a "safe" rather than a dynamic leader. His backers credit him with "constructive ideas" but not even Eden has defined them very sharply. The Tories have accepted him as their future leader. Another top Tory, asked if Eden's accession was certain, answered: "We don't think about it any more than about Princess Elizabeth being the next queen of England. It's just one of those things that's now accepted as inevitable."

No leading Conservative is very new or exciting. R. A. ("Rab") Butler is probably the ablest. He is considered the brain behind the reorganization of the party machinery; Lord Woolton, who made a fortune in merchandising before he entered politics, actually administered the reorganization. Butler's chief liability is a certain aloofness of manner and appearance; he could not make a wide popular appeal at the polls. But he is an able administrator and has become a more effective speaker than Eden, who is beginning to display the tendency to ramble that marked Ramsay MacDonald's later years. Butler cannot be lightly dismissed as a potential premier. Harold Macmillan is considered a "little too clever"—a serious accusation among Britons, who associate cleverness with unreliability. Oliver Stanley is able but lazy; "bone idle" is a British phrase often applied to him. Sir David Maxwell Fyfe, the British prosecutor at Nuremberg, is a good speaker but untested executive.

There is not—unfortunately—a single Liberal left in Britain who can be considered as a major, active political possibility.

4

A housewife in Birmingham kept telling me how "lucky" she and her family were. "We were lucky when we lost our house in a German raid. The bomb landed next door and ruined everything there, but we saved all our clothes and most of our furniture, even though the walls were so cracked the house had to be pulled down.

"My hub was lucky. When he got back from his four years in India, his suits still fitted. Lots of men's sizes had changed when they got out of the army and they couldn't wear their old clothes. And how lucky I was to get him back! No, he doesn't want to emigrate. He says he saw quite enough of the world.

"We were lucky to get this house. The overcrowding did it; a family full of in-laws, and this got too small for them. So they managed to find a larger house. We were lucky to be around just when they decided to sell. Otherwise we'd still be looking. It took every penny my hub and I had, but anyway we have a roof of our own—and that's luckier than lots."

I told her that many Britons seemed more pessimistic than herself. She tossed her head. "The British are always moaning," she said. "We even get a bit of pleasure out of moaning. But afterward we say, 'That was a good moan, wasn't it?'—and get on with the job. We're great workers, you know, when we put our mind to it."

A man in Plymouth told me: "I'll be sixty next birthday. I've saved all my life and have laid by a few thousand pounds. I don't even smoke now, it's so expensive. And food is so scarce and dreary. I've been waiting a year for passage to Australia. I'll go soon as I can get it. I didn't work and save all my life to have my old age in England as she is now."

There was the Coventry housewife with three small children: her husband works in the Alvis automobile plant. They lost their home when the Germans blitzed Coventry, and now live in a small prefabricated house, "I like this prefab; it's cozy, and easier to keep clean than the old house." Her children were plump and pink cheeked. When I praised their looks she said: "Children get better care now than I did. I never had this orange juice or cod-liver oil, and those days my family couldn't afford milk for me. We're allowed a pint a day each for Peter, Brenda, and Susan— and we can pay for it."

A Coventry bricklayer was disgusted at the coal shortage, ragged planning, and red tape: "My dad was mortal sick last autumn, and the doctor gave us a priority order for extra coal to keep him warm. The coal came five weeks after we buried him. Mum was sick too. When she got worse, the doctor gave us another priority order. She died in March; her coal came three weeks later. What do you do? You can't refuse coal, even if the reason for it is gone. You need it too bad. At least dad's coal helped mum."

There was the Welshman of eighteen who had served six months of his two-year army draft, and was eager to get back to his bride and his carpenter's job in Carnarvonshire. I asked if any of his family were coal miners.

"My dad is," he said. "He's sixty-three and still down the pit. He went down fifty years ago, and he's been at it ever since. You don't catch me going down the mine. Maybe Britain does need coal, but somebody else can dig it. I had one brother in the RAF; he was killed over Cologne. But my other two brothers are miners. They both hate it, but with families to support they can't break loose. They were caught in the 30s, when there wasn't much other work to be had. Me, I got apprenticed to a carpenter on purpose, soon as I left school."

At an aircraft plant near Gloucester I talked to a man of thirty-eight who was helping build jet planes. "How's Britain doing? My belly tells me she's doing damn badly. We need jets, with Russia around, but right now we're selling most of these to Argentina. I guess the government wants some beef from there, even if it takes our jets to get it."

The graying master of the ancient Oxford college that Attlee attended told me: "The Oxford type is changing. Many more are here on state scholarships, from the so-called lower-middle and working classes. England's old squirearchy is vanishing. It had good, sometimes great qualities to offer the country and we are sorry to see it go. But the Oxford type has been changing ever since plow boys came here to become priests. Both England and Oxford go on."

The same afternoon I heard of an American woman who had visited in the Wedgwood home. The day she left, Mrs. Wedgwood took her to a china closet. "It has always been a tradition for us to give visitors in our home something from the potteries as they were leaving," she said. "Now everything we make goes for export. So please select a piece you like from my personal collection."

A black marketeer (Britain has some, though far less than the Continent) said: "The trouble here is that people won't work and have no incentive to work." It sounded funny, coming from him, but he was quite sincere: "Now take me. If I worked like the devil for a year and somehow scraped up the money for a car, I still couldn't get it. There aren't any cars for sale. We export them. I wish England was like Belgium. They put goods in the shops, gave people an incentive to work—and Belgians have worked."

The Labor government is trying to make over-all plans for

forty-nine million British lives as varied as these nine. The chief single impression I got in Britain is that Britons are being individualistic despite any and all plans. The most revealing illustration was the tale of the tiddleywinks I heard from a minor executive in the London head office of one of Britain's biggest firms:

"Before the war I had considerable faith in the probable efficacy of schemes which depend on the capability of human nature to stand the test of co-operating in difficult circumstances, involving some self-sacrifice for the common good. My faith has faded. There are times when the state, or some other form of control depending on the problem concerned, has to crack down because voluntary controls aren't enough.

"The lunchroom at my office showed me the unreliability of human nature. We are a group of several hundred men of varying ages, but similar background, employed in the same building as part of the same organization. You'd think such a group would provide the most likely field for voluntary co-operation. Not so. These men are not starving. A petty personal advantage is as much as they can derive. The most they can get out of it is grabbing the best item on the menu. But our little greeds show the world in miniature.

"The trouble started when the lunchroom could not get enough supplies to provide a main meat course for every person every day. Some people always had to take fish, cheese or other less attractive alternative.

"The first result was that as many people as possible rushed up to the first sitting. The lunchroom is open from 11:30 to 2:00. There was a notable increase in business from 11:30 to 12:00— or even 11:30 to 11:32. The one o'clockers of the second sitting had to be vegetarians. All the meat went with the first sitting.

"This was countered by saving half the meat courses for one o'clock. The lunchroom is normally closed from 12:30 to 1:00 while the waitresses clean and set the tables for the second sitting. It's also a matter of company organization; we get an hour for lunch. I go to lunch at one; my colleague has to go at 11:30 so we can take over for each other. Now, from 12:45 onward, rows of men were sitting there with tongues hanging out, to be the first to get their orders in. Anyone who came at the normal one o'clock hour was again a vegetarian.

"Further brain racking on the part of the lunchroom committee produced a biscuit tin with a hole in its lid. Pushing their hands through the hole, the diners groped in the tin and pulled out a tiddleywink—red or green, little flat disks like gambling chips. Red for the meat course, green for the unlucky vegetarian diner (he might be able to get fish or cheese). But luck was still against the one o'clockers, who never seemed to draw anything but green disks. The committee switched the colors. Red was now vegetarian, and red was now what the one o'clockers almost invariably drew. I drew fifteen greens in a row when green was undesirable. This invariable sequence on the part of almost every one o'clocker did seem curious. The committee viewed with suspicion and investigated.

"It emerged that some members plunging their hands into the box brought out a generous handful of disks, retaining one of a suitable color. Frenzied ringing of changes in the color of the disks was quite unavailing. It was not until someone thought of removing the disk markings from the menu, that is, the colors which qualified for the various dishes, that matters began to improve, because men had to turn in their disks before they knew what a given disk would rate that particular day.

"But there was a sort of grapevine intelligence that crept down from the first lot to the second lot that red was a good color that day—like inside information that lets you cheat on a school exam.

"One of the ways the committee worked out what people were doing was when, after my fifteen straight greens, I triumphantly drew a red. Not a single portion of any red dish was left. How, that day, those vegetables stuck in my throat! I looked up the steward and asked, 'How come?' The steward, who by this point was nearly as keen that I should draw a red as I myself, was startled and furious. Investigation showed there had been one other unfortunate whose red disk could not be honored—but despite this there were ninety-six red disks originally in the biscuit tin, ninety-six red disks had been presented and honored, so the steward on checking up found he had ninety-eight. Clearly there had been some hanky-panky. It developed that some people had built up a little nest egg of disks by drawing two at a time, then using whichever disk seemed most favorable any day.

"Now, with the steward watching madly all the time, with

members of the committee growing eyes in the back of their heads, there are always several eyes on anyone who puts his hand into the biscuit tin. The position is as good as it can be got. It's not foolproof even so, but one has a reasonable chance.

"A new threat looms on the horizon. One of my colleagues told me the other day that he can tell the colors by minute differences in the thickness. The green tiddleywinks are slightly thicker than the reds. This was one of my own close associates and I didn't even dare say what I thought, which was, 'Do *you* do that?' Which is the sort of thing you very rarely *do* say to a colleague."

The last two sentences make it clear that the British are still a silent people; most Americans would come right out with such a crack.

The whole story shows postwar Britain: the shortages, the little jockeyings for the drab little advantages which are all that life now offers, the plans, the partial breakdown of the plans when put into practice. Here was an effort at what Churchill called "equal sharing of miseries." Whenever the slightest loophole was left for incentive, fair or unfair, men took advantage of it to get unequal rewards.

The plan was voluntary—democratic. There was no totalitarian decree from above as to which men should eat meat and which become vegetarians. This, on a nation-wide scale, is the central dilemma of Britain's democratic Socialism. Because of the nation's desperate economic position, Socialism cannot possibly offer Britons before 1960 (if then) any more palatable variety of rewards in life than the rewards symbolized by that lunchroom menu. All of Cripps' capital levies on Britain's few remaining rich people will not raise the national average enough to make it comfortable. Only incentives will make people work harder and longer for the red tiddleywink—and the better housing, clothing, and advantages for one's family that it implies. If the incentive is no more than mere chance, men will then be underhand to make the chance come in their favor.

Britain's democratic Socialism seems to be falling between the stools of Russian Communism, which has ways to enforce its plans on people, and American capitalism, which gives them various incentives to work well. If the Labor government does not find some way out of that dilemma, Britain may need a new set of tiddleywinks. Britons' instincts are still toward individualism, but if their plight grows too terrible, a turn further left can never be excluded.

With integrity and stubbornness, the Socialists still emphasize the equality Communists abandoned long ago. Stalin and the other Kremlin leaders have country houses near Moscow, southern villas by the Black Sea, their choice of the best food and consumer goods Russia has to offer, and a screen of guards to keep ordinary Russians from getting anywhere near them. They offer some similar incentives, as well as punishments, to other Russians. In May 1948, on the closing day of the annual Labor Party conference at Scarborough, Premier and Mrs. Attlee ate as usual in the hotel's public dining room, of the usual drab British food. When they left the room Premier Attlee, the most powerful man in Britain, carried the old mayonnaise jar of sugar they had brought with them from London. If the Attlees had not fetched their own scant ration, they would not have had any sugar in their tea.

This integrity, decency and care for the small essentials is as British as it is admirable. If there is some middle way for Britain, the Socialists—who do embody their countrymen's great, unassuming strength—may find a way out of their dilemma.

PART V

◎

Chapter 17. WHO FORMS A FOREIGN
POLICY?

IN AMERICA, most of the questions on foreign policy are about
Russia. In Europe, most of them are about America. Europeans
have the right slant.

The aims, even the methods of Russian policy are clear and
direct compared to those of America. The men in the Kremlin
attempt to be enigmatic. They mix mild words and aggressive
actions even more skillfully than Hitler. They can throw the
world into a hopeful tizzy, as they did with their "peace offensive"
in May 1948, when Molotov suggested that the Big Two settle
world affairs by themselves and Stalin proposed as the basis
for settlement a letter from Henry Wallace which at most 10
percent of the American people endorsed. Molotov knows that
world affairs cannot be settled by any two nations, even the most
powerful, and Stalin knows that the way to start genuine negotiations is not to address the out-of-office messiah of a minority
but elected officials, like the president of the United States and
the premiers of Britain, France, Italy and other nations. The
Stalin-Molotov maneuvers cannot conceal the basic Russian policy,
which is an effort to make the whole world as Communist as
it is now making Czechoslovakia.

America is the real riddle. America is the most mysterious
country of all. Nobody, not even we Americans can be certain
of what enigmatic America will do next. This is why Europeans
ask so many more questions about us than about Russia, why
we so greatly puzzle Europe, and why Russian policy thrives
on the confusion we Americans create by our unpredictable
actions.

In country after country, people said to me: "We would like to support America, if only we knew what your policy actually was. Do you yourselves know?" I had to admit that we didn't.

Whenever Europeans think they see a consistency in American policy, and start to follow it, we do just the opposite. European democrats, for example, began to believe that America really did oppose totalitarianism of any type. We had just about convinced them that they could trust our sincerity in this—when the House of Representatives added totalitarian Franco Spain to the list of ECA beneficiaries. The Senate hastily removed Spain, but the action had caused an immediate repercussion all over Europe and the effects will be felt there a long time.

Many Europeans feared that we were interested in them only as a place to dump our surplus goods. The slow process of persuading them that America really did want world trade on fair terms—a persuasion that had to start from scratch after the Republican Hawley-Smoot tariff in 1930 and a Democratic president's torpedoing of the London Economic Conference in 1933 —was just about won after fourteen years of the Hull reciprocity program, American leadership in the International Trade Organization, and the passage of ECA without any crippling trade amendments. In May 1948 the House of Representatives overnight wiped out almost all of the progress we had gradually made in fourteen years by amending reciprocity out of recognition. It is economic idiocy for us to spend billions on billions of dollars through ECA attempting to restore Europe and simultaneously ruin any hope of permanent European recovery by raising our tariffs so that Europe can never sell goods here for the dollars that will enable it to buy goods here. When we show ourselves capable of such incredible inconsistency, many Europeans naturally decide we are stupid, short-sighted fools who cannot be trusted to look after our own or anybody else's interests.

Every such action as aiding Franco Spain, or pulling the pillars of our own economic temple down upon ourselves and every nation associated with us, confirms Europeans in their deep-seated assumption that we Americans are so unpredictable in our foreign policy as to be virtually impossible to live with. In their despair, many of these Europeans then tend to turn toward Russia, which has great faults but, for all its zig-zag tactics, is at least basically consistent.

The difference is in how the two great magnets form their foreign policy. Russian moves as the men in the Kremlin dictate. A few leaders tell 200,000,000 Russians what to do. No leaders dictate to us 145,000,000 Americans. When we fail to make up our minds, or change our minds for no apparent reason, the whole world is mystified.

An American foreign policy, if it is to work and to last, must be formed by ourselves—the American people. No administration, of any party, can do the job for us. Our elected officials can suggest or initiate policy, and leaders in both major parties can insure its being executed in bipartisan fashion. But fundamentally, we the people must *form* it. If we fail to approve it, to understand it, or to back it, no American foreign policy is worth the paper on which it is written. But if we form a policy which is firm and farsighted, it can meet any contingency. It can even handle the seeming contradiction that should be the base of American foreign policy: to prevent the next war, if humanly possible, but to win it if it must be fought.

2

For the first 150 years of our national existence, we Americans shrank from developing any positive foreign policy, though we did evolve a backhanded one by a series of negative actions. We took Washington's advice to avoid entangling alliances and later adopted the Monroe Doctrine, which told Europeans not to meddle with the American hemisphere. After World War I had made it clear that we were one of the two or three most powerful nations on earth, we reaffirmed our negative, isolationist policy by refusing to join the League of Nations. The most characteristically American act of foreign policy between the two world wars was our arms embargo, by which we unrealistically hoped (1) to keep others from breaking the peace and (2) to keep war away from our shores if others started it.

The brutal reality of World War II began to trouble our isolationist dream. After Pearl Harbor, we slowly awoke to a realization that we needed a new, positive American policy.

The man who best personified our change was a Republican senator from the formerly arch-isolationist midwest. After Germany invaded Poland, Arthur H. Vandenberg announced: "This so-called war is nothing but about twenty-five people and propaganda." He led the fight against relaxing the Neutrality Act and voted against lend-lease, the draft, and renewal of the draft. After Pearl Harbor, he loyally supported wartime measures, but remained an isolationist so far as postwar plans were concerned. When he saw how the world had shrunk in an air age, he began to change his mind. At the Mackinac Island policy meeting of Republican leaders in September 1943, Vandenberg produced the word "participation" to express the increasing Republican view that America must stay in world affairs after the war. On January 10, 1945 he rose in the Senate, publicly abandoned isolationism, and urged a treaty with Russia and Britain to keep Germany and Japan forever disarmed.

Vandenberg did not change us Americans so much as we changed him. It was our response to his speech—the warmest response that any single American speech has received in recent years—which spurred him into the constructive, bipartisan course he has followed in foreign policy ever since. It was the enthusiasm of our response to Vandenberg's speech which caused Roosevelt to appoint him a delegate to the San Francisco Conference which organized U.N. He has been attending major foreign meetings ever since. "I have sat," he says somberly, "for 213 days across the table from Mr. Molotov."

It was in a marathon series of across-the-table meetings with Russia, Britain, and France that America first tried to hammer out its postwar foreign policy. The sessions began with the first meeting of Big Three foreign ministers (Hull, Molotov, and Eden) at Moscow in October 1943, continued through the meetings of governmental heads (from Roosevelt, Stalin and Churchill at Teheran and Yalta, to Truman, Stalin and Attlee at the end of Potsdam), and closed with the weary meetings of the Council of Foreign Ministers from September 1945 to December 1947. At first held in the deepest secrecy, these meetings gradually developed into the most fully reported diplomatic encounters in history. Almost entirely through a series of Western concessions, they did finally produce a set of five unsatisfactory peace treaties (Italy, Finland, Rumania, Bulgaria and Hungary) which America would already revise if it could. They produced a U.N. so weakened by compromise that it has never been able to take any decisive action. They produced (at Potsdam) an apparent economic agreement on Germany which the Russians have vetoed ever since. They have failed to produce any peace treaties for Germany, Austria, or Japan. They have utterly failed to produce any working agreement between Russia and the West.

The one major place where the Big Four met regularly from 1945 to 1948 was in the Allied Control Council at Berlin. This ended in stalemate when the Russians refused to call a regularly scheduled meeting in March 1948. About the same time, the four foreign ministers' deputies, meeting in London, failed to reach any agreement on the Austrian peace treaty. Russia had already declined the American invitation to a peace conference on Japan.

The era in which the Big Four (or Big Five, counting China in the Pacific settlement) had tried to agree on peace terms, and find a means of close postwar co-operation among themselves, was over. It is unlikely that Big Four meetings will be revived. When the Russians are really ready to co-operate, there are other channels—ambassadors in the various capitals, contacts in U.N., and peace conferences—through which the remaining treaties can be negotiated and other outstanding differences settled.

The Big Three and Big Four methods of negotiation were tested amidst difficulties few of our delegates can ever forget. One difficulty was the endless repetition of the same arguments by the Russians, sometimes several times the same day and often a dozen times the same week. A tired American delegate announced that he could not even go to the opera without hearing a voice wailing above the woodwinds: "The Soviet Union demands a liberal, democratic, peace-loving central government for all Germany." (This was the tune the Russians sang as they vetoed all proposals to bring it about.)

Another difficulty was translation. This ranged from American bewilderment in Berlin at having the Russians charge that American GIs were "biting old men and women" (later it developed that they meant "beating," which was still bewildering), to Bevin's attempt to tell jokes to Molotov. At the Moscow Conference in March 1947, Bevin three times tried vainly at the buffet after the meeting to get one story across to Molotov. It concerned an eighty-year-old man marrying a twenty-year-old girl. Asked if his bride was heir-minded, the groom answered that it didn't make much difference, since he was not heir-conditioned. The interpreter never could translate this well enough to make Molotov smile.

Molotov tends to snap at his slight, unhappy-looking interpreter Pavlov. At one Paris meeting, Pavlov distorted one of Molotov's sentences. Molotov looked at him bleakly and then remarked that eventually he would have to have Pavlov executed. The foreign official to whom Molotov was talking took this as a labored jest; Pavlov turned red and then pale, evidently considering it a very poor joke indeed. Pavlov still appears at foreign meetings, but Molotov is now more frequently translated by Oleg Troyanovsky, son of a former Soviet ambassador to America, who studied at Cornell while his father was at Washington and has a good command of American slang.

Charles E. Bohlen, a top American diplomat, whose command of Russian made him Roosevelt's and Truman's interpreter to Stalin, was asked after Postdam which president had been easier to translate. He diplomatically said that both used such clear sentences that they were fairly easy to put into Russian. Then he added, "Mr. Truman did give me one bad moment."

"What was that?"

"A meeting had been going on for hours, getting nowhere. Finally someone suggested that we all adjourn to the buffet next door for fifteen minutes, to see if refreshments might ease the tension. Truman and Stalin reached the door simultaneously. The president turned to me and said, 'Tell the generalissimo it's the seventh inning; we'll all stretch.' "

"How did you ever get that baseball term across to the Russians?"

"I thought fast," said Bohlen, "and then said—in Russian—'The president has just made a very American joke. You will all please laugh.' The Russians did."

Molotov supervises delegates from the Russian satellites about as closely as his own subordinates. At the Paris Peace Conference,

Ales Bebler of Yugoslavia, who had been dozing, roused with a start to realize that he had been summoned to vote on a clause in the Rumanian treaty. "No," he said, and looked at Molotov, who frowned. "I mean yes," said Bebler. Molotov frowned harder. "I mean I abstain," babbled the Yugoslav. Molotov smiled.

It is easy to see why the Communists even have a hierarchy of toil. When someone remarked to Madame Gromyko that her husband was a hard worker she answered: "Yes, Andrei does work hard, yet not as hard as Comrade Vishinsky, and even that is not so hard as Comrade Molotov works."

"A revolutionary," Molotov has observed, "must work fourteen hours a day—and sixteen hours a day after the revolution succeeds." Molotov says he has worked his sixteen hours almost every day since the October Revolution in 1917. To break the monotony, he shifts to an entirely different subject every few hours (oftener if possible) and does some of his work sitting, some standing, some pacing about his office.

Molotov and Vishinsky manage to exhaust any Westerner who works with them. At the New York meeting of the Council of Foreign Ministers in November 1946, which coincided with a meeting of the U.N. General Assembly, five hours of tense debate in the CFM left Byrnes limp, but the Russian team would shuttle right out to Flushing or Lake Success and be ready to go on all night. One reason for their freshness, of course, was that they usually had their orders from Moscow and simply worked within that framework, while Bevin and Byrnes had a fairly wide latitude, which forced them to weigh their words far more carefully.

Even polite George Bidault lost his temper with Vishinsky at the Paris Peace Conference after one especially wearing series of obstructions. Toward the end of the debate came this passage at arms:

Vishinsky: "I ask for the floor on a point of order."

Bidault: "I wish to speak first."

Vishinsky: (Not translated from the Russian.)

Bidault: "I have the floor."

Vishinsky: (Not translated from the Russian.)

Bidault: "I am obliged to insist on respect for the chair."

Vishinsky: (Not translated from the Russian.)

A voice from the left: "Translate it."

Bidault: "There is no reason to translate what Monsieur Vishinsky says, since he does not have the floor." (The conference translators spoke only when the presiding officer gave the signal.)

As Vishinsky continued in Russian, Bidault banged his gavel. When that had no effect, he rang the chairman's bell, which is used only to open and close sessions. Finally Vishinsky got the floor and said he had merely been attempting to withdraw a Russian objection. He added: "I am very sorry the president was disturbed, and particularly that he disturbed the august bell at his elbow."

Bidault answered: "I did not ring the bell. It was rung by article 62 of our rules of procedure."

The delegates, who had had little to laugh about, laughed.

In more restricted sessions, the chiefs of state or foreign ministers sit round a circular table, each flanked by an interpreter and several key assistants. Behind them are serried rows of specialists, who can sit back playing tick-tack-toe or reading newspapers when their particular topic is not up for discussion, as often it is not for days and weeks at a time. They have to stand by in case. Sometimes they can help their chief make a touchdown run. This occurred when Molotov accused America of holding back reparations from Germany and announced—reading from a document Vishinsky had handed him—that John C. Green of the U.S. Department of Commerce had publicly emphasized the great value of German patents which America had obtained.

Charles P. Kindleberger, an American economic adviser sitting in the third row of seats, remembered a letter from John Green which he had filed in a brief case crammed with all kinds of documents for emergencies. He passed it up to H. Freeman Matthews in the second row, who passed it to Benjamin Cohen in the first row, who passed it to Marshall. Marshall quietly read Green's letter to a taken-back Molotov. Green stated that all German scientific data discovered by America was being published in pamphlets that anyone could buy, that Russia had been one of the biggest buyers but had published no data whatever on its own technological discoveries in Germany, and asked Marshall to look into the matter at Moscow. Vishinsky's face reddened. But he turned to his boss with a grin—which sickened and died when he saw the grim expression on Molotov's face.

That evening, at a banquet Molotov gave, Marshall appropriately wore Russia's Order of Suvorov, awarded him in 1944 for "strategic and tactical skill."

Sometimes the Americans were caught off base by lack of a document. When Molotov suddenly quoted a Truman speech of August 1945 about the part of Germany given Poland to administer, Marshall motioned for a copy of the speech to be passed up to him. That appalled his aides, for they had no text of it in the room. Cohen, who had drafted this Truman speech including the quoted passage, whispered into Marshall's ear and then scribbled frantically. Snapped Marshall (rightly, as it later proved): "President Truman has been quoted out of context."

By the end of the Moscow Conference in April 1947, the deadlock on the German and Austrian treaties—and on the whole Big Four relationship—was practically complete. General Mark Clark, then American commander in Austria, put it in a military metaphor: "Russia gave us impossible demands, echeloned in depth." When the Big Four foreign ministers finally met again in London in November 1947, the stalemate was so much worse that the London *Times* compared them to "men trying to play polo in an Atlantic swell." Bevin was still attempting to joke with Molotov in the conference's lighter moments. This time he put one across. When Lord Pakenham, British minister in charge of German affairs, was asked by Molotov whether he had ever read Karl Marx, Lord Pakenham said, "I have, though I am anything but a Marxist." Molotov suggested that one was unlikely to find a good Marxist in the House of Lords. Bevin cut in: "That's just where you're wrong. The House of Lords are the only people in England who have the time to read Karl Marx."

At the end of three weeks of fruitless wrangling in London, Marshall listed the long record of frustration and then moved adjournment. Bidault said it was his "painful duty" to agree that deadlock had been reached. With a wintry smile, Molotov said he had no remarks and no objections. Bevin, as chairman, observed: "I must say with a deep feeling of regret that our experience here makes me wonder—I put it no higher than that— whether this is the body that will ever be able to settle the European and German problem." Then he pronounced the formal adjournment. No date was set for another meeting. The direct Big Three and Big Four conference method will not be tried again unless Russia is really ready to co-operate.

3

Only sustained effort can make a foreign policy. It takes money and materials, as in ECA. It takes thought. And it takes men.

The chief reason why, up to now, we Americans have never possessed more than a negative foreign policy in peacetime is that, once a war was over, we were unwilling to back our policy with men. The classic instance came after World War I, which we fought "to make the world safe for democracy." By itself, war never makes anything safe. At best, it creates the conditions which unremitting peacetime action can then safeguard through the years. In 1919, the world did seem safe for democracy. An American president, Woodrow Wilson, proposed a League of Nations to keep it safe. A natural, inevitable part of the League was a small international police force, since no human society in history has ever enjoyed complete, voluntary co-operation. (Even some of the angels in heaven once rebelled.) America's isolationists then led a successful fight against our joining the League, using as their main argument, "Do you want your boy to die over an obscure quarrel in some far country?" Americans didn't. Later, British and French isolationists took up a similar cry, "Why die for Danzig?"

The result, in less than twenty years, was what Churchill rightly calls "the unnecessary war"—the bloodiest ever fought. History has a sense of irony. World War II began when Hitler drove across Poland toward Danzig, and for six years men died for Danzig, all over the world, on a scale that made the League's little, still-born international police force—which could have kept the peace had it been in action from 1919 onward—seem like a Boy Scout troop.

Any foreign policy, however global, comes down to specific sore points in specific places like Danzig. They may seem obscure to most of us Americans at the start, but they can soon become terribly important. Some of the sore points between Russia and the West, any one of which might quickly cause a major war if Russia or its satellites attacked, are Spitsbergen, Finland, the Ruhr,

Trieste, northern Greece, the Dardanelles, Kars and Ardahan, Azerbaijan, China, and Korea.

Trieste could well be the Danzig of World War III. It is a perfect example of the type of problem we Americans will repeatedly meet, and must solve to avoid war. My own experience has made me keenly aware of the potential danger of Trieste. In 1945 I handled, day by day, the secret documents which showed how America nearly lost the peace there before we had even won the war.

Like Danzig, Trieste is a great European port, overwhelmingly inhabited by one nationality but serving a hinterland of other nationalities. Since Roman times, Trieste has been a city inhabited by people from the Italian peninsula, speaking Latin and later Italian. In 1382 it passed from the control of Venice to Austria and was almost uninterruptedly a part of the Austrian Empire until 1918. It was an Austrian imperial free port from 1719 to 1891; then and later it was the great port for northern Yugoslavia and southern Germany, as well as for land-locked Austria, Hungary, and Czechoslovakia.

At Versailles, Italy claimed Trieste and the Italian-speaking area around it. This was granted, but unfortunately Versailles also awarded the Slovene-speaking section of this former province of the Austrian Empire to Italy, instead of Yugoslavia.

In 1941 Yugoslavia joined the Allies and was promptly overrun by Germany. Italy had entered the war on the Axis side in 1940. The leaders of the two rival Yugoslav partisan groups, Mihailovich and Tito, both made territorial claims on Italy around Trieste. Yugoslavia was our Ally and Italy was not; ethnologically Yugoslavia did have a clear claim to a couple of thousand square miles and several hundred thousand people.

In 1943, Italy changed sides and became "our gallant co-belligerent." The Nazis held the northern half of Italy and most of Yugoslavia; it was a slow, bitter battle to push them back. They still held a lot of Italy and most of Yugoslavia when America's 1944 presidential campaign took place. Angling for the large Italo-American vote, both Roosevelt and Dewey issued resounding pledges for the sanctity of Italian soil, and American aid for Italy's just claims as a co-belligerent. These pledges included Trieste and the area round it.

In the late fall of 1944, the State Department sent the draft of its proposed policy on the Trieste region to the White House for approval. This was a summary of territorial policy, an outline of Tito threats already made to occupy the whole disputed area, and the proposed policy of stopping such conquest by force if necessary. It was, in short, a paper on a foreseeable crisis of arms and of American conscience. It sought to answer in advance the question: "Do we yield our principles and the foundations of peace, or do we support our principles with action?" Presently the draft returned, with these words in the president's handwriting: "I concur. F.D.R."

America wished to see the disputed province divided as fairly as possible along ethnological lines, giving Yugoslavia about three-fifths and Italy about two-fifths including Trieste which is 80 percent Italian. The British agreed.

In February 1945, Field Marshal Alexander, the Allied supreme commander in the Mediterranean, sent his chief of staff, Lieutenant General W. D. Morgan, to Belgrade with the American map. Morgan's mission was to have Tito, who had just been recognized by the Big Three at Yalta with Mihailovich discarded, agree to this line as the occupation boundary for the province. Allied troops were to occupy the Italian part and Tito troops the Yugoslav part, i.e., occupation zones resembling those the great powers had agreed upon for Germany and Austria. Tito demanded that Yugoslavia occupy more territory. Morgan, who was a general and not an ethnologist, yielded. On February 27, he and Tito formally signed an occupation agreement defining the Morgan Line (see map, page 381) as the zonal boundary. This left Trieste and about one-fifth of the province on the Italian side of the line. Neither the State Department nor the British Foreign Office liked Morgan's agreement—they did not see its terms until after it was signed—but it did specify that the final disposition of the province would not be made until the peace treaty.

In April, Roosevelt died and Truman became president. In his last years, as Hull aged and especially after Stettinius was appointed, Roosevelt was increasingly his own Secretary of State. His long presidential service had given him a great deal of background for it. I was then working in the State Department's Office of European Affairs, seeing practically every document that came or went, including those labeled Top Secret, since one of my duties was to write items for a daily summary of developments that circulated to a few top people at the State and War departments and the White House.

For Roosevelt, one did not have to provide more than the merest thumbnail of background explanation for a foreign-policy development; he knew the earlier stages. Truman was different. Like most Americans, he had concerned himself very little with foreign affairs. A key official at State dropped in to see me two days after the changeover and we made arrangements to provide fuller background in summarizing for the new president. As the official started toward the door he paused, turned toward me, and said: "Remember, President Truman knows nothing."

In foreign affairs, it was almost literally true.

Ten days later, the German armies began a hasty withdrawal from northern Italy and Yugoslavia. The Allied troops, who for two years had been fighting peak by peak up Italy, rushed forward. Tito's partisans, who despite their boasts had been waging little more war than Mihailovich in the last year, finally began rushing too. They rushed straight for Trieste and points west— all beyond the Morgan Line which Tito had solemnly agreed to observe. A British general took the surrender of the German garrison in Trieste (Tito is still falsely claiming that his partisans took the city), but the province and Trieste itself were overrun by partisan bands.

When Tito was sharply reminded of his signed agreement to the Morgan Line, he replied, in Hitler's words: "Conditions have changed."

The State Department sent full summaries and background to the White House and War Department. Truman answered: "This is a Balkan affair that does not concern America." The War Department stated: "The lives of American soldiers should not be risked in this unimportant matter."

Why die for Trieste? At that time, most of us Americans would probably have sided with the White House and the Pentagon. But an agreement among allies is an agreement. We had Tito's signed pledge to observe the Morgan Line, and we had a fair, ethnically-based policy which would give Tito most of the province but save the Italian part for the Italians. If we surrendered such principles, in the very moment of victory, to a little Hitler's unilateral claim that "conditions have changed," could there be any hope of a durable peace?

The White House and War Department reaction meant that no effective protest was sent Tito. He realized that he could probably go farther. He set up his own Yugoslav governments in such Italian cities as Trieste, Monfalcone, Pola, and Gorizia, and had the effrontery to complain at "the presence of American and British forces in this Yugoslav territory." He then ordered thirty thousand of his troops to infiltrate the next Italian province, Udine. The Yugoslavs marched off nine thousand Italian civilians, few of whom have ever been heard of again though Allied investigators later recovered over eight hundred of their bodies from an abandoned coal mine at Basovizza near Trieste, seized banks and other property, arrested the Italian archbishop of Gorizia and many priests, requisitioned all the food in the area, and used the full range of terror tactics.

On May 9, Tito, rejecting Allied protests that he had completely broken his word, said "Yugoslavia intends to keep what it has conquered," and added that he would demand the Italian province of Udine. Like other dictators before him, Tito made one territorial demand too many. Americans might, weakly, have swallowed his presence in Trieste, but these further demands on Italy brought him practically to Venice. The State Department's daily messages to the White House and Pentagon finally had some effect; like other Americans, Truman and the War Department knew that Venice was an Italian city, well inside Italy. On May 13, the administration agreed that the Yugoslav forces should be pushed back to the Morgan Line, even if it took the lives of American men.

When this ultimatum was presented to Tito on May 15, he whined that it was "unfair." The next day he dropped his demand for the province of Udine, ordered his troops to withdraw from it, and—again taking a leaf from Hitler—claimed that Trieste was his "last territorial demand." The day after, he rejected the ultimatum.

By now it was clear that only force could make Tito keep his signed word. On May 21, after due warning to Tito, American and New Zealand troops moved through the Tito garrisons and took up their posts all along the Morgan Line. Other Allied

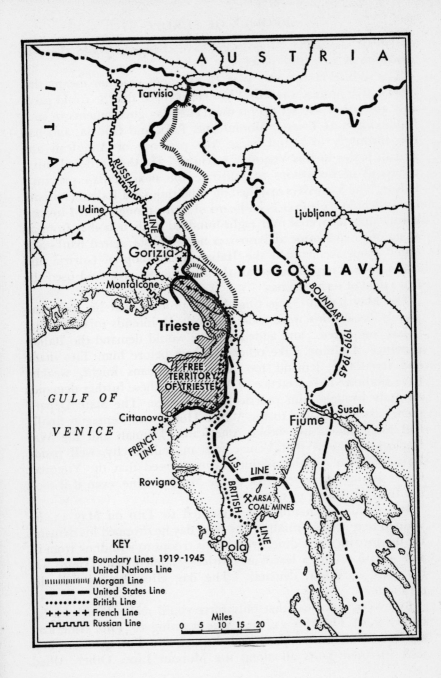

AUSTRIA

Tarvisio

ITALY

RUSSIAN LINE

Udine

Ljubljana

Gorizia

YUGOSLAVIA

Monfalcone

Trieste

BOUNDARY 1919-1945

FREE
TERRITORY
OF
TRIESTE

GULF OF

VENICE

Cittanova

Susak

Fiume

FRENCH
LINE

Rovigno

U.S. LINE

BRITISH

ARSA
COAL MINES

LINE

Pola

KEY

—··—··— Boundary Lines 1919-1945
———— United Nations Line
ııııııııııı Morgan Line
— — — United States Line
•••••••• British Line
+++++ French Line
⌐√⌐√⌐√ Russian Line

Miles
0 5 10 15 20

troops camped alongside every Yugoslav detachment in the area. In two days, Allied planes flew five thousand sorties over the area, in peaceful, silvery formations of fifty or so at a time. On June 12, after one more ultimatum, Tito withdrew his troops to his side of the Morgan Line.

All this was done without a single casualty—once Tito realized that the Allies meant what they said. The State Department breathed a sigh of relief. This was premature. Before June ended, there was a new Secretary of State, James F. Byrnes, who knew almost as little about foreign affairs as Truman had. Byrnes had been a skillful and effective horse trader in the Senate, where if you make a concession to the other fellow you can count on his giving you something in return. Byrnes learned, slowly and expensively, that you can't trade this way with Russia. One of the most expensive lessons was Trieste.

This is what Byrnes successively yielded on Trieste *without getting anything for anybody in return*, which one should get if one is going to horse-trade:

(1) September 1945 meeting of the Council of Foreign Ministers in London. Byrnes agreed that there should be an international area in Trieste port with "free transit" of goods to and from the hinterland. He added, "But Trieste must always be Italian."

(2) April-May 1946 meeting of the CFM in Paris. The four-power commission of experts recommended four different lines for the Yugoslav and Italian areas. Byrnes quickly abandoned the American and British lines in favor of the "compromise" French line, thus giving 138,000 Italians to Yugoslavia, plus the Italian-developed Arsa coal mines, bauxite and mercury deposits, and all the Italian coastal ports including Pola. Byrnes further agreed that Italy must demilitarize its border with Yugoslavia—the same border that Yugoslav troops had crossed in 1945 before we insisted on their withdrawal.

Byrnes repeated that his stand on keeping Trieste itself Italian was one of principle and therefore not subject to change.

(3) June-July 1946 meeting of the CFM in Paris. Supported by Vandenberg, Byrnes agreed to take Trieste away from Italy and internationalize it under U.N. In order to insure Molotov's agreement to this "compromise," Byrnes further agreed that Russia should receive $100 million in reparations from Italy! As Byrnes

explained it on page 133 of his book *Speaking Frankly*: "Molotov then asked whether the problem of reparations could be disposed of 'in a positive fashion' if the Trieste issue were settled [i.e., by internationalization]. I stated that I did not think this would create insuperable difficulties." On page 148, Byrnes reports that the Council of Foreign Ministers did agree to give Russia $100 million in reparations from Italy.

American and British troops were in the Trieste area all during these negotiations—as they still are, since Russia has thus far not agreed to a governor for the Free Territory of Trieste and the peace treaty provides that Allied soldiers remain there until a U.N. governor requests them to leave. We had pushed Tito back to the Morgan Line he himself had agreed to. Molotov and Tito could argue until they were blue in the face that Trieste should be given to Yugoslavia—but we occupied this Italian city and merely had to state that it would stay Italian. Instead, Byrnes and Vandenberg internationalized it.

Unbelievable as the whole negotiation now seems, we Americans must not be too hard on Byrnes and Vandenberg. They genuinely thought that such concessions to Russia should at least produce Russian good will toward America in return. Most of us Americans thought the same thing at the same time.

Our American concessions gave 87 percent of the province to Yugoslavia, and did not even leave the Free Territory of Trieste enough space to grow its own garden produce. Of the three railways Trieste had for its prewar trade with central Europe, two (which carried 79 percent of the trade) were put entirely in Yugoslavia. Except for a two-mile opening into Italy, Trieste is completely enclosed by Yugoslavia. Its water supply and electric power stations are in Yugoslavia. The Triestini sardonically call their state "Topolino" (Mickey Mouse). Since it is no longer part of Italy and receives no aid from that country, America has had to give Trieste $20 million worth of food a year. Since the Yugoslavs are building up Fiume as a rival port for the trade from central Europe, the U.N. is having to underwrite Trieste's annual fiscal deficit. In sum, the Free Territory of Trieste is a political and economic monstrosity.

Tito is still trying to get Trieste or, if he can't have it, cripple it completely. In November 1946 he offered, through Italian Communist leader Palmiro Togliatti, to let the Italians have Trieste if they would give him the Italian city of Gorizia. Tito repeated the offer in March 1948. If Tito held Gorizia, he would control all three railway lines into Trieste, and could cut off all its rail traffic whenever he wanted. The Italians have consistently refused this one-sided offer.

On September 15, 1947, the day the Italian peace treaty went into effect, Tito massed ninety thousand troops outside Trieste, where the Americans and British had only five thousand soldiers apiece. The Yugoslavs tried to force their way into the city, and told the American sentries they were "coming through." The American answer was that any soldier who crossed the line would be shot. The Allied troops were hopelessly outnumbered; they could have been overwhelmed. But Tito knew the American troops had orders that they were expendable.

American troops—American lives—are in Trieste because the American administration knew in the autumn of 1947 what it had not known in the spring of 1945. It knew that, if a treaty which Russia and Yugoslavia had signed and ratified could not be enforced from the day it went into effect, no agreement anywhere would be safe. President Truman no longer thought Trieste "a Balkan affair that does not concern America." The War Department no longer thought that "the lives of American soldiers should not be risked in this unimportant matter." Washington was ready in advance to "die for Trieste" as it had never been ready in advance to "die for Danzig."

Are most of us Americans ready to die for Trieste? Probably few of us were prepared to do so in September 1947. More of us were prepared in March 1948, when America—in an effort to influence the Italian election—proposed restoring Trieste to the Italy from which we should never have allowed it to be taken. It was ironic to have ex-Secretary Byrnes and Senator Vandenberg applaud this proposal, since without their approval Trieste could not have been internationalized in the first place. They, like the rest of us Americans, are still learning.

We Americans tend to look on Trieste as Metternich looked on Italy—"only a geographical expression." But the sore points of the world are more than mere political and geographic symbols. They have people of flesh and blood. Every hill and valley in them has its majorities and minorities, its dead heroes and live arguments, its habits, slogans and heartaches. Finland or the Ruhr, northern Greece or the Dardanelles, Azerbaijan or Korea, might just as readily see the start of a world war as Trieste.

When we recognize a Trieste when we see it, and take steps to insure that no Trieste gets out of hand, we will have gone a long way toward preventing war. We Americans will then have formed a true and realistic foreign policy. We will have learned the truth we tried to ignore for 150 years: that we matter to the world and the world matters to us. We will realize that a foreign policy is not only thought and effort, money and materials, but men. We will know that our men, at Trieste, or ready to go to other Triestes, can do what we failed to do after World War I.

Then there should be no World War III. Then the Henry Pages of this earth should live out their peaceful span.

Acknowledgments

This book is based on five years in Europe, between 1935 and a recent eight-month trip. In connection with it I owe a particular debt to: E. K. Hollingshead, Max Ways, Trine Dreyer, Mitchell Page, John Fischer, Geoffrey Gorer, and Mark Vishniak; people in eastern and central Europe who gave me information at risk to themselves; others who helped me in many places; and the press corps of the countries I have visited, notably my Time Inc. colleagues. None of these can be held responsible for my views— nor can *Time*, which kindly gave me leave of absence to write the book and permission to use some material it has published.

I can never sufficiently thank my father and mother. She taught me to read, he taught me to think; both taught me to see, to feel, and to try to understand.

S.W.

Set in Linotype Baskerville
Format by A. W. Rushmore
Manufactured by The Haddon Craftsmen
Published by HARPER & BROTHERS, *New York*

3782

DATE DUE
